CP

BEYOND MAGNA CARTA

The 800th anniversary of Magna Carta falls in June 2015. In this work Dr Blick argues that this event should be the occasion for a reassessment of the past, present and future of the UK constitution. He draws on his experience as research fellow to the first ever parliamentary inquiry into the possibility of a written constitution for the UK. Dr Blick considers a series of English and UK historical texts from Anglo-Saxon times onwards, among which Magna Carta is the most prominent, which sought to set out arrangements for the governance of England and later the UK as a whole. He argues that they comprise a powerful tradition of written constitutional documents, and stresses the importance of the European dimension to their introduction and content. The author then considers the present nature of the UK constitution, describing the period of immense flux through which it has passed in recent decades, and the implications of this phase of change. Dr Blick identifies a need for a full written constitution for the UK as the next appropriate step. Finally, he discusses the democratic processes suitable to devising such a text, and what its contents might be.

Beyond Magna Carta

A Constitution for the United Kingdom

Andrew Blick

·HART·
PUBLISHING
OXFORD AND PORTLAND, OREGON
2015

Published in the United Kingdom by Hart Publishing Ltd
16C Worcester Place, Oxford, OX1 2JW
Telephone: +44 (0)1865 517530
Fax: +44 (0)1865 510710
E-mail: mail@hartpub.co.uk
Website: http://www.hartpub.co.uk

Published in North America (US and Canada) by
Hart Publishing
c/o International Specialized Book Services
920 NE 58th Avenue, Suite 300
Portland, OR 97213-3786
USA
Tel: +1 503 287 3093 or toll-free: (1) 800 944 6190
Fax: +1 503 280 8832
E-mail: orders@isbs.com
Website: http://www.isbs.com

© Andrew Blick 2015

Hart Publishing is an imprint of Bloomsbury Publishing plc.

British Library Cataloguing in Publication Data
Data Available

ISBN: 978-1-84946-309-6

Typeset by Compuscript Ltd, Shannon
Printed and bound in Great Britain by
CPI Group (UK) Ltd, Croydon CR0 4YY

For Nicola, George and Frederick

Acknowledgements

The following people and institutions have helped me, whether they knew it or not, in conceiving of, researching and writing this book. All interpretations and errors of fact or omission are my own.

Graham Allen, Robert Blackburn, Karen Blick, Robin Blick, Vernon Bogdanor, Democratic Audit, Brendan Donnelly and the Federal Trust for Education and Research, Stephen Haseler, Peter Hennessy, the International Institute for Democracy and Electoral Assistance, George Jones, Stephen Pittam and the Joseph Rowntree Charitable Trust, Giles Radice, my colleagues at the Institute of Contemporary British History, Nat le Roux and The Constitution Society, Anthony Tomei and the Nuffield Foundation, Unlock Democracy, Stuart Weir, Richard Whitman, Stuart Wilks-Heeg, and Robert Worcester. I am grateful to Richard Hart and the team at Hart Publishing including Mel Hamill, Tom Adams and Charlotte Austin for making this work possible.

Finally I must thank my family—Frederick, George and Nicola Blick—whose tolerance this project must have tested to its fringes, as I fear will my future endeavours.

Andrew Blick
Acton
London
January 2015

Contents

1

Introduction

FUTURE HISTORIANS WILL certainly regard 18 September 2014 as an important date in the history of the United Kingdom (UK). On this day, they will record, Scotland voted (by approximately 55 per cent to 45 per cent) to reject independence. What is not yet clear is whether, in such narratives, the decision will appear as a lasting reprieve for the UK, or a stage in its unravelling. The referendum and its aftermath revealed fundamental flaws in the UK system. In retrospect, it may even be seen as a crisis of legitimacy. Methods through which constitutional change could come about were unsatisfactory. The system of governance as a whole was becoming imbalanced. A viable means of stabilising it was difficult to discern, and the task of doing so made more problematic by conflicting sectional interests. An exemplar of these defects came with a joint statement in the closing stages of the campaign by the leaders of the main parties in Westminster: the Conservative Prime Minister David Cameron; the Liberal Democrat Deputy Prime Minister Nick Clegg; and the Labour Leader of the Opposition Ed Miliband. It was called the 'Vow'.[1]

Issued at a point when the outcome of the vote seemed in doubt, the Vow made a series of pledges regarding the autonomy of Scotland. They would come into force if the referendum produced a 'no' verdict. Rather than through an official outlet, it appeared as a statement in the *Daily Record* newspaper on 16 September 2014. Despite the informal setting it immediately assumed a quasi-constitutional status. The three politicians began by iterating their agreement that the 'Scottish Parliament is permanent'. This statement, in the UK context, was dramatic. The *Cabinet Manual*, an official publication dating from 2011 describing itself as a 'guide to the laws, conventions and rules on the operation of government' puts forward what is a conventional—if contested—view on this subject. Its first paragraph refers to the existence of a 'sovereign [UK] Parliament, which is supreme to all other government institutions'. Shortly afterwards, the manual claims that 'Parliament is sovereign and it has provided by Acts of Parliament—which, by their nature, may be repealed—for certain issues to be considered and determined at different levels'. Among the beneficiaries of this contingent benevolence were 'the Devolved

---

[1] *Daily Record*, 16 September 2014.

Administrations'.[2] The Vow, though not in itself amounting to a legal curb on the Westminster legislature, surely suggested a need to qualify such accounts of UK parliamentary authority. If Parliament genuinely was in possession of a theoretical legislative omnipotence, what was to prevent it overriding the Vow at some point in the future, even if it had gone as far as to enact it in statutory form?[3] And if the Vow did prove to be in some way binding, how valuable was the doctrine of parliamentary sovereignty as a means of describing the UK constitution?

The Vow not only promised security for the Scottish Parliament, but guaranteed it the transfer of 'extensive new powers', in accordance with a tight timetable that would commence the day after the referendum. In a passage resembling the preamble of a written constitution, the text then went on to describe the purpose of the UK as being 'to secure opportunity and security for all' with 'resources' shared 'equitably' among Wales, Scotland, Northern Ireland and England. The end goal was the 'defence, prosperity and welfare of every citizen'. This suggestion of a fundamental socio-economic purpose was in conflict with more orthodox UK constitutional conceptions. The statement also referred to the maintenance of the 'Barnett' formula for allocating expenditure between the four components of the UK, and guaranteed Scottish parliamentary control over expenditure on the National Health Service.

While the Vow arose in the circumstances of a vote held in Scotland it had sprawling implications for the UK. The manner of its appearance served to demonstrate some of the problems associated with constitutional change in this country. As the late 'yes' surge that occurred during the referendum campaign demonstrates, sometimes popular dynamics can develop that are hard to control from above. Nonetheless, the Vow—though the product of panic—was a manifestation of the discretion that political leaders can wield in shaping the underlying system, potentially to detrimental effect. A hurried product, it had no prior authorisation from the UK Parliament or anyone else outside the group of politicians responsible for it. Only the Scottish electorate was given the chance to approve or reject it, and then only in the negative sense that it would be implemented if it chose not to support independence.

As soon as the 'no' result was known on the morning of 19 September, a number of constitutional issues immediately appeared on the agenda for the whole UK. Cameron announced his intention that accompanying the changes foreshadowed in the Vow would be a package for the entire UK, proceeding at the same pace as the Scottish reforms.[4] It would include enhanced devolution for Wales and improvements for the system of self-government of Northern Ireland. The most significant portion of his announcement related to the part of the UK where there

---

[2] Cabinet Office, *The Cabinet Manual: A guide to the laws, conventions and rules on the operation of government*, 1st edn (London, Cabinet Office, 2011) 2.

[3] See: The Smith Commission, *Report of the Smith Commission for further devolution of powers to the Scottish Parliament* (Edinburgh, The Smith Commission, 2014) 5; 13.

[4] Statement by the Prime Minister, 19 September 2014.

was as yet no devolution outside Greater London: England. Cameron knew that he would be under pressure from Conservative English MPs who felt he had ceded too much to Scotland, in particular over public expenditure. He needed to quell these criticisms by showing he was asserting the cause of England. Stating that the 'millions of voices of England must … be heard', Cameron indicated his support for the adoption of a system known as 'English Votes for English Laws' (EVEL) in the UK Parliament. At his party conference the following month he confirmed this position, describing his 'vow to the people of England … English votes for English laws—the Conservatives will deliver it'.[5] This untried concept involved giving English MPs in the Commons an exclusive role in determining business that affected only England. Depending on the precise method of implementation it could mean the appearance of a Parliament within a Parliament at Westminster, and even a government within a government at Whitehall.[6] It would also create problems for the Labour Party if it held a majority of UK but not of English MPs. If Labour formed a government in such circumstances its non-English representatives would not be able to support it in the Commons in crucial policy areas such as English education and health.

With this concern surely influencing him, Miliband came forward with his own proposals later on the same day.[7] While Cameron had expressed a desire for 'cross-party' and 'civic' involvement in the process of change, the Miliband scheme placed far greater emphasis on the importance of inclusiveness, calling for a programme of national and regional discussion involving both politicians and the wider public, leading to a Constitutional Convention. Miliband focused primarily on the ideas of regional and 'sub-national devolution', not—as Cameron had done—an 'English voice'. The Miliband time frame was longer than that of Cameron, with the full Constitutional Convention projected for October 2015. Miliband believed that there might be a need for a 'regionally representative Senate'—presumably replacing the House of Lords. This view pointed towards a federal system for the UK, though he did not define it expressly in these terms. Finally, Miliband suggested his process could possibly lead to 'codifying the constitution'. Earlier in his career, Miliband had been a special adviser to Gordon Brown when Brown was the Labour Chancellor of the Exchequer. As Prime Minister from 2007–10, Brown had explored the possibility of a written constitution. He made no progress. But during the referendum campaign in 2014 it was Brown who brokered the Vow. In doing so, he triggered wider developments that might in turn lead on to the attainment of this earlier idea.

At the time of writing, the outcome of this constitutional upheaval is impossible to predict with certainty, involving a complex interaction of ideas and political

---

[5] Speech to Conservative party conference, 1 October 2014.

[6] For some variants, see: First Secretary of State and Leader of the House of Commons, *The Implications of Devolution for England* (London, HM Stationery Office, 2014); Society of Conservative Lawyers, *Our Quasi-Federal Kingdom* (London, Society of Conservative Lawyers, 2014).

[7] Labour Party, 'A Constitutional Convention for the UK; a dynamic new political settlement for England and for Britain' press release (19 September 2014).

forces. Many concepts, not all of which are compatible, are in play. They include accelerated devolution, EVEL, the promotion of English regions, the holding of a constitutional convention, the increased adoption of a federal model for the UK, and the establishment of a written constitution. It is clear that dynamic and desta-bilising tendencies are at work. Serious systemic malfunction is a possibility. The Union, despite the 'no' vote in Scotland, remains insecure. The UK reached this difficult position at the very moment when it was poised to celebrate the 800th anniversary of a document—of English provenance—often held as central to a supposedly superior and steady constitutional system. This book argues that, by taking Magna Carta as our cue, we can use the past to assist us in understanding how we came to be where we are, and the way forward. Problems the UK faces at present are part of a process that stretches back to the 1950s and the beginnings of the full post-imperial era. The hunt for clues to potential solutions can begin far earlier still, in the sixth or seventh centuries. Rather than imprisoning us, the past can offer release.

CONSTITUTIONAL PERCEPTIONS

Many common understandings of our constitution are flawed. So too is the system itself. The 800th anniversary of Magna Carta presents an opportunity to begin correcting these defects. This ancient text is regarded as emblematic of democracy and liberty not only in its home country but internationally. We are right in the UK to mark its importance. Yet in doing so we should not only celebrate, but take the opportunity for a critical assessment of the way we are governed. The agreement that John Lackland and the leaders of the rebellion against him struck in June 1215 provides us with a portal. Through it we can perceive at once the constitutional past, present and possible future. But what is the nature of the set of understandings in need of reconsideration, and the dif-ficulties requiring attention? They are discernable through some of the words of our political leaders spread over nearly seven decades down to the present, within the time span that historians delineate as the contemporary period. Not all the accounts considered in the passages that follow are entirely flawed, nor do they represent a single consistent stream of thought. Nevertheless, each of them is chosen because it is a statement by a holder of a prominent political position (or a leading party), for the particular ideas it presents, and because of the important tendencies and developments which it serves to accentuate. They begin with a speech given at a time when the democratic future of the UK and the whole of Europe was uncertain.

On 4 June 1940, following the British Expeditionary Force evacuation via Dunkirk, Churchill made his 'fight on the beaches' speech in the House of Commons.[8] He referred to 'long centuries of which we boast' when conquest had

---

[8] For analysis of Churchill's June 1940 speeches in context see: Roy Jenkins, *Churchill* (London, Macmillan, 2001) 611–21.

not taken place, though stressing that such safety had never been certain. Here is the first example of a widespread, misleading perception. In reality foreign invasion has been as much a defining feature of the history of the British Isles as avoidance of it. Moreover, the sea surrounding the 'island' Churchill referred to repeatedly in his address to the Commons (though the state he governed occupied more than one island) could in earlier times facilitate rather than protect against incursion. As the historian Jonathan Scott writes: 'In pre-modern Europe, where transport was efficient only upon water, the Channel was (as it were) a bridge, not a moat'.[9]

Two weeks later, on 18 June, France had a new Prime Minister, Marshal Philippe Petain, replacing Paul Reynaud, and was seeking peace terms from the Germans. Churchill gave his 'finest hour' address to the Commons. He asserted that 'we in this island and in the British Empire' were in solidarity with the conquered European nations. The 'Battle of France' had come to an end and Churchill anticipated that the 'Battle of Britain' would follow. The outcome would determine the survival of 'the long continuity of our institutions and our Empire'. He concluded that if it was possible to achieve victory, then 'if the British Empire and its Commonwealth last for a thousand years, men will still say, This was their finest hour'.

The power and value of the speech at the time Churchill delivered it are beyond question. Yet the claim about the 'long continuity of our institutions' does not withstand close scrutiny. The UK state began with the union between England (including Wales) and Scotland of 1706–07, too recent to claim a history of 'long centuries'. Churchill may have had English 'institutions' in mind, but their incorporation with Scotland was itself an abrupt change, particularly if it is accepted that the Union was not simply an English absorption of the kingdom lying to the north. A further jolt came in 1800–01, with the joining of Great Britain with Ireland—most of which then left the Union in 1922. These changes alone serve to deny a smooth existence. Moreover, Churchill himself was at times an advocate of further dramatic shifts. In 1912, in a speech in his Dundee constituency (a city that would vote for independence in 2014), he had proposed a system intended to reconcile Irish pressure for Home Rule with UK constitutional balance, through a symmetrical decentralisation of power. Building on ideas he had put forward within government the previous year, Churchill argued that Ireland, Scotland and Wales should each have parliaments, with perhaps between 10 and 12 English regional bodies, all under the Westminster Parliament. Here was a quasi-federal model similar to that later pursued, not wholly successfully, under the Labour government first elected in 1997. Churchill left open the possibility of an even grander project, a politically integrated empire.[10]

---

[9] Jonathan Scott, *England's Troubles: Seventeenth-Century English Political Instability in European Context* (Cambridge, Cambridge University Press, 2000) 10.

[10] John E Kendle, *The Round Table Movement and Imperial Union* (Toronto, University of Toronto Press, 1975) 149–50.

The Home Rule idea of which this scheme was a manifestation did not ultimately succeed in preventing the most blatant interruption of continuity in UK history: the departure of all but six counties of Ireland that Churchill witnessed from the vantage point of the coalition Cabinet of David Lloyd George. Two decades later, as the Germans overran Western Europe in the early phase of his premiership desperate circumstances drove Churchill to become associated with further plans that, if implemented, would have meant further ruptures with past practice. In May, the War Cabinet sought to bring about Irish entry into the conflict through offering the Republic subsequent reunification with the North. The Republic declined.[11] Then on 16 June 1940, two days before the 'Finest Hour' speech, the War Cabinet had agreed a proposal intended to create a basis for continued French participation in the war. The terms were that 'France and Britain shall no longer be two nations, but one Franco-British Union' with 'joint organs of defence, foreign, financial and economic policies'. It would have linked legislatures, a single form of citizenship and a unified War Cabinet.[12]

The Reynaud Government fell and the plan faltered with it. But the idea of European supra-nationalism persisted, manifesting itself in a continental integration project after the war. The UK was reluctant to participate in some of the key early initiatives such as the European Coal and Steel Community (ECSC) and the European Economic Community (EEC) (1957). But in 1961 the UK applied for EEC membership, following a reorientation of policy under the Conservative Prime Minister Harold Macmillan. Speaking to his party conference in October 1962, the Labour Leader of the Opposition, Hugh Gaitskell, explained his reservations about this development.[13] His words demonstrate that the ideas and interpretations regarding the UK constitution this book seeks to reassess are not connected to any one party.

Gaitskell cast doubt on the idea that membership of the EEC was an economic imperative for the UK, and stressed the consequent impact on trade connections with the Commonwealth, which he claimed was a more dynamic entity than widely supposed. He recognised the power of the claim that it would be better to participate in a body as formidable as the EEC, than to choose to remain outside. But he asserted the need to balance other concerns in any decision. Gaitskell discussed the possibility that the customs union would develop into a 'political union'. The prospect of an expanding practice of majority decision-taking within the Community would heighten the need for caution: it created potential for the imposition on the UK of measures it had opposed. He then moved to the 'idea and ideal of Federal Europe'. Gaitskell argued that, while some in the UK were

---

[11] Michael Burgess, *The British Tradition of Federalism* (London, Leicester University Press, 1995) 120.

[12] See: Richard Mayne and John Pinder, *Federal Union: The Pioneers: A History of Federal Union* (Basingstoke, Macmillan, 1990) 27–29.

[13] *Britain and the Common Market: Texts of speeches made at the 1962 Labour Party Conference by the Rt Hon Hugh Gaitskell MP and the Rt Hon George Brown MP together with the policy statement accepted by Conference* (London, Labour Party, 1962).

keen to minimise the importance of European federalism, it was important to the founders of the EEC. In an important passage, he asked: 'What does federation mean? It means that powers are taken from national governments and handed over to federal governments and to federal parliaments'. One example he cited was of the United States (US), another was Australia. The UK would become, he held, the equivalent of a state within one of these federations, like Texas, California, Western Australia or New South Wales:

> We should be like them. This is what it means; it does mean the end of Britain as an independent nation state. It may be a good thing or a bad thing but we must recognise that this is so.

Later in his speech, re-emphasising the point about 'the end of Britain as an independent European state', he added the famous phrase: 'It means the end of a thousand years of history'. Once again, there was confusion about the precise state he was referring to. The UK was certainly not a thousand years old; moreover, it is important to be cautious about labelling it a nation—as opposed to a multination—state.

A particular problem for Gaitskell was the threat that the EEC posed to UK links with the Commonwealth. The empire Churchill spoke of was passing, but the global outlook that came with it lingered, along with a heritage organisation of former colonies. A federal Europe meant 'the end of the Commonwealth'. It was not possible for the UK as 'a province of Europe' to continue as the 'mother country of a series of independent nations'. While accepting that it was for other Western European countries to decide if they wished to combine in a federal system, it was 'not necessarily the answer' for the UK: 'For we are not just a part of Europe—at least not yet. We have a different history. We have ties and links which run across the whole world'. He wished to 'cherish' the Commonwealth. He favoured, therefore, a looser arrangement that allowed the UK to enhance its association with the EEC states while also preserving its connections with the Commonwealth: 'the building of a bridge between the Commonwealth and Europe'.

The political school now known as 'Euroscepticism' may now be more associated with the Conservative Party (and the United Kingdom Independence Party). But the Gaitskell speech shows that Labour has long historical connections with this outlook, which has at times permeated Labour more than the Conservatives. Another intervention on the subject came from the future Labour leader and Prime Minister, James Callaghan. In May 1971, with the Conservative Prime Minister Edward Heath in the process of taking the UK into the EEC, Callaghan complained that membership might entail 'a complete rupture of our identity'. He warned that French plans could pose a threat to the 'language of Chaucer, Shakespeare and Milton'. The appropriate answer, he proposed, was 'Non, merci beaucoup'.[14]

---

[14] Hugo Young, *This Blessed Plot: Britain and Europe from Churchill to Blair* (London, Macmillan, 1998) 273.

On 20 September 1988 the Conservative Prime Minister Margaret Thatcher gave a speech to the College of Europe in Bruges.[15] It would become a focus for the rise of hostility towards European integration within her party. The argument it presented involved propositions about the European dimension of the UK constitution. She opened by stressing that 'We British are as much heirs to the legacy of European culture as any other nation. Our links to the rest of Europe, the continent of Europe, have been the dominant factor in our history'. The UK drew constitutional influence from Europe, and exerted the same upon it, as part of a wider process of cultural exchange. Her account drew largely on examples predating the existence of the UK, and mainly dealing with English history. For instance, she referred to the Roman Empire, and how 'Our nation was ... "restructured" under the Norman and Angevin rule in the eleventh and twelfth centuries'. She stated that 'We in Britain are rightly proud of the way in which, since *Magna Carta* in the year 1215, we have pioneered and developed representative institutions to stand as bastions of freedom'. She described 'Christendom', 'with its recognition of the unique and spiritual nature of the individual' as an important part of the constitutional heritage of Europe, including an emphasis on 'personal liberty and other human rights'. Another shared feature was that 'Europeans explored and colonized—and yes, without apology—civilized much of the world'. A particular contribution of the 'British' to Europe was in resisting the emergence of a 'single power' achieving continental hegemony. The UK was, therefore, a committed European, she held. But the European Community was not synonymous with Europe. Budapest, Prague and Warsaw were 'great European cities', and 'European values' had helped establish the US in the role of 'valiant defender of freedom'.

Turning to the future Thatcher insisted 'Our destiny is in Europe, as part of the Community'. But this outlook did not preclude other external relationships, for the UK or any other member. The Community was 'not an end in itself'. Neither was it 'an institutional device to be constantly modified according to the dictates of some abstract intellectual concept'. It should not be 'ossified by endless regulation'. The Community should avoid expending effort on 'internal disputes or arcane institutional debates'. For her the purpose of the Community was to provide for security and attain economic success through 'individual initiative and enterprise'. She cautioned against forcing the Member States 'into some sort of identikit European personality'. The US constitutional system—federal in nature—was not an appropriate model because of the more diffuse identity across Europe. She supported the idea of Community members working more closely together. But doing so did not 'require power to be centralized in Brussels or decisions to be taken by an appointed bureaucracy'. She went on to remark that at a time when even the Soviet Union was beginning to understand the value of 'dispersing power and decisions away from the centre' within the European Community there existed support for the reverse. Thatcher went on: 'We have not successfully rolled back the frontiers of the state in Britain, only to see them

[15] Margaret Thatcher, speech to the College of Europe ('the Bruges Speech') 20 September 1988.

re-imposed at a European level with a European super-state exercising a new dominance from Brussels'.

Thatcher supported the process then under way for the establishment of a European single market, calling for 'action to *free* markets, action to *widen* choice, action to *reduce* government intervention. Our aim should *not* be more and more detailed regulation from the centre: it should be to deregulate and to remove the constraints on trade'. She called for developments including 'a genuinely free market in financial services in banking, insurance, investment'. She stressed that 'we certainly do not need new regulations which raise the cost of employment and make Europe's labour market less flexible and less competitive with overseas suppliers'. A problem with her outlook was that she advocated a single market, but seemed uncomfortable with the measures needed to attain it. Her repeated use of the word 'action' showed that the dissolution of barriers to commerce required intervention at European level to ensure that all Member States conformed to agreed rules and did not pursue their own divergent policies. The speech—though subtle in its recognition of the UK as a European power—also displayed a more general disquiet with the European integration project, for instance through the reference to the importance of continuing bilateral extra-European relationships, and to Europe not being encapsulated in the Community alone. The eventual accession of states formerly within the Soviet sphere of influence meant that by the early twenty-first century the 'great European cities' to which she referred of Budapest, Prague and Warsaw were all within the European Union (EU). Yet this transformation did not ease the concerns of the Eurosceptics for whom Thatcher was an inspiration. Indeed, the widening of membership that many on the Right had advocated provided a focus for those who disliked the EU, who regarded new Member States as a problematic source of inward migration to the UK.

In the following decade, the Labour Party contested and won the May 1997 General Election on an extensive programme of constitutional reform including: devolution to Wales, Scotland and Northern Ireland; the incorporation of the European Convention on Human Rights (ECHR) into UK law; freedom of information legislation; and the removal of hereditary peers as a first stage of House of Lords reform. Important changes had taken place in preceding decades under governments of varied complexion. Nonetheless, there were significant divisions between the parties that respectively gained and lost office in 1997, and this election marks an important moment in UK constitutional development. For this reason it is apt to consider the campaign statements of the two main parties at this time, and what they reveal about perceptions of the UK constitution.

The 1997 Conservative Party General Election Manifesto was an important statement of constitutional orthodoxies about to become subject to new challenges.[16] In a section headed 'The Constitution' it held: 'Alone in Europe, the history of the United Kingdom has been one of stability and security', much of which

---

[16] Conservative Party, *You can only be sure with the Conservatives* (London, Conservative Party, 1997).

derived from 'the strength and stability of our constitution—the institutions, laws and traditions that bind us together as a nation'. This claim of UK exceptionality founded in 'stability and security' with a strong constitutional dimension was dubious. It ignored, for instance, the palpitations involving Ireland, the status of which has also been a source of internal conflict that has sometimes made the UK appear an outlier on the European scene for its levels of violence rather than its guarantee of security to its own population.

While the constitution was 'stable' the manifesto went on, it was not 'static'. It has been woven over the centuries—the product of hundreds of years of knowledge, experience and history. Radical changes that alter the whole character of our constitutional balance could unravel what generations of our predecessors have created'. For this reason the party sought 'to continue a process of evolution, not revolution'. One problem with such a stance is that doubt can surround whether a particular change is only incremental or something more substantial. Furthermore, there have been developments that it would be entirely reasonable to describe as 'radical changes' with important consequences for the 'constitutional balance', including in the decades immediately preceding the 1997 General Election. In 1973 the UK had—under a Conservative government—joined the EEC, a constitutional event important, not only in its own right, but connected to other developments suggested in the Conservative Manifesto. It pledged not to bring about UK membership of a European single currency without first obtaining the agreement of the electorate through a referendum. This commitment showed that such votes—which many once considered inappropriate to the UK political culture—were now an accepted part of the system, surely a challenge to the traditional 'balance'?

The document identified 'Parliament ... the Crown and our legal system' as the 'three key institutions that uphold our constitution' and stressed that the 'supremacy' of Parliament was 'fundamental to our democracy, and the guarantee of our freedoms'. The manifesto opposed 'radical reform that would undermine the House of Commons'. One such threat came from the Labour proposal (agreed with the Liberal Democrats) for domestic incorporation of the ECHR that the Conservatives described as a 'new Bill of Rights'. Such a measure would, the manifesto held, bring with it the danger of a shift of authority from Parliament to the courts. This outcome would entail 'undermining the democratic supremacy of Parliament as representatives of the people'. The manifesto did not consider whether EU membership had the same supposedly undesirable impact, though it had become clear by this point that it involved courts being able to disapply Acts of Parliament in as far as they were incompatible with European law. The text went on: 'Whilst this may be a necessary check in other countries which depend upon more formalised written constitutions, we do not believe it is appropriate to the UK'. Here the manifesto suffered from a confused account of causality. A Bill of Rights or similar instrument is often an intrinsic part of a written constitution. Therefore to suggest that because the UK does not rely on the latter, the former is not applicable, seems a circular proposition. This passage did, however, serve to highlight the existence of a genuine divergence between the UK and all other significant democracies bar two: the absence of a written constitution.

Another possible change the Conservatives opposed was the adoption of an electoral system that would 'break the link between an individual member of parliament and his [sic] constituents'. The party opposed 'proportional representation' on the grounds that it would lead to 'unstable, coalition governments that are unable to provide effective leadership'. Arrangements of this kind would involve 'crucial decisions being dependent on compromise deals hammered out behind closed doors. This is not the British way'. One problem with this claim was that coalitions of various sorts have been a frequent occurrence in UK history, including the celebrated wartime government of Churchill. Indeed, the next time the Conservatives held office it was in conjunction with another party—the Liberal Democrats. Furthermore, the striking of confidential bargains at the highest level, far from being unknown, is central to traditional understandings of the UK constitution: this practice is precisely what takes place in Cabinet, the supreme executive organ, regardless of whether one party or more forms the government. Indeed, recent evidence suggests that the details of intra-government negotiations are more likely to become public under a coalition.

The manifesto stated that the 'Union between Scotland, Wales, Northern Ireland and England underpins our nation's stability'. It acknowledged their 'distinctive individuality' as 'different nations'—suggesting a view of the UK as both a nation and comprising other nations (though how Northern Ireland fits within such a formula is unclear—is it a nation, part of a nation, or something else)? The Conservatives opposed Labour plans for devolution to Wales and Scotland, on the grounds it would have a destabilising impact, and call into question the role of Westminster MPs elected from constituencies in those nations. The overall judgement of this proposal was that it would 'unravel a constitution that binds our nation together and the institutions that bring us stability'. Here the Conservatives displayed a degree of prescience, as recent developments in Scotland demonstrate. The Conservative position on Northern Ireland was—in accordance with a cross-party approach—different. While noting that 'we cherish the Union and Northern Ireland's place within it', it accepted that the unusual position required a return to self-government (in abeyance since 1972) in the Province, on a basis of consensus and the protection of the rights of different groups within it.

A notable quality of the manifesto Labour issued in 1997, given that it was a party about to embark on a constitutional reform programme of historic significance, was its concern to stress the limitations on its plans.[17] Labour identified a 'national crisis of confidence in our political system'. Yet it then stressed that it would 'respond in a measured and sensible way'. The party would remove hereditary peers from the House of Lords, as part of a programme to make the second chamber 'more democratic and representative'. But it had 'no plans to replace the monarchy': not a fervent endorsement of this institution, but intended to reassure.

---

[17] Labour Party, *New Labour: Because Britain deserves better* (London, Labour Party, 1997).

The party stressed that its proposals for 'decentralisation of power to Scotland and Wales' amounted to 'devolution not federation. A sovereign Westminster Parliament will devolve power to Scotland and Wales. The Union will be strengthened and the threat of separatism removed'. So far, the latter prediction has proved to be the opposite of reality. Through its proposals for local government Labour presented itself as seeking to remove some of the central controls upon this tier. But much of its programme in this area consisted of placing requirements upon local government rather than removing them. While Labour promised it would be more constructive towards the EU and seek to become a leader, it described a 'vision of Europe' as 'an alliance of independent nations ... We oppose a European federal superstate'. The Labour Party appeared to have accepted the premise and language of Thatcher.

The prominence of constitutional reform in the Blair governments might suggest that he saw the subject as important and worth discussing. Yet in July 2000 the Conservative Leader of the Opposition, William Hague, called a Commons debate on the relationship between Parliament and the executive. In his response Blair, though acknowledging that the subject Hague addressed was 'serious' suggested that rather than delivering the 'eccentric speech' he did, he might have addressed issues such as 'jobs, the economy, schools, hospitals or even crime'. Blair noted that he did 'not know whether people in his pubs and clubs are talking about pre-legislative scrutiny, but they are not in mine'. Hague had delivered a speech, Blair concluded, worthy of his reputation as someone who, when 16 years old, used to 'read Hansard underneath the bedclothes'.[18] Here is an example of how those who seek to raise constitutional issues in the United Kingdom risk ridicule for obsession with technicalities.

In May 2010 the Conservative and Liberal Democrat Parties formed a coalition. The published document setting out their agreed platform announced: 'our political system is broken. We urgently need fundamental political reform'. The government would hold a referendum on whether there should be a change in the electoral system for the UK Parliament, though the agreement did not bind the two parties to a single position on which side to take in the campaign. Other stated policies were to introduce fixed-term parliaments of five-year's duration and to bring about a reduction in the number of MPs, combined with an equalisation in the number of voters in each constituency. Further constitutional commitments included to establish a committee on reform of the House of Lords, producing proposals for a mainly or wholly elected second chamber of Parliament, 'on the basis of proportional representation'. The coalition would set up a commission to examine the so-called 'West Lothian question' that involves the consequences for Parliament of devolution. It would hold a referendum in Wales on an extension in the powers of the National Assembly for Wales and implement the 'Calman Commission' proposals for enhancements to Scottish devolution.[19] The New

---

[18] HC Deb 13 July 2000, vol 353, col 1097.
[19] Cabinet Office, *The Coalition: Our programme for government* (London, Cabinet Office, 2010).

Labour reform momentum, then, was to continue under the coalition. But the Conservative Party was not content with all the existing patterns of development, and its leader sought to frame his concerns in historical terms.

In January 2012 the Conservative Prime Minister of the Coalition Government, David Cameron, gave a speech regarding the UK chairmanship of the Council of Europe. He stressed that his central interest would be 'reform' of the European Court of Human Rights, the organ of the Council that heard appeals from citizens within Member States claiming they had suffered violations under the ECHR. He opened with the assertion that 'Human rights is a cause that runs deep in the British heart and long in British history. In the thirteenth century, the *Magna Carta* set down specific rights for citizens, including the right to freedom from unlawful detention'. He went on to note two further texts (that, like Magna Carta, were English and predated 'British history') that are often included in the same historic legal canon as Magna Carta: the Petition of Right and the Bill of Rights. Yet these claims were a preliminary to Cameron setting out a programme, the intended impact of which was to restrict the scope of the European Court of Human Rights, and the access of individuals to it, though presented as part of an agenda for efficiency and democracy.[20]

In September 2012, Cameron appeared on the David Letterman television chat show in the US. Letterman surprised the Prime Minister with a quiz on UK history, the content of which was less light-hearted than the tone. Much of Letterman's questioning involved constitutional issues, clearly taken more seriously in the US than the UK. It underlined the persistence of Magna Carta as a revered text in the US, again to a greater extent than in the UK. The following year the American hip-hop artist Jay-Z released an album entitled *Magna Carta Holy Grail*, a juxtaposition suggesting a status in US popular culture akin to that of a mythical relic. The questions Letterman put to Cameron in 2012 were evidence of how outsiders might perceive the UK constitution as in some senses peculiar, how they might understand the historic trajectory of the UK as a whole, and the implications in turn for its system of governance. Some of the answers Cameron provided—or was unable to provide—were revealing also, though the media response at the time focused excessively on his errors and ignorance.

Noting that the UK was once a great power but had lost this position, Letterman asked whether the British Empire was 'just awful'. Cameron responded 'there were some good bits and less than good bits. Obviously we [the UK and the American colonies] had a bit of a falling out at that time'. Letterman probed the complex multinational quality of the UK. Asked about Wales, Cameron stated: 'it's a small country, a very proud nation … There are people who speak Welsh as a first language but it's very much part of the United Kingdom'. On whether the Welsh voted 'for you' Cameron replied 'Some of them did, but my party tends to do better in England'. Letterman asked the UK Prime Minister to explain the division in Ireland, and Cameron recounted that in the past 'all of Ireland was part of

---

[20] Speech by the Prime Minister, 25 January 2012.

the United Kingdom. Then a movement formed for Irish independence and when that happened, Northern Ireland wanted to stay part of the United Kingdom'. When Letterman pressed him on the role of religious divisions there, Cameron presented them as a part of a complicated historic process.

The questioning then turned to Magna Carta. The Prime Minister was able to name the year of the agreement, and that it was made in Runnymede. However, the premise of the question put by Letterman that Magna Carta was 'signed' was false. Literacy at the time was limited in its spread, and though he could read, King John was unable to write, so could only signal agreement through speech or gesture. Cameron did not know what Magna Carta meant in English ('great charter'—though the term 'great' only began to attach to it after 1215 and initially referred not to importance but to its size relative to another document associated with it, the Charter of the Forest, first issued in 1217).[21]

In October the following year Cameron returned to the subject of Magna Carta once more. At his conference speech he complained about 'some Russian official' who had supposedly said that the UK was 'just a small island that no one pays any attention to'. In response he posed a series of questions intended to emphasise the importance of the UK. Cameron opened by asking: 'When the world wanted rights, who wrote Magna Carta?', as well as other constitutionally orientated queries, including: 'When they wanted representation, who built the first Parliament?'; 'When they searched for equality, who gave women the vote?'; 'Whose example of tolerance ... of people living together from every nation, every religion, young and old, straight and gay ... whose example do they aspire to?'. His implications were in each case dubious. They involved errors such as conflating England with the UK, and then making on behalf of this composite entity excessive claims about pacesetting achievements. In the process he demonstrated the endurance of a need to depict the UK constitution as exceptional and superior.[22]

At conference a year later, the last before the next general election, Cameron again invoked Magna Carta. Speaking in the wake of the Scottish referendum, he opened by referring to himself as 'proud to stand here today as Prime Minister of four nations in one United Kingdom'. While recognising the internal complexity of the UK, this statement implied that Northern Ireland was a nation. The idea of 'this special country', as he put it, was central to his narrative once more. Cameron made a series of policy pledges for implementation in the event of his party winning an overall Commons majority in 2015. One of them involved the European Court of Human Rights. He claimed that the ECHR, which the Court was responsible for enforcing, was important and valuable at the time of its introduction after the Second World War. But he held it had come to be interpreted in ways that were 'frankly wrong', involving 'rulings to stop us deporting suspected terrorists', the application of the Convention 'even on the battle-fields of Helmand' and pressure 'to give prisoners the vote'. Cameron stated: 'This is

---

[21] 'David Cameron on David Letterman: his history test in full' *Daily Telegraph*, 27 September 2012.
[22] Speech to Conservative party conference, 2 October 2013.

the country that wrote Magna Carta' and had 'time and again ... stood up for human rights'. He insisted 'We do not require instruction on this from judges in Strasbourg'. He promised a 'new British Bill of Rights' and the abolition of 'Labour's Human Rights Act'.[23]

Close consideration of the historical record suggests a series of reservations regarding this analysis. As already noted, attaching Magna Carta to a 'country' that did not exist in 1215 is problematic. Furthermore, deploying this document as part of a narrative of separateness from Europe raises numerous difficulties. In many ways it was an archetypal European text. Magna Carta was one of a number of manifestations of a trend for the issuing of legal texts setting out the privileges of subjects that prevailed widely across the continent around the time of its production. It was written not in English but in the shared European language, Latin. The Angevin monarch who issued it was not clearly English and he was the head of a (dwindling) European empire. Military and political difficulties in Europe, in which the Church, a European 'supranational' (to deploy current terminology) institution played an important part, were crucial to the introduction of Magna Carta. Furthermore, the papacy—after initially attempting to destroy Magna Carta—went on to become its guarantor, making excommunication a penalty for its violation. In this instance, 'instruction'—as Cameron labelled it—came from Rome, as it would later come from Strasbourg.

External intervention, then, was important to the development of English legal norms. Further confirmation of this observation comes with the Dutch invasion of 1688—otherwise known as the 'Glorious Revolution'—leading on to the Bill of Rights of the following year. This epochal instrument was partly an expression of principles that William of Orange brought with him from his homeland, the United Provinces, masquerading as an assertion of ancient English law. This distortion of past concepts to serve the needs of the present is an important theme in itself. Cameron was correct in his view that the ECHR had changed over time through reinterpretation. Yet to enlist Magna Carta in the cause of human rights, as he did, is to subscribe to one of the greatest manipulations of a text ever to have taken place, dwarfing any transformations of the ECHR to date. The authors of Magna Carta would find unrecognisable the document as it exists in contemporary popular conceptions. Yet, overall, this conversion of its original meaning has—as Cameron's argument obliquely attests—been a great benefit to the world. Why is a similar approach to the ECHR, executed far more cautiously, not apt? Advocates of the traditional UK constitution often hold flexibility to be a systemic virtue. They seem unwilling to admit the same outlook when considering the ECHR. The curious extension of such logic is that as part of an exercise in asserting independence within or from Europe, the UK should move towards a more codified Napoleonic style system, and away from an adaptive model of judicial interpretation, despite the latter being a feature of the common law system so prized as distinguishing England within its continent.

---

[23] Speech to Conservative party conference, 1 October 2014.

Consideration of this set of political statements suggests a number of themes and questions for consideration in this book. As a whole they amount to a challenge to the idea, prevalent in the United Kingdom, that to take the constitution seriously is somehow pedantic or diversionary. The first involves continuity and change, and the idea that through a unique combination of the two, the UK is exemplary in its stability. Second is that of internal identity. How should we understand the UK as a state, given its complex make-up? Third is the relationship with the outside. What is the best way of interpreting the European dimension of the UK constitution, and what is the significance of the global empire and its passing? Fourth is that of accepted constitutional doctrines. How viable is parliamentary sovereignty in theory and in practice, and how might we assess attitudes towards federal structures, both as a means of internal UK organisation and at European level? Fifth—and the focal concern for this work—comes the exalted status of Magna Carta. This book will not dispute the importance of Magna Carta—indeed it will amplify it, but through reconfiguring interpretations of the kind that Thatcher and Cameron have suggested. It will consider, for instance, the aptness of the present day tendency to perceive Magna Carta through a civil and political lens, and to neglect its socio-economic dimensions. I will also discuss the role of the Church and of religion in Magna Carta, as in other constitutional developments. Sixth, and following on from the revered status of Magna Carta, which is a text of a constitutional nature, it is appropriate to question definitions of the English and UK constitution as, from an historical point of view, 'unwritten'. Seventh and last, a critical examination of the notions of UK exceptionality and superiority is necessary.

The outlooks this book interrogates have a deep cultural resonance, with the most eloquent advocacy possible, stretching over centuries. In *Richard II*, written late in the sixteenth century, Shakespeare put in the mouth of John of Gaunt a speech about England, the 'other Eden, demi-paradise'. England is, Gaunt states, a 'fortress built by Nature for herself/Against infection and the hand of war'. The 'silver sea' acts as 'a wall/Or as a moat defensive to a house,/Against the envy of less happier lands'. Gaunt closes with the exaltation: 'This blessed plot, this earth, this realm, this England'. The Shakespeare/John of Gaunt praise suggests themes that remain familiar today: a polity better than others, separate from the continental mainland in physical and other ways, and thanks to its geography enjoying security and stability. Churchill deployed similar concepts in 1940 and the John of Gaunt oration provided the journalist and contemporary historian Hugo Young with the title—*This Blessed Plot*—for his 1998 study of the difficult relationship between the UK and European integration since the Second World War.[24] Had he chosen to, Shakespeare probably could have provided a stirring account of the importance of Magna Carta that we might draw upon today. However, he notoriously failed specifically to refer to it in his *Life of King John*. Someone with as wide a range of knowledge as the author of the plays of Shakespeare surely knew about

---

[24] Young, *This Blessed Plot* (n 12).

Magna Carta. In Act II Scene 7 of *As You Like It*, Jaques exclaims 'I must have liberty/Withal as large a charter as the wind'. But perhaps Shakespeare chose to omit it from his account of John for political reasons: the text was inconvenient from the point of view of the Tudor centralising urge.

Archetypal praise of supposed constitutional traditions came from other authors in later periods, such as Alfred Tennyson in the nineteenth century. He made assertions about the international exceptionality and superiority of the British (he used the term Britain rather than England) system, and its ability to combine continuity with gradual change, in his poem 'You Ask Me Why, Tho' Ill At Ease', published in 1842. Tennyson referred to 'the land that freemen till,/ That sober-suited Freedom chose,/The land, where girt with friends or foes/Man may speak the thing he will,/A land of settled government,/A land of just and old renown,/Where Freedom broadens slowly down/From precedent to precedent'. This poem espoused the so-called Whig narrative. In this outlook the whole of English and then UK history—including Magna Carta—was a progressive attainment of the unique freedom that set the country apart from others. While this idea has long since lost academic credibility it lingers in political culture, including in the speeches of present day political leaders.[25]

Shakespeare and Tennyson promoted ideas that have commanded a wide following. But they are not the whole of our constitutional tradition. For instance, John Donne wrote in 1624:

> No man is an island, entire of itself; every man is a piece of the continent, a part of the main; if a clod be washed away by the sea, Europe is the less ... any man's death diminishes me, because I am involved in mankind.

Lying behind this call for human solidarity was Donne's direct experience of the European conflict that began in 1618, eventually gaining the label of the 'Thirty Years War'.[26] It had direct links to the prolonged conflicts of seventeenth-century England, a period that calls into question claims regarding a continuous, resilient constitution. The impact of the Thirty Years War—and the sentiment that Donne expressed—suggests that English systemic development was characterised by close connection with, rather than separation from, the continental mainland. Another player within and observer of the tumult of this era was John Milton. As we have seen, he was one who James Callaghan invoked when expressing concern about the supposed threat that European integration posed to the English language. Milton himself had a different attitude towards constitutional influences derived from elsewhere in the continent. In 1670, discussing the experience of the Civil War, Milton—who had been a supporter and employee of Oliver Cromwell—expressed regret that those responsible for governing during the 'Interregnum' (as it was subsequently labelled) were not wholly capable

[25] For critical analysis of this school, see: Herbert Butterfield, *The Whig Interpretation of History* (New York, WW Norton & Co, 1965).

[26] Brendan Simms, *Three Victories and a Defeat: The Rise and Fall of the First British Empire, 1714–1783* (London, Allen Lane, 2007) 7–9.

of performing the task. They would have benefited, he believed, from obtaining outside knowledge:

> [T]he sun, which we want, ripens wits as well as fruits; and as wine and oil are imported to us from abroad, so must ripe understanding and many civil virtues be … from foreign writings and examples of best ages; we shall else miscarry still and come short in the attempts of any great enterprise.[27]

A century-and-a-half later, in response to the August 1819 'Peterloo' massacre of franchise reform demonstrators in Manchester, Percy Shelley wrote 'The Masque [or Mask] of Anarchy'. In this poem he prefigured debates about whether rights should focus only on civil and political activity—that Tennyson had highlighted— or also be socio-economic in character. Shelley asked 'What art thou Freedom?'. It was not, he felt, 'A shadow soon to pass away/A superstition, and a name/Echoing from the cave of Fame'. 'For the labourer', Shelley concluded, freedom was 'clothes, and fire, and food'.[28] Events of 1819 provided evidence, anyway, that even 'civil and political' rights were less firm than might be supposed. The protestors in Manchester in August 1819 sought the expansion of a tiny franchise; though they were peaceful, some of them were killed. Furthermore, Shelley had difficulty securing publication for his poem, because of its politically sensitive nature, and it did not appear until 1832, a decade after his death. Even then those daring to reproduce it faced the threat of legal harassment.

The proposition that the English or UK constitution was innately better than others lacked universal acceptance. For ironic effect, Charles Dickens has the Mr Podsnap character in the novel *Our Mutual Friend* describe how 'We Englishmen are Very Proud of our Constitution … It was Bestowed Upon Us by providence. No other Country is so Favoured as this Country'. Real people, outside the pages of Dickens, held similar views. Vernon Bogdanor observes 'Mr Podsnap's view was to be echoed not only in Britain but also by observers in other countries, who studied the British constitution to discover the secret of success- ful government, the secret of how to combine freedom with stability'.[29] Yet as the attitudes of Dickens, Shelley, Milton and Donne show, a constitutional counter- tradition exists, awaiting discovery. If found it can help unlock a different percep- tion of the English/UK constitution as it has been, is and could be.

The book divides into three parts. Part one considers a series of documents from English and then UK history that share some of the features we might asso- ciate with a written constitution. Part two assesses the current constitution. It does so through identifying and analysing a period of change of historic significance beginning in the 1950s, and continuing to the present. I consider the causes and main manifestations of this phase of transformation, the tensions associated with

---

[27]   Scott, *England's Troubles* (n 7) 37–38.

[28]   For analysis from this perspective, see: Peter Linebaugh, *The Magna Carta Manifesto: Liberties and Commons for All* (Berkeley CA, University of California Press, 2008) 20–21. See also: K Kullen, 'Shelley's "Mask of Anarchy" and the Problem of Modern Sovereignty' (2011) 8 *Literature Compass* 95.

[29]   Vernon Bogdanor, *The New British Constitution* (Oxford, Hart Publishing, 2009) 3.

it, and where it might be leading. Part three then argues in favour of the introduction of a written UK constitution. It goes on to consider how such a text might come into being and what it might include.

Certain caveats are required. First, when the present author uses the term 'unwritten constitution', it is not intended to convey the idea of a system none of which is included in any official document. As the political commentator Sidney Low wrote in 1904: 'It is not so much that our constitution is unwritten, for of course much the largest part of it is written and printed'.[30] I find the label 'unwritten constitution' useful as a means of distinguishing from its opposite, a 'written constitution'. The latter term implies an act of conception through language. The UK constitution has not passed through an embracing process consciously deployed in pursuit of such an end. In the following work, the term 'unwritten' is intended to convey also that the UK lacks a single document, or connected series of documents, that are expressly a constitution, possessing some kind of special legal status and setting out fundamental social rules. Some prefer to contrast 'codified' and 'uncodified' constitutions, but the codification label could convey a more functional and less inspiring exercise of compilation, seeking to collate that which exists rather than to create anew. Second, this work does not pretend fully to consider Welsh, Irish or Scottish constitutional history in their own right, not because they are unimportant, but for the opposite reason, because others are better placed to do so in the proper fashion they merit. However, a key theme in the consideration of the UK polity is the complex and multinational nature of its composition. Third, I take seriously those who caution against the literal reading of earlier documents as though they are fully-fledged modern texts.[31] We should not inject into the declarations of yesterday the values of today. Yet neither should we dismiss the contemporary significance of efforts of the past using the standards of the present. The historic survey that follows will demonstrate that these earlier documents express some of the same urges as later written constitutions in different parts of the world: to set out overriding, enduring rules on a basis of consultation. Moreover, they had an important if sometimes indirect or distorted influence on the appearance of the concept of the written constitution, and the contents of these texts, as well as other important later declarations of a constitutional quality.

A senior legal academic has remarked that 'writing about Magna Carta at all requires a measure of presumption'.[32] My justification for doing so on this occasion is that, since the 700th and even 750th anniversaries, the UK constitution has passed, and continues to move, through an exceptionally pronounced phase of change. This period of development can provide enlightening perspectives

---

[30] Sidney Low, *The Governance of England* (London, T Fisher Unwin, 1914) 2.

[31] Martin Loughlin, *The British Constitution: A Very Short Introduction* (Oxford, Oxford University Press, 2013) ch 1.

[32] RH Helmholz, 'Magna Carta and the *ius commune*' (1999) 66(2) *The University of Chicago Law Review* 297.

on Magna Carta, which can in turn enable a better understanding of present trajectories. Some might object that, in the following pages, I enlist Magna Carta for purposes other than those who originally created it intended, or could have conceived. Yet, while over the centuries those seeking to procure Magna Carta for their own causes have subjected it to misrepresentation and distortion, a more subtle approach is available. It is possible to identify perennial concerns surrounding the text and the circumstances of its introduction in 1215 without committing acts of violence to the historical record. Moreover, the story of Magna Carta from the outset has involved the deployment of legend in pursuit of particular goals. In as far as I do exploit rather than merely analyse, it is the mythology surrounding Magna Carta and some of the values associated with this lore that I appropriate. Since 1215 Magna Carta has served many—often good—causes. This book is written in the belief that there is yet more value still to be extracted from it. In this endeavour I will be in good company.

Part I

The Written Constitutional Tradition

2

Before Magna Carta: Early Law Codes and Charters

WRITING AND CONSTITUTIONALISM are inextricable in English history. Long before 1215 and Magna Carta, a series of texts had appeared in England setting out fundamental social rules and principles. They began—as far as is known for certain—around the turn of the sixth and seventh centuries in Kent. Law codes subsequently appeared in two other early English kingdoms, Mercia and Wessex. A ruler of the latter territory, Alfred 'the Great' (a label that he merited, but which he only gained a millennium after his own lifetime) produced a long and celebrated entry in the genre. Alfred began the establishment of a unified English realm, in the face of Viking incursions, over which his descendants presided, continuing his practice of literate lawgiving. Conquest, first by Vikings, then by Normans, followed. But the practice of issuing written statements of basic law continued. From the contemporary standpoint, Magna Carta may seem the beginning of an 800-year-old tradition. In 1215, it was an example of a practice already five centuries old.

THE ETHELBERT LAW CODE

Bede, a monk based in Jarrow, enjoys the reputation of being the first English historian. He completed his most famous work, *Ecclesiastical History of the English People*, in 731. In it Bede tells of the death, following a 56-year reign, of King Ethelbert of Kent, in 616. For the final 21 years of his life, Bede recounts, Ethelbert had been a Christian, who converted following the arrival of Augustine in England. Ethelbert controlled all the territory south of the river Humber, the third ruler to attain this geographic reach, and the first of his adopted faith. Bede describes the 'many benefits that [Ethelbert's] wisdom conferred on the nation'. Among these achievements Bede singles out one in particular. He notes how Ethelbert 'introduced with the consent of his counsellors a code of law inspired by the example of the Romans, which was written in English, and remains in force to this day'.[1] We do not have a precise date for this event. William Stubbs offers a range of 601–04[2], FL Attenborough

---

[1] Bede, *Ecclesiastical History of the English People* (London, Penguin, 1990) 111–12.
[2] William Stubbs, *Select Charters and Other Illustrations of English Constitutional History from the Earliest Times to the Reign of Edward the First*, 9th edn (Oxford, Clarendon Press, 1929) 66.

tentatively proposes 602–03[3], while some point further back, to even before 595.[4] But whatever the exact point of appearance, beyond doubt is the importance of the text.

The account Bede gives introduces a number of themes important to this work. First is that of English and UK constitutional traditions. Ethelbert's document was not a written constitution as we would understand it today. Concepts that inform such texts—including representative democracy, universal rights and popular sovereignty—were more than a millennium away. Nor was the Ethelbert code a comprehensive definition of the official institutional framework. Nonetheless, it is written and it is constitutional, and it shares some of the essence of a written constitution. The document reaches us in the present thanks to Ernulf, Bishop of Rochester. In the first half of the 1120s he instigated the reproduction of a series of legal documents, in a volume known as *Textus Roffensis*. In addition to the Ethelred law code, it featured two more from seventh-century Kent; among other texts it included, from the late ninth century, the law code of King Alfred, and the charter of Henry I—issued in 1100 at the time of his coronation and known as his 'Charter of Liberties'. This final document went on to have a direct influence upon Magna Carta. *Textus Roffensis* demonstrates the existence by this time of an awareness of a continuum of such instruments in England: a written constitutional tradition. By the early twelfth century, it already stretched back around 500 years. Ethelbert's work was the inaugural entry in the canon. It is possible that others predated it, but were lost. Two historians of early English law suggest: 'Some earlier Kentish king may have led the way. We can but speculate whether it was Eormenric or the shadowy Octa or the shadowy Oisc and whether laws were being written in Kent in the early sixth century'.[5] Regardless, the Ethelbert code is what remains.

What are the qualities that the Ethelbert document shares with contemporary constitutional texts? Most obviously, it was written. It is common to regard Augustine's appearance in Kent in 597, after which he became the first Archbishop of Canterbury, as marking both the introduction of Christianity and of literacy to England (some suggest, however, that the Ethelbert text predated 597, and therefore Christianity in England, and—as we have seen—even that other, necessarily non-Christian, codes existed before it).[6] The ability to produce written texts was a prerequisite for a project such as Ethelbert's. But rather than possession of this skill leading to the production of the code, it seems that a powerful desire to seek to clarify fundamental social rules actually drove the English to create their written language. The Ethelbert document is credited as easily the first work

---

[3] FL Attenborough (ed), *The Laws of the Earliest English Kings* (Cambridge, Cambridge University Press, 1922) 1.

[4] HG Richardson and GO Sayles, *Law and Legislation: From Aethelberht to Magna Carta* (Edinburgh, Edinburgh University Press, 1966) 9.

[5] Ibid.

[6] Lisi Oliver, *The Beginnings of English Law* (Toronto, University of Toronto Press, 2002) 14–15.

produced in English (though in a form only specialists can read). Indeed of all the other Teutonic languages, none produced any surviving texts this old, apart from 'short inscriptions'. It contrasts with equivalent documents produced on the continental mainland around this time, which used Latin.[7] Writing and the constitution, therefore, were intertwined at the earliest possible stage in England, and this entanglement helped bring about the written English language and the English legal system.

What precisely did Ethelbert have written down? As with many of the documents discussed in this part of the book, an initial reading of this code might create doubt about its constitutional credentials. On the surface, its primary purpose is stipulating levels of recompense for criminal acts. In part it was probably setting out various rules which already existed in unwritten form. The text, for instance, goes into considerable detail about the amount of money that must be paid by assailants to victims for a range of physical injuries: a removed thumbnail costs three shillings; a severed shooting finger nine shillings; a lost big toe 10 shillings; a punch on the nose three shillings. The document describes the price of incapacitation of genitalia as 'three person payments'.[8] Those who complain about a supposed 'compensation culture' in contemporary society deride an ancient English tradition. The advertising slogan 'where there's a blame there's a claim' would fit this document well.

Behind the specifics the code possesses a number of qualities also associated with written constitutions. It deals with fundamental issues involving the fabric of society. In his lecture on Ethelbert's document given in 2003, Patrick Wormald explained that enforcing a clear system of compensation was essential to prevent a descent into a protracted, escalating vendetta between clans that was a danger in the Anglo-Saxon world.[9] Another function of the code was to act as propaganda. Unlike later documents we will consider, it seemingly did not name the king as its progenitor (though it may once have had a preamble that is now lost, describing how Ethelred produced the declaration with the advice of senior counsellors).[10] Either way, the code was known to be his product, as Bede's account establishes. It showed he was a peer of other continental kings who were issuing similar texts around this time, bringing himself into line with emerging best practice. Ethelbert 'wished to ensure his importance to the future by means of a permanent memorial in the technology of the future, that is, writing. These laws of the Kentish people may well have been intended ... as a monument to the king'.[11]

---

[7] Attenborough, *The Laws of the Earliest English Kings* (n 3) 3. See also: AWB Simpson, 'The Laws of Ethelbert' in Morris S Arnold et al (eds), *On the Laws and Customs of England: Essays in Honor of Samuel E. Thorne* (Chapel Hill NC, University of North Carolina Press, 1981) 4.

[8] The translation used here comes from Patrick Wormald, *The First Code of English Law* (Canterbury, Canterbury Commemoration Society, 2005) 3–10.

[9] Ibid, 11–13.

[10] Richardson and Sayles, *Law and Legislation* (n 4) 11.

[11] Oliver, *The Beginnings of English Law* (n 6) 20.

Ethelbert achieved a lasting impact, greater than he could have imagined. The code came to be regarded as a core component of English law long after the passing away of the king who instigated it, with Bede describing it as still 'in force to this day' more than a century later (though the texts considered in this chapter were not fully justiciable in a contemporary sense). Later, similar Anglo-Saxon documents would refer back to their predecessors, including that of Ethelbert. In the preliminary passage to his law code of the late ninth century King Alfred described how he had consulted with 'many of the ones that our forefathers observed' including those of Ethelbert 'who first among the English people received baptism'.[12] This lasting status for the text bears comparison to that sought by written constitutions, which usually attempt legally to entrench themselves.

Further senses in which this code is constitutional arise from its subject matter. It deals with such issues as 'the status of government agencies', personal security and 'women's rights'.[13] It protects property, and sets out to ensure welfare provision for those prevented physically from supporting themselves because of injury, through making assailants pay for medical treatment and subsistence. The text also implies a principle that the monarch has a role in ensuring the safety of public gatherings.[14] It handles these subjects through treating different institutions and groups in turn, describing the particular acts against them for which recompense must be made, and what precisely it should be. In some instances the code sets out the responsibilities and internal relations of these social categories. It starts with the Church and clergy and then moves to the king and his retinue, followed by the aristocracy, free and partially free common men, physical injuries, women, workers and slaves.

The code delineates rights of a sort, though they are neither equal nor all-embracing as we would understand the term today. Individuals' worth varies according to their particular characteristics. Differentiation takes place between and within groups. Sexual relations with a 'king's maiden' incur a penalty of 50 shillings, but if she is a 'grinding slave' on the royal staff, the tariff drops to 25 shillings. In the Church, compensation for the property of a bishop is set at 11 times its value, a priest at a multiple of nine, a deacon six and a cleric three. For transgression against the king and his immediate circle, compensation is generally fixed at 50 shillings, the earl 12, and the 'ceorl' (or common man) six.

The treatment of women appears anachronistic and unfair if judged using contemporary standards. For instance, Ethelbert's text stipulates that if a freeman sleeps with another freeman's wife, the offending freeman must buy the wife concerned and purchase a replacement for the freeman whose spouse he has acquired, delivering her to the home of her new husband. Yet the code sets out a series of protections, in particular for the status of widows. Interestingly, it accepts

---

[12] Simon Keynes and Michael Lapidge, *Alfred the Great: Asser's Life of King Alfred and Other Contemporary Sources* (London, Penguin, 1983) 164.

[13] Wormald, *The First Code of English Law* (n 8) 10.

[14] Oliver, *The Beginnings of English Law* (n 6) 105, 85.

the idea of divorce—perhaps because Christian influence had not yet become fully pervasive in this regard or perhaps because the text was not in fact the work of Christians[15]—and seems to imply that women have a role in the decision, in such circumstances, over who should keep any children there may be. The woman is entitled to half of the property of the ex-husband if she takes custody of the offspring, and a smaller amount if she does not. If there are no children, she has no property rights.

Later law codes in the Anglo-Saxon era also dealt with women.[16] Indeed, historians traditionally tended to hold that the social status of women enjoyed greater protection in this age than it did following the Norman conquest, whereupon it deteriorated. However, Anne L Klinck has suggested a different pattern. She indentifies a decreasing legal subordination to men, in some respects at least, over the Anglo-Saxon period, and a higher degree of continuity from the late Anglo-Saxon to the Norman period than previously supposed. She notes that law codes issued under Ethelred II and Cnut in the eleventh century (both of which Wulfstan, Archbishop of York, drafted)[17] gave greater independence to women, in such areas as whether widows should marry again, be single, or become nuns, and in ruling out forced marriages. Condemnation of women for the crimes of their husbands became less likely. Yet clear inequalities existed: females risked greater penalties for adultery than males.[18]

To return to the Ethelbert code: Bede's reference to the king introducing it 'with the consent of his counsellors' is significant. Nineteenth-century historians were mistaken when they transplanted contemporary ideas of representative government to a time when they did not exist.[19] Nonetheless, Bede's account promotes the view that the Ethelbert text rested in consultation of some kind. The ruler could not produce law 'of his sole authority'. When seeking to take advice on and validate important decisions, Anglo-Saxon kings turned to a body comprising their senior magnates that came to be known as the 'Witan', a body of real if vague and variable power. One account speculates that the Witan would have considered a proposed text, produced by royal scribes, and put forward possible alterations. After a process that was possibly longer than a day in duration the officials would create a revised version, with a number of copies for reading out in public across the realm.[20] That the Ethelbert code rested on the participation of the Witan, and that successors to it in the Anglo-Saxon era make a point of

[15] Richardson and Sayles, *Law and Legislation* (n 4) 1.

[16] Theodore John Rivers, 'Widows' Rights in Anglo Saxon Law' (1975) 19 *American Journal of Legal History* 208.

[17] For the role of Wulfstan and the extent of his personal influence, particularly on the latter code, see: Stephanie Hollis, '"The Protection of God and the King": Wulfstan's Legislation on Widows' in Matthew Townend (ed), *Wulfstan: Archbishop of York, The Proceedings of the Second Alcuin Conference* (Studies in the Early Middle Ages 10) (Turnhout, Brepols, 2004).

[18] Anne L Klinck, 'Anglo-Saxon women and the law' (1982) 8 *Journal of Medieval History* 107.

[19] For analysis of this error see: Patrick Wormald, *The Making of English Law: King Alfred to the Twelfth Century*, Vol 1, *Legislation and its Limits* (Oxford, Blackwell, 1999) 4–14.

[20] Richardson and Sayles, *Law and Legislation* (n 4) 11–12.

stating in their texts that they were issued on such a basis, shows that contemporaries regarded these documents both as important, and deriving the high level of legitimacy they needed from (by the standards of the time) wide participation. After the Conquest of 1066 the Normans replaced the Witan with a smaller group of royal advisers.[21] Nonetheless, though government became more streamlined, texts of a constitutional nature continued to emphasise that they rested on broad consultation, albeit within the altered context of Norman rule.

The idea of restoring supposed traditional values was an important component in the post-Conquest documents discussed in this part of the book. Indeed, Norman centralisation provided the factual but slender basis for an extravagant mythology—fully developed in the seventeenth century—about representative, limited government in England's Anglo-Saxon past, that became subject to a 'Norman yoke'.[22] Furthermore, participants in the movement which led to the introduction of the most influential of written constitutions—that of the United States (US)—believed they were asserting their rights as free Anglo-Saxons. While such representations of Anglo-Saxon governance were distorted, the notion of the need for an inclusive procedure that genuinely informed Ethelbert's project (and successors to it) remains relevant, albeit adapted and augmented. The creation and subsequent amendment of full written constitutions often involves special processes designed to obtain wide assent. These documents generally assert that they are expressions of the will of the whole people—the doctrine of popular sovereignty—and seek to ensure that government is limited and founded in democracy and representative institutions.

Bede encourages a further observation through his claim that Ethelbert was 'inspired by the example of the Romans'. Ethelbert's text was European. The term 'Romans' could imply both those who had governed the old Roman Empire, and the Frankish kings who succeeded them, among whom Ethelbert sought to assert his leadership credentials. Ethelbert had advisers with connections to the continental mainland. Moreover, around 580, before he converted, he had married Bertha, a Christian, who was the daughter of Charibert, a Frankish king. She was literate and her personal chaplain, Liuhard, would also have been, and possibly attempted to transfer his Frankish writing into Anglo-Saxon. The structure and some of the details of the code resemble the contents of other texts issued elsewhere in Europe around this time. The Anglo-Saxons themselves originally came from the mainland, bringing certain principles with them, anyway. On a more practical level, even the currency unit the text refers to—the shilling—was of Germanic derivation, confirming continental entanglement. Before the Anglo-Saxons began manufacturing their own coins, which did not become a regular

---

[21] See eg: James Fosdick Baldwin, *The King's Council in England during the Middle Ages* (Oxford, Clarendon Press, 1969).

[22] For a classic account of this tradition, see: Christopher Hill, 'The Norman Yoke' in Christopher Hill, *Puritanism and Revolution: Studies in Interpretation of the English Revolution of the 17th Century* (London, Secker & Warburg, 1958).

practice until around 630, they 'used Merovingian gold coins imported from the Frankish territories'.[23]

In his assessment of Ethelbert's code and its successors, Wormald argues that 'pronouncements by any regime obviously need to be understood in terms of its own political culture. The political culture of the first English kingdom was European'.[24] The provenance of the law code demonstrates that not only does England have an ancient and important tradition of writing down constitutional arrangements, but that in doing so it has expressed its developing European identity. A European consciousness as later understood did not exist by this time (though neither did an English awareness).[25] Yet the production of these documents and their contents can only be understood if English and UK constitutional history is placed within a continental continuum. Its role—like that of all the parts of Europe—has been distinctive. For instance, while Ethelbert innovated by using a written form of the native Anglo-Saxon language, the equivalent Frankish documents were in Latin. In coming centuries, the British Isles remained outside the Carolingian realm which expanded through mainland Western Europe and reached its peak under Charlemagne early in the ninth century. Nonetheless the position of England and the UK has never been one of isolation from the broader continental environment. Carolingian practices, for instance, exerted influence on the legal initiatives of Alfred and subsequent English kings.[26] In fact there has been a continuous and fertile process of two-way influence, in constitutional areas as in others. To deny it is to belittle both sides of this equation and their combined achievement.

Awareness of this European dimension leads on to a final set of remarks that Bede's commentary prompts. He stresses the Christian nature of the text (though as we have seen some dispute this interpretation).[27] For many historians, the arrival in England of the Church—a pan-continental entity—was vital for its promotion of the use of writing, a prerequisite to the production of this text. The Church also spread ideas about kings being lawgivers and taught about biblical codes, encouraging the creation of statements such as that of Ethelbert. Given its possession of literacy, a rare quality at the time, the Church was a source of the expertise necessary to carry out the drafting. This position was useful both from the point of view of rulers and clerics. The latter were able not only to pursue spiritual goals, but also to secure their institutional self-interest through Ethelred's document. Bede notes approvingly of Ethelbert that the 'first of his laws is designed to protect those whose persons and doctrines he had embraced, and prescribes what satisfaction must be made by any person who steals property

---

[23]   Oliver, *The Beginnings of English Law* (n 6) 8–9, 13, 15, 82.

[24]   Wormald, *The Making of English Law* (n 19) 30.

[25]   See: Chris Wickham, *The Inheritance of Rome: A History of Europe from 400 to 1000* (London, Allen Lane, 2009) 3–5.

[26]   David Pratt, 'Written Law and the Communication of Authority in Tenth-Century England' in D Rollason et al (eds), *England and the Continent in the Tenth Century* (Turnhout, Brepols, 2011).

[27]   Richardson and Sayles, *Law and Legislation* (n 4) 9.

from the Church, the bishop, or other clergy'.[28] Another interpretation of the assertion of the position of the Church is that it was not in the original text but a later insertion, made some time before Bede gave his account.[29]

Numerous subsequent English constitutional documents and written constitutions internationally have dealt with the place of religious institutions within society (though they may do so through specifying their separation from the public sphere) and the related issue of religious faith, including individual belief. Of further importance is the role of the Church as provider of expertise. Whatever its precise role in the Ethelbert text, it was definitely important to the creation of later such texts. Clerics can be seen as precursors to the experts and the officials who inevitably play a part in devising any written constitution. They are essential to such a process, and may well make valuable contributions to it, but at the same time are likely to have certain agendas of their own, which can skew the outcome. Finally, the Church was what would now be termed a supranational institution, distinct from domestic authority. At different points in history the relationship between the two could become tense and played an important part in constitutional development, in England as elsewhere in Europe, while disputes between domestic clergy and the Rome hierarchy were also possible.

ANGLO-SAXON CODES AFTER ETHELBERT

Other codes followed Ethelbert's. Hlothaere and Eadric of Kent issued a document that Stubbs dates to 685–56.[30] Its stipulations include that there is a need to follow the findings of the 'judges of Kent' in resolution of disputes. In this sense it was providing for the role of an official institution, the judiciary (of an undoubtedly primitive kind). It sets out the right for mothers to keep their children if the father dies, with a guardian from the family of the father acting as custodian of the property of the child until they are 10. Alongside rules applying to violent crime, it includes measures to protect private property from theft and regulations regarding the purchase of 'property in London',[31] a vexing task even in the Anglo-Saxon era.

Another Kentish effort came around 700 (perhaps 695) from King Wihtred. It includes a preamble describing the gathering in a place called Barnham of 'a deliberative council of the notables'. They unanimously agreed upon a set of 'decrees, and added them to the legal usages of the people of Kent'. The first provisions deal with the crucial constitutional compact between monarch and Church, whereby the former affords privileges to the latter in return for the conferral of legitimacy. It states that 'The Church shall enjoy immunity from taxation' (prefiguring the

---

[28] Bede, *Ecclesiastical History of the English People* (n 1) 112.
[29] Richardson and Sayles, *Law and Legislation* (n 4) 2–4.
[30] Stubbs, *Select Charters* (n 2) 67.
[31] Attenborough, *The Laws of the Earliest English Kings* (n 3) 21, 18–23, 19, 23.

privileged fiscal status provided to religions today) and that 'The king shall be prayed for, and they shall honour him freely without compulsion'. The remainder of the document deals extensively with enforcing Christianity, as well as imposing rules upon slaves and other workers, the protection of property, and the swearing of oaths, an important binding component in the society of the time.[32]

Law codes had by this point spread beyond Kent. Some time between 688 and 694, Ine of Wessex had produced a text. It opens by proclaiming that he—'by the grace of God king of Wessex', drawing on the advice of his father, his bishops, his aristocrats and the 'chief councillors of my people', as well as a large body of clergy, had pondered 'the salvation of our souls and the security of our realm' in order to ensure that 'just law' and judgments should pervade throughout, and that no one should undermine them in future.[33] This preamble resembles those which are found at the beginning of contemporary codified constitutions, establishing the legitimacy and values underpinning the document. It is, however, issued in the name of the king, as became the practice in the texts that came after Ethelbert, and appears intended as a means of proclaiming and enforcing Ine's divine authority. At the same time, the need to consult—and to be seen to do so—is apparent. After Ine and the Kentish code-makers, Offa of Mercia, who ruled from 757 to 796, possibly produced a lost document. Its existence can be inferred from a reference in the law code of King Alfred, alongside citations of those of Ethelbert and Ine, the last of which texts Alfred included as a supplement to his own.

During his reign Alfred fought off Viking incursions, eventually becoming king of all those parts of England not under occupation. Emerging from this crisis, probably some time after 893, was a substantial law code issued in his name. It was by far the longest of its kind in the period preceding the Norman Conquest. Through this document Alfred sought to achieve greater certainty following difficult circumstances, bolster his own kingship, promote a particular set of values, and unite the different peoples who had come under his rule.[34] Some see it as part of a project that had the effect of encouraging the development of England as a self-aware political entity.[35] The text presents itself as the continuation of an historic mission of transposing the biblical rules applied in Israel to Christian societies. In the document Alfred describes how he initiated among his advisers an evidence-gathering process, ordering them to assemble a range of scriptural rules, and laws from the times of Ine, Offa and Ethelbert. Through drawing on Kentish and Mercian sources as well those of Ine who, like Alfred, was a West Saxon Alfred incorporated varied traditions from his newly expanded territory. He probably had wider European influences too, and in conventional accounts assembled a team of expert advisers drawn from across the continent. Alfred states

---

[32] Ibid, 3, 25, 24–31.

[33] Ibid, 37.

[34] Keynes and Lapidge, *Alfred the Great* (n 12) 39, 304–05, 163–70.

[35] Sarah Foot, 'The Making of *Angelcynn*: English Identity before the Norman Conquest' (1996) 6 *Transactions of the Royal Historical Society* 25.

in the document that he was reluctant to create many laws of his own, but instead preferred to choose those from the earlier English codes that seemed to him 'most just',[36] leaving out the remainder. Once he had completed his task, he showed them to his advisers, who showed approval.

The account Alfred gave of how he composed his text raises another important theme. Authors of documents such as his code sought to derive legitimacy from the past, by purporting to restate already established rules. But the reality was never so straightforward. When writing down regulations that were previously related only by word of mouth (as possibly took place under Ethelbert), there was likely to be doubt about what precisely the rules were. Those producing texts had no choice but to impose some of their own interpretations. Even when working with written sources, a strong temptation existed to bring about change through distorting, fabricating or omitting previously existing rules. Alfred seems to have deployed these sorts of techniques. He describes dispensing with certain past laws and ordering them to be followed in different ways, and his account of the process he used does not fully preclude that he added some provisions. Wormald judges that a quarter of the Alfred code did not derive from existing English law, though a significant quantity of the additions were focused on narrow issues.[37] Self-interest could encourage adjustments in the law. Successive texts that followed the Ethelbert code amplified the role of the king, including as a recipient of fines, and Ethelbert's text itself may have enhanced the position of the ruler as it was under pre-literate arrangements. But while kings could exploit the potential for executing change while emphasising continuity, these methods could also turn against them.

Alfred had already helped produce a shorter document, in a pause between fighting with the Vikings, that is suggestive of the potential constitutional importance of treaties. Drafted some time between 886 (when Alfred captured London) and 889 at the latest, it was a peace agreement between him and Guthrum, king of the Vikings in East Anglia. It underlines that the existence of England—like that of any state in later times—was not purely an internal matter, but involved recognition from others. The text opens with the usual nod to inclusion, referring not only to Alfred and Guthrum but 'the councillors of all the English race and all the people who are in East Anglia'.[38] Though Alfred expressed concern in his law code that he did not want to impose unwelcome stipulations on future generations, not knowing what their requirements might be, this treaty states that it applies to the 'living and the unborn', if they wanted to have the favour both of God and of those who promulgated it. In this sense, the text sought to be self-entrenching. Next the agreement fixes the border, running along the Thames, then the Lea to its source, direct to Bedford, then along the Ouse as far as the old Roman road, Watling Street. It then sets out to establish equal treatment under

---

[36] Keynes and Lapidge, *Alfred the Great* (n 12) 164.
[37] Wormald, *The Making of English Law* (n 19) 281–82.
[38] Keynes and Lapidge, *Alfred the Great* (n 12) 171. For a translation of the text see: 171–72.

the law of Englishmen and Danes, through stipulations about compensation for manslaughter. There follows an agreement that neither side will poach men from the other for their armed forces. Counterbalancing this restriction on transfers of labour is the undertaking that both parties will permit trade in 'cattle and goods', provided those crossing the border supply hostages to guarantee that their intentions are peaceful, and that they do not intend to perpetrate 'fraud'. The combined intent of these provisions can be seen as the introduction into an area previously rent by military conflict of a common, entrenched set of legal, social and commercial standards intended to facilitate mutually beneficial, regulated trade, underpinned by a shared normative outlook, that of Christianity (to which Guthrum had converted). Unfortunately, the treaty failed to achieve sustained peace. In 892, two years after the death of Guthrum, the Vikings mounted another invasion.

The Anglo-Saxon law code production-line continued running after Alfred. Between 900 and 1035, all but 13 kings issued texts.[39] During his reign from c925 to c939, Aethelstan issued six. They raise subjects of constitutional interest. Among them was 'the first social legislation in England, providing for the relief of the poor'.[40] A short instrument entitled 'Ordinance Relating to Charities', it was intended to enforce the king's desire that his 'reeves ... shall always provide a destitute Englishman with food'. Those who failed to perform this duty were subject to a fine of 30 shillings, for division between the 'poor' within the 'estate' concerned. Alongside this social regulation another, longer, Aethelstan text, his 'Ordinances', includes numerous economic provisions. In combination with trade regulations it states that 'there shall be one coinage throughout the king's realm'. When a 'moneyer' is found to have produced defective coins, 'the hand shall be cut off with which he committed the crime, and fastened up on the mint'. A further document from the Aethelstan period applied to a specific sub-unit of the kingdom. It comprised 'ordinances which have been agreed upon ... by the bishops and reeves who belong to London'. Attenborough writes 'This document is of considerable importance as the first example of what may be called the by-laws of an association'. Its application may have stretched beyond London, to cover the whole of Middlesex and possibly further still: an early form of a 'Greater London' city-region. The provisions of the text include commitments that 'each one of us shall annually contribute four pence for our common benefit'; that 'we shall all stand together, both in friendship and in feud'; and that leading figures 'shall assemble once every month ... and we shall take cognisance of how our various statutes are being observed'. We can detect in these statements some of the features of self-financing, autonomous local government, though the document closes with some proclamations from the central authority, the king.[41]

---

[39] Wormald, *The Making of English Law* (n 19) 286.
[40] Richardson and Sayles, *Law and Legislation* (n 4) 18.
[41] Attenborough, *The Laws of the Earliest English Kings* (n 3) 127, 135, 157, 212, 159, 163, 169.

A notable document appeared under Cnut, in 1020 or 1021. It is the last, of those that survive, from the pre-Norman era.[42] This code deals with a spread of subjects of a constitutional character: the powers of the king; legal processes; religion; the Church; and the rights of assorted groups. The circumstances of its introduction and its content illustrate many important themes. It appeared from a long period of conflict between Anglo-Saxons and Viking invaders. Following the death of Ethelred II in 1016, Cnut, a Dane, began to establish himself as ruler. The importance of a wider European perspective to English constitutional development is, therefore, plain: the document emerged in the context of foreign conquest. Also apparent is the role that discontinuity and crises can play in the creation of such texts. The code was part of an attempt to establish peace between the two groups. An inclusive process was involved: a joint Danish–English Witan at Oxford of 1018 seems to have been significant to the instigation of the document.[43]

Furthermore, the text suggests limitations on official authority, especially that of the king. A late section opens with a commitment from Cnut to prevent the repetition of previous oppressions. To this end it seeks to proscribe arbitrary taxation and punishment in various manifestations. For Cnut, agreeing such terms probably seemed worthwhile as a means of securing his position. His commitment took place against the background of a trend towards coronation pledges that had developed in Western Europe from the second half of the ninth century. Much of the content of the document derives from previous law, and was intended to demonstrate continuity under the new ruler. But Pauline Stafford identifies the latter passages covering 'abuses of lordship ... specifically those of the king' as innovatory (though possibly drawing on lost sources).[44] Statements issued by kings intended to serve their own interests were now beginning to become limitations upon them.

Consideration of the sources of the code leads on to the matter of who produced it. Wulfstan, Archbishop of York, widely credited with drafting the text,[45] was an important legal adviser both to Ethelred II and after him Cnut. He seems to have used the circumstances of transition to new political leadership to promote agendas of his own, some of which he had already expressed through laws of the Ethelred period. As the occupant of an administrative support role to successive regimes of different complexions, there are parallels between Wulfstan and the permanent civil servants of recent times. Positions of the sort Wulfstan and more contemporary staff held can afford significant influence, including in constitutional matters, to those who fill them. There is debate, however, about

---

[42] Pauline Stafford, 'The laws of Cnut and the history of Anglo-Saxon royal promises' (1981) 10 *Anglo-Saxon England* 173. The text is known as I and II Cnut.

[43] Ibid, 173–74.

[44] Ibid, 185, 174–77, 181–82.

[45] See: Dorothy Whitelock, 'Wulfstan and the laws of Cnut' (1948) 63 *English Historical Review* 433; and Dorothy Whitelock, 'Wulfstan's authorship of Cnut's laws' (1955) 70 *English Historical Review* 72.

how far Wulfstan was insulated from other influences, or was obliged to canvass and reflect wider opinion.[46] Whatever the precise authorship, the outcome was impressive, for the way it compiled diverse existing rules and particularly in its apparently more original features. Noting that scholars have found precedent for Magna Carta in the *post*-conquest period, Stafford—in an article drawing particular attention to the passages in the code that seek to impose terms on those in positions of power—remarks that the 'journey towards Runnymede may have begun earlier'.[47]

POST-CONQUEST TEXTS

The kingdom William acquired in 1066, then, not only possessed a long-established set of constitutional characteristics, but regularly presented key features of them in written form. While the Normans and their successors, the Angevins, operated a more centralised system of governance than that which preceded them, they felt obliged to at least acknowledge values associated with the Anglo-Saxons, and often did so in writing (though there was a shift away from Old English to the use of Latin). In his 'Ordinance separating the Spiritual and Temporal Courts'—of unknown date—William describes himself as acting on the counsel of churchmen and the 'chief men of the realm'.[48] A more substantial and important document was that known as the 'Charter of Liberties of Henry I'.[49] The king issued it upon his coronation in 1100, which the charter describes as taking place 'by the common counsel of the barons of the whole kingdom of England'. In the document Henry promises to correct certain injustices and oppressive actions to which his brother (who was possibly murdered) and to some extent his father had subjected the realm when each of them was king. Principally, the activity he promises to end—or return to a traditional level—involved raising extra money through selling vacant church posts, charging aristocrats for receiving inheritances and selling women from this social group as brides. He also pledges to annul a 'common tax on money' collected through counties and cities. A recurring theme in the charter is the restoration of practices and laws prevailing in the time of Edward I—though curiously Edward is an Anglo-Saxon king who has no surviving law code to his name. Here Henry pays heed to the idea of legitimacy deriving from the past, through his promise to restore continuity with the pre-Conquest era, though not providing specifics about what it meant in practice. He combines this promise to revive Anglo-Saxon norms with a pledge to re-establish security in his kingdom, following disruption under his brother.

---

[46] See eg: Hollis, '"The Protection of God and the King": Wulfstan's Legislation on Widows' (n 17).

[47] Stafford, 'The laws of Cnut and the history of Anglo-Saxon royal promises' (n 41) 190.

[48] Translation in: George Burton Adams and H Morse Stephens (eds), *Select Documents of English Constitutional History* (London, Macmillan & Co, 1959) 1–2.

[49] Translation in ibid, 4–6.

In 1135, Stephen issued a charter guaranteeing 'all the liberties and good laws' agreed by his uncle, Henry, as well as 'all the good laws and good customs' prevailing under Edward. He commits both himself and his successors to honouring this guarantee, to his people and their descendants.[50] The following year Stephen issued a further charter stating that the Church was 'free', invoking reverence to 'good laws and ancient and just customs'.[51] Then in 1164, under Henry II, came the 'Constitutions of Clarendon'.[52] The product of conflict between the king, the Church and the barons, it presents itself as restoring an earlier order, on this occasion naming Henry I, himself a supposed reviver of continuity in his own time. A record made by ecclesiastical and other notables in the presence of Henry II, the constitution asserts a variety of rights possessed by the king with respect to the Church, and his position as a resolver of disputes. It did not end the tensions that produced it: in 1170 Thomas Becket, the Archbishop of Canterbury upon whom the Clarendon text was forced, died in his own cathedral at the hands of people who believed they were implementing the wishes of Henry II.

By the close of the twelfth century certain tendencies were well established in England. They centred on the production of texts that share certain features with modern written constitutions. With roots in the seventh century (or earlier) and the Anglo-Saxon period, this practice survived and even strengthened under occupation by the Vikings and following the establishment of Norman government. Crises such as foreign invasion or internal disruption often precipitated the introduction of these documents. Their authors could see their work as a means of providing stability and might seek lasting existence for it. Kings played a prominent part in instigating these texts, generally issuing them in their own names, and often using them to assert or increase their own authority. Yet the texts rested on advice and perhaps even consent from a wider group of social notables, and presented this dependency as desirable. The Church was often important to their creation. Clerics could provide the expertise that was vital to what could be a demanding task of drafting. These officials could in turn influence the content, which often dwelt on Christian values and the privileges of the Church.

The codes dealt with matters that were fundamental to the functioning of society, such as basic values, and rules to discourage violence, facilitate economic activity and promote social welfare. They set out to provide for certain privileges and protections, including for women, though not 'rights' in the contemporary sense of the term. The texts defined some official powers and functions, and could at the same time serve to constrain public authority through imposing conditions upon it. These documents were part of a wider European tendency, and broader continental events, such as military conflict, helped bring them about. Texts could make a lasting impact on the consciousness of those who came after. They

---

[50] Translation in ibid, 7–8.
[51] Translation in ibid, 8–9.
[52] Translation in ibid, 11–14.

between them form the beginning of a constitutional chain stretching from the seventh century and onwards—as we will see—to the present. Drafters of codes were aware of and drew upon their predecessors, doing so openly and making a virtue of it. Yet the texts do not represent an unchanging set of practices and values. They are part of a tradition, but one that involves transformation as well as continuity, with references to the upholding of established values sometimes disguising change. All of these characteristics would find their fullest expression in an agreement imposed upon the Angevin ruler, John, in June 1215.

3

Magna Carta: The Life, Death and Afterlife of a Text

MAGNA CARTA HAS the capacity both to disappoint and to surpass expectations. There was no single document signed by King John, who could read but not write. But multiple copies bearing his seal were dispatched across the realm. Of them, four are known to survive, in the possession of Lincoln and Salisbury cathedrals with one apiece, and the British Library, holding two. Magna Carta was not a statement of universal rights, but it has inspired innumerable such texts internationally, that often echo its actual words. Though sometimes claimed as British, it is more appropriate to call it English. Yet—written in an abbreviated legal Latin—it was European in nature, and has gained global currency. It survived little more than two months in its original 1215 form and was never properly implemented. Yet William Stubbs typified a common view of it when he stated in 1870 that 'the whole of the constitutional history of England is a commentary on this Charter'.[1] Indeed for some, Magna Carta is one of the 'two secular documents' that are the most important in world constitutional history. It occupies this category, according to such assessments, alongside the Twelve Tables of Rome, dated to the middle of the fifth century BCE. From these Roman texts runs a thread that leads on to the collection issued under Justinian in the sixth century, later known as the Corpus Juris Civilis, through to the Napoleonic law code of 1804, and from there to the present.[2] More esteemed company is impossible. Some might detect hyperbole. So much of Magna Carta as widely understood—from the numbers subsequently attached to the paragraphs to the meaning of the words—is owed to retrospective reinterpretation and even fabrication. But a central source of the historic importance of Magna Carta has been the very claims made on its behalf. Moreover, the text itself was a distortion of that which preceded it.

As this consideration of contradictions suggests, there are many Magna Cartas: it is a physical artifact (or rather a number of them); a (failed) peace treaty reached in 1215 between king and rebelling subjects; a time-specific legal

---

[1] *Why Commemorate the 800th Anniversary?* (Magna Carta 800th Anniversary Commemoration Committee, London, 2014).

[2] Henry Sherman Boutell, 'The Seventh Centenary of Magna Carta' (1914–15) 3 *Georgetown Law Journal* 49.

document focused to a significant extent on detailed arrangements of the time; and a symbol of freedom in England and beyond with centuries of endurance. The present task—a reassessment of English and UK systemic traditions from the perspective of a series of texts—suggests another manifestation of Magna Carta: as an entity sharing some of the qualities, in embryonic form, of a written constitution. In her account of the historic legacy of Magna Carta, Anne Pallister describes it as 'often regarded as the nearest equivalent to a written constitution which the English possess'.[3] But any such comparisons require careful handling. Magna Carta predated the full appearance of the concept of a written constitution by half a millennium, and the portions for which Magna Carta is most well known deal with only one part of the likely content of such a document. However, Magna Carta—particularly in its 1215 version—is wider in its coverage than generally known, treating a substantial range of the sorts of issues typically dealt with in systemic texts. The circumstances in which it came into being, expired and then revived are also instructive regarding the subject of a written constitution. Moreover, the idea of Magna Carta and the principles with which it came to be associated drove the international development of this kind of instrument—one of the main claims that Magna Carta has to immortality.

THE MAGNA CARTA MOMENT

By 1215 it was a firmly established practice for kings of England to issue documents that shared features with the written constitutions of later eras. Magna Carta drew upon and augmented this tradition. At the same time the text was, like those considered in the previous chapter, of a European quality, confirming English and UK development as part of this wider continental continuum. It was one of a number of such sets of concessions issued by kings, setting out limits on their powers, around this time, though it had its own special character, and subsequently it has become the most celebrated and influential of them all. In his great work on the 1215 document JC Holt writes that: 'England was no exception in twelfth- and thirteenth-century Europe, and Magna Carta was far from unique, either in content or in form'. He describes how Emperor Frederick Barbarossa had in 1183 afforded privileges to the group of northern Italian conurbations that comprised the Lombard League. King Alfonso IX of Leon decreed certain rights for his subjects five years later. King Peter II of Aragon contemplated but did not execute similar provisions for Catalonia in 1205. Emperor Frederick II created new rights for some of his princes in 1220, while King Andrew II of Hungary issued his famous Golden Bull, stipulating privileges for some of his people, in 1222. The list continues. By the end of the thirteenth century, France was the most significant realm not to have seen a grant of this kind. Then in 1303 it too entered

---

[3] Anne Pallister, *Magna Carta: The Heritage of Liberty* (Oxford, Clarendon Press, 1971) 1.

the field when Philip IV issued a 'great reforming ordinance', followed by Louis X, introducing regional allowances in 1315.[4] Charters were in the air.

A tendency in the varied cases Holt cites was for rulers to make concessions when faced with political difficulties connected to military conflict. So it was in England in 1215, and by this point the Angevins were already party to the continental trend of charter making. Their administration was increasingly literate, with less left unwritten. There was a tendency for the royal granting of municipal charters of liberties. Certain areas managed to acquire more autonomy in their local self-governance, sometimes through payments to the king. Before he came to the throne, as Count of Mortain, John issued a set of privileges to Bristol in 1189–91 that prefigured many of the contents of Magna Carta. A London commune formed in 1191 forced acknowledgement of the privileges of the city. In April 1215 John granted a charter to Bayonne, a city within his remaining French territory.[5] Two months later at Runnymede, he augmented this practice further. Not only was the act of issuing Magna Carta part of a continental trend, according to one author wider European influences were important to its actual drafting. In this account, it is possible that a number of specific portions of the text display the imprint of the *ius commune*, a combination of canon and Roman law that took hold in educational institutions on the continental mainland from the twelfth century onwards.[6]

Magna Carta, then, was a European document. Moreover, it was the product of difficulties associated with the maintenance of a European empire. The Angevin or Plantagenet dynasty began in 1154 when Henry II, who was grandson of Henry I, succeeded Stephen, who was grandson of William I (the Conqueror), and the last of the Normans. Like the Normans, it is hard to describe the Angevins as 'English'—or indeed to attach to them any other national label (this indeterminacy is a long-standing feature of the nobility generally, because of the practice of dynastic intermarriage). Henry II constructed a vast collation of territories, running from northern England, taking in Normandy, and down to the south west of France. Sustaining this empire was costly in financial and personnel terms. Angevin kings all had to tax their realms heavily. They did so utilising a legal system subsequently labelled 'feudalism'. The precise character of feudalism and how it developed remain matters of controversy. But it is possible to describe it as by this point involving the principle that the king was the ultimate owner of land. Senior magnates held it from him, and were obligated to their ruler, including in the provision of military service and money. This pattern extended downwards through society, with a chain of sub-tenancies and reciprocal duties. Lords—with

---

[4] JC Holt, *Magna Carta*, 2nd edn (Cambridge, Cambridge University Press, 1992) 25–26. See also: Nicholas Vincent, *Magna Carta: A Very Short Introduction* (Oxford, Oxford University Press, 2012) 61–62.

[5] Holt, *Magna Carta* (n 4) 50–74; Vincent, *Magna Carta* (n 4) 61–62.

[6] RH Helmholz, 'Magna Carta and the *ius commune*' (1999) 66(2) *The University of Chicago Law Review* 297, 300–01.

the king at the summit—were subject for their part to an expectation that they would ensure a minimum level of security, justice and good governance. The details were unclear, but there was a general understanding that if monarchs failed manifestly in performing these tasks, subjects were entitled to break with their loyalty and rebel. The vagueness of this overall system meant that rulers could exploit it to their advantage, as the Angevins did, increasing their demands for taxes, military service, or payment in place of military service. The consequent breakdown in tacit rules led to an attempt to make a more definite statement of the position in writing.

The Angevins had a further means of raising money. Henry II is credited as the main instigator of the system known as the common law, the beginnings of which are traceable to Anglo-Saxon times. The common law meant royal justice imposed from the centre, potentially usurping its equivalents carried out under the auspices of local lords. Common law provided the king with fees from those taking part in the cases. Sometimes the king deliberately forced delays, to encourage participants in proceedings to offer financial inducements to secure the outcome they wanted. Monarchs did not regard themselves as bound by the common law and treated it as their privilege. If they chose they could refuse to provide it. Nonetheless, it offered rationalised law to those who used it, and carried the potential of future use as a curb on rulers.[7]

The Angevin system entailed friction, particularly when it involved the contortion of established social customs to suit royal purposes. For instance, the Angevins could expand the 'forest'—meaning the land under direct royal control, rather than simply wooded areas—exploiting it for their financial gain, and overriding whatever systems were previously in force in the areas concerned. An assortment of other devices available included arbitrary fines, charging people exhorbitant sums for receiving inheritance and even selling widows into new marriages. These activities created tension with the barony. Another social institution with which the Angevins came into conflict was the Church. The Constitutions of Clarendon of 1164, seeking to assert royal over religious authority, arose from this tension, as did the murder of the Archbishop of Canterbury, Thomas Becket, in 1170, the event for which the reign of Henry II is best remembered. The potential for insurrection and disturbance under the Angevins was apparent long before 1215, and in 1173 a major uprising against Henry II took place, involving members of his immediate family, the barony and foreign powers.

Long-term trends interacted with more specific issues during the reign of John Lackland. In 1199 he succeeded his brother, Richard Lion-heart, who had come to the throne following the death of Henry II in 1189. Richard was an absentee king who had squandered riches on military adventures, but he at least commanded some degree of popularity. One of John's most remarkable achievements was in standing out as exceptionally unpleasant and arbitrary even in the company of

---

[7] See: David Carpenter, *The Struggle for Mastery: The Penguin History of Britain 1066–1284* (London, Penguin, 2004) 233–42.

medieval English kings. As AA Milne put it, 'King John was not a good man—/ He had his little ways.'[8] Not only was he abrasive, paranoid and ruthless, perhaps more importantly still, John met with military failure. Magna Carta opens with John describing himself as King of England, Lord of Ireland, Duke of Normandy and Aquitaine, and Count of Anjou. Already by this time the list was partly fantasy. John had lost large portions of his French possessions and his thwarted efforts to regain them created circumstances conducive to the introduction of Magna Carta. Commencing with the fall of Chateau Gaillard in March in 1204, a sequence of defeats saw Philip II of France seize all formerly Angevin possessions in France north of the river Loire. Consequently John had a greater need to raise money and men to recapture the lost lands, yet a smaller remaining group of territories from which to obtain these resources, forcing him ever harder to stretch his privileges and squeeze his subjects in England.[9]

Added difficulties came when a dispute developed with Pope Innocent III, with John objecting to the appointment of Stephen Langton as Archbishop of Canterbury. Between 1208 and 1213 England was subject to a papal interdict, formally denying to the kingdom the 'sacraments of the Church: no Mass, no burial in consecrated ground'. Most bishops hastily left the kingdom.[10] Eventually John achieved reconciliation with the Pope. In May 1213 he took the drastic step of submitting the whole of England to the vassalage of the papacy. Later, in March 1215, he committed himself to going on a crusade (a pledge he had no intention of honouring). Relations with Rome may have improved, but the earlier tensions must have undermined the legitimacy of the king. Then a further military emergency manifested itself. Faced with a looming French assault on England in 1213, John had some initial maritime success. In 1214 he landed in France. However, a cataclysm came in July with Philip II's victory over the group of European allies John had assembled at the Battle of Bouvines, in Northern France. John's only remaining French possessions were now Gascony and Poitou. Maine, Touraine and Anjou were gone. Normandy was already lost and John had no chance of winning it back.

Defeat overseas translated into crisis in England. By this time a group of barons known as the 'Northerners' (though not all who resisted John were actually from the North) felt nervously drawn closer and closer to rebellion. On 5 May 1215, at a tournament in Northamptonshire, they finally disavowed their loyalty to the king. After his subjects declined his offer of some kind of third party adjudication, John moved to confiscate their castles, marking the beginning of an armed conflict. Then crucially allies of the barons took control of London. The possibility of invasion from France revived, with a threat that the barony might invite Philip to supplant John. Magna Carta was from this perspective a peace treaty between the king and his rebelling subjects, an attempt to prevent escalation into full civil war.

---

[8]   AA Milne, *Now We Are Six* (London, Egmont, 2013) 2.

[9]   Claire Breay, *Magna Carta: Manuscripts and Myths* (London, The British Library, 2010) 8–11.

[10]   Vincent, *Magna Carta* (n 4) 48.

John granted it, the final passage of the text states 'in the meadow which is called Runnymede' lying part way between Windsor, where John was staying, and Staines, where the barons were based, on 15 June 1215. This date is as good as any for marking the Magna Carta moment, though we will never know exactly what was agreed at this point, and how, precisely, it fitted into the overall process. The desperation of the rebels is apparent in chapter 62 of the text. John promises not only to forgive all offences committed during the uprising, but to abandon all 'ill will, grudge and rancour' towards those with whom he had conflicted.[11] It was one of number of excessively optimistic provisions in the document.

Magna Carta, then, was the product of a short-term crisis exacerbating underlying tensions. In this sense it bore similarity to numerous written constitutions of later times. This overlap continues in other areas. English law codes and charters had long contained preambles stating that they were the outcome of consultation with senior lords and religious figures. Such declarations were the product of practical necessity and an associated principle that government, and in particular the setting out of fundamental rules, should rest on some kind of engagement with society beyond the monarch. These texts therefore offered limited precursors to a concept that achieved full fruition as the popular sovereignty doctrine, entailing the entire body of people in a society acting as the source of systemic legitimacy. The preamble to Magna Carta maintained the existing forms. John announced that he was acting on the advice of a series of churchmen and nobles. Yet it was not John but the magnates who provided the impetus for the text on this occasion—a contrast with earlier circumstances when kings such as Alfred seemingly took the decision to produce codes themselves, and then engaged in a consultation of some kind. John proclaimed Magna Carta as a consequence of intense pressure from a broad social coalition, including barons, the commercial classes in London and church figures, bound together by the objective of obliging the king to rule differently. Given these origins, a prominent motif of Magna Carta is the acceptance by John of limitations and terms of conduct applying to him and his heirs. The history of Magna Carta as an agreement imposed upon John from underneath (though leading participants in the process were all members of the elite) would contribute to its standing in time to come.[12] This quality suggests a connection between the extent of involvement in the creation of a constitutional text and the legitimacy it enjoys.

The near mythical status of Magna Carta might create a temptation to view the words of the text as having appeared fully formed from nowhere, or as being the work of a single inspired mind. Langton once enjoyed the reputation of being the main author. In fact the creation of the document took place over a prolonged

---

[11] The translation used here is found in Holt, *Magna Carta* (n 4) 448–73.
[12] See: Faith Thompson, *The First Century of Magna Carta: Why it Persisted as a Document* (Minneapolis MN, University of Minnesota, 1925).

period of time, probably incorporating diverse influences, and was a group effort, with contributions from numerous players from different sides of the dispute.[13] Fragmentary records of this process survive. The French national archives hold a text now labelled the 'unknown charter' that UK historians did not appreciate until late in the nineteenth century. It comprises a version of the charter of liberties of Henry I from 1100, with what appear to be additional provisions agreed by John. Verifying and dating the document is difficult, but it seems to provide us with a glimpse of the creation of Magna Carta while it was in process, and suggests the importance of the Henry I declaration to its 1215 successor. One explanation of the 'unknown' charter is that it represents an agreement John struck with the barons in November 1213 that did not hold. A larger body of opinion has supported the view that it is an account of negotiations from some point in the first half of 1215.[14] A later stage in the process of devising and negotiating terms manifests itself in a document known as the Articles of the Barons. Bearing the seal of John, this text survives in the British Library where it is displayed alongside two copies of the 1215 text. The Articles may be a record of a provisional agreement between the two camps, possibly dating from 15 June 1215 itself, or perhaps earlier.[15]

These texts are indicative of a task—devising and agreeing Magna Carta—that was demanding, large-scale and protracted. They demonstrate the importance of process to the creation of any constitutional document. Just as the breadth of the coalition involved in events leading to Magna Carta contributed to its eventual effectiveness, so did the approach of those involved in devising the text. Their desire to work from an evidence-base, and incorporate expertise and research, as suggested by the use of the 1100 charter, would be appropriate for a contemporary exercise of this nature. It is reasonable to speculate that they drew upon other previously existing instruments, contained in the growing corpus of such documents that was then manifesting itself in England and across Europe. But this use of past declarations suggests that, in another way, the Magna Carta process possibly differed from modern constitution-building exercises. It sought to justify itself through past precedent to an extent that might not be necessary now. As William McKechnie put it, the 'barons and royal officials who helped in framing it were ignorant of the abstract principles of political science'.[16] However much they might want change, the conceptual setting within which those who produced Magna Carta had to operate did not permit them overtly to do any more than assert that to which they were already supposedly entitled. The tension inherent in an effort to restrain the Angevins in a way not yet achieved, while avoiding open innovation, became an important quality of the text itself.

[13] Vincent, *Magna Carta* (n 4) 63.
[14] Holt, *Magna Carta* (n 4) 418–28.
[15] Breay, *Magna Carta* (n 8) 25–28.
[16] William Smart McKechnie, *Magna Carta: A Commentary on the Great Charter of King John*, 2nd edn (Glasgow, James Maclehose and Sons, 1914) 110.

THE 1215 TEXT

While documents similar to Magna Carta appeared in Europe during this era, qualities that set it apart were its length and detail. It comprised 63 chapters. At the time they were not numbered. The appearance to contemporary eyes of disorganisation intensifies because the text lacks clear structure. Sometimes groups of provisions fit together well, such as a series dealing with the position of women,[17] but incongruous jumbles also occur. In the space of four chapters the text moves from the handling of land belonging to convicted criminals, to a prohibition on fish weirs, to the issuing of writs, to measurements of food and drink.[18] Consequently the most helpful form of analysis is thematic, rather than dealing with the contents in order. The best starting point is that noted above: the relationship of Magna Carta with the past. In many ways, Samuel Johnson's characterisation of Magna Carta as 'born with a grey Beard' is apt.[19] The text contains references to the assertion of long-existing standards, for instance municipal liberties in chapter 13, in limiting the extent of knights' duties in chapter 16, and the insistence in chapter 23 that particular forms of forced labour be in accordance with established (unspecified) norms. The repeated references to the 'law of the land' (for instance in chapter 55) create the impression that Magna Carta simply seeks to restore a proper order violated under John in particular and the Angevins in general. In the text, John commits to correct both his misdeeds and eventually those of Richard and Henry II, for instance with regard to property seizures.[20]

Nonetheless, change was inherent in the Magna Carta project. It sought to make a difference—and it did, in ways and on a scale unimaginable in 1215. Even as far as it was restorative in its intent, this objective entailed change, even if only through a reversion to prior arrangements. Anyway, recreating the past is by definition impossible. Magna Carta was something new. It was not simply a reissue of a previous document such as the charter of Henry I, or even a compilation of such texts. It was an addition to the law: clarifying, elaborating—and transforming. Attempts to codify established understandings are rarely as straightforward as they might seem. A constitutional version of the uncertainty principle applies here: an exercise in observing the system can lead to it changing. Different parties to the process are likely to have divergent views of the existing position. Through imposing a particular interpretation, the documents they produce are vehicles for a form of change. Furthermore, participants in such discussions are likely—unconsciously or consciously—to conflate what they think the norms *are* with what they think they *should be*. This tendency leads readily to substantive transformation.

---

[17] Chs 6–8.
[18] Chs 32–35.
[19] Cited in Peter Linebaugh, *The Magna Carta Manifesto: Liberties and Commons for All* (Berkeley CA, University of California Press, 2008) 21.
[20] Ch 52.

Magna Carta moved into new territory in areas such as its requirement in chapter 12 that scutage should be one of the forms of taxation subject to consent, and in its demands (contained in chapters 50 and 51) that John remove from England named allies and defined military personnel he had imported from France. Perhaps most innovative of all were the enforcement provisions contained primarily in chapter 61, discussed below. The assessment of Holt is that:

> Sometimes Magna Carta stated law. Sometimes it stated what its supporters hoped would become law. Sometimes it stated what they pretended was law. As a party manifesto it made a party case with scant regard for fact or existing practice.[21]

Indeed the ambition and novelty of Magna Carta contributed to its initial failure: John found it an unacceptable imposition on what he saw as his established and proper prerogatives. However, though it contained a powerful if cloaked radicalism, Magna Carta was in keeping with tradition in another way. There was already an ancient practice of producing legal texts that stressed a foundation in the past while achieving at least some innovation at the same time. As on these earlier occasions, it is likely that some of those involved in producing the text were pursuing this approach as a deliberate tactic. Magna Carta was part of a grand English tradition of hiding change behind continuity. It is fitting that this text would itself come to be incorporated into similar such projects, with future efforts at transformation presenting themselves as asserting the principles of Runnymede. In a sense they did, but not in the way they advertised. As McKechnie put it in his account of those who challenged the Stuarts in the seventeenth century on a basis of Magna Carta, they were 'disguising revolutionary projects by dressing them in the garb of the past'.[22]

The idea of Magna Carta as confirming already existing privileges would much later on become central to a debate about its value. This discourse in turn connected to wider constitutional issues. In his *Reflections on the Revolution in France* of 1790 Edmund Burke stressed the desire 'to derive all we possess as *an inheritance from our forefathers*'. Any 'reformations' were 'carefully formed upon analogical precedent, authority, and example'. Burke went on to record that 'Our oldest reformation is that of Magna Charta [sic]'. Yet he noted the view that 'the antient charter, the Magna Charta of King John, was connected with another positive charter from Henry I'. Moreover, both of these texts 'were nothing more than a re-affirmation of the still more antient standing law of the kingdom'. This historic background confirmed for Burke 'the powerful prepossession towards antiquity ... and the stationery policy of this kingdom in considering their most sacred rights and franchises as an *inheritance*'.[23] By contrast, Thomas Paine, in *The Rights of Man* of the following year, with Burke in his sights, identified what

---

[21] Holt, *Magna Carta* (n 4) 300–01.

[22] McKechnie, *Magna Carta* (n 15) 133.

[23] Edmund Burke, *Reflections on the Revolution in France* (London, Penguin, 2004) 117–18.

he saw as the 'error of those who reason by precedents drawn from antiquity'. The problem for Paine was that such advocates

> do not go far enough into antiquity ... They stop in some of the intermediate stages of an hundred or a thousand years, and produce what was then done, as a rule for the present day. This is no authority at all.

For Paine it was necessary to proceed 'to the time when man came from the hand of his Maker' and when 'Man was his high and only title, and a higher cannot be given him'. Given this outlook Paine viewed Magna Carta as 'no more than compelling the Government to renounce a part of its assumptions. It did not create and give powers to Government in a manner a Constitution does'.[24]

Another way in which Magna Carta lent itself to later adaptation was its vagueness. Some of the text is precise. John states in chapter 2 that on the death of an earl or a baron, the heir must provide an 'ancient relief' amounting to £100 to obtain his inheritance. Chapter 33 orders the removal of all fish weirs from England, other than those on the coast. John specifies in chapter 50 the names of the favoured officials he has agreed to remove from their posts (one of whom— intriguingly from the point of view of subsequent mythology—was Philip Mark, his Sheriff of Nottingham). But in other areas the charter is more nebulous. There is reference, for instance, to the maintenance of existing privileges, such as those attached to London and other conurbations, without their being defined (chapter 13). Indeterminacy was probably useful as a means of securing agreement between John and the rebels at Runnymede in areas of intense controversy.

The most famous provisions of all exemplify the perversely powerful uncertainty of Magna Carta. Chapters 39 and 40—which were eventually merged into one and numbered chapter 29 in its final 1225 issue—provide that free men will not be punished other than 'by the lawful judgement of his peers or by the law of the land' (chapter 39), and that John will not 'sell ... deny or delay right or justice' to any one (chapter 40). A term such as 'peers' is obviously important in this context, yet at the same time it is not apparent what it means. Similar doubt clouds the phrases 'lawful judgement' and 'the law of the land', though they are once again clearly pivotal from the perspective of the operation of the rule, and the fate of the individuals involved.[25] The potential for interpretation and transformation that these two chapters—in particular chapter 39—presented is probably the main reason that anyone today would write, publish or read a book with the words Magna Carta in the title. To help these provisions attain the status they ultimately did, some adaptation was necessary, most notably through the so-called 'six statutes' introduced in the period from 1331 to 1368. These fourteenth-century enactments included a stipulation that 'lawful judgement of his peers' meant jury trial, something that was not yet fully developed in 1215; that 'law of the land' meant 'due process of law'; and that a 'free man'—a label that could

---

[24] Thomas Paine, *Common Sense and the Rights of Man* (London, Phoenix, 2000) 204.
[25] Vincent, *Magna Carta* (n 4) 76.

only have encompassed a tiny proportion of the population in 1215—was a 'man of whatever estate or condition he may be'.[26] The drafters of Magna Carta could not have anticipated such developments, but the mode of expression they wilfully adopted helped make them possible.

A central thrust of Magna Carta is the protection of baronial interests against the arbitrary behaviour of the king in his financial demands, through the violation of property and personal security, his manipulation of the law, and his exclusive style of government.[27] It was an effort by an established group to prevent perceived abuse of the system on which its own privileges rested. This perspective is essential to a comprehension of the attainment of Magna Carta in 1215 and the text itself. But it does not provide a complete understanding. Magna Carta is a multidimensional entity, demanding further complementary interpretations. It is not only the interests of the barony that found expression in Magna Carta; the Church was clearly a beneficiary. While the influence of Langton was not as great as once believed, the imprint of his institution upon Magna Carta is clear. A difference between the Articles of the Barons and the final Magna Carta of 1215 is the appearance in the latter of an opening chapter in which John commits to the freedom of the Church in England and to maintaining its (unspecified) privileges, also pledging not to interfere in ecclesiastical appointments.[28] Other groups are represented. A number of chapters deal with the position of women. Like the Anglo-Saxon charters, while not involving the modern concept of equality, they supply certain protections, specifically for widows. Chapters 7 and 8, for instance, provide for widows to receive their inheritance and choose whether or not to remarry. Chapter 54, however, is less generous to women, restricting their ability to take legal action.

The social scope of Magna Carta extends further. Below the barony, portions of Magna Carta explicitly address the position of knights and free men beneath this level.[29] To be effective the rebellion of 1215 must have rested on this wider base of support. Towards the close of Magna Carta, chapter 60 calls for a cascade of obligation, stating that all the grants made in the preceding text from the king to his 'men' should pass in turn from these church leaders and lords to 'their own men'. Other parts of society may have an implicit presence in Magna Carta. In his 2008 work, *The Magna Carta Manifesto*, Peter Linebaugh urges consideration of the document from the perspective of marginalised groups.[30] As he explains, some of the more obscure provisions, for instance involving fish weirs and river banks,[31] were relevant to the large mass of the population in their daily

---

[26] Holt, *Magna Carta* (n 4) 10.
[27] AE Dick Howard, *Magna Carta: Text and Commentary* (Charlottesville VA, University Press of Virginia, 1964) 9–12.
[28] Breay, *Magna Carta* (n 8) 28.
[29] See eg: chs 2, 39.
[30] Linebaugh, *The Magna Carta Manifesto* (n 18).
[31] Chs 33, 48.

subsistence struggles.[32] Furthermore, provisions regarding the regulation and retrenchment of the royal forest[33] were important to these unprivileged peoples, since expansion of these zones of arbitrary monarchical dominion entailed disruption of the customs governing their livelihood. Linebaugh likens the utilisation of royal privileges in these areas to a privatisation programme. It involved, in effect, central government requisitioning land previously available for use by the people in common to raise money from private sources. Magna Carta was an intended barrier to this practice.

The Linebaugh thesis requires a further reflection on the scope of Magna Carta. Chapters 39 and 40 provide its most renowned content, and have come to be associated with what we would now describe as civil and political rights. But there is another side to Magna Carta, engaging with what would be termed—again to employ concepts not in use in 1215—social and economic issues, into which category fall provisions dealing with such matters as taxes, property and the royal forest. It also contains numerous commercial stipulations. Chapters 10 and 11 set out regulations involving the borrowing of money from Jews. The commitment in chapter 13 to the privileges of London and other urban areas was presumably desirable from the point of view of some of the occupants of these municipalities in allowing them to carry on business without unwanted interference. John calls in chapter 35 for standardisation of weights and measurements throughout the kingdom, including for wine, ale, corn and cloth. Chapter 41 provides for the equal treatment of all merchants, whether domestic or foreign, with some limitations if they come from an enemy realm at a time of war.[34] These stipulations entailed an effort to impose new rules applying throughout the territory, but with the objective of eliminating a multiplicity of diverse local regulations, thereby attaining uniformity of trading conditions. The concept would recur in later centuries at UK and European levels.

Another premise of Magna Carta that remains at the core of the tradition depicting it as a source of the principle of limited government, is the concession by John of constraints upon himself and those acting on his behalf. Alongside numbers 39 and 40 precluding features of arbitrary justice, other chapters seek, for example, to control the extent of the financial extractions he can make from subjects for inheriting property,[35] and on the amounts that local royal officials can acquire for themselves in the course of their duties.[36] The king pledges in chapter 12 to observe constraints on his power to raise taxes. But it is also possible to view Magna Carta as a creative, positive document. Limitations could be part of a wider system. The chapter 12 requirement is not only a restriction, but also a requirement to adhere to a more inclusive process of decision-taking. Provisions

---

[32] For an account of English society in 1215, see: Danny Danziger and John Gillingham, *1215: The Year of Magna Carta* (London, Hodder & Stoughton, 2003).

[33] See eg: chs 47–48.

[34] For comment, see: Howard, *Magna Carta* (n 26) 18–20.

[35] See eg: chs 2, 4.

[36] See eg: chs 25, 28, 29, 30, 31.

intended to contain the encroachments of John into baronial inheritance also stipulated what were the entitlements of heirs.[37] Chapters 39 and 40 suggest commitment to an equitable system of justice. This idea gains force in other parts of the text. Chapter 20, for instance, requires that punishment of free men should be proportionate to the crime. In chapter 17, John pledges that the court of common pleas will be held in a fixed place, rather than following him on his travels. This provision entailed a requirement to provide for easier access to justice. So too did chapters 18 and 19, which set out to ensure that local legal cases took place in the relevant area, and chapter 40, with its prohibition on delaying, denying or selling justice. Another chapter, 45, was in part a promise to bring about improved professional standards and higher levels of competence among legal officials. In seeking to end the oppressive Angevin system, or at least its more extreme manifestations, Magna Carta also outlined what those who forced it upon John saw as the appropriate model.

Another theme of Magna Carta is the role of different institutions of governance. At the centre is the monarchy. The text is issued in the name of the king, taking the form of a series of pledges about how he and those who come after him will conduct themselves in future. It also deals with the position of local governance. Angevin rule had a centralising dimension, for instance through the development of common law, the expansion of the forest, and the assertion of increased financial demands on the kingdom. Through its efforts to secure the status of groups that provided local leadership including the clergy and the barony, to impose conditions on John and his agents, to curtail the forest, and to assert the privileges of London and other conurbations, Magna Carta set out to offset this tendency. But it was not wholly centrifugal in character. Some of the commercial chapters aspired to ensure single regulatory measures across the kingdom. Magna Carta did not seek to dissolve the royal common law system, rather to reform it. Chapter 12, dealing with taxation, did not abolish scutage and aid, but insisted that the raising of it rested on consent. John describes in chapter 14 the gathering required to obtain this approval. He specifies the substantial group of barons and churchmen who will meet at a fixed location. John or his officials will provide all those eligible to attend with notice of at least 40 days, and explain in advance the purpose of the assembly. McKechnie judged that the idea of this gathering was not sufficiently developed, its powers not fully explored.[38] Nonetheless, here Magna Carta—though building on existing practice—partially anticipated an institution that did not yet exist: Parliament. It would come in time to be the expression of a centralised yet consultative system.

Constitutional texts often endeavour to entrench themselves in some way, to express their fundamental importance, immune from casual modification. They may do so through establishing amendment procedures. Magna Carta simply asserts its own perpetuity—more sophisticated mechanisms would come later.

---

[37] See: chs 2, 4.
[38] McKechnie, *Magna Carta* (n 15) 129–30.

John asserts repeatedly that his pledges will apply forever, to him and his descendants.[39] Another common feature of fundamental texts is that they contain some kind of enforcement mechanism, often involving the courts. Magna Carta sought to ensure it operated in practice through a system proposed in chapter 61. The king allows his barons to select 25 from among their own ranks, whose task it will be to uphold the text and ensure the monarch and his officials abide by it. This body will have flexible ways of operating and substantial scope for action. It will be authorised to reach decisions on a basis of majority votes, with all members obliged to abide by and act to implement the decision taken. If violations of Magna Carta came to their attention, any four of the barons will be able to require action from the king within a 40-day period. After this point, if the problem is still not resolved, the four can bring the matter to the attention of the whole body of 25. This group would then be permitted 'with the commune of all the land' to 'distrain and distress' the monarch until it achieved an outcome it deemed satisfactory. The barons can act in any way they choose, subject only to a prohibition on their attacking the king or his immediate family. Chapters 52 and 55 attach to the committee specific adjudicatory responsibilities involving property that John had seized and fines he had applied. This was a remarkable blueprint for a formidable committee. It would never come fully into being. The attempts of those who forced Magna Carta on John to fix its existence were futile. At the close of chapter 61 John promised not to seek a revocation of Magna Carta—then immediately commenced doing so.

MAGNA CARTA AFTER 1215

On 24 August 1215 Innocent III rescinded Magna Carta. Having resolved their earlier disputes he and John were now in alliance. The Pope found unacceptable a text disruptive to the control of a kingdom of which he was now custodian. Magna Carta came to an end slightly more than two months after it was agreed. But it would return. Civil war erupted, and Prince Louis, son of Philip of France, invaded. On 18 October 1216 John died, supposedly after guzzling rich food and drink. His son, only nine years of age, succeeded him as Henry III. Advisers to the young monarch decided to revive the charter. They reasoned that to do so would promote the idea that the passing of John meant transition to a more inclusive, moderate form of government, and help win back subjects to the Angevin side.[40] Redrafted versions appeared three times under Henry III: in November 1216; November 1217; and—in its final form—February 1225.[41] Along the way textual changes—specifically deletions—occurred,[42] of which Ralph V Turner presents a

---

[39] See: chs 1, 61, 63.

[40] For the 1216 re-issue as a propaganda device, see: William F Swinder, *Magna Carta: Legend and Legacy* (Indianapolis, Bobbs-Merrill, 1965), 104–5.

[41] Thompson, *The First Century of Magna Carta* (n 11) 116.

[42] Dan Jones, *Magna Carta: The Making and Legacy of the Great Charter* (London, Head of Zeus, 2014), ch 10.

dissection. In 1216 stipulations that disappeared included the requirement that demands for aids and scutage be subject to consultation with a defined group of magnates (chapters 12 and 14). The chapter providing for enforcement by barons (61) vanished also. Thus, while royal advisers sought to stress a change from the arbitrary approach of John Lackland, they were careful to limit the restrictions upon the monarchy. Parts of the 1216 text also contained more precise language than that deployed in 1215, with a view to reducing the scope for it forming a basis for legal action.[43] This outlook finds a contemporary equivalent in the constant fears among Whitehall officials of the executive being exposed to judicial review.

The 1217 issue was a conciliatory gesture following military victory for the royal cause. Again, some modification took place with a view to avoiding legal action. At this point the separate Charter of the Forest appeared simultaneously, removing from Magna Carta chapters dealing with forests, and elaborating upon them. After the joint issue of Magna Carta with the Charter of the Forest in 1217, the two texts became firmly linked. This coupling seems to have provided the 'great' charter, as the longer of the two, with the name by which we now know it. Initially, Magna denoted relative size, not absolute importance. In 1225, the third and final redraft of Magna Carta appeared. The less than wholesome motive for this act of immense constitutional significance was Henry III's need for money, following another period of civil conflict. Recommitting to Magna Carta was the concession he had to make to the senior figures of his kingdom in return for their providing him with a new grant. The two entries in the 1215 text that are most famous today, 39 and 40, dealing with punishment by the law and not delaying or denying justice, became one. In the 1225 text they are attributed the shared number 29.[44]

Given these complex changes, combined with the nature of the technology of the time, it is not surprising that even in its first century a substantial degree of confusion developed about Magna Carta and its precise contents. The existence of four different versions, from 1215, 1216, 1217 and 1225 (the final text) was a problem, compounded by the circulation of numerous unofficial renderings that were not rigorous in their search for accuracy.[45] Even the 1297 confirmation of Magna Carta—purportedly replicating the 1225 version—differs from its supposed source, suggesting that the scribe used one of these unofficial documents. Alongside faulty reproductions, distorted interpretations soon commenced also. Possibly appearing around 1290, the anonymous work *The Mirror of Justices* backdated the supposed origins of the principles contained in Magna Carta to the legendary Trojan origins of the kingdom, and misrepresented and exaggerated the extent of the constraints it imposed on the monarchy. Its author promoted Anglo-Saxon and parliamentary ideals. While it seems to have made little impact

---

[43] Ralph V Turner, *Magna Carta: Through the Ages* (Harlow, Longman, 2003) 81.
[44] Ibid, 81, 82, 85–87.
[45] Geoffrey Hindley, *A Brief History of the Magna Carta: The Story of the Origins of Liberty* (London, Robinson, 2008) 274–76.

at the time it first appeared, the *Mirror* would significantly influence perceptions in the seventeenth century, with weighty consequences.[46] Only as late as
1759 did methodical versions of the different texts appear: the work of William
Blackstone.[47]

During the course of the thirteenth century Magna Carta became important as
a legal instrument and a symbol. Faith Thompson stresses the importance of the
exceptionally broad coalition of support that produced the text. Even after their
initial alliance subsided, the different groups could find in Magna Carta something to appeal to them. Though utilising it in a partial, self-interested way, they
nonetheless served to promote the document as a whole. Thompson stresses that
it was a combination of causes that facilitated the survival and rise of Magna Carta
as the embodiment of proper constitutional values in the thirteenth century. It
appealed both as a written, legal statement, and as a restatement of long established freedoms. The text had protection through the courts. Moreover, though
Innocent III had annulled Magna Carta in 1215, the Church subsequently came
to perform a supportive role. Langton and other bishops issued a declaration of
excommunication for those who transgressed Magna Carta (and the Charter of
the Forest) at the time of the third edition of 11 February 1225. Numerous similar
statements followed, sometimes from figures in the domestic church hierarchy,
others under the explicit authority of the Pope—as in 1254 (by Innocent IV) and
1257 (by Alexander IV). The Church, therefore, provided Magna Carta with what
we might describe today as a supranational enforcement mechanism, similar to
those associated with the European Convention on Human Rights (ECHR). It
was also confirmed by kings in 1237, 1253, 1258, 1264 (by Simon de Montfort),
1265, 1266 and 1276. A 1297 assertion found its way onto the chancery rolls, an
action that eventually gained for it the reputation of being the first English statute
(though it was, as we have seen, a slightly faulty copy of the 1225 text). In 1301, the
Lincoln Parliament produced a further affirmation.[48] Continuing her account in a
follow-up work, Thompson records the number of parliamentary affirmations of
Magna Carta (in statutes and Parliament rolls) as being 23 under Edward III, 13
for Richard II, six in the reign of Henry IV, and two under Henry V.[49]

Assertions of Magna Carta could come in documents that themselves contained some of the qualities of a written constitution. In 1311, Edward II—subject
to baronial coercion—agreed to the New Ordinances.[50] An ambitious document
comprising 41 articles, it includes a number of specific references to Magna Carta.

---

[46] William Justice Whittaker (ed), *The Mirror of Justices* (London, Selden Society, 1895) ix–lv;
Turner, *Magna Carta* (n 40) 110.

[47] Ivor Jennings, *Magna Carta and its Influence in the World Today* (London, HM Stationery Office
1965) 12.

[48] Thompson, *The First Century of Magna Carta* (n 11) 106, 116.

[49] Faith Thompson, *Magna Carta: Its Role in the Making of the English Constitution, 1300–1629*
(London, Sutton, 2008) 10.

[50] Abridged text in: George Burton Adams and H Morse Stephens (eds), *Select Documents of English
Constitutional History* (London, Macmillan & Co, 1901) 92–95.

It contains a stipulation that the king should 'live of his own' and not obtain funds other than those to which he is customarily entitled.[51] Article 9 demands that the king should not make war or leave the 'realm' except with the 'common assent of his baronage, and that in parliament'. Here the document engages an area of constitutional controversy that remains current in the present era. The conduct of armed conflict has been a central part of the discretionary power of the monarchy, known as the Royal Prerogative. In 1215, Magna Carta approached this power tangentially through asserting limitations and qualifications on the ability of the king to raise money to pay for war. Article 9 of the New Ordinances was more direct. The struggle to achieve this encroachment upon executive privilege continues today (though ministers—particularly the Prime Minister—now wield the power in practice, with the position of the monarch merely formal); Parliament has still not achieved firm or legally binding specific authority over military conflict.

A further assault on the discretion of the monarch comes in Article 14. It produces a long list of senior office holders, including the chancellor, chief justices of both benches, the treasurer and the chancellor of the exchequer. When making their appointments, the king must obtain 'the counsel and assent of his baronage, and that in Parliament'. If for some reason there is a need to fill one of these posts when Parliament is not sitting then the king must act on 'the good counsel which he shall have near him, until the Parliament'. Such provisions entail an enhanced role for Parliament. Consequently it is apt that Article 29 requires that a parliament take place at least once and if necessary twice each year, 'in a convenient place'. The text also seeks to prohibit royal interference, under the privy seal, in the justice system. It attempts to prevent the imposition of delay and the violation of established legal norms by such means.[52]

In the Tudor period Magna Carta lacked recognition at high political level. During an era of centralised government, its attempts to impose limitations on royal authority did not fit with the official agenda. Notoriously, as discussed in the introduction, Shakespeare's *King John* did not specifically mention Magna Carta. But it was never completely forgotten. Indeed, the printing press that arrived in England late in the fifteenth century would make it more possible to spread awareness of Magna Carta, that first appeared in print in 1508. Then in the seventeenth century it received renewed attention as a central part of a narrative deployed by opponents of Stuart absolutism. This approach repeated the familiar pattern of drawing on supposed ancient principles to make a case against governmental practices of the present. Those engaged in this campaign presented privileges arising from royal concessions as fully-fledged rights, the origins of which they claimed stretched back as far as Ancient Britain.[53]

---

[51] Art 4.
[52] Art 32.
[53] Hindley, *A Brief History of the Magna Carta* (n 42) 281–85.

The most important figure in this school was the jurist and parliamentarian Sir Edward Coke. He sought to present the idea of an ancient constitution that dated back even to before Roman occupation, under which all in England enjoyed a set of rights. Believing that the *Mirror of Justices* was 'a treatise which set forth the law of King Arthur's day'[54] he held that a proto-parliament had sat in this mythical time, and that Parliament had agreed the 1225 edition of Magna Carta. This document was critical to his thesis, and he made impossible claims on its behalf, exaggerating the extent to which its authors had intended to require consultation on decision-taking and place curbs on executive power. Coke suffered royal persecution for his stance. But the ideas he advocated lasted, and others continued this approach when resisting Stuart methods.[55] As McKenchie put it:

> If the vague and inaccurate words of Coke have obscured the bearing of many chapters, and diffused false notions of the development of English law, the service these very errors have done to the cause of constitutional progress is measureless.[56]

The disputes between advocates of more limited government and the Stuarts eventually led to two revolutions, and the early emergence of the concept of the written constitution.

Magna Carta entered the eighteenth century with its status waxing. Granville Sharp, most famous as a campaigner against slavery, referred in 1774 to Magna Carta as having over time become 'stamped ... with an authority equal to the *Constitution* itself, of which it is, in reality, a most essential and *fundamental* part'. Because of this quality 'any attempt to repeal it would be treason to the State!' In his view, therefore, the 'glorious Charter must ... ever continue un-repealed: and even the articles which seem at present useless, must ever remain in force'.[57] By this time developments that would eventually confound this outlook were already taking place. In the period since 1215, Parliament had emerged as the central institution of the English constitution. Continual parliamentary confirmations may have helped re-enforce the importance of Magna Carta, but also suggested that this document was dependent upon the legislature. Some interpret a statute of 1368, during the reign of Edward III, as seeking to entrench Magna Carta, instructing that it and the Charter of the Forest 'be holden and kept in all Points; and if there be any statute made to the contrary, it shall be holden for none'. Possibly this provision sought to ensure that Magna Carta prevailed over not only earlier law, but subsequent parliamentary enactments.[58] However, it transpired that Parliament could, if it chose, override Magna Carta, at least as a legal instrument.

Pallister catalogues how the legislature went about realising this latent power. Starting in the sixteenth century demands emerged for a rationalisation of English

---

[54] Whittaker, *The Mirror of Justices* (n 43) x.
[55] Turner, *Magna Carta* (n 40) 146–51.
[56] McKechnie, *Magna Carta* (n 15) 133.
[57] Pallister, *Magna Carta* (n 3) 89.
[58] Howard, *Magna Carta* (n 26) 24–25.

law, which a number of influential thinkers felt had proliferated excessively to the detriment of its overall effectiveness. The utilitarianism of Jeremy Bentham provided special impetus. Eventually, in the second half of the nineteenth century, Parliament began passing Acts aimed at abolishing redundant laws, beginning in 1861 with the Statute Law Revision Act. Its sequel from 1863 covered older statutes, including Magna Carta, repealing either wholly or partially 18 chapters, held either to be archaic or already in effect almost revoked. Two more clauses disappeared in 1879, two in 1887 and one in 1892.[59]

The First World War furnished evidence of parliamentary supremacy over the principles associated with Magna Carta as well as its existence as a statute. The advent of the conflict in 1914 proved inconvenient from the point of view of attempts to mark the 700th anniversary of the text the following year. A committee formed early in 1914 had made various plans involving international participation, most of which it abandoned after the commencement of the war. The only event that took place in 1915 was a lecture McKechnie gave to the Royal Historical Society. Two years later a volume of *Magna Carta Commemoration Essays* appeared. However, it was not as extensive as initially intended. The introduction refers to a series of unnamed foreign contributors who removed themselves from the project. They included a 'German professor' pointedly described as 'once a friend of England' who communicated his inability to take part via Sweden. Circumstances also precluded French, Hungarian and Belgian contributions. The author of the introduction, Henry Elliot Malden, found a 'peculiar satisfaction ... in an English celebration of a thirteenth century document and event'.[60] But the lost entries might have provided a European perspective that is often lacking from assessments of Magna Carta.

The same circumstances that depleted the official commemoration also helped to mark the anniversary in an unfortunate way. In accounting for the missing portions of the book, Malden described how the 'memory of the assertion of the principle of government by law was overclouded by the cares of the immense struggle to maintain that principle through force of arms'.[61] Even if we accept the dubious characterisation of Britain as fighting for 'government by law' it is important to note how far it violated these principles during the course of the conflict. Less than a week before the 700th anniversary of the agreement of Magna Carta, on 10 June 1915, an Order was issued under the authority of the Defence of the Realm Act 1914. Known as Regulation 14B, it allowed the Home Secretary, on advice, to impose restrictions upon or imprison people on security or defence grounds, if they were of 'hostile origin or associations'. The regulation created a sweeping power of detention without trial applying to British subjects and foreigners alike, simply because they were deemed to have the wrong background

---

[59] Pallister, *Magna Carta* (n 3) 89–101.
[60] Henry Elliot Malden (ed), *Magna Carta Commemoration Essays* (London, Royal Historical Society, 1917) xx–xxii.
[61] Ibid, xix.

or connections. Hundreds became its victims. In this instance, Magna Carta had clearly failed to provide protection against the delaying or denial of justice.[62] The Second World War saw a magnified version of this policy.

After the First World War, to return to Pallister's account, pruning of Magna Carta continued. In 1925, one chapter disappeared (with a saving proviso), and part of another, which Parliament completely expunged in 1947. A further three vanished in 1948. 'Thus, within the space of some 100 years, twenty-eight clauses of Magna Carta were removed from the statute book'.[63] In 1965, the same year that Lord Denning described Magna Carta as 'the greatest constitutional document of all times—the foundation of the freedom of the individual against the arbitrary authority of the despot',[64] the Law Commission came into being. Charged with reviewing and rationalising the entirety of legal measures, in 1966 it secured the abolition of a further Magna Carta chapter: number 14 in the enacted version of the 1225 text. A lasting interpretation of this provision had been that it expressed the tenet that the level of punishment should be appropriate to a given crime. The Commission began to take a more expansive approach to its task. It brought forward a Bill designed to remove another eight chapters from Magna Carta. Under this plan the only chapters left completely intact would have been number 9 (dealing with municipal rights) and 29 (the portion dealing with punishment only by trial and not delaying or denying justice). Parliamentary scrutiny led to the removal of chapters 1 and 37 from the Bill, preserving their existence. Chapter 1 dealt with the liberty of the Church and—ironically given the plan to remove it—contained a commitment in perpetuity to the contents of the document. Chapter 37 was what is known as a 'General Saving' provision containing another commitment to uphold Magna Carta—and a less salubrious reference to the payment Henry III received from his magnates in return for this guarantee.[65] The four components remain in force to the present day.

THE GLOBAL STATUS OF MAGNA CARTA

Though whittled down as a legal instrument in its territory of origin, Magna Carta had attained spectacular success as an export. The first market was in North America. So great a status did the text attain in the United States (US) that in the early phase of the Second World War the UK Government contemplated gifting to the Americans the 1215 Lincoln Cathedral copy, that was on display in the US. The idea was that it symbolised the values that were at stake in the conflict, and the presentation would be an important gesture at a time when good relations

---

[62] AW Brian Simpson, *In the Highest Degree Odious: Detention Without Trial in Wartime Britain* (Oxford, Clarendon Press, 1994) 5–33.

[63] Pallister, *Magna Carta* (n 3) 97.

[64] *Why Commemorate the 800th Anniversary?* (n 1).

[65] Pallister, *Magna Carta* (n 3) 89–101.

were crucial. Any such proposition was unpalatable to Lincoln Cathedral.[66] But how had Magna Carta attained such stature that an ancient sheet of parchment with the text written on it could be considered a lever of foreign policy?

At the same time that England battled over its constitution in the seventeenth century, with Magna Carta frequently playing a central role in debates, it was colonising North America. Many of those who took part in this migration tended to believe that they took with them the rights they thought they enjoyed under Magna Carta, which was in turn a reassertion of Anglo-Saxon privilege. Charters of these settlements expressed these sentiments, commencing with the Virginia text of 1606. As well as providing for institutions of colonial government, it included the statement that colonists would 'have and enjoy all liberties, franchises and immunities ... as if they had been abiding and borne within ... Englande'.[67] The Massachusetts Body of Liberties of 1641 contained a clear adaptation of portions of Magna Carta, including in the requirement for punishment by the law. Copies of Magna Carta itself (from 1687), and works promoting prevailing if anachronistic interpretations of it, began to disseminate.[68] In the following century, a common view among those who became increasingly resistant to British imperial rule was that they were asserting rights associated with Magna Carta. Even for those who were not necessarily Magna Carta enthusiasts, it was a useful brand. In his hugely influential *Common Sense*, published at the outset of 1776, Thomas Paine called for a continental conference that would 'frame a ... Charter of the United Colonies ... answering to what is called the Magna Charta [sic] of England'.[69]

The quest to realise the principles of Magna Carta eventually led the Americans not only to free themselves from British rule, but to dispense with monarchy and aristocracy, with parliamentary sovereignty and with established religion. In place of these features they created, on a continental scale, a secular, federal republic in which all institutions—including the federal legislature—were subject to an entrenched written constitution grounded in the principle of popular consent. A principle soon developed that the courts were able to annul even congressional primary laws if incompatible with the text. Constitutional standards of the late eighteenth century were not the same as those of today. Slaves and women were not within the scope of the system. Yet, like Magna Carta, it could adapt, in accordance with demands that it expand its coverage, partly drawing on its own words for inspiration. The US version of Magna Carta, however, has tended to focus on civil and political liberties and limitations on government, and not socio-economic protections.

---

[66] *The Magna Carta* (New York, Sotheby's, 2007) 86–89.

[67] AE Dick Howard, *The Road from Runnymede: Magna Carta and Constitutionalism in America* (Charlottesville, VA, The University Press of Virginia, 1968) 15.

[68] William F Swindler, 'Runnymede Revisited: Bicentennial Reflections on a 750th Anniversary' (1976) 41(2) *Missouri Law Review* 1.

[69] Paine, *Common Sense and the Rights of Man* (n 23) 32.

From 1776, the year of the Declaration of Independence, the states began producing bills of rights that once more consciously modelled themselves on the provisions making up chapters 39 and 40 of the 1215 Magna Carta. An important feature of the US Constitution drafted in 1787 was that it created a potentially more powerful central authority than that which previously existed, but set out to limit it—in accordance with the principle of constrained government connected with Magna Carta—with safeguards for the rights of states. The first set of amendments to the Constitution, applied in 1791, comprised the US 'Bill of Rights'. It contained the by-now predictable mirroring of portions of Magna Carta, for instance in Article 7, stipulating that no one shall be 'deprived of life, liberty, or property, without due process of law'. As well as influencing constitutional documents, Magna Carta itself has retained greater hard legal relevance in the US than in the UK. In the words of RH Helmholz writing in 1999:

> The number of chapters that survive in today's English statute book can be counted on the fingers of one hand, but across the Atlantic the Charter continues to be widely cited in judicial opinions for the great principles, and even some of the mundane details, it contains.[70]

Proceedings in recent times in which Magna Carta figured include the case taken by Paula Jones against the then-US President, Bill Clinton, in which she alleged sexual harassment.

Consequently many observers in the US treat Magna Carta as a heavy influence upon or even direct ancestor of their Constitution, and by extension linked to further subsequent developments of great import. As Henry Sherman Boutell wrote at the time of the 700th anniversary in 1915: 'The most illustrious documentary offspring of Magna Carta is the Constitution of the United States, the oldest written national constitution now in force, and the progenitor of all modern constitutions'.[71] As the Boutell comment suggests, traces of Magna Carta can be found in many constitutions internationally, reaching them both via the US model and more directly from the UK. In his essay marking the 750th anniversary of Magna Carta, Sir Ivor Jennings even detected its influence on the French *Declaration of the Rights of Man* of 1789 (not strictly a constitution, but certainly constitutional, and fundamental). Article 7 of this historic statement stipulates that legal proceedings should take place in accordance with defined legal and procedural norms.[72] Jennings' observation was suggestive not only of far reaching impact for Magna Carta, but was further evidence that any notion of a firm dichotomy between English/UK and mainland continental constitutional development is false. Beyond Europe, British imperialism spread a text that could at the same time present a threat to the Empire, as events in the American colonies from 1776 demonstrated. After the Second World War, various former colonial

---

[70] Helmholz, 'Magna Carta and the *ius commune*' (n 6) 299.
[71] Boutell, 'The Seventh Centenary of Magna Carta' (n 2) 49.
[72] Jennings, *Magna Carta and its Influence in the World Today* (n 44) 39.

territories—such as India, Pakistan and Malaya—also echoed Magna Carta in their constitutions.[73] At the supranational level, Magna Carta had a direct impact upon the United Nations Universal Declaration of Human Rights of 1948 and the ECHR. The UK is itself a signatory to both. When presenting the declaration to the UN in 1948, Eleanor Roosevelt speculated that it might become 'the international Magna Carta for all men everywhere'.[74] The UK had a prominent influence on drafting the ECHR. Yet, just as the 700th anniversary of Magna Carta saw some unfortunate developments from the perspective of the ideals it had come to symbolise, it is possible that the 800th anniversary could see another grotesque commemoration; it could take place shortly after the election of a government intent on diluting provision of the ECHR in UK law, and reducing the impact of the European Court of Human Rights on the UK, or possibly withdrawing from the ECHR altogether. In these circumstances, participants on both sides of the argument will cite Magna Carta in support of their case.

Given that Magna Carta has achieved vast domestic and international impact, but in a complex and circuitous way, it is unsurprising that the text remains both renowned and a subject of confusion within the UK. A survey conducted in 2012 revealed that an impressive 85 per cent of British adults were aware of its existence. But when asked which rights from a list they thought it provided, those who knew of Magna Carta showed they were not necessarily well informed about its precise significance. For instance: 38 per cent chose 'democracy'; 36 per cent 'freedom of speech'; 21 per cent the 'right to vote'; 9 per cent 'equal rights for women'. However, the single most popular option—'rule of law', at 60 per cent—was at least a defensible claim, as was 'trial by jury' (49 per cent), and 'Freedom from arbitrary arrest' (30 per cent). Those who knew that Magna Carta existed but said they did not know its function comprised 12 per cent. Those aware of it but who picked none of the options—most of whom were presumably not constitutional purists wedded to the literal meaning of the 1215 text—made up 2 per cent.[75] This research shows that Magna Carta has a very high rate of recognition for a failed 800-year-old peace treaty written in Latin. It is also apparent that many people make a connection between it and one or more of a bundle of democratic and human rights principles, that elsewhere we might expect to find in a written constitution. Yet in the UK, the practical realisation of values—like Magna Carta—is subject to the authority of the Westminster Parliament.

Magna Carta emerged from a crisis produced by an intersection between the general problems of Angevin rule and specific difficulties connected to the reign of John Lackland, stimulating a broad coalition to subdue him. It was part of a European trend of the time, and built on ongoing tendencies within England. It was also something new, despite the attempt to justify itself from precedent.

---

[73] Ibid, 40–41.

[74] *Why Commemorate the 800th Anniversary?* (n 1).

[75] *Magna Carta 800th Briefing* (London, Magna Carta 800th Commemoration Committee, 2014) 5–6.

Producing and agreeing the text was an impressive feat. The document itself deals with much we might expect to find in a written constitution: rights (of a sort); limitations on power; and the roles of institutions of government. It restrains and creates; and engages in socio-economic as well as civil and political matters. The text suggests an important connection: between government that is conducted by some kind of consent, and is subject to limitations. This general linkage remains relevant today, with the mutual dependency of democracy and human rights. Magna Carta also aspires towards entrenchment, though the objective is to remain in force for ever rather than be amendable subject to a special procedure. Finally, it sought to establish mechanisms that would enforce it, comparable with the judicial constitutional review that takes place in many countries today, and often takes precedence over all other authority, signifying the supremacy of the constitutional text.

The demise of Magna Carta so soon after its creation in 1215 contains an important lesson. Features in the surrounding environment can serve to undermine the effectiveness of a constitutional document. A severe lack of trust between key players is a problem, and if any of the most prominent individuals or groups involved is in some way hostile to the text, it is unlikely to succeed. The desire of John to evade limitations upon him doomed Magna Carta. Wide involvement and acceptance, then, are vital. In the longer term, it was the width of the collection of individuals and groups with a vested interest in the document that helped provide for its survival as an operative legal instrument. Some degree of self-interest will motivate representatives of any category. The key to success is to balance and bind them all together. Just as the alienation of an important group can create problems, so can its over-privileging: Henry III and his advisers were able to remove some of the more inconvenient provisions from their reissued versions of Magna Carta. The external setting beyond the territory itself is also crucial. The annulment of Magna Carta came from the Pope in Rome—and later, important support for the text came from the same source.

While the social and political context is crucial to constitutional texts, words— both as part of legal enactments, or simply on their own—can also change their environments. Magna Carta is the best imaginable illustration of this principle. The impact of the words of Magna Carta is complex and came about partly because sections of it were drafted in an open-ended way. It created a potential for reinterpretation with huge consequences for English constitutional development, especially in the seventeenth century. Of equal importance was the impact overseas. Magna Carta helped inspire the concept of the written constitution, and the content of many such texts worldwide. Yet to date it has not come home in this form. Magna Carta reaches us today in both augmented and diminished condition. It is a symbol of the rule of law: of limited government and freedom from arbitrary punishment. Magna Carta embodies the idea of including the fundamental rules of a society in a single text. That it arose from pressure from below upon a king adds to its credibility, but the socio-economic concerns it addressed are now forgotten or dismissed as archaic. Furthermore, mechanisms for enforcement were stripped from the text with the first revision in 1216, and Parliament soon began to appear as a supreme body, that had the power to protect or repeal it as it chose.

The role of Parliament in constitutional change suggests tensions within the traditional constitutional model of England and the UK. On the one hand, ours is depicted as an ancient system containing within it customs and rights that—though lacking special legal protection in a single formal text—are nonetheless real, perhaps even more powerful than they would be if entrenched in the way they are under other systems. Yet alongside this supposition exists an omnipotent parliament, limited only by practical and psychological considerations. While some may hold that these constraints are sufficient to protect the former component of the constitution, the fate of most of Magna Carta at the hands of a legislature infused by utilitarian zeal from the nineteenth century could suggest otherwise. Consequently, as a constitutional document with true legal force in the UK, Magna Carta is negligible. For full expression of the values we link to it we must look elsewhere, and to some extent begin again.

4

Revolutionary Century

O F ALL PERIODS in English history the seventeenth century was the most
fertile for the production of constitutional documents. These efforts to
state fundamental principles of governance and liberties punctuated an
era of expansive constitutional dispute, civil war, revolution and foreign invasion.
They gave expression to a then emergent conceptual framework that remains
recognisable in the contemporary United Kingdom (UK). The texts considered
here fit into a time frame beginning in 1628 with the Petition of Right and running to the beginning of the eighteenth century and the Act of Settlement 1701.
In the intervening years a full-scale civil war took place between 1642 and 1646
and again in 1648. January 1649 saw King Charles I tried and then executed. For
most of the so-called 'Interregnum' that followed, Oliver Cromwell was the definite leader, until his death in 1658. His son, Richard, succeeded him but left office
the following year. In 1660, Charles II returned from exile to take the throne his
father had held before him. James II succeeded his elder brother Charles II in
1685. His reign was brief. With the 'Glorious Revolution' of 1688, James II fled and
William of Orange, of the United Provinces (the Dutch Republic), took his place,
becoming William III, ruling jointly with his wife, a daughter of James, Mary II.
Policymakers then took steps to exclude Catholic Stuarts from the throne. In the
process they inaugurated the Hanoverian succession that came into force—within
a new state, the United Kingdom of Great Britain—following the death of Queen
Anne in 1714, when George Ludwig of Hanover became George I.[1]

The causes of this tumult were complex, but a sequence of interlocking themes
characterises the period.[2] One was religion. Doctrinal disagreement could have
pronounced constitutional resonance, because of the implications for the organisation and policy of the Church of England, a crucial official institution. Hostility
towards Catholicism was a powerful force in England, within Parliament and
beyond. Perceptions of a Stuart lean towards Catholicism were a regular source
of discontent during the seventeenth century. Apprehension about royal intentions in this area contributed to the removal of Charles I and James II, and was
important at other times. It is important to stress that the break from Rome

---

[1] For a definitive history of this period, though from a British rather than strictly English perspective, see: Mark Kishlansky, *A Monarchy Transformed: Britain 1603–1714* (London, Penguin, 1997).
[2] For an assessment of key tendencies, see: Jonathan Scott, *England's Troubles: Seventeenth-Century
English Political Instability in European Context* (Cambridge, Cambridge University Press, 2000) 27–33.

executed in the Tudor period did not have the effect of isolating England from the continental mainland. Rather, it provided a particular perspective from which to assess European developments, and was an influence upon alliance-forming, security policy, and decisions over whether to intervene militarily. Attachment to Protestantism even linked England to the development of a principle that rulers had a duty to act—even to the point of deploying armed force—to prevent tyrannical behaviour in foreign lands, a precursor of the 'responsibility to protect' theory of today.[3]

As this external dimension to religion shows, the outside world made a critical contribution to the English constitutional trauma of the seventeenth century. The archipelagic, Britannic context was significant. The English (including Wales), Scottish and Irish kingdoms shared a monarch, and developments in one could impact upon others. For instance, a rebellion in Scotland, followed by a Scottish invasion of England, triggered the English Civil War of the 1640s. Mainland Europe was equally important. England was part of the continent and shared in its struggles. In particular the so-called 'Thirty Years War', commencing in 1618, impacted upon England. At its outset it involved a confrontation between Catholic Habsburgs and Protestants. For many in England active pursuit of the Protestant cause at this time and later in the century was essential. In practice the engagements such advocates of action favoured could involve aligning with Catholic as well as Protestant powers, if deemed necessary to the protection of the liberty of their religion in Europe. Unrest over royal European policy and the manner in which it was executed could spill into disputes about the constitutional position of the monarchy and its prerogatives, and the role of Parliament. The Thirty Years War created immense problems for James I and his son Charles I, in time compromising the office they held. At this time the Habsburg powers presented the main threat to the European balance. Later, with the wearing down of Spain, France became the greater force. Favourable inclination on the part of Charles II and James II towards their cousin, Louis XIV, King of France, caused consternation in England.

Concepts and principles could straddle the English Channel. One recent study of the so-called 'Glorious Revolution' of 1688 presents it as a moment at which England chose between two competing systems in operation elsewhere in Europe: absolutist Catholicism (with minimal interference from Rome) of the Louis XIV ilk, and Dutch-style, Protestant limited government. The latter approach won through.[4] Indeed, William of Orange made the banishment of arbitrary Stuart methods an explicit part of his public appeal to the English when setting out from the United Provinces.[5] William was only the first foreign import acquired to

[3] See: Brendan Simms and DJB Trim (eds), *Humanitarian Intervention: A History* (Cambridge, Cambridge University Press, 2011).

[4] See: Steve Pincus, *1688: The First Modern Revolution* (New Haven CT, Yale University Press, 2009).

[5] Jonathan I Israel, 'William III, the Glorious Revolution and the Development of Parliamentary Democracy in Britain' in John Pinder (ed), *Foundations of Democracy in the European Union: From the Genesis of Parliamentary Democracy to the European Parliament* (Basingstoke, Macmillan, 1999) 36–38.

banish the threat of Stuart Catholicism (and the Stuarts were themselves obtained from outside England early in the sixteenth century, though from elsewhere on the island of Great Britain). In 1701, to permanently exclude Catholic monarchs, England committed to a Hanoverian future, creating a dynasty that persists to the present. Events in England had external repercussions. The rise to power of Cromwell, for instance, was instrumental in tilting the European balance of power against Spain and in favour of France. Later American and French revolutionaries drew inspiration from the replacement in 1688 of James II. It is possible to go as far as to identify pan-continental synchronicity at play. Christopher Hill once depicted 1648 as a year of European revolution, akin to that which occurred precisely two centuries later.[6]

Any attempt to depict English constitutional history as distinguished by its stability and continuity does not survive a proper assessment of the seventeenth century. After much conflict, in the middle decades of this period, the monarchy collapsed. So too in time did the system that replaced it. Though a Restoration then took place, Charles II often seemed in peril and his brother lost power in 1688. The traditional presentation of the so-called 'Glorious Revolution' in English historiography was of a smooth reassertion of established principles. More recent interpretations have disputed this account. Steve Pincus has put forward the idea that 1688 should be seen as the first in a series of revolutions that would take place around the world, which it both prefigured and helped inspire.[7] In this narrative, England emerges as special not because it has avoided abrupt discontinuities such as those experienced by France from 1789, but for its precociousness, reaching them first, and influencing their subsequent occurrence elsewhere.

Another perspective on 1688 that conflicts with conventional versions is that it involved a Dutch invasion, again undermining the myth of English constitutional insulation from external intervention. Foreign conquest has been pivotal. In the words of Brendan Simms: 'The old England had been founded in 1066 by a Frenchman; the new England in 1688 by a Dutchman'.[8] Like the earlier conquest, the later had systemic implications. By 1688, England resembled—to apply the terminology of the present—a failed state. It had suffered from a prolonged period of internal conflict and violent disputes with its neighbours, all coloured by religious, ideological and ethnic divisions. Government could be arbitrary and unstable. Human suffering was widespread. The declaration William issued in October 1688 in advance of his operation—arranging its distribution in vast quantities among his future subjects—deployed concepts similar to those advanced by proponents of contemporary liberal interventions. He asserted his intention to promote governmental best practice, ensure fair elections, and protect individual

---

[6] Christopher Hill, *Puritanism and Revolution: Studies in Interpretation of the English Revolution of the 17th Century* (London, Secker & Warburg, 1958) 133.

[7] See: Pincus, *1688: The First Modern Revolution* (n 4).

[8] Brendan Simms, *Three Victories and a Defeat: The Rise and Fall of the First British Empire, 1714–1783* (London, Allen Lane, 2007) 39.

rights. Having effected regime change and installed himself in power (though this outcome was not necessarily his initial intention), William permanently altered the course of development of England, importing into it external norms. He showed that such humanitarian military actions can succeed. Of course William had other, more self-interested, motives. He urgently needed England to ally with the Dutch against France. But he could not simply dismiss the expectations he had created before taking power, even if they proved inconvenient. One way in which they found expression was through the Bill of Rights 1689.[9]

The final theme is that of conflicting models of government. Pronounced disagreements appeared over the proper balance between, on the one hand, monarchical rule drawing on the Royal Prerogative and, on the other, Parliament, comprising the king or queen, Lords, and Commons, acting together. Also pertinent to the position of the monarch was the development during the seventeenth century of the idea that government comprised a contract between people and their ruler, who was consequently not absolute and whose authority rested on continued adherence to the conditions of the agreement. John Locke became the most important exponent of this theory with the second volume of his *Two Treatises of Government* in 1690. Further struggles took place between the different components of the legislature and between supporters and opponents of the very existence of monarchy. Another tension was between more arbitrary and more limited government. Criticism of the Stuarts often held that they favoured the former approach, but it was also possible to make this charge against the system that supplanted the monarchy of Charles I. Furthermore, the connection between support for religious tolerance and government by consent was complex. A monarch such as James II might take up the cause of more freedom of belief (even claiming he had introduced a new Magna Carta) but dislike relying on Parliament, while his opponents could fear in his religious programme a shift towards Catholicism, as well as disliking an assertion of the Royal Prerogative over Parliament.

Various constitutional texts appeared in efforts to resolve these disputes in particular directions, some of which resemble, in important respects, written constitutions; others, which go further, could be said fully to merit such a description. This tendency takes us to a further area of contention of this period, and requires some terminological clarification. During the seventeenth century the use of the word 'constitution' to mean the system of governance began to come into use, though it did not immediately achieve the wider application it eventually attained, and did not imply a single encompassing text. The word 'constitution' is Latin in origin. In Roman times *constitutiones* was a formal description applied to the laws of the emperors (though in usage it could convey a wider concept). Subsequently the Church adopted this label to describe its internal directives. By the twelfth

[9] Israel, 'William III' (n 5) 36–38.

century, *constitutiones* was imported back into the secular domain, though still to describe individual measures rather than the systemic whole.[10]

While 'constitution' began to acquire a broader application during the seventeenth century, another phrase of similar connotation was more frequently deployed: 'fundamental law'.[11] Today 'fundamental law' often implies the core rules embodied in a written constitution, probably entrenched through special amendment procedures and enforced through judicial review. In this earlier era it did not have so specific a connotation. While the term conveyed the idea of a set of underlying values, it was not clear precisely what they were, though they might well include some crucial common law principles and Magna Carta. Often those who described such norms seemed to regard them as of powerful moral force but lacking in firm legal existence. According to this school of thought, in the most extreme circumstances, it might be permissible to rebel against governors who violated the rules, but no other specific recourse existed. Yet when sitting as judge in *Dr Bonham's Case* of 1610, Edward Coke spoke some famous words that seemed to endorse the idea of fundamental law being fully justiciable, to the point of allowing the negation of statute. He claimed that 'in many cases the common law' could control statutes and might 'adjudge them to be utterly void'. If an Act of Parliament was 'against common right and reason' or if it was 'repugnant, or impossible to be performed' then common law could rule that it was 'void'.[12] However, what precisely Coke had in mind is disputed; on other occasions he asserted parliamentary supremacy.

Coke was a leader of the drive against Stuart absolutism. Yet versions of the fundamental law concept, in hard legal form, could figure in royalist argumentation also. At his trial Charles I rejected 'the illegality of this pretended court'. No 'freeborn subject of England', he held, could enjoy security if 'power without right daily make new, and abrogate the old fundamental laws of the land'.[13] Describing the period following the Restoration, Jeffrey Goldsworthy states: 'Supposedly immutable fundamental laws were appealed to more often by monarchists than anyone else, to protect the succession and prerogatives of the Crown from statutory control'.[14] Conversely, those seeking to restrain or eliminate the monarchy often advocated a supreme legislature, free from limitations. This disposition fitted with a radical Protestant tendency to suppose that the people were not bound to any one kind of government, and could alter it as they saw fit, in pursuit of and

[10] See: Charles Howard McIlwain, *Constitutionalism: Ancient and Modern* (Ithaca NY, Cornell University Press, 1947) 22–24.

[11] JW Gough, *Fundamental Law in English Constitutional History* (Oxford, Clarendon Press, 1955) 51.

[12] Citied in Gough, ibid, 31–32.

[13] 'The King's reasons for declining the jurisdiction of the High Court of Justice', reproduced in Samuel Rawson Gardiner (ed), *The Constitutional Documents of the Puritan Revolution* (Oxford, Clarendon Press, 1906) 374.

[14] Jeffrey Goldsworthy, *The Sovereignty of Parliament: History and Philosophy* (Oxford, Oxford University Press, 1999) 142.

limited by higher universal values.[15] John Milton posed the rhetorical question in 1660: 'How could our forefathers bind us to any certain form of government ... more than we can bind our posterity?' For him Parliament was 'above all positive law'. It could make and unmake both 'civil or common law'. Furthermore, a later Parliament was 'above the former' and above all previous 'lawgivers' and without doubt was 'above all precedent laws'.[16]

This dynamic provided impetus for the rise of the doctrine of parliamentary sovereignty. But among those who overthrew Charles I it is also possible to identify another strand that leads to the written constitution. The most important intellectual development in this direction took place within the 'Levellers', a loose radical egalitarian grouping with a following in the rank and file of the parliamentary army. Sometimes Leveller pronouncements shared in the revolutionary scepticism regarding legally binding fundamental law. Yet at other points different views manifested themselves.[17] As the 1640s progressed the threat appeared, in place of arbitrary royal government, of an oppressive Parliament. One leading Leveller, John Lilburne, looked to existing instruments, including Magna Carta, as sources of protection. He followed in an established practice of asserting supposedly ancient liberties. But another prominent Leveller, Richard Overton, disagreed. He argued in 1646 that 'the laws of this nation' were 'unworthy a free people'. Overton held there was a need for them all 'to be considered and seriously debated and reduced to an agreement with common equity and right reason, which ought to be the form and life of every government'. He judged Magna Carta to be 'but a beggarly thing, containing many marks of intolerable bondage'. Moreover, the laws produced by parliaments since the thirteenth century had 'made our government much more oppressive and intolerable'.[18] Such ideas pointed towards a constitutional text, with overriding legal authority, drawing not on the past, but first principles, and deriving legitimacy from the people. They soon found, to a degree, concrete form—for a limited period—domestically, and over time achieved far wider international influence.

THE PETITION OF RIGHT 1628

The background to the Petition of Right was an atmosphere of rising tension around the use of the Royal Prerogative. In 1626, Charles I imposed extra-parliamentary taxation to fund an ultimately unsuccessful military operation in France the following year. He also imprisoned without charge prominent individuals refusing to pay a forced loan, leading to the celebrated *Five Knights* case

---

[15] JC Davis, 'The Levellers and Christianity' in Brian Manning (ed), *Politics, Religion and the English Civil War* (London, Edward Arnold, 1973) 237.

[16] Cited in Gough, *Fundamental Law in English Constitutional History* (n 11) 138.

[17] Davis, 'The Levellers and Christianity' (n 15) 237.

[18] Cited in: ASP Woodhouse, 'Introduction' in ASP Woodhouse (ed), *Puritanism and Liberty* (London, JM Dent & Sons, 1938) 95–96.

of 1627. The imposition of troops returning from the failed mission to France on private residences compounded discontent. In areas in which they clustered, military discipline extended to apply to civilians. Then in 1628 the need for further financial support drove Charles I to call a Parliament. With Edward Coke playing a prominent role, it set out to curtail excesses in the use of royal authority. After resisting an agreement Charles I finally succumbed to the Petition of Right.

The text takes the form of an address to Charles I from the House of Commons and House of Lords.[19] It seeks to secure the principle of government by consent, exercised in conformance with core legal norms. This combination casts light on present day concepts. At times the relationship between democracy and human rights can appear antagonistic. Some might regard entrenched rights as an inappropriate restriction on the legislative capacity of elected representatives, while others could perceive mechanisms of majority rule as posing a threat to the rights of minorities. But closer inspection dispels this supposed dichotomy. It is a crucial part of the rights of individuals in a society that they are all permitted to participate in political processes on some kind of basis of equality. Equally, proper involvement in democracy is dependent upon the possession of various rights. Magna Carta provided both for specific privileges and inclusive government of some kind. The Petition of Right renders more explicit the interconnection suggested in the earlier text by dealing only with these twin qualities. Arbitrary government, such as that towards which Charles I was disposed, tends to resist all constraints, whether they involve consulting over policies or legal procedures. The Petition of Right sought to remedy this difficulty. In doing so it continued the grand tradition of advancing into new territory while claiming to state or reassert existing principles.

Clause 1 refers to laws from the reigns of Edward I and Edward II, along with other 'laws of this realm' and 'the good laws and statutes of this realm'. They meant, the text claims, that the subjects of Charles I had 'inherited' a 'freedom' from an obligation to pay 'any tax, tallage, aid, or other like charge' that was not 'set by common consent in Parliament'. Having asserted a (dubious) historical basis for inclusive decision-making, the Petition seeks the same source of authority for royal conformance with legality through invoking Magna Carta. It quotes the stipulation from 'The Great Charter of the Liberties of England' that a 'freeman' cannot be punished except 'by the lawful judgment of his peers, or by the law of the land'. The Petition locates similar authority in the laws of Edward III. It cites Magna Carta again in clause 7 when establishing the need for executions to take place in accordance with the 'law of the land'.

The document asserts that Charles I and his officials were failing to meet these standards. Across a number of counties commissioners were demanding loans from members of the public (clause 2). The king was issuing special orders to imprison subjects without charge (clause 5). The Petition noted critically a policy

[19] Text reproduced in: George Burton Adams and H Morse Stephens (eds), *Select Documents of English Constitutional History* (London, Macmillan & Co, 1959) 339–42.

of scattering soldiers and sailors across the country, forcibly taking up residence in private homes (clause 6). Commissioners, acting under the sanction of the king's Great Seal, were using 'martial law' powers, intended for application to members of the armed forces in times of conflict, to impose the death penalty on individuals without due process (clauses 7 and 8). Behind the same cloak some alleged offenders were escaping punishment (clause 9). The picture is of a parallel system of arbitrary royal justice. Clause 10 'humbly' asks Charles I to terminate these abuses and clause 11 that he issue a declaration including in it a commitment that his 'officers and ministers' would proceed in accordance with the 'laws and statutes of this realm'. The Petition was, like Magna Carta in 1215, a stipulation the king felt obliged to accept. He did so after it was read on 2 June, in a statement of his resolve 'that right be done according to the laws and customs of the realm'. Whatever Charles meant by these words, the Petition failed to impose on him the approach sought by those who drafted it. Between 1629 and 1640, Charles I governed without calling a Parliament. He raised finance through novel deployments of the Royal Prerogative, leading to the landmark *Ship Money* case of 1637 that found in favour of the king in utilising an extraordinary source of revenue, but only by seven judges to five. Charles I eventually felt forced to reconvene Parliament, and it turned upon him.

BLUEPRINTS: THE ARMY AND THE LEVELLERS

Written constitutions imply limitations on legislatures. It is understandable, then, that some of the early impetus for the development of documents of this kind came from sources other than Parliament: the army and the Levellers. They produced texts that—though not enacted—merit consideration because of the ideas they proposed and the influence they had. By 1647, out of the tumult of the Civil War, the parliamentary army had become a political player in its own right. In August of that year it issued its Heads of Proposals, setting a proposed working accommodation with Charles I.[20] It calls for firmly enforced biennial parliaments (clause I(1)), sitting for at least 120 days, unless they consent otherwise, and not longer than 240 days (or another agreed limit). The king would be able to dissolve the Parliament after 120 days (clause I(2)). The text provides for the monarch to hold emergency parliaments but not in a fashion that interrupts the electoral cycle (clause I(3)). It calls for the distribution of seats 'according to some rule of equality or proportion'. A suggested formula is that the number of members attached to each county should be 'proportionable to the respective rates they bear', but the Heads of Proposals seems to allow for 'some other rule of equality or proportion'. The purpose is to 'render the House of Commons (as near as may be) an equal representative of the whole' (clause I(5)). Another requirement is for measures to ensure elections are free and there is 'certainty of due returns' (clause I(6)).

---

[20] Reproduced in: Gardiner, *The Constitutional Documents of the Puritan Revolution* (n 13) 316–26.

The Commons will have the power to modify election rules in future. The Heads of Proposals provides for freedom of speech and voting in the Commons without fear of recrimination (clause I(7)), and for the Commons and Lords to possess 'judicial power, or power of final judgment' that the king cannot overturn unilaterally (clause (8)).

The Heads sets out a series of detailed provisions to ensure that for an interim period the Commons and Lords have control over the disposition of the armed forces and senior appointments within them, and that parliamentary consent is required for war and peacemaking. It requires protection for freedom of religious belief. The text also calls for a series of immediate changes. They include: guarantees for a public right of petition; the removal of duties from products upon which the poor are dependent; the reassertion of the laws of the forest; that 'monopolies ... and restraints to the freedom of trade' are removed; greater clarity in legal proceedings; that no one 'may be compelled by penalty or otherwise to answer unto questions tending to the accusing of themselves ... in criminal causes'; and that it should not be possible to execute someone 'under two witnesses'.

The event known as the 'Putney Debates', a discussion between representatives of the Levellers and the army, took place in October and November 1647. If these meetings were a prototypical constitutional convention,[21] then the Levellers supplied it with a draft text for consideration in the form of the 'Agreement of the People for a firm and present peace'.[22] The Levellers produced this document by surprise on the second day of proceedings. Over the next two years numerous other texts using this or a similar title would appear. Two historians of the Agreements contend: 'At the root of all versions of the *Agreement* was the device of a written agreement between the people and their representatives settling immutable fundamentals of governance, or "foundations of freedom"'.[23] The title suggests legitimacy derived from below. It opens with a statement of the intention to 'avoid both the danger of returning into a slavish condition and the chargeable remedy of another war'. To this end the Agreement seeks to avoid what the authors saw as the fundamental source of difficulties: infrequent gatherings of Parliament, or the undermining of the institution when it was in session. Notably absent from the model this document envisages are the monarchy and the House of Lords. Article I, complaining that 'the people of England, being at this day very unequally distributed ... for the election of their deputies in Parliament', proposes that constituencies be 'more indifferently proportioned according to the number of the inhabitants'. Here was a distinction from the less radical army proposal that the formula for constituencies might be based on tax bracket, rather than treating all people as equal. To end problems associated with 'the long continuance of

---

[21] See: Richard Gordon, *Repairing British Politics: A Blueprint for Constitutional Change* (Oxford, Hart Publishing, 2010) 16.

[22] Gardiner, *The Constitutional Documents of the Puritan Revolution* (n 13) 333–35.

[23] Philip Baker and Elliot Vernon, 'Introduction: The History and Historiography of *the Agreements of the People*' in Philip Baker and Elliot Vernon (eds), *The Agreements of the People, the Levellers and the Constitutional Crisis of the English Revolution* (Basingstoke, Palgrave Macmillan, 2012) 2.

the same persons in authority' Article II calls for the dissolution of the current Parliament at the end of September the following year (it had sat since 1640, earning the name the 'Long Parliament'). Elections to the Parliament, with the new boundaries in place, will then take place every two years, on the first Thursday in March.

Once again suggesting popular sovereignty, Article IV states that the 'power of this, and all future Representatives of this Nation, is inferior only' to those who select them, that is the people. The article lists various authorities Parliament possesses, none of which are subject to 'consent or concurrence of any other person or persons'. This power encompasses creating, amending and repealing laws, forming and abolishing executive and judicial institutions, controlling public appointments and holding to account those who fill them, war and peacemaking, and the conduct of diplomacy. But Parliament is to be subject to limits, with a number of areas beyond its legislative reach. First came 'matters of religion and the ways of God's worship'. Parliament can, however, promote religion in a way it sees fit, though not in a manner that is 'compulsive'. Second, 'impresting and constraining any of us to serve in the wars' is without the power of Parliament, since to do so is 'against our freedom'. Representatives are, however, able to use finance to raise forces 'to engage in any just cause'. Third, recriminations for actions during 'late public differences' are excluded. Fourth, 'all laws made or to be made' must apply equally to all, with no distinction according to 'tenure, estate, charter, degree, birth, or place'. Judicial processes are also to apply in the same way whoever is involved. Fifth, and exceptionally subjectively, laws should be not only 'equal' but also 'good, and not evidently destructive to the safety and well-being of the people'. These entrenched principles resemble those of later written constitutions, though there is no accompanying amendment procedure or stated means of enforcement, judicial or otherwise. The Agreement of the People closes with the claim that it has stated 'our native rights'. The authors feel compelled to defend them 'not only by the examples of our ancestors, whose blood was often spent in vain for the recovery of their freedoms ... but also by our own woeful experience'. Even a text so advanced in anticipating modern democratic and constitutional principles presented itself as seeking to regain a distant past.[24]

Leveller ideas, including some expressed in this text, prefigured constitutional developments on the other side of the Atlantic. The Levellers receive credit in US sources for originating the principles of protection from self-incrimination and that an accused person should be aware of the charge made against them, enunciated respectively in the Fifth and Sixth Amendments of the US Constitution. They certainly pre-empted concepts that took hold in the US, such as firm legal protection for rights and fundamental texts grounded in popular as opposed to parliamentary sovereignty. The Levellers may also, partly via the Quaker movement,

---

[24] See: D Alan Orr, 'Constitutionalism: Ancient, Modern and Early Modern in the *Agreements of the People*' in Philip Baker and Elliot Vernon (eds), *The Agreements of the People, the Levellers and the Constitutional Crisis of the English Revolution* (Basingstoke, Palgrave Macmillan, 2012).

have had a specific influence upon such thinking, though it is difficult precisely to prove.[25] Yet however prescient they would prove to be, the Levellers could not secure a consensus for their ideas at Putney in the autumn of 1647. Henry Ireton, a leading figure in the army, objected to provision for the size of constituencies based on population rather than tax take, because of the width of franchise it implied. Colonel Thomas Rainborough (now often known as Rainsborough), speaking for the Leveller cause in this dispute, uttered the famous words 'the poorest he that is in England hath a life to live, as the greatest he'. But he was an isolated voice at senior level in the army. A further irresolvable point of contention arose because the army had committed to preserving Charles I in office.[26] Yet in January 1649 the army brought forward its own Agreement of the People, derived partly from the earlier Leveller document.[27] Like this prior document it dealt with matters including the election of Parliament, the composition and control of the executive and religious freedom. Also like the Leveller text, it did not provide for a monarchy (Charles I was executed later in the month it appeared), and included entrenched provisions beyond the reach of Parliament. In the following decade the developing concept of a written statement of fundamental rules found concrete legal form, under particular influence from this army version of the Agreement of the People.[28]

CONSTITUTIONS UNDER CROMWELL

A typical description applied to the Instrument of Government of 1653 is that it was 'England's first and ... only written constitution'.[29] In fact it covered not only England, but an area larger than the present UK, encompassing England (including Wales), Scotland and Ireland and the 'dominions thereunto belonging' (preamble).[30] Yet it endured not much more than three years (from 1653 to 1657) and 'was soon cast aside and all but forgotten' following the demise of Cromwell and eventual return of the monarchy.[31] Oliver Cromwell sought through the Instrument of Government to bring about a more secure political system after protracted upheaval. He seems not to have found the embryonic idea of a written constitution attractive when the Levellers were developing it. In many ways, he was of conservative outlook.[32] Subsequently Cromwell accepted the idea of

---

[25] Michael Kent Curtis, 'In Pursuit of Liberty: The Levellers and the American Bill of Rights' (1991) 8 *Constitutional Comment* 359.

[26] Kishlansky, *A Monarchy Transformed* (n 1) 175–76.

[27] Gardiner, *The Constitutional Documents of the Puritan Revolution* (n 13) 359–71.

[28] David L Smith, 'The *Agreements of the People* and the Constitutions of the Interregnum Governments' in Philip Baker and Elliot Vernon (eds), *The Agreements of the People, the Levellers and the Constitutional Crisis of the English Revolution* (Basingstoke, Palgrave Macmillan, 2012).

[29] George D Heath, 'Making the Instrument of Government' (1967) 6(2) *Journal of British Studies* 15.

[30] Reproduced in: Gardiner, *The Constitutional Documents of the Puritan Revolution* (n 13) 405–17.

[31] Heath, 'Making the Instrument of Government' (n 29) 15.

[32] HN Brailsford, *The Levellers and the English Revolution* (London, The Cresset Press, 1961) 490–91.

what became the Instrument in the hope that it could provide the firm basis for government that he wanted. When parliamentarians asked for changes to the text in 1654, Cromwell told them that 'In every government there must be somewhat fundamental, somewhat like the Magna Carta, that should be standing and unalterable'.[33] As ever, Magna Carta could at times serve as a useful rhetorical tool for political leaders—and also be an annoyance to them. The following year, when judges referred to it in support of a case against his government for seeking to raise funds without parliamentary approval, Cromwell warned them that 'their *Magna Farta* should not controle [their] Actions'.[34]

It is once again significant that the army, not the legislature, was the source of the Instrument, given that this document in some ways specifically sought to constrain Parliament, which some in the military felt had taken excessive authority upon itself.[35] The main author of the Instrument was Major-General John Lambert, who had previously worked with General Henry Ireton on the army Heads of Proposals. Some have believed that Lambert was possibly the only drafter.[36] It is more likely that a group of five to eight prominent army figures carried out the task, of whom Lambert was one. Production and formal acceptance of the Instrument took place 'amid strict secrecy and in great haste' with the process 'known only to a very select few, none of whom ever divulged details. Little information reached the public'. There were only 'confidential, top-level consultations'. Peter Gaunt argues that though an official public reading of the document took place in Westminster Hall on 16 December, with the new government installed at the same point, Cromwell and his Council then altered the Instrument before issuing it in printed form on 2 January. One area of change seems to have been in allowing Cromwell more time to appoint his initial full complement of Council members. It was possible to doctor the Instrument in this way without political reprisal precisely because the initial process producing it was so secretive and the original content was not widely known.[37] This exclusive approach may have made the production process more efficient, but did not aid the legitimacy of the document.

The Instrument begins by setting out a constitutional model different from that of parliamentary sovereignty, under which ultimate legal authority rests with a Parliament incorporating the monarchy within it. Instead it vests this power in two distinct places: the institution of Parliament, and an office holder who is separate from it. Further on the text places limitations upon the Parliament. Yet the Instrument also provides powers and protections for the legislature that it

---

[33]   Barbara Silberdick Feinberg, 'The Political Thought of Oliver Cromwell: revolutionary or conservative?' (1968) 35(3) *Social Research* 460.

[34]   Ralph V Turner, *Magna Carta: Through the Ages* (Harlow, Longman, 2003) 160; Anne Pallister, *Magna Carta: The Heritage of Liberty* (Oxford, Clarendon Press, 1971) 24.

[35]   Heath, 'Making the Instrument of Government' (n 29) 18.

[36]   Ibid.

[37]   Peter Gaunt, 'Drafting the Instrument of Government, 1653–54: A Reappraisal' (1989) 8(1) *Parliamentary History* 29, 38–42, 39, 28.

did not previously possess, demonstrating that a written constitution that curbs the law-making authority of Parliament can strengthen it in other ways. Clause 1 describes the 'supreme legislative authority of the Commonwealth' as present within 'one person, and the people assembled in Parliament'. The 'one person' the Instrument referred to is the 'Lord Protector of the Commonwealth of England, Scotland, and Ireland', that is, Cromwell. This stipulation is a reminder that at this point in English history there was no king. Not only was Charles dead, but an Act of 1649 had abolished the monarchy altogether, prohibiting 'his issue and posterity, and all others pretending title under him' from becoming king or queen. Such an office, the Act went on, had proved 'unnecessary, burdensome, and dangerous to the liberty, safety, and public interest of the people'. The 'nation' was now released 'to return to its just and ancient right, of being governed by its own representatives'.[38] However, the idea of making Cromwell king recurred during the Interregnum. He never succumbed to it, formally at least, but the post the Instrument created for Cromwell shared some similarities with that of a monarch.

It is also notable that the institution with which the Lord Protector shares legislative power is described as 'the people assembled in Parliament', suggesting that the authority of Parliament is derived from below—a step towards popular sovereignty. The Parliament was unicameral. In March 1649, the Commons, acting on its own, had abolished the House of Lords, describing it as 'useless and dangerous to the people'. In doing so, the Commons provided a possible answer to an argument that supporters of the second chamber continue to advance today. The Act stresses that worthwhile members of the Lords who have a contribution to make will not 'be excluded from the public councils of the nation', since they will be able to participate in Parliament 'if they shall be thereunto elected'.[39]

The Instrument provides for the office of a Lord Protector, supported by a council of between 13 and 21 members. Clause 33 names Cromwell as holder of the title. Though occupied for life, the post of Lord Protector is 'elective and not hereditary', with the council responsible, when the time came, for choosing 'another fit person', by majority verdict, to succeed Cromwell (clause 32). Nonetheless, following the death of Cromwell his son Richard followed him in the post. It was difficult to conceive of any other way of proceeding, though events of this period would help in time to develop different conceptions. After listing 15 initial council members, clause 25 sets out the procedure for selecting further participants, which involves Parliament providing a long-list of six, whittled down to two by the council, from which the Lord Protector chooses one. A joint procedure between Parliament, council and Lord Protector can punish council members for improper behaviour (clause 25).

The text vests in the Lord Protector what is in effect executive power (clauses 2 and 3). One of the consequences of this feature of the Instrument is that a

---

[38] 'The Act abolishing the office of King', text reproduced in Gardiner, *The Constitutional Documents of the Puritan Revolution* (n 13) 384–87.

[39] 'The Act abolishing the House of Lords'; text reproduced in Gardiner, ibid, 387–88.

number of authorities that up to the present are still exercised under the Royal Prerogative were briefly in the 1650s derived from a written constitution instead. The responsibilities include the 'chief magistracy and the administration of the government' (clause 2) and the granting of pardons (clause 3). The Lord Protector directs the armed forces and the reserves, subject to the 'consent' of Parliament, if it is in session, or, if it is not, the majority of the council (clause 4). This requirement affords Parliament an authority it lacks today, since the disposition of the armed forces is exercised under the Royal Prerogative without a legal necessity for the support of the legislature (though the regulation of the armed forces is partly a matter of statute, and Parliament votes on its finance). However, as at present, the Instrument makes conduct of diplomacy and the 'power of war and peace' exclusive to the executive, the Lord Protector acting with the approval of the council (clause 5). Nonetheless, clause 23 requires the Lord Protector to convene Parliament 'forthwith' for its 'advice concerning' any conflict that may take place in future. To this day, the recall of the Commons remains, under a Standing Order of the House, within the gift of the executive, even in times of military emergency.

Clause 6 sets a limit on the Lord Protector, iterating that legislative and tax-raising authority is exercised only with the consent of Parliament. The exception to this constraint comes with clause 30, the equivalent to the emergency powers provision of a modern constitution. This portion of the Instrument mandates the Lord Protector to raise money and make laws to deal with military threats before the meeting of Parliament, which shall have force until it convenes. The Lord Protector can summon Parliament early in emergencies. Once convened in this way it cannot disband for three months without its own consent (clause 23). The text guarantees funding for military purposes, the judicial system, and the functions of the executive branch, a reduction in which is prohibited without consent of both Parliament and the Lord Protector (clause 27).

The Instrument devotes most space to the position and composition of Parliament. It stipulates that a Parliament will be called on 3 September 1654 and summoned once every three years (clause 7). After meeting, Parliament cannot be suspended in any way for the first five months unless it agrees (clause 8). The number of members is fixed at 400 (clause 9). The Instrument lists the geographical constituencies and number of members to be returned from each (clause 10). Summons to Parliament are under the Great Seal (clause 11). Those involved in the conflict with Parliament since 1641 are prohibited from being elected or voting for a set period (clause 14), while individuals connected to the Irish rebellion and Roman Catholics are permanently excluded in this way (clause 15). The Instrument makes detailed provision for the oversight of electoral procedures. Members of Parliament must be 21-years-old, and 'of known integrity, fearing God, and of good conversation' (clause 17). Sixty or more of the people returned in the manner determined in the Instrument qualify as the 'Parliament of England, Scotland and Ireland' (clause 22). Though most public appointments are in the hands of the Lord Protector, Parliament has the power to select the holders of the posts of Chancellor, Keeper or Commissioners of the Great Seal, the Treasurer, Admiral, Chief Governors of Ireland and Scotland, and the Chief Justices of the Benches (clause 34). In this sense a power which traditionally and up to the present has been a matter of Royal Prerogative came to a significant extent under parliamentary control.

In addition to providing for the Lord Protector and Parliament and the relationship between them, the Instrument deals with religion. Clause 35 states that Christianity 'as contained in the Scriptures' is the 'public profession' and requires its vigorous promotion. Yet at the same time it guarantees the right to follow a different version of the Christian faith to that officially promulgated. However, the Instrument rules out 'Popery or Prelacy', 'licentiousness', and abuse of rights to the detriment of others (clause 37). The Instrument strengthens the requirement of tolerance by stating that all laws violating religious liberty are deemed 'null and void' (clause 38). This provision does not specify whether or not it applies to future as well as existing legislation. If it did, it would be of a similar status to many written constitutions, in overriding more regular law with which it is incompatible, even if the offending statute was enacted after the constitution.

Determining that a constitution takes precedence over other laws is one form of entrenchment. Another is creating a heightened procedure for alteration of the constitutional text itself. The legislative process set out in clause 24 allows Parliament to force Bills into law if the Lord Protector has not agreed to them within 20 days. But this power does not apply to laws 'contrary to the matters contained in these presents'. The historian, Samuel Rawson Gardiner, though regarding the Instrument as a substantial achievement of drafting, criticised the supposed overlooking of the need for an amendment procedure.[40] However, it is possible to construe the intended effect of clause 24 as being to make changes to the Instrument possible, yet more demanding to execute than standard laws, through the necessity for approval from the Lord Protector. A further suggestion of fundamental status comes in clause 12. It requires officials responsible for overseeing parliamentary elections to obtain from voters an agreement that the candidate they chose was not empowered to alter the basic system of dual government by Lord Protector and Parliament. Finally, clause 41 places on the Lord Protector a duty to swear before the council and any others they summon to attend that he will uphold this text, as well as the well-being of the nations and other legal norms.

Though production of the Instrument was the work of a small group operating in secret, once introduced Cromwell strained to promote the text, stressing transparency as a virtue. As he put it to Parliament 'The thing is open and visible, to be seen and read by all men, and therefore let it speak for itself'. The Instrument attracted wide comment both from advocates and opponents. In February 1654 Marchamont Nedham issued a supportive account of the text intended for

---

[40] Gardiner, 'Introduction' in *The Constitutional Documents of the Puritan Revolution* (n 13) lv–lvi, lviii.

wide public consumption.[41] The Instrument formed part of the Cromwellian European propaganda campaign, with a special edition produced for continental distribution.[42] (Exporting the revolution through texts was a concerted policy: the regime had also dispatched its agent Edward Sexby to France in 1651, where he promoted an abbreviated translation of a Leveller Agreement, alongside a manifesto intended to court Hugenot support.)[43] The Instrument also provided inspiration for a work by the poet Andrew Marvell, a Cromwell supporter, containing the couplet 'Such was that wondrous Order and Consent,/When Cromwell tun'd the ruling Instrument'.[44]

A hostile pamphlet of the time held that Cromwell had through the Instrument taken on 'all those Powers, and maintains all those principles of Tyranny against which' the army had struggled when the monarchy wielded them.[45] Analysis by historians has to some extent supported this strand of criticism. One author concludes that the Instrument was an executive-loaded text, and that the only significant protections it included for the position of Parliament were providing it with a position in the process of appointing senior office-holders, giving it the ability to veto alienation by the Protector of public land, and guaranteeing parliaments on a triennial basis.[46] A particular area of academic interest regarding the practical operation of the Instrument of Government has been its use as a means of preventing returned candidates from serving in Parliament.[47] Initially deployment of this power was sparing. But Carol S Egloff describes how in 1656 the Council of State denied over 100 individuals entry into Parliament and that it did so for narrow political reasons that the original drafters of the text did not envisage. This purge represented a response to eroding support for the government, but in turn came at a cost of further criticism and negative feeling.[48]

Problems of design and usage certainly existed. Yet understood in the context of its time and what followed, the Instrument is of transcendent importance, both for its implications and—though not as well remembered now as it should be—its influence. The text offered a different constitutional model from that ultimately adopted in England and the UK: a limited but protected Parliament with powers of executive oversight, no monarch, an executive head separate from the legislature, a unicameral system without unelected second chamber, and individual freedoms, set out in a single entrenched document. It is arguably the first operational written constitution in world history (though there is also an older Islamic tradition in this field, and developments were already gaining their own momentum

---

[41] Joad Raymond, 'Framing Liberty: Marvell's "First Anniversary" and the Instrument of Government' (1999) 62(3–4) *Huntington Library Quarterly* 324.

[42] Hill, *Puritanism and Revolution* (n 6) 133.

[43] Baker and Vernon, 'Introduction' in *The Agreements of the People* (n 23).

[44] For quotes and analysis see: Raymond, 'Framing Liberty' (n 40) 315–50.

[45] Ibid, 323.

[46] Heath, 'Making the Instrument of Government' (n 29).

[47] See eg: Heather Falvey, 'Interpreting the Instrument of Government: Objections to the 1654 Election in the Isle of Ely' (2012) 31(2) *Parliamentary History* 133.

[48] Carol S Egloff, 'The Search for a Cromwellian Settlement: Exclusions from the Second Protectorate Parliament. Part 1: The Process and its Architects' (1998) 17(2) *Parliamentary History* 178.

in America, through such texts as the Fundamental Orders of Connecticut of 1639). Maurice Vile argues that one of the principal underpinnings of the US text produced in 1787, the so-called 'separation of powers' concept, originated in 'English political thought at the time of the Civil War'. Vile holds that to this end the American document 'mirrored the structure of the Cromwellian Constitution, the *Instrument of Government* of 1653'.[49] An idea discarded in England thereby flourished later in a former British colony.

The army Council of Officers authorised the Instrument on 15 December and the following day Cromwell took up post as Lord Protector.[50] Parliament met on 3 September 1654. But instead of working the system, members showed more interest in challenging it. Some of them argued that only Parliament had the authority to pass a measure such as the Instrument. Members sought to secure amendments to the text.[51] This development confirmed the initial apprehensions of Cromwell about written constitutions. A composite set of parliamentary proposals—recorded by the Clerk of the Parliaments, John Browne—survives, which Gardiner reproduced as the Constitutional Bill of the first Parliament of the Protectorate, along with an analysis of the ways in which it differed from the Instrument of Government.[52]

Unsurprisingly given its provenance, a characteristic of the Constitutional Bill is that it seeks to assume more powers for Parliament relative to the Lord Protector. This approach manifests itself in a key distinction between the Instrument and the Bill: their respective approaches to entrenchment. The former stipulates that any changes to its provisions require approval from the Lord Protector (and some of it appears to be unalterable by any means). However, the latter text reduces the scope of this protection. It states that 20 days after Parliament presents them to the Lord Protector, Bills can become law even without his approval, so long as they do not contravene specified matters over which he possesses a veto (clause 1). Under the Bill, therefore, amendments in areas not protected, even within the Bill itself, would be ultimately in the hands of Parliament alone. The first exception to the general rule comes with clause 2, setting out that the requirement for agreement from the Lord Protector applies to measures intended to change the system of combined government by 'a single person and a Parliament'. Further protections involve religious freedom. Such differentiations in status exist in present day written constitutions, which sometimes employ varied degrees of entrenchment.

A further shift towards Parliament comes with the provision that it, not the council, would elect a Lord Protector to succeed Cromwell, in a manner which Parliament, furthermore, would determine (clause 3). Clause 39 deals with the

---

[49] Maurice Vile, 'British Influences on the American Founding Fathers: Lessons for Europe' in Stanley Henig (ed), *Federalism and the British* (London, Federal Trust, 2007) 20.

[50] David L Smith, 'The Struggle for New Constitutional and Institutional Forms' in John Morrill (ed), *Revolution and Restoration: England in the 1650s* (London, Collins & Brown, 1992) 22.

[51] Kishlansky, *A Monarchy Transformed* (n 1) 208.

[52] Gardiner, *The Constitutional Documents of the Puritan Revolution* (n 13) 427–47. For his comparison with the Instrument see table in 'Introduction' lviii–lx.

appointment of council members. The Instrument gave the Lord Protector the right to make the final decision from a shortlist of two, which the council chose from six candidates that Parliament initially presented. With the Bill, Parliament sets out to give itself the right to approve nominations, made by the Lord Protector. Symbolically, they are to swear in to office in Parliament, if it is sitting—the Instrument did not require that they do so in this location. The Bill also stipulates that the tenure of members of the council is dependent upon parliamentary consent, which must be obtained within 40 days of the convening of each new Parliament (clause 40). Clause 25 of the Instrument provided that the initial quorum of the council was seven and that the Lord Protector and council could determine its new level as the membership grew, but the Bill stipulated that the minimum attendance was 11 (clause 39).

The Instrument granted Parliament certain rights in the exercise of powers which have traditionally been—and are today—provided for under the Royal Prerogative, with no parliamentary input formally required. Parliament could make certain major public appointments and the Lord Protector needed its approval (or if Parliament was not sitting, that of the council) for his actions in directing the armed forces. The Bill extends this particular parliamentary power, by stipulating that the size of the forces must be agreed between Parliament and Lord Protector (clause 48), and that after the death of Cromwell they will come under the control of Parliament (clause 46). The Bill also sought to restrict the provision for funding of the armed forces and civil government, a particularly objectionable idea from the point of view of Cromwell (clauses 18 and 49). The Bill encroaches further into executive privilege with clause 53: 'The power of making war is only in the Lord Protector and the Parliament'. There is no mention of arrangements for periods when Parliament is not in session. Nonetheless, this idea was, and remains, radical. At the time of writing, the ability to declare war, or enter into armed conflict without a formal statement of hostilities, remains a Royal Prerogative. Under the Bill, peace can only be made with the agreement of Parliament, or—if Parliament is not sitting—the council, subject to subsequent parliamentary consent (clause 53). The handling of foreign relations remains a responsibility of the Lord Protector, advised by and with the approval of the council (clause 54).

As noted above, there is a strong interrelationship between government by consent and the protection of freedoms. The principles involved are mutually dependent and not fundamentally in conflict. However, tensions can develop between them. In this case a power-grab by Parliament, though it might have a basis in what would now be seen as democratic values, could have posed a threat to rights. The Bill retains a degree of commitment to religious tolerance, but dilutes it as compared with the Instrument. Clauses 42 and 43 provide generally that Bills intended to restrict the freedoms of those not subscribing to the public religion (set out in clause 41) are subject to possible veto by the Lord Protector. But the Bill presents such measures as a possibility provided they meet with procedural requirements, while the emphasis in the Instrument was on their not being permitted. Moreover, the Bill provides that Parliament may produce laws without the agreement of the Lord Protector intended to repress 'damnable heresies' as well as 'atheism, blasphemy, popery, prelacy, licentiousness, and profaneness' and attacks on the endorsed parameters of Christianity. Though unable to veto such legislation, the Lord Protector is to have a role, along with Parliament, in defining what are 'damnable heresies' and public 'doctrines' (clause 43). The potential threat of expansive parliamentary power to personal freedom remains with us. In the present day, advocates of the doctrine of parliamentary sovereignty can see the legal entrenchment of freedoms as an improper constraint.

Cromwell responded to the Constitutional Bill by disbanding Parliament at the soonest permissible point. He then set up a military dictatorship. Discontent followed, and in the autumn of 1656 Cromwell felt obliged to convene another Parliament. In February 1657 it presented him with a proposed new system of government under the title Humble Petition and Advice. Central to this blueprint was that Cromwell should become king, an idea he considered but ultimately rejected. But most of the other components of the initial Humble Petition and Advice came into force as what David L Smith calls 'England's second—and last—paper constitution'.[53]

The Petition is a less comprehensive text than the Instrument or the Constitutional Bill, focusing more on resolving specific contentions that had arisen between Lord Protector and Parliament. It was the work not of the army but Parliament, perhaps explaining its more conservative quality. Nonetheless, it has some of the features of a written constitution. It presents itself as aimed at promoting certain values—in this case a particular form of Christianity—tempered by a (limited) tolerance, and it establishes institutions and procedures of governance. The Petition is an address by the 'Knights, Citizens and Burgesses now assembled in the Parliament of this Commonwealth' to 'his Highness the Lord Protector'. After a grovelling preamble worthy of the monarch it was initially intended to praise, clause 1 once more establishes Cromwell as Lord Protector. In this role he is to act as 'Chief Magistrate' of England, Ireland and Scotland, in accordance with the Petition, other laws, 'and not otherwise'. An important change from previous arrangements is that the text permits Cromwell while he is alive to determine who will become Lord Protector after he dies. Clause 2 signals the return of a Parliament 'consisting of two Houses' which must be called at least every three years. The council becomes the Privy Council once more. New Privy Council members require approval by the council and then Parliament, and expulsions need parliamentary consent. The maximum membership is 21, the quorum seven. The council is responsible for approving military appointments and advises the Lord Protector in his administrative role (clause 8).

---

[53] Smith, 'The Struggle for New Constitutional and Institutional Forms' (n 49) 22–25. Reproduced in: Gardiner, *The Constitutional Documents of the Puritan Revolution* (n 13) 447–59. 'The Additional Petition and Advice' is at 459–64.

The more traditional nature of the Petition is present in its treatment of Parliament. Clause 3 insists upon the upholding of the 'ancient and undoubted liberties and privileges' of this institution. Clause 4 deals with qualifications for membership of Parliament. The Petition re-establishes bicameralism. There is to be an 'other House' consisting of between 40 and 70 individuals nominated by the Lord Protector, initially with the consent of the Commons, and in future the House itself. The quorum is 21. This 'other House' then begins to become curiously similar to the House of Lords, though—much like the present Lords—with members appointed for life rather than inheriting their position. The Petition seems to take a judicial function for this chamber as a given, and goes on to regulate its activities in this area. Both Houses of Parliament have a role in giving consent to the Lord Protector—in his Chief Magistrate guise—in his direction of the armed forces (clause 8). The Petition does not deal specifically with war or peacemaking. The two chambers take on the responsibility previously assumed by the unicameral Parliament for approving major public appointments (clause 9). Parliament now seems to comprise the House of Commons, other House, and Lord Protector, judging by the reference in clause 7 to the 'three Estates in Parliament'. The experiment set out in the Instrument of a legislative power divided between a unicameral Parliament and a separate Lord Protector was over.

The Petition agrees to provide a fixed income for civil government and military expenses, unalterable except with the agreement of both houses of Parliament and the Lord Protector (clause 7). In dealing with religious belief, the Petition largely reverts to the more tolerant flavour of the Instrument and away from that of the Constitutional Bill. However, it extends the list of tenets to which individuals who do not follow the official line must nonetheless subscribe (clause 11). In January 1658 the legislature reconvened. But objections to the existence of the 'Other House' from within the Commons prompted Cromwell to disband Parliament the following month. He died later in the year, having failed to put in place a lasting constitutional structure.[54] Yet viewed from a longer-term perspective, the constitutional achievements of Cromwell and others in the mid-seventeenth century were immense.

THE BILL OF RIGHTS 1689

At the turn of 1688/1689 England was passing through an archetypal constitutional moment. A major political, constitutional and military crisis was underway. Some of the motivation was of a long-term nature. It arose from problems often associated with the Stuart period: arbitrary government, disputes about confessional matters and European orientation, and difficulties involving the other kingdoms over which the Stuarts presided. Tensions became more immediate because of the nature of the rule of James II. His Catholicism and the way he

---

[54] Smith, 'The Struggle for New Constitutional and Institutional Forms' (n 49) 27.

chose to express it, alongside his wider political programme, prompted objections. Late in 1688, William of Orange—the husband (and cousin) of James II's daughter, Mary, who was not a Catholic—invaded, and then James II fled. It was not clear who was in charge. Civil war seemed possible. External security threats came from Ireland, where rebellion was possible, and from Louis XIV, who threatened to attain hegemony on the continental mainland. A flurry of pamphlets, advocating various different constitutional approaches, informed public debate. Parties were developing. The Whig group leaned towards radical models, even to the point of removing monarchy; some of them sought a text along the lines of the Leveller Agreement.[55] Tories were more conservative.

Against this background a Convention met from January 1689. Outsiders had applied this term colloquially to the body that had brought about the Restoration in 1660, but the 1689 version initially attached this term to itself.[56] Like a parliament, the Convention of 1689 included peers and elected members (with a relatively even balance between Whigs and Tories among the latter). But no king had summoned it. It had to decide it was a parliament for itself, and retrospectively asserted that it had been so all along. On 23 February 1689 the Convention produced a Bill declaring it was a parliament, authorised with the signature of William.[57] Regardless of whether or not the label 'Parliament' was correct, it was an irregular gathering. The acts it carried out matched its extraordinary status. One was to place William and Mary jointly on the throne. (Through including Mary Parliament sought to present a semblance of continuity, but in doing so exerted its authority in an unprecedented way.) Another was to produce a constitutional text that remains of foundational significance in the contemporary UK, and a powerful influence elsewhere in the world.

Unlike the Instrument of Government, the Bill of Rights was not simply devised and imposed by a small group. The Bill, that began as the 'Declaration of Rights', had a challenging passage through the Convention.[58] A Commons committee of 12 Tories and 28 Whigs drew up the initial draft, with modifications from the Commons sitting in full, and the Lords.[59] An important point of debate involved the distinction between the assertion of ancient law, and the creation of new measures: an issue that remains important to historical analysis of the Bill. The Declaration was initially conceived of to a significant extent as a list of grievances and a sketch of a legislative programme for fuller subsequent expression. But it subsequently gained importance as law in its own right.[60] The Bill of

---

[55] Baker and Vernon, 'Introduction' in *The Agreements of the People* (n 23) 9.

[56] J Franklin Jameson, 'The Early Political Uses of the Word Convention' (1898) 3(3) *The American Historical Review* 477.

[57] Lois G Schwoerer, *The Declaration of Rights, 1689* (Baltimore MD, The Johns Hopkins University Press, 1981) 267.

[58] Ibid, 284.

[59] Tim Harris, *Revolution: The Great Crisis of the British Monarchy, 1685–1720* (London, Penguin, 2006) 331.

[60] Geoffrey Lock, 'The 1689 Bill of Rights' (1989) XXXVII *Political Studies* 540, esp 541–42.

Rights describes itself as the product of the Lords and Commons 'assembled at Westminster, lawfully, fully and freely representing all the estates of the people of this realm'.[61] This body presented, as the Bill puts it, 'a certain declaration in writing' to William and Mary on 13 February 1689. The timing is crucial. It was a preliminary to William and Mary taking up the throne. Acceptance of the Declaration was not an express condition of assumption of the monarchy, but was implied. Furthermore, the Declaration predated the determination that the Convention was a parliament. To remove any doubts arising from its provenance as a product of the Convention, the Declaration became the Bill—in slightly altered form—in December 1689, when it was enacted as a statute.[62]

The text begins by noting how James II—supported by 'divers evil' advisers, judges and ministers—had undermined Protestantism and the 'laws and liberties' of the kingdom. His transgressions included taking upon himself and executing a power, without parliamentary approval, to dispense with or suspend laws. He had created a 'court of commissioners for ecclesiastical causes' using the authority of the Great Seal. James II, the Bill of Rights claims, had improperly raised money using the Royal Prerogative. He had, again without consent from the legislature, raised and maintained a standing army in peacetime. A further offence was removing weapons from Protestants while simultaneously giving them to Roman Catholics. James II had intervened in parliamentary elections, used prosecutions to interfere with parliamentary business, brought unsuitable people onto juries, and required 'excessive bail' and 'excessive fines', along with 'illegal and cruel punishments'. He had pre-empted judicial processes by promising people that they would benefit from 'fines and forfeitures' applied to others before they were even convicted. All such behaviour, the Bill of Rights holds, was inimical to law and liberty.

The text then describes James II as having 'abdicated', leaving the 'throne … vacant'—a crucial part of the revolutionary narrative of constitutional legitimacy. At this point, the Bill of Rights recounts, William ('the Prince of Orange')—with the advice of Lords and senior MPs—summoned the members of the Lords 'being protestants' and sent letters to constituencies calling on them to select individuals 'to represent them, as were of right to be sent to parliament, to meet and sit at Westminster' on 22 January 1689. The purpose of this gathering was to ensure 'that their religion, laws, and liberties might not again be in danger of being subverted'. The document seeks to present itself as the outgrowth of a domestic, historic continuity. Members of this body, it asserts, were acting 'as their ancestors in like case have usually done' in 'vindicating their ancient rights and liberties' by making a declaration. Towards the end the document reasserts this point with the statement that 'the rights and liberties' to which it refers are 'true, ancient, and indubitable rights and liberties of the people of this kingdom'.

---

[61] Reproduced in EN Williams, *The Eighteenth Century Constitution* (Cambridge, Cambridge University Press, 1960) 26–33.

[62] Schwoerer, *The Declaration of Rights, 1689* (n 56) 267.

As with Magna Carta, the invocation of supposed historic freedoms served the purpose of restraining the executive, with these principles applying to 'all officers and ministers whatsoever shall serve their Majesties and their successors according to the same in all times to come'. Again like Magna Carta, this constitutional text asserted perpetuity.

In clauses 1 to 4, the Bill of Rights declares 'illegal' certain practices under James II it has already outlined: nullifying laws without parliamentary consent; creating special legal commissions; and raising money without appropriate parliamentary approval. It asserts the 'right of the subjects to petition the King' without harassment (clause 5): a statement of the need for public engagement in government. Recruiting or maintaining a 'standing army within the kingdom' in peacetime, the text holds, is only legal with the agreement of Parliament (clause 6). Like Magna Carta, the Bill of Rights can present to the modern-day reader curious juxtapositions of obscure anachronism and timeless universal principle. Fitting in the former category, it states that Protestant subjects are allowed 'arms for their defence suitable to their conditions' within the law (clause 7). In the latter, the following stipulation is that parliamentary elections 'ought to be free' (clause 8). But at the time both conditions were judged necessary to create a barrier to a return to the experience of James II as ruler. As well as seeking to prevent interference with the process of determining who should sit in the Commons, the Bill of Rights is concerned with ensuring that parliamentarians can fulfil their duties without legal retribution. The 'freedom of speech, and debates or proceedings in parliament, ought not to be impeached or questioned in any court or place out of parliament' (clause 9). This provision is vital to a healthy legislature, despite the potential for abuse. In 2013, the report of the Joint Committee on Parliamentary Privilege confirmed that this feature of the Bill of Rights continues to have direct legal significance.[63]

The Bill of Rights, like the Petition of Right earlier in the seventeenth century, presents government by consent and the preservation of rights as part of a whole, as a modern constitution can deal with the institutions of democratic governance and the protection of human rights. With clause 10, the text moves on from the role of Parliament and prohibits 'excessive bail' and 'excessive fines', and the use of 'cruel and unusual punishments'. Clause 11 requires jurors to be 'duly impaneled and returned', and that in cases of high treason jury members should be freeholders. While this latter provision would now seem inappropriately exclusive, at the time a degree of financial independence was seen as some kind of guarantee of impartiality, a protection against trial-rigging. Through clause 12, the Bill of Rights prohibits the practice of offering people the proceeds of fines or confiscations before an individual is convicted. Finally, in clause 13 a direct connection is made between representative government and maintenance of rights. It requires frequent parliaments to be held to enable 'redress of all grievances' as well as for the 'amending, strengthening and preserving of the laws'. A parliament in regular

---

[63] Joint Committee on Parliamentary Privilege, *Parliamentary Privilege* (2013–14, HL 30, HC 100).

session was a barrier to possible monarchical tyranny and undermining of the integrity of the legal system.

The text insists that all its stipulations are unquestionable entitlements and should not be violated. It expresses optimism in the light of pronouncements by William that he shares their objectives. The 'lords ... and commons' then declare William and Mary to be King and Queen of England, France (on which they still had an optimistic claim), and Ireland; and determine that no Roman Catholic or spouse of a Roman Catholic can ascend to the throne in future. But what was the true intent lying behind this text, and what did it truly achieve? A long-standing debate surrounds how far the Bill of Rights was a radical, creative instrument, or a conservative reassertion of that which already existed.[64] It may be that—as the document claims—the authors sought only to assert established law. Yet even if they did, and even if they were correct in believing that they were doing so, they intended to make a difference. They were at least addressing perceived malpractice that had taken place, whether legal or otherwise, and wanted to prevent it from happening in future. But a more convincing interpretation comes from Lois G Schwoerer:

> The authors of the Declaration of Rights asserted that they, like their ancestors before them, were doing nothing more than restoring old, acknowledged rights of Englishmen which had been grievously violated. There is nothing surprising about such an assertion ... What is surprising is the willingness of historians to accept this claim at face value.

The Declaration was, Schwoerer goes on, a 'radical reforming' text, 'resolving long-standing disputes in ways favourable to Parliament and the individual'.[65]

Crucially, the Bill of Rights contributed to the containment of the Royal Prerogative as a constitutional power source. A conventional view is that 1689 was the vital turning point in the assertion of the ultimate superiority of Parliament over the monarch acting alone[66] (though some emphasise a need for caution in regarding it as a precise cut-off point).[67] Events of this time also seem to have established firmly the principle that Parliament can regulate even the succession to the throne. The Bill of Rights is, for these reasons, often regarded as key to the development of the doctrine of parliamentary sovereignty. It was also part of a wider, pronounced change in the governance of England, to which the Dutch dimension was crucial. England moved decisively towards a system of limited government similar to that of the United Provinces, though it did not utilise the same territorial dispersal of power that characterised Holland, focusing instead on the use of Parliament as a brake on the monarchy. This model persisted in England and the UK even after Napoleonic occupation eradicated it in its country

---

[64] Harris, *Revolution* (n 58) 328–48.

[65] Schwoerer, *The Declaration of Rights, 1689* (n 56) 283.

[66] See eg: Hilaire Barnett, *Constitutional and Administrative Law*, 9th edn (Oxford, Routledge, 2011) 95.

[67] Sebastian Payne 'The Royal Prerogative' in Maurice Sunkin and Sebastian Payne (eds), *The Nature of the Crown: A Legal and Political Analysis* (Oxford, Oxford University Press, 1999).

of origin. The new order in England attained expression in the Bill of Rights, and in subsequent policies, such as allowing legislation providing for pre-publication censorship to lapse. England sided clearly with the Dutch in their struggle against Louis XIV. Other measures of historic importance, such as the formation of the Bank of England, clearly emulated the model of William's homeland.[68]

As well as representing the absorption of outside ideas, the Bill of Rights achieved international impact on the etymology and nature of constitutions. The Convention, though it decided it was a parliament, provided an example for future attempts at the re-founding of political systems, and influenced the use of the word 'convention' to describe bodies established for this purpose. When Americans began utilising this term they consciously imitated the language as well as the experience of 1689.[69] Furthermore, components of the Bill of Rights are mirrored in the US Constitution, including the first group of amendments to it that are known as the 'Bill of Rights', a phrase that has become synonymous with such declarations. Another text upon which the Bill of Rights made a clear imprint is the European Convention on Human Rights (ECHR). The ECHR has itself become an important component of the UK constitution, particularly following its incorporation into domestic law under the Human Rights Act 1998.[70] Criticisms of the EHCR for importing undesirable foreign norms perhaps overlook its important English sources, including the Bill of Rights and Magna Carta. Furthermore, while the ECHR entails some external influence manifesting itself within the UK, so too did the Bill of Rights. Far from being a negative feature, that they channelled forces from outside is central to the value of both.

THE ACT OF SETTLEMENT 1701: ALTERNATIVE CONSTITUTIONAL MODEL?

A further document of broad and deep constitutional implications—some of which it fulfilled, others it did not—appeared at the outset of the eighteenth century. It arose from a biologically induced crisis. The Act of Settlement 1701 describes itself as 'An Act for the further Limitation of the Crown and better securing the Rights and Liberties of the Subject'. A long opening narrative recaps the main contents of the Bill of Rights. It notes that the subjects of William and Mary 'had no greater temporall Felicity or hope' than for their rulers to produce a 'Royal Progeny'. The idea of a continental confessional-security agenda connected to a programme of limited government appears with a description of the ancestors of William as 'for many Years ... principal Assertors of the reformed Religion and the Liberties of Europe'. Mary was now dead with no heir. An arrangement already existed for the Crown to pass to 'Princess Ann [sic] of Denmark', the younger sister of Mary, and a Protestant. But her son Prince William, Duke of

---

[68] Israel, 'William III' (n 5) 33–40; Scott, *England's Troubles* (n 2) 474–96.
[69] Jameson, 'The Early Political Uses of the Word Convention' (n 55).
[70] Lock, *The 1689 Bill of Rights* (n 59) 542–44.

Gloucester, was now deceased also: the line was not secure. A threat came from the son of James II, also James, a Catholic and Pretender in exile. He had the backing of, among others, Louis XIV, who recognised him as James III of England (VIII of Scotland) following the death of his deposed father in 1701.

Consequently, in the interests of the 'Safety Peace and Quiet of this Realm' and to 'obviate all Doubts and Contentions', a need existed for 'further Provision of the Succession of the Crown in the Protestant Line'. The Act therefore determined that 'the most Excellent Princess Sophia Electress and Dutchess Dowager of Hannover' should be 'the next in Succession in the Protestant Line to the Imperiall Crown' of England, France, Ireland and the 'Dominions and Territories' in its possession. Sophia had a claim—though weak—through her mother, Princess Elizabeth, who was the daughter of James VI/I. This progeny embodied lasting English entanglement with the European conflicts of the seventeenth century: Elizabeth was the wife of Frederick V of the Palatinate, a central figure in the outbreak of the Thirty Years War in 1618. In 'Default of Issue' of 'Ann' and of William, the succession would pass through Sophia and 'Heirs of her Body being Protestants'. Section II provides that those subscribing to the 'See or Church of Rome' or married to a 'Papist' were barred from the throne, while section III requires the monarch to be 'in Communion with the Church of England'.

The new succession arrangement pointed to a lasting and firm connection between England and the continental mainland. Accordingly the Act sets out a series of safeguards to come into place upon a Hanoverian transition. The Act stipulates that if someone 'not being a Native of this Kingdom of England' should inherit the Crown, the 'Nation' will not be 'obliged to ingage in any Warr for the Defence of any Dominions or Territories which do not belong to the Crown of England without the Consent of Parliament' (section III). Another problem the Act seeks to avert is that of an absentee monarch. It states that 'Consent of Parliament' is required before a ruler can leave 'the Dominions of England Scotland or Ireland' (section III). Parliament repealed this provision in 1716 when George I wanted to travel to his territories in Germany.[71] Another fear was that the Hanoverians would bring with them a sizeable entourage to implant into positions of authority and social standing, as William of Orange had done. The 1701 Act accordingly forbids foreigners from joining the Council, sitting in either House of Parliament, gaining public office, or receiving grants of land (section III).

Having made exclusions from the Privy Council, the Act then deals in more detail with this royal advisory and extra-parliamentary legislative body. The Act requires that 'all Matters and Things relating to the well governing of this Kingdom which are properly cognizable in the Privy Councill by the Laws and Customs of this Realme shall be transacted there' (section III). The purpose of this stipulation was to ensure that key government business took place fully within the Privy Council, precluding the use of more informal conclaves that might in effect

---

[71] Mark A Thomson, *A Constitutional History of England: 1642–1801* (London, Methuen, 1938) 181.

bypass it. By this time a body smaller than the Council, advising the king, known as the Cabinet or Cabinet Council, was operating. The Cabinet of later years had its origins as a sub-group of this then emergent entity. A secret body, the early Cabinet was the subject of suspicion; Parliament felt it was harder to hold to account the actions of individuals within the Cabinet as compared with the Privy Council. The purpose of this provision in section III of the Act was to re-establish the position of the Privy Council and therefore afford Parliament an improved purchase on government.

The Act then goes on immediately to state: 'and all Resolutions taken thereupon shall be signed by such of the Privy Councill as shall advise and consent to the same' (section III). Lying behind this requirement was a desire to ensure that, with the preceding stipulation renewing the centrality of the Privy Council to government, it would be possible more effectively to monitor those who partici- pated in this group. To this end the Act sought to prevent members of the Privy Council from submitting collective advice, and ensure they remained individually responsible for their counsel.[72] Parliament repealed these stipulations regard- ing the Privy Council in 1706. Members had seemingly formed the opinion that such requirements would have made the holding of a ministerial post intoler- able. Parliament would constantly have insisted on access to the individual views submitted. Ministers might consequently have proved coy about expressing an opinion at all, and if they did do so differences between them would have received unwelcome exposure.[73]

Section III then prohibits any 'Person who has an Office or Place of Profit under the King or receives a Pention from the Crown' from sitting in the House of Commons. The apparent motive was to prevent executive patronage from compromising the integrity of the Commons. The long-term effect would have been to prevent 'MPs from becoming ministers at all',[74] though at this stage senior members of government tended to sit in the Lords, with few based in the Commons. Whigs disliked this prohibition in the Act, fearing that it imposed such limits on the Royal Prerogative as to make the taking up of the English monarchy appear unattractive, possibly preventing the Hanoverian ascendancy they desired and enhancing the Jacobite threat.[75] In 1706 Parliament abolished this prohibi- tion, and it then introduced in its place a requirement for Members taking up ministerial posts to seek re-election to the Commons, a practice that only ended fully in 1926 (after being restricted in 1919).[76]

Another branch of government, the judiciary, receives protection from section III, determining that it is possible to 'remove' judges only 'upon the Address of both Houses of Parliament'. The intention was to secure judicial independence

---

[72] Betty Kemp, *King and Commons: 1660–1834* (London, Macmillan, 1957) 116–19.
[73] Thomson, *A Constitutional History of England* (n 70) 217.
[74] See: Paul Langford, 'Prime Ministers and Parliaments: The Long View, Walpole to Blair' (2006) 25(3) *Parliamentary History* 382.
[75] Kemp, *King and Commons* (n 71) 57–59.
[76] Thomson, *A Constitutional History of England* (n 70) 187.

from the influence of the monarchy. Section III closes by ruling out the possibility of appealing against impeachment by the Commons for a pardon under the Great Seal of England. Presumably this rule sought to prevent the monarch from shielding ministers from parliamentary punishment. Finally, the Act requires all rulers and their agents to act in accordance with the 'Laws of England', which are the 'Birthright of the People thereof' (section IV).

Some of the content of the Act of Settlement—such as the provision it makes for royal succession—is well known and retains relevance today (subject to some alterations in the rules). The protection it creates for the tenure of judges remains central to an impartial legal system and by extension the rule of law. Other components of the Act are revoked and long forgotten, yet they remain of interest because of the alternative constitutional structure they pointed towards, if not entirely consciously on the part of the creators. The sections prohibiting office holders from sitting in the Commons and dealing with the operation of the Privy Council come within this category. Had these provisions come into force they would have placed a block on the development of key features of the contemporary UK constitution: governments with key members sitting in the Commons, resting primarily on the confidence of that chamber, and collective government through Cabinet. Nor could the office of Prime Minister have emerged in the way it did.[77] Subsequent amendments to the Act reopened the path towards a system of central government that remains with us in the UK today.

During the final century of its existence as a separate state, England experienced conflict, instability and discontinuity. These circumstances encouraged the production of a series of constitutional texts of profound importance. Most importantly, they helped decisively to constrain—though not eradicate—the Royal Prerogative. They also promoted the idea of legal due process and individual rights as integral parts of English political culture, and guaranteed a Protestant succession. Further ideas had currency in this period of English history but did not ultimately make sufficient progress in England. Most significantly, the idea of a text containing entrenched political rules appeared. But the advance of the concept of parliamentary supremacy—a means of containing monarchical authority within a legislative trinity also comprising Commons and Lords—did not fit with the idea of enforceable fundamental law. While the mid-seventeenth century texts contained limitations on Parliament, the Bill of Rights emphasised and sought to advance the strength and privileges of this institution.

Other paths presented themselves that England did not take. Both the Instrument of Government and Act of Settlement suggested a clearer distinction between executive and legislature than ultimately emerged, and the latter instrument sought to prohibit collective government. In the century that followed the Act of Settlement, some of the same forces that had driven constitutional turmoil

---

[77] See: Langford, 'Prime Ministers and Parliaments' (n 73) 382–83; Thomson, *A Constitutional History of England* (n 70) 217; Kemp, *King and Commons* (n 71) 57–59.

in England during its twilight as a distinct entity forced it to integrate with Scotland, to form the United Kingdom of Great Britain, which in turn incorporated with Ireland to create the United Kingdom of Great Britain and Ireland. The choices made—both consciously and unconsciously—in seventeenth century England had consequences for these successive new entities. But the arrangements they embodied did not achieve full acceptance, and remain controversial to the present.

5

Union and Parliament

THE UNITED KINGDOM (UK) began on paper. As he lay dying in 1702, one of the final wishes William III expressed was for the merging of his kingdoms, England and Scotland. His arrival from the United Provinces to seize power had occasioned a key English constitutional document, the Bill of Rights of 1689 (mirrored by an equivalent statement in Scotland). When executed, his deathbed recommendation would create a new state, with a further text at its core. England brought with it considerable constitutional baggage. Over the two centuries that followed, one developing component within the English tradition would gain increasing acceptance as supplanting the authority of all other legal norms within the UK, which comprised Great Britain and Ireland following the 1800 Act of Union. This doctrine of parliamentary sovereignty filled conceptual territory that a written constitution might otherwise have occupied. Its most renowned explicator, Albert Venn Dicey, used it explicitly to contrast the domestic system with those of other countries. For some his work acquired a status similar to that of a constitutional text. Given the degree of authority the model Dicey promoted vested in the Westminster legislature, control of this institution was of exceptional importance. The eventual outcome was a battle that in turn led to a further constitutional document, the Parliament Act 1911.

THE CREATION OF A UNION

External threats, especially from France, have repeatedly supplied impetus for constitutional development. From the standpoint of England, Louis XIV provided the most powerful immediate incentive for the union with Scotland.[1] It took place in 1706–07 in the midst of the War of Spanish Succession (1701–14). Jacobite sentiment—that is support for the line of James VII/II—persisted in Scotland, and Louis XIV might seek to capitalise upon it, launching an attack on England using Scotland as a base. Senior policymakers in England wanted to neutralise this threat and ensure a Scottish contribution to the military effort. Yet in 1703 an increasingly independent Scottish Parliament (the 'Estates'), through the Act

---

[1] For discussion see: Allan I Macinnes, 'Anglo-Scottish Union and the War of the Spanish Succession' in William Mulligan and Brendan Simms (eds), *The Primacy of Foreign Policy in British History, 1660–2000: How Strategic Concerns Shaped Modern Britain* (Basingstoke, Palgrave Macmillan, 2010).

Anent Peace and War, made its agreement necessary for the entry into and settling of armed conflict, encroaching on the Royal Prerogative. Another initiative from the Estates provided England with a further motive for union. The Estates had not accepted the fixing of the succession to Sophia of Hanover and her heirs, provided for by the English Act of Settlement. Then in 1704 the Scottish Act of Security stipulated that the Estates had the right to choose the successor to Queen Anne when she died. It added that if certain guarantees were not obtained from England for the rights of Scotland, the ruler the Estates selected would be a different person from the monarch of England. Added to these security issues, the independent trade policies of Scotland were disturbing English operations. Dealing with these problems through conquest was a difficult proposition: a negotiated agreement was preferable.

Scottish politicians instrumental in fusion had their own distinct rationale. Union would protect the position of Protestantism. It could provide access to an empire, something Scotland lacked—and was clearly not able to attain for itself. Scotland had recently embarked upon a colonial adventure in Darien, Panama, beginning in 1698. Partly thanks to English intervention it was a scandalous failure. The Darien episode created financial pressure and gave added momentum to the idea of union. Furthermore, a trade war with England was developing. The English in 1705 passed the Alien Act, threatening a series of sanctions if Scotland did not begin to negotiate a union. An escalation in tensions possibly leading to military conflict seemed possible.[2]

Historians disagree over whether union was inevitable.[3] But these more immediate motives for each party certainly interacted with protracted tendencies. The continental context is important. Christopher A Whatley identifies a European trend towards the fusion of states, with the number of 'independent polities' in Europe declining from approximately 1000 in the fourteenth century to 350 by the close of the eighteenth. Driving this sharp drop was a need to consolidate resources and expand administrative machinery, in pursuit of further territorial and economic aggrandisement.[4] European examples had an impact on the Union discourse. For instance, the formation of Protestant confederations within the Holy Roman Empire during the seventeenth century was a direct influence on the development of the idea of some kind of British incorporation.[5] At a British level, combination of the two kingdoms had long been a subject of consideration.

---

[2] For recent accounts of the Union drawn on here, see: Elizabeth Wicks, *The Evolution of a Constitution: Eight Key Moments in British Constitutional History* (Oxford, Hart Publishing, 2006) esp 31–34; Allan I Macinnes, *Union and Empire: The Making of the United Kingdom in 1707* (Cambridge, Cambridge University Press, 2007) esp 277–78; Iain McLean, *What's Wrong with the British Constitution?* (Oxford, Oxford University Press, 2009) 47–75.

[3] For the opinion that union was fated to come about, see eg: TC Smout, 'The Road to Union' in Geoffrey Holmes (ed), *Britain After the Glorious Revolution: 1689–1714* (London, Macmillan, 1969) 193. For the opposing view, see eg: Christopher A Whatley, *Bought and Sold for English Gold? Explaining the Union of 1707* (East Lothian, Tuckwell, 2001) 89.

[4] Whatley, *Bought and Sold for English Gold?* (n 3) 21.

[5] Macinnes, *Union and Empire* (n 2) 71.

Personal fusion, when James VI of Scotland became James I of England 1603, increased the salience of this concept. He even announced that he was the king of 'Great Britain'—but those who succeeded him did not. In the middle of the seventeenth century fusion under a single system came about briefly under Cromwell. A number of other efforts to instigate it took place before the final success of 1706.

During the extended build-up to union a full public debate took place. It is possible therefore to hold that the thorough discussion often deemed important to the creation of a constitutional text occurred. However, there are also reasons for regarding the union process as flawed. England was in a clear position of strength in the negotiations relative to Scotland. Yet Scotland was not completely lacking in leverage, and in areas where Scotland obtained unfavourable outcomes the fault may lie with the performance of the Scottish commissioners. A further problem with the process was that those selected to serve as commissioners on both sides represented only a partial slice of the views present in the Estates and Parliament. Proceedings, moreover, took place in secret. Yet it was not possible for the commissioners wholly to ignore outside opinion.[6] Moreover, the agreement had to obtain the approval of the Scottish and English legislatures, with the former institution making certain additional clarifications. Connected legislation protected the churches of both countries, and the Scottish universities. (The final Act of Union with Scotland that the English Parliament passed in 1707 is the version used here.) Scrutiny, modification and consent from representative institutions (of the early eighteenth century variety), therefore, took place. But a long-standing challenge to the integrity of the process alleges that the Crown improperly used payments to members of the Estates as a political lubricant, easing the passage of the Union through the Scottish legislature. Others dispute whether such inducements were decisive. Another debate involves how far it was in keeping with Scottish constitutional standards for the Estates to make such an agreement without wider direct involvement of the Scottish people.

In England, widespread celebration marked the coming into effect of the Treaty on 1 May 1707 (though there had been significant English resistance to the project). But the response in Scotland was subdued.[7] For a significant group in Scotland the system the Union inaugurated was not legitimate.[8] Jacobite insurrections of varying scale took place during the eighteenth century. In 1713, there was a serious effort in the House of Lords to disband the Union. Yet—as Linda Colley shows—though it may not have built on initial enthusiasm, the period following the Union saw a development of British identity, albeit founded in large measure on hostility to France.[9] This phenomenon is evidence of the importance a formal text, and the structures it sets out, can attain. The cultural circumstances

---

[6] Jim Smyth, *The Making of the United Kingdom: 1660–1800, State, Religion and Identity in Britain and Ireland* (Harlow, Longman, 2001) 95.

[7] Macinnes, *Union and Empire* (n 2) 313.

[8] Smyth, *The Making of the United Kingdom* (n 6) 109.

[9] Linda Colley, *Britons: Forging the Nation 1707–1837* (New Haven CT, Yale University Press, 2009).

prevailing at the time of the introduction of such a document are significant to its viability, and an absence of consensus and popular support is a problem. Yet the position is not one of determinacy and dependency: a constitutional document can stimulate a change in its wider environment.

A degree of uncertainty surrounds how, precisely, to categorise the Union text, and whether it is a treaty as normally understood. In 2013, the UK Government published specially commissioned legal advice on the constitutional consequences of Scottish independence, in advance of the 2014 Referendum. The paper concerned, by James Crawford and Alan Boyle, two legal academics, expressed the view—partly on the grounds that the UK Parliament had subsequently amended parts of the text—that 'neither the *Treaty* nor the *Acts of Union* currently operate as a treaty in international law'.[10] Whatever their precise status, the Treaty and Acts seem to make for curious documents to provide the grounding for a polity. Yet still they contain some of the key features that often attach to a written constitution.[11]

The 1707 Act opens with a preamble recounting events leading to its production and including a commitment to the 'Protestant religion and Presbyterian Church Government within the Kingdom of Scotland'. Then in Article I comes the fundamental purpose, which, like that of written constitutions, is to provide the basis for a state, in this instance one that did not previously exist. It stipulates that from 1 May 1707 'the Two Kingdoms of England and Scotland ... shall be ... united into One Kingdom'. It does not mention Wales, which had been incorporated into England since the Tudor period, through a process completed with the Laws in Wales Act 1536 (now sometimes known as the Act of Union 1536). The English Parliament had Welsh representation within it and the same legal system covered both territories. In 1746, the Wales and Berwick Act 1746 stipulated that references to 'England' should read as encompassing Wales (and Berwick-upon-Tweed). Some might hold that in 1706–07 England was in practice absorbing Scotland too, though the precise legal position at least was different.

The 'One Kingdom' would have 'the name of Great Britain'. While the term 'United Kingdom' is regarded as only becoming relevant later, this text goes on repeatedly to describe the new entity using this phrase. Article I, for instance, refers to 'said United Kingdom', and Article II to 'the Monarchy of the United Kingdom of Great Britain'. The merger was to receive symbolic expression through a combination of the crosses of St George and St Andrew, in a manner for the monarch to determine, for use in banners, ensigns, flags, and standards on land and at sea. The Queen (Anne), under the terms of the document, also chose the 'Ensigns Armorial'—the heraldry. There would be (as required in Article XXIV) a new 'Great Seal for the United Kingdom of Great Britain'.

---

[10] James Crawford and Alan Boyle, 'Opinion—Referendum on the Independence of Scotland—International Law Aspects' in Secretary of State for Scotland, *Devolution and the Implications of Scottish Independence* (Cm 8554, 2013) Annex A76.

[11] For an assessment of the idea of the Union text as a constitution, see: Wicks, *The Evolution of a Constitution* (n 2) esp 37–52. See also: N MacCormick, 'Does the United Kingdom have a Constitution? Reflections on *MacCormick v Lord Advocate* (1978) 29(1) *Northern Ireland Law Quarterly* 1; TB Smith, 'The Union of 1707 as Fundamental Law' [1957] *Public Law* 99.

Article II deals with the office of head of state, and in particular who can occupy the role in future. That the holder of the post is a ruler of an imperial power is clear from the reference to 'the Monarchy of the United Kingdom of Great Britain and of the Dominions thereto belonging'. The Treaty and Acts came about in circumstances of a European power struggle, which had global colonial amplification, spilling over into the Americas. Once again, the constitutional history and pre-history of the UK demonstrates an inescapable continental influence. Consideration of Article II undermines the cult of separateness in a further sense. Not only was union partly a product of European dynamics, it ensured that the state it created had a firm place within them, through reiterating the rules regarding the royal line contained in the English Act of Settlement 1701. After the now heirless Anne, Article II fixes the 'Succession' to 'the most Excellent Princess Sophia Electress and Dutchess [sic] Dowager of Hanover and the Heirs of Her Body'. Anne narrowly outlived Sophia, so the Crown passed to Sophia's son, George Louis, who became George I, ruler of Great Britain in 1714. The new kingdom thereby passed to a House that also ruled a territory—Hanover—that was part of the Holy Roman Empire. The Treaty and Acts served to subject the new state to rulers with a fixed interest in the continental mainland, who would bring this perspective to policy formation. In the words of Brendan Simms, 'by virtue of Hanoverian succession Britain, or Britain-Hanover ... lay ... at the heart of Europe. For the next forty years or so, Britain became indisputably a German power, reigned over by Germans'.[12]

Reflecting interlinked security and confessional concerns of the time, the new kingdom set out in the text contains a systemic form of discrimination that persists—subject to slight alterations—to the present. Article II introduces (or restates from English legislation) a qualification regarding those descendants of Sophia that succeed to the monarchy. Succession is dependent upon their 'being Protestants'. The Article excludes 'Papists and Persons marrying Papists' from possessing the Crown. If the individual who would otherwise qualify does not meet the religious requirements then the succession proceeds as though 'such Papist or Person marrying a Papist was naturally dead'. Recent reforms have applied to these stipulations. The Succession to the Crown Act 2013 (section 2(2)) provides that: 'A person is not disqualified from succeeding to the Crown or from possessing it as a result of marrying a person of the Roman Catholic faith'. Section 4(3) of the 2013 Act states that Article II of the Acts of Union between Scotland and England (and similar provisions in the Union between Ireland and Great Britain) are subject to the 2013 Act. But the requirements regarding the faith of the monarch (as opposed to her or his spouse) remain intact.

Article III requires 'That the United Kingdom of Great Britain be represented by One and the same Parliament to be stiled The Parliament of Great Britain'. This provision is suggestive of a centralised union (though certain other characteristics of the new state to some extent offset this tendency). Was this particular form of

---

[12]   Brendan Simms, *Three Victories and a Defeat: The Rise and Fall of the First British Empire, 1714–1783* (London, Allen Lane, 2007) 79.

fusion inevitable? At the time of the drafting of the Treaty of Union, an idea in vogue in Scotland was that the preferable combination between the two nations was one of 'federal union'. Broadly speaking, this concept meant that both the Scottish and English Parliaments would persist, but there would be some areas of shared activity, such as foreign policy. It would have been of a looser nature than systems labelled 'federal' today. Those who advocated this model defined it as being the opposite of an 'incorporating union'. They responded to a widespread fear in Scotland that this latter approach would mean the English Parliament simply absorbing the Estates, and Scotland itself. Lord Somers, one of the English representatives in the talks leading to the Union, had written a pamphlet advocating the maintenance of both Parliaments, with an overlap of membership between them, though under which England would dominate foreign and economic policy.[13] However, in the talks leading to the Union, the English commissioners would not entertain the idea of 'federal union'.[14] At the outset of negotiations the Scottish team put forward this solution, though they knew they would not secure agreement to it.[15] Scotland would have to wait around three centuries before making significant progress towards this objective, through devolution from the late 1990s. The 'Vow' of September 2014, and the report of the Smith Commission that followed, promised to extend the principle further.

Provision for the precise level of Scottish representation within the Parliament comes later. Article XXII states that there will be 16 'Peers of Scotland' in the House of Lords. This figure was small compared with the 83 nobles who had taken part in the final session of the Scottish Estates (99 peers were active in the English House of Lords).[16] Article XXIII confirms that Scottish peers will have the same rights as their English equivalents. The House of Commons, Article XXII states, will include 45 MPs from Scottish seats. This figure compares with a total of 513 members from England and Wales. If Scotland had received MPs in proportion to its population, it would have had around 100. However, to apply such a standard in this period is inappropriate. If worked out in relation to taxes paid—the accepted conversion measure of the time—the number of Scottish MPs would only have been about 28.[17]

After the short Article III providing for the Parliament, there follows a series of economic provisions. They have the effect of creating a single trading bloc removing both internal duties and what in the terminology of today are 'non-tariff barriers', that is, internal regulatory variations that can serve to restrict competition. Viewed from one perspective, the Union created a new central authority imposing rules on a vast geographical domain. But from another point

[13] Macinnes, *Union and Empire* (n 2) 281.
[14] PH Scott, *1707: The Union of Scotland and England: In Contemporary Documents with a Commentary* (Edinburgh, Chambers, 1979) 22–26.
[15] PWJ Riley, *The Union of England and Scotland: A Study in Anglo-Scottish Politics of the Eighteenth Century* (Manchester, Manchester University Press, 1978) 182–84.
[16] Macinnes, *Union and Empire* (n 2) 315.
[17] McLean, *What's Wrong with the British Constitution?* (n 2) 73.

of view, it had the effect of reducing the overall burden of regulation across the territory through eliminating differences between Scotland and England, creating the potential for a truly integrated market with uniform trading conditions. Article VI states 'That all Parts of the United Kingdom for ever from and after the Union shall have the same Allowances Encouragements and Drawbacks of Trade and liable to the Same Restrictions and Regulations of Trade and the Customs and Duties on Import and Export' as those previously in force in England, subject to limited exemptions. Article XVI stipulates that 'the Coin shall be of the same Standard and Value throughout the United Kingdom', while Article XVII requires the use of the 'same Weights and Measures' across the whole territory (an example of a provision that took some time to become effective in practice, not properly coming into force until the following century). The impact of the particular economic framework the Union created on each party was complex. In some areas the English economy was at a clear competitive advantage over the now exposed Scottish, which had to come into line with English arrangements. Yet Scotland gained access to new colonial markets (in America), and obtained benefits such as the ability to move cattle into England unimpaired.[18]

Though union brought about a high degree of political and economic harmonisation, at the same time it preserved significant heterogeneity, to ameliorate Scottish sensitivities about being devoured by a neighbour. It is possible to see the arrangements for the Scottish legal system in this light. Article XVIII notes that all Scottish laws existing prior to union are retained afterwards, unless they conflict with the agreement itself. While the new Parliament is able to change law in future, it is subject to a qualification. It is not permitted to alter 'Laws which concern private Right except for evident Utility of the Subjects within Scotland'. Article XIX preserves the Scottish courts system 'in all Time coming', subject to modification by Parliament only 'for the better Administration of Justice'. Feudal 'Offices' and 'Jurisdictions' are upheld (Article XX), and the distinctive Scottish system of local government is preserved also: 'the Rights and Privileges of the Royal Burghs in Scotland as they now are do remain entire after the Union' (Article XXI). Despite such allowances for variation, the fusion of 1706–07 produced arrangements that were significantly more centralised than the 'federal union' or confederation some had envisaged. Nonetheless, they suggest that implicit in the Union from the outset was a principle that England would make concessions to Scotland, to ensure that the relationship was not one of simple domination and therefore make the arrangement acceptable to Scotland. This logic has continued to manifest itself in different ways down to the present.

The final Article (XXV) states that all existing 'Laws and Statutes' either in Scotland or England that conflict with the agreement will 'cease and become void'. This statement deals with the then existing contents of the statute book of each party to the agreement. But what was the effect of the Treaty and Acts on future legislation of the new Parliament? The text seemingly seeks to entrench itself,

---

[18] Macinnes, *Union and Empire* (n 2) 317–21.

and unlike some efforts assessed in the previous chapter from the seventeenth-century revolutionary period and in later states elsewhere, it does not provide for an amendment procedure. Article I states that the union of the kingdoms will apply 'for ever after'. Article II excludes 'Papists' and their spouses from attaining the monarchy 'for ever'. The provisions for an integrated market apply 'for ever from and after the Union', and so on. This wording might point to the conclusion that the Parliament of Great Britain cannot amend the terms of union, or at least is restricted in the extent to which it can do so. Moreover, since the text creates the Parliament, how can this institution have primacy over the source of its own power? In these senses, the Treaty and Acts once more resemble a written constitution. However, the UK Parliament has subsequently legislated contrary to the terms of the Treaty and Act, using regular procedures, most recently with the Succession to the Crown Act 2013. In a submission to the House of Lords Select Committee on Privileges in 1999, the UK Government asserted that

> the United Kingdom Parliament has complete sovereignty to amend any provision of the Articles of the Acts of Union. This is true even in relation to those Articles which are expressed to be entrenched for all time ... such as the creation of the United Kingdom, the succession to the Monarchy, the Scottish Courts and the Church of Scotland.[19]

Yet debate persists about whether the fundamental features of the Union are lawfully subject to repeal and amendment from Westminster. This issue is a component of a discussion of crucial importance to conceptions of the UK constitution: the doctrine of parliamentary sovereignty. Within this school Parliament is able to amend or repeal any statute, including the Acts of Union and all their contents, using regular legislative procedures. Some maintain, however, that the Scottish Estates did not possess any such power, and therefore even if the English Parliament did, it does not follow that the Parliament created in 1707 would assume this authority. As Lord Cooper put it in 1953:

> Considering that the Union legislation extinguished the Parliaments of Scotland and England and replaced them by a new Parliament, I have difficulty in seeing why it should have been supposed that the new Parliament of Great Britain must inherit all the peculiar characteristics of the English Parliament but none of the Scottish Parliament.[20]

Others might argue that 1706–07 in fact saw the English Parliament consume the Scottish Estates. Meetings continued in Westminster, following the timetable and rules of the English Parliament. A further possible view is that a doctrine of parliamentary sovereignty previously existed in Scotland as well as England. Yet in the contemporary UK a shared presumption exists that Scottish independence, entailing a complete revocation of the Treaty and Acts, would require affirmative support from the Scottish people, expressed in a referendum. This consensus

---

[19] 'Case for Her Majesty's Government' in Select Committee on Privileges, *Second Report* (HL 1998–99, 108) App 3, para 62.
[20] Reproduced in: Wicks, *The Evolution of a Constitution* (n 2) 47, fn 77.

suggests that, whether for strict legal reasons or political expediency, an Act of Parliament alone is not enough.

Great Britain and Ireland

The United Kingdom emerged fully in 1800 when the Union extended to take in Ireland. The circumstances and terms of this agreement are notable both for their similarities to and differences from their 1706–07 predecessor. Since the sixteenth century Ireland had been a dependent kingdom, effectively an English colony. A union of some kind had been a serious option for a century before it took place.[21] The decision to incorporate Ireland with Great Britain had, once again, an important European dimension to it. Just as Louis XIV prompted England to incorporate with Scotland, Napoleon drove Great Britain towards union with Ireland.[22] The prevalence of the Roman Catholic religion among the population of Ireland marked it out as a security risk, from which the French might launch an assault. Economic concerns played a part, as they had in the incorporation of England and Scotland. Financial difficulties for Great Britain and Ireland encouraged a merger between them. An expanded free market area could yield benefits. Ireland was also seen as a potential source of personnel and resources for the British imperial cause.[23]

The British first minister (the term Prime Minister lacked formal existence at this point), William Pitt the Younger, carried out detailed preparatory work, including commissioning an historical survey of the construction of the earlier Union between England and Scotland. He liaised with Irish politicians, and in December 1798 the government promoted debate through an anonymous pamphlet entitled 'Arguments For and Against an Union', akin to a consultation document. A heated public discussion followed. Like the Union of 1706–07, some have regarded the project as tainted because of unsavoury political management methods. As the politician and playwright Richard Sheridan said in Parliament at the time, 'a union effected by fraud, by intrigue, by corruption, by intimidation, would ultimately tend to endanger the connexion between the two countries'.[24]

The Union agreement was not as concerned with the preservation of pre-existing Irish institutions and systems as was the 1706–07 text for those of Scotland. Suggesting some regard for Irish autonomy, early in the genesis of the scheme those developing it considered creating a 'subordinate assembly' based in Dublin, sending on representatives to the UK Parliament. But the idea was rejected.[25]

---

[21] James Kelly, 'The Act of Union: Its Origins and Background' in Daire Keogh and Kevin Whelan (eds), *Acts of Union: The Causes, Contexts and Consequences of the Act of Union* (Dublin, Four Courts Press, 2001) 46.

[22] Colley, *Britons* (n 9) 328.

[23] RB McDowell, *Ireland in the Age of Imperialism and Revolution: 1760–1801* (Oxford, Clarendon Press, 1979) 682–83, 687.

[24] Smyth, *The Making of the United Kingdom* (n 6) 213, 217.

[25] McDowell, *Ireland in the Age of Imperialism and Revolution* (n 23) 680.

Another important omission from the Act involves the position of Roman Catholics.[26] Those in London conducting preparatory work for the Union considered including at least limited provision for the rights of Catholics within it. But this issue was controversial among Protestants in Ireland and from the perspective of the overall orientation of the contemplated new state. The Cabinet came to the view that it would be better to leave the matter to one side, to resolve after incorporation. The monarch, George III, firmly opposed conciliation of the Catholics. Yet, as GC Bolton describes, fearing fatal opposition to union, in autumn 1799 the Cabinet gave permission to its representatives in Dublin to inform Catholics they were lobbying that the government in London was broadly favourable to their inclusion in the political system, though subject to limits. The government allowed the creation of a certain impression but failed to deliver. In February 1801 after George III proved unwilling to modify his stance, Pitt the Younger resigned. Pitt returned as head of government in 1804, remaining in place until his death in 1806, but avoided any attempt to force the issue, at a time when he was more focused on the conflict with Napoleon and did not want to generate internal divisions.[27] Consequently the new state suffered a major flaw from the outset; Iain Mclean describes the refusal of George III to accept emancipation as 'the first great tragedy of the union'.[28]

The preamble to the Act of Union with Ireland 1800 describes itself as expressing terms agreed by the Parliaments of Ireland and Great Britain. It states the purpose as being 'to promote and secure the essential interests of Great Britain and Ireland, and to consolidate the strength, power, and resources of the British Empire'. To this end it sets out 'to unite the two kingdoms of Great Britain and Ireland into one kingdom'. Article I provides for the creation of the state, with the name 'The United Kingdom of Great Britain and Ireland'. It asserts that it will exist 'forever after'. The text prescribes the succession to the Crown (Article II), the existence of a Parliament (Article III), and the representation of Irish lords and MPs in that Parliament (Article IV). Article V merges the churches of the two countries into 'the established church of England and Ireland'. It holds that this arrangement is integral to the Union as a whole, yet in 1869 Parliament legislated to disestablish the Church in Ireland. Article VI incorporates Ireland into the economic bloc, while Article VIII provides for the laws of the entire UK to be subject to the Parliament.

In as far as it did seek to entrench the existence of the UK 'forever after', the departure of all but six counties from the UK in 1921–22, forming the Irish Free State, represented a far more severe rupture of this entrenchment principle than any to which the Union between England and Scotland has yet been subject. This event led—though only by 1927—to the UK formally becoming the United

---

[26] Colley, *Britons* (n 9) 328–29.
[27] GC Bolton, *The Passing of the Irish Act of Union: A Study in Parliamentary Politics* (Oxford, Oxford University Press, 1966) 66–67, 207–08, 211–12, 214.
[28] McLean, *What's Wrong with the British Constitution?* (n 2) 85.

Kingdom of Great Britain and Northern Ireland. Partly because of this break, this Union receives less attention from constitutional scholars as a fundamental document than that between Scotland and England. But as the foregoing description shows, it performs some of the functions of a written constitution. The text of 1800 has further significance from the point of view of this work. It puts into effect the final stage in the establishment of a multinational state comprising Wales, Scotland, Ireland and England. From this perspective it is difficult to assert that the European integration project that began in the post-1945 period is conceptually alien to the UK. Indeed, a chief difference between the unions of Europe and of the Atlantic archipelago is that the latter—which involved express rejection of the less centralised federal model favoured in Scotland in the early eighteenth century—was far more politically concentrated at a single point than the former has been.[29] Ironically, those who portray the European Union as incompatible with UK constitutional traditions often dwell on the idea of an excessive allocation of authority to Brussels. Perhaps the constitutional form taken at the outset of the UK has encouraged a conceptual framework within which it is difficult to accommodate the idea of multinational conglomeration based on the sharing of power between pre-existing units and the new centre. The dissolution of dispersed points of authority may as a consequence seem an inevitable outcome.

The history of Ireland in the UK provides further reason to qualify more conventional constitutional narratives. The eventual departure of most of Ireland undermines the idea of continuity. Moreover, for long periods during the existence of the UK, Ireland and then Northern Ireland has been the site of a conflict, with associated violence taking place in Great Britain also. This historic tendency is difficult to reconcile with the image of a state untroubled on its own soil by armed combat or uprising. Furthermore, from the point of view of one group, a foreign conquest and occupation had taken place. These problems produced political pressure, with constitutional consequences. Since the nineteenth century a variety of systemic experiments have taken place in response to Irish-related security problems. Policymakers have tried to treat Ireland and subsequently Northern Ireland as distinct cases, not part of the UK mainstream. But a number of experiments have transferred to Great Britain. They include: extraordinary security powers; devolution; proportionate voting systems; the use of referendums; and the idea of a right of secession from the UK. The so-called 'Irish question' also prompted conceptual thinking about constitutional issues in the UK, encouraging the development of federal proposals. It led to dilemmas about fundamental issues such as the nature of parliamentary sovereignty. In short, the Union between Great Britain and Ireland both created a state and incorporated into it a dynamic that would drive change and challenge some of its principal constitutional precepts, including those involving the Union itself.

---

[29] For an historical consideration of similarities and differences between Great Britain as formed in 1706–07 and the EU, see eg: Brendan Simms, 'Towards a mighty union: how to create a democratic European superpower' (2012) 88(1) *International Affairs* 49.

ALBERT VENN DICEY AND PARLIAMENTARY SOVEREIGNTY

The state constructed between 1706 and 1801 had internal problems, but successfully attained the external security objectives that drove it. Invasions, that had characterised English history and heavily conditioned its constitutional development, ceased. Bourbon and Napoleonic threats were overcome. Had it occurred, an occupation by a country outside the UK might have led to the introduction of a new constitutional text, but it did not happen so the issue did not arise. After 1815, the UK became the pre-eminent world power, with a vast formal and informal empire. This entity provided an outlet for internal tensions, without which some kind of revolution, again possibly leading to the creation of another fundamental document, might have been more likely. During a period when countries around the world were adopting fuller written constitutions, influenced by English ideas and subsequent developments in late eighteenth century America and France, the UK had no compelling reason to do so. Writing in 2006, in an analysis of the historic data, Donald S Lutz discerned a pattern whereby, over the past 200 years, 'we have moved from a situation where almost no country had a written constitution to one where almost every country has one'. From 1800 to 1900 there was a 'gradual, fitful process' that gained pace thereafter, only decelerating 'as there are fewer and fewer countries remaining without a written constitution'.[30] The UK, by default, began to appear an oddity. A feature of its system that had long roots in the English tradition—parliamentary supremacy—appeared more distinct because it was a way of comprehending UK difference, both to outsiders and internally. In a work first published in 1835, the French theorist and politician Alexis de Tocqueville famously remarked that 'In England [sic] Parliament has the right to modify the constitution. In England, therefore, the Constitution can change constantly, or rather it does not exist at all.'[31] The supremacy of Parliament was not entirely a homemade invention, and had its origins partly in concepts derived from the continental mainland,[32] but those who observed and promoted it within the UK overlooked this provenance. The theorist most closely associated with this doctrine in popular understanding encapsulated it precisely in terms of international contrast.

Albert Venn Dicey was Vinerian Professor of English Law at Oxford University. In 1885, he published the first edition of a work, based on lectures, entitled *Introduction to the Study of the Law of the Constitution*.[33] It became perhaps the most influential account of UK (or English, the term he insisted on using) arrangements ever produced. The particular version it promoted of one doctrine

---

[30] Donald S Lutz, *Principles of Constitutional Design* (Cambridge, Cambridge University Press, 2006) 4.

[31] Alexis de Tocqueville, *Democracy in America* (London, HarperCollins, 1994) 101.

[32] JWF Allison, *The English Historical Constitution* (Cambridge, Cambridge University Press, 2007) 103–04.

[33] AV Dicey, *Introduction to the Study of the Law of the Constitution* (Indianapolis IND, Liberty Fund Inc, 1982).

became so widely absorbed into political consciousness as to become by proxy a constitutional text itself. Parliamentary sovereignty, as Jeffrey Goldsworthy convincingly argues, had conceptual origins in the Middle Ages; and the term existed before Dicey used it.[34] Dicey's impact was to popularise the phrase and widely promote his specific interpretation of its meaning. Other authors, such as William Blackstone in the eighteenth century and Walter Bagehot in the nineteenth, achieved great impact on constitutional understandings through their work. But Dicey was probably the most important of all because his thought became a focus for such a pervasive, powerful—and eventually controversial—concept.

The first chapter opens with the words: 'The sovereignty of Parliament is (from a legal point of view) the dominant characteristic of our political institutions'. Dicey begins by clarifying that Parliament comprises three components: the monarch, the House of Lords and the House of Commons. He then defines the sovereignty this institution possesses as entailing that it has, 'under the English constitution, the right to make or unmake any law whatever; and further, that no person or body is recognised by the law of England as having a right to override or set aside the legislation of Parliament'. Dicey goes on to cite authorities and historic examples supporting his view and dismisses rival claims to legislative authority. He describes a series of what he holds to be false views of the limitations on parliamentary sovereignty: that laws are invalid if they conflict with fundamental moral values or international law; or if they override the Royal Prerogative. Dicey argues that it is not possible for a parliament to pass a law protected from amendment by a future parliament. In this regard he draws attention to the various Acts of Union. He acknowledges that those who devised them sought to give them a special status. However, he records, Parliament subsequently changed provisions within them, for instance relating to Scottish university professors. Having dismissed supposed impediments upon it Dicey insists that Parliament can legislate however it chooses, and there is 'no power which, under the English constitution, can come into rivalry with the legislative sovereignty of Parliament'. Dicey describes the practical as opposed to legal limitations upon the doctrine. One is the prospect that a law will produce outright disobedience among those to whom it is intended to apply. The other involves the disposition of those producing the legislation, who may feel constrained for reasons of their own.

In the second chapter Dicey draws comparisons between Parliament and legislatures not possessing sovereignty. Here he emphasises the supposed exceptionality of the 'English' system. Parliament, he holds, can alter any law, including enactments of a constitutional character, using the same procedure in each case. None of them take precedence over any other. No separate category of constitutional law exists. He observes that modifying some legislation—such as that providing for the Union between England and Scotland—without good reason would be poorly advised. On other hand, there are also laws, such as the Dentists Act 1878, that Parliament

---

[34] Jeffrey Goldsworthy, *The Sovereignty of Parliament: History and Philosophy* (Oxford, Oxford University Press, 1999) esp 22–235.

could happily alter or repeal as it saw fit. Yet neither law could claim higher legal status than the other. Consequently, if the Dentists Act happened 'unfortunately [to] contravene the terms of the Act of Union, the Act of Union would be *pro tanto* repealed, but no judge would dream of maintaining that the Dentists Act 1878, was thereby rendered invalid or unconstitutional'. Here we encounter what is now known as the doctrine of 'implied repeal'—that, if there is conflict between them, a later Act always supersedes an earlier one, regardless of whether or not it explicitly states that it does so, or of their respective political importance.

For Dicey the lack of differentiation between higher and lower law was directly associated with the absence of a written constitution. He rejected the idea that the malleability of the constitution arose from it lacking definition in this way. Dicey suspected a reverse chain of causality: there was no purpose in creating a text, because it was subject to change at will from Parliament. It would be possible, he held, to devise an Act of Parliament setting out the constitution, provided that Parliament remained able to alter it in the usual way. Indeed one writer, Sheldon Amos, had already published, in 1873, just such an account of the 'English' constitution as (in his view) it was, entitled *A Primer of the English Constitution and Government*.[35] Having denied the existence of entrenchment and discussed the absence of a written constitution, Dicey then described the inability of the judiciary or any other institution to 'nullify an Act of Parliament, or to treat it as void or unconstitutional'. The consequence of these features of the constitution was that it was 'the most flexible polity in existence'. Dicey contrasts a 'flexible' constitution, under which Parliament can change any legislation using an identical process in every case, with a 'rigid' arrangement, prevailing in such countries as Belgium and France. Dicey notes that while the model in 'England' allows for much formal change, the more static systems tend either to block such development or provoke uprisings through their very inflexibility.

The third chapter is a comparison between the English system and federal constitutions of the sort in force in the US. He observes a polarity between 'England' and the US in that the former had an unrestrained parliament, while in the latter a dispersal of authority applied. Yet, nonetheless, for Dicey the US system represented a realisation of the same concepts that applied in 'England'. Both constitutions were founded in similar principles of 'law, of justice, and of the relation between the rights of individuals and the rights of government, or the state'. After a discussion of the historic motives that might lie behind the formation of both a federal and a unitary system, he identifies three key features of the former. First is 'supremacy of the constitution'. Second is the sharing of power between institutions. Third is the role of the courts in interpreting the constitution. It is nearly inevitable, Dicey judges, that a federal constitution will be 'written' and legally entrenched ('rigid', as Dicey has it). He expresses the view that 'Federal

---

[35] Sheldon Amos, *A Primer of the English Constitution and Government* (London, Longmans, Green and Co, 1873).

government means weak government'. The existence of various competing power bases entails the pointless consumption of effort. Consequently, Dicey concludes, federations are at a systemic disadvantage when faced with rival unitary states. A further problem he identifies is that the judiciary might not be suited to performing the special task that a federal constitution would entrust to them. The personal proclivities of judges could influence their decision-making—however good their intentions—undermining their credibility, and party political considerations might determine their appointment.

Dicey goes on in the second part of his work to discuss the rule of law and constitutional conventions. These latter passages had a huge impact on perceptions of the UK system of government. Yet it is parliamentary sovereignty with which Dicey has the strongest public connection, and his version of the doctrine, in direct or received—and possibly corrupted—form, has had a greater influence than any other account of it. He has had deep and prolonged impact upon views within the executive and inside Parliament. It is not difficult to understand his appeal in these spheres, since Dicey's ideas maximise the potential for a government, with support in the legislature, to give expression to the policies it chooses, while they promote to parliamentarians the notion that they share in an institutional legal omnipotence.

In April 1886, William Gladstone, the Liberal Prime Minister, promoted the reputation of Dicey shortly after the first edition of his masterwork appeared. He praised the 'valuable work of Professor Dicey on the Law of the Constitution' on the grounds that 'No work that I have ever read'—and Gladstone had read many—'brings out in a more distinct and emphatic manner the peculiarity of the British Constitution in one point to which, perhaps, we seldom have occasion to refer'. This 'point' was 'the absolute supremacy of Parliament'. The only restrictions on this authority were 'such as human nature in a Divinely-ordained condition of things imposes'. There was 'nothing that controls us, and nothing that compels us, except our convictions of law, of right, and of justice'.[36] Nearly nine decades later, in March 1975, Margaret Thatcher, a future Conservative Prime Minister who was then Leader of the Opposition, referred in the Commons to the view expounded by Dicey that 'parliamentary sovereignty is supreme'[37] and said: 'Do read him. Both the eighth and tenth editions are full of good stuff'.[38]

Adherence to Dicey in Westminster–Whitehall circles persisted further, as a June 2006 government evidence submission to the parliamentary Joint Committee on Conventions shows.[39] In a discussion of the role of Parliament it argued that Parliament—composed of the monarch, the House of Lords and the House of Commons—was 'the sovereign body of the UK constitution'. Having

---

[36] HC Deb 8 April 1886, vol 304, col 1048.
[37] HC Deb 11 March 1975, vol 888, cols 307–08.
[38] Ibid, col 308.
[39] 'Memorandum by Her Majesty's Government', 8 June 2006, to Joint Committee on Conventions, *Report* (2005–06, HL 265-II, HC 1212-II).

echoed Dicey the government then named him as providing the 'classic expression of parliamentary sovereignty', quoting his passage about Parliament possessing 'the right to make or unmake any law whatever' and not being subject to any kind of override. The government went on to assert that it was 'generally accepted' that the account Dicey provided applied not only to the 'English constitution', but 'equally to the UK constitution'. The government believed 'It remains a true description. Even if Parliament should agree to make itself subordinate to some other jurisdiction, it remains open to it to resume its sovereignty at any time. It therefore remains the sovereign body of the constitution'.

Yet though Dicey has had a profound and protracted influence, there are complexities. Deeper analysis of praise for him helps reveal them. The speech Gladstone gave in 1886 introduced his government's Bill for Irish Home Rule. Gladstone saw Dicey as offering a reassurance that the creation of a subordinate assembly in Ireland need not undermine the position of the Westminster Parliament and was not, therefore, a threat to the stability of the UK constitution. The work of Dicey was, as Gladstone put it to the House, a 'favourable starting point' to the debate.[40] However, Home Rule brought Gladstone into public conflict with Dicey, who soon become one of the most prominent opponents of this policy. In his later career Dicey became an advocate of referendums as a means of approving—or blocking—legislation. On the surface this idea might seem difficult to reconcile with the idea of absolute authority of Parliament. The 1975 endorsement from Thatcher came in a debate on the then forthcoming plebiscite on whether the UK should continue to be a member of the European Economic Community. She introduced him by noting that 'some names ... can be quoted in support of both sides of the argument'. Thatcher described how one facet of Dicey, where 'parliamentary sovereignty is supreme', came from the main text of his book. The other involved considering his perspective 'as a political activist who hated the party system and thought what he called the absolutism of a party possessed of parliamentary majority needed to be curbed'.[41]

Dicey was a great thinker. But as a constitutional source he presents some problems.[42] Perhaps these difficulties are of a sort that might arise from using the output of any one individual in this way. The idiosyncratic qualities that a wider process might have removed become magnified by the special importance attached to the work. Certainly Dicey, for all his brilliance, left himself open to attack on grounds of inconsistency. The government submission to the Joint Committee on Conventions of 2006 probably overplayed the degree of consensus to which the ideas of Dicey are subject. Furthermore, it failed fully to acknowledge the difficulties in sustaining the relevance of his theories in the wake of subsequent constitutional developments.

---

[40] HC Deb 8 April 1886, vol 304, col 1048.

[41] HC Deb 11 March 1975, vol 888, cols 307–08.

[42] For recent debate concerning the consistency or otherwise of Dicey see: Vernon Bogdanor, 'The Consistency of Dicey: A Reply to McLean and McMillan [2008] *Public Law* 19; Iain McLean and Alistair McMillan, 'Professor Dicey's Contradictions' [2007] *Public Law* 435; McLean, *What's Wrong with the British Constitution?* (n 2) 128–40.

Aside from discussion specifically of Dicey, the intellectual viability of the doctrine of parliamentary sovereignty in general has become a long-standing subject of controversy. For some the concept is invalid, and a term such as 'parliamentary supremacy' more apt.[43] One criticism involves the relevance of the word 'sovereignty'; it had a traditional use as a description of the individual power of a monarch and could be difficult to transfer to a body—Parliament—with members numbering in the hundreds.[44] Parliament has to operate in accordance with a complex set of procedural requirements, and is in this sense limited. A further area of debate involves two different versions of parliamentary sovereignty. According to the 'continuing' account, Parliament is unable to bind itself. But if this theory is correct, then Parliament is not omnipotent, because a limitation applies to it. The alternative to 'continuing' sovereignty is 'self-embracing'. In this model, Parliament is able to impose restraints on its own power. Yet, if it exercises this ability, its sovereignty will cease to exist, and is therefore only transient in nature.[45] For some, Parliament is subject to fundamental curbs, though they do not exist in explicit form.[46] Yet another dissenting view is that, while parliamentary sovereignty may have a place in English constitutional traditions, it does not apply in other parts of the UK, particularly Scotland.[47] Recent practical developments have served further to call into question parliamentary sovereignty, both its legal persistence and practical relevance, as we will see.

Another line of attack on parliamentary sovereignty has been to hold that it is undesirable. Even at the time Dicey first set out his account of parliamentary supremacy, some—while believing the doctrine prevailed in practice—disliked it, and advocated the establishment of different constitutional norms. Writing in *Contemporary Record* the year before the publication of *Law of the Constitution*, Herbert Spencer stated that the 'great political superstition of the past was the divine right of kings. The great political superstition of the present is the divine right of parliaments'. He described how an insistence upon the supremacy of Parliament served as a response to any who queried the properness of 'some arbitrary State-interference', leaving the opponent 'paralyzed'. Spencer identified a need to 'ask the how, and the when, and the whence, of this asserted omnipotence bounded only by physical impossibilities'. He suggested that while 'Liberalism in the past' had sought to restrict the authority of monarchs, 'true Liberalism in the future' ought to address itself to 'putting a limit to the powers of Parliaments'.[48] Such views, though they have never yet come to dominate, have endured.

---

[43] AW Bradley and KD Ewing, *Constitutional and Administrative Law* (Harlow, Longman, 2011) 49.

[44] W Ivor Jennings, *The Law and the Constitution* (London, University of London Press, 1959) 148; RTE Latham, *The Law and the Commonwealth* (Oxford, Oxford University Press, 1949) 523.

[45] Jeffrey Goldsworthy, *Parliamentary Sovereignty: Contemporary Debates* (Cambridge, Cambridge University Press, 2010) 106.

[46] Wicks, *The Evolution of a Constitution* (n 2) 19–20.

[47] See: McLean and McMillan, 'Professor Dicey's Contradictions' (n 41).

[48] Reproduced in: HJ Hanham (ed), *The Nineteenth-Century Constitution: 1815–1914* (Cambridge, Cambridge University Press, 1969) 20–21.

THE PARLIAMENT ACT 1911

Writing in 1913 Sidney Low held: 'The Parliament Act of 1911 is a definite step towards the enlargement of the "written" at the expense of the unwritten, or conventional, constitution'.[49] The Act certainly possesses some of the features of a written constitution. It straddles different parts of the system: the internal arrangements of the legislature; the frequency of elections; and, perhaps most significantly for present purposes, deals with processes involved in the changing of fundamental rules. The Parliament Act 1911 arose because a relationship reliant upon informal understandings failed, necessitating legislative intervention. The crisis leading to the Act involved a clash between the elected Liberal majority in the House of Commons and the permanent, hereditary Conservative majority in the House of Lords. For most of the nineteenth century, the Tories then the Conservatives were numerically dominant in the Lords, a position first established during the ascendancy of Pitt the Younger. If a different group held a majority in the Commons, problems could arise. By the early eighteenth century the House of Lords had accepted that it could not amend Finance Bills. During the course of the nineteenth century some in the Lords seemed to acknowledge that the Commons had some kind of seniority over it that was at its greatest immediately following a general election.[50] But in legal terms, the Lords retained an equal status with the Commons. The second chamber could block legislation, and used this power in a partisan fashion against Liberal majorities in the Commons. The radical Liberal Government that took office in 1905 and won a substantial general election victory the following year experienced serious disruption of its legislative programme in the Lords. Then in 1909 the Lords vetoed the so-called 'People's Budget'. It had overplayed its hand, an error leading to a lasting, formal reduction in its authority.

Eventually, the Parliament Act 1911 emerged from this conflict, the purpose of which was to give statutory expression to the supremacy of the Commons over the Lords. A full public debate of the options preceded it. Popular engagement came through two General Elections held in January and December 1910. There are limits to how far such events can be said to have provided authorisation for constitutional change since they are not referendums (which admittedly have their own problems as decision-taking devices). Moreover, the Liberal Party won neither election outright, though was able to secure the support needed for a Commons majority in both cases. During the first campaign matters other than the clash between the two Houses—such as tariff reform—became prominent. The Lords then backed down over the particular issue, passing the budget. But the Liberal Government then introduced a Parliament Bill containing measures for the curtailment of the power of the Lords, which the second chamber would not accept. For the second poll of 1910, therefore, the plan for the Lords was set before

---

[49] Sidney Low, *The Governance of England* (London, T Fisher Unwin, 1914) viii.
[50] Roy Jenkins, *Mr Balfour's Poodle: People v Peers* (London, Pan Macmillan, 1999) 36.

the electorate and the constitution was paramount in debate.[51] Ultimately, the threat that the monarch would execute a mass creation of Liberal peers secured the consent of the Lords to what became the Parliament Act.

In between the two elections, an event with some of the character of a constitutional convention took place. Edward VII died in May 1910 and was succeeded by George V. It seemed appropriate to endeavour to avoid embroiling a new monarch in the dispute. In May 1910, Lord Curzon, a leading Conservative, called for discussion between the parties, with the purpose of creating 'a draft of a new Constitution for this country', resolving the unstable interactions between Commons and Lords.[52] The talks ran from June to November. Four senior figures each from the Liberal and Conservative Parties took part, including the leaders of both—Herbert Asquith and Arthur Balfour respectively. While the occurrence of the meetings was a matter of public record, the actual content of the discussions was confidential.[53] The Conservatives were willing to entertain the idea of the Commons gaining a right to override the Lords, but they wanted safeguards in some areas. Negotiations therefore dealt with the idea of defining different classes of parliamentary Bill. One of the categories would be that of 'constitutional' legislation. Unlike other laws, over which the Commons could have the final say, if there was deadlock between the two Houses over a Bill within this group, the dispute would pass to the electorate to resolve in a referendum.

In seeking agreement over this issue, an obstacle arose over how to define home rule. The January General Election had left the Liberals dependent upon Irish nationalists for their majority (as did the December poll). To obtain the support of the nationalists, the Liberals would have to introduce Home Rule to Ireland, and they knew that the Lords would try to block it. Indeed, from the Liberal point of view, the need to secure legislation giving effect to this policy was a primary motivation for the Parliament Act. Within the scheme under discussion with the Conservatives, the Liberals could not allow Home Rule to come within the 'constitutional' definition. Equally, the Conservatives wanted to be able to block Home Rule, through passing the issue to voters throughout the UK, whom, the Conservatives assumed, would reject it. The talks failed. Had they succeeded, and in the process established a class of constitutional legislation that would be subject to special procedures, the comparisons with a written constitution, entrenching its contents, would have been clear. Ultimately, the Parliament Act heavily diluted this concept—though a trace of it remained.

The Act opens with a declaratory statement about the necessity of 'regulating the relations between the two Houses of Parliament'. It then states an objective of replacing the hereditary Lords with a 'Second Chamber constituted on a popular ...

---

[51] Neal Blewett, *The Peers, the Parties and the People: The General Elections of 1910* (London, Macmillan, 1972) 105, 168.

[52] *The Times* (6 May 1910). Cited in: Peter Dorey and Alexandra Kelso, *House of Lords Reform Since 1911: Must the Lords Go?* (Basingstoke, Palgrave Macmillan, 2011) 19.

[53] Jenkins, *Mr Balfour's Poodle* (n 49) 149.

basis': a term that implied elections of some kind. But the Act notes that this change 'cannot be immediately brought into operation'. Moreover, any 'measure' creating an elected second chamber would need to include 'provision ... for limiting and defining the powers of the new Second Chamber'. While waiting on this more sweeping transformation, the present Act would bring about those limitations that seemed 'expedient' upon the 'existing powers of the House of Lords'. On a literal reading, then, the Act is a stopgap measure, quelling the existing hereditary chamber before supplanting it.

In reality, the idea of an elected second chamber did not appeal to the Liberal Government that introduced the Parliament Act, for reasons it is possible to infer from the preamble, with its reference to the necessity of 'limiting and defining the powers' of such a body. A chamber with a popular mandate would have more legitimacy than an hereditary House in asserting itself against the Commons. The reductions in the powers of the Lords contained in the Act, discussed below, might not be enough. The Liberal Government was more interested in imposing terms on the House that had created such difficulties for it than creating a potentially even more problematic replacement chamber. It was in the business of expanding the relative powers of the Commons, not reducing them, as suggested by section 6 of the Act, stressing that none of the content of the Act 'shall diminish or qualify the existing rights and privileges of the House of the Commons'.

The claimed intention of achieving a 'popular' House has not yet come about. In the century since the 1911 Act, countless and varied parliamentary initiatives have sought to introduce a directly or indirectly elected component to the Lords. All have failed.[54] An obvious reason for this course of events is that the Lords itself is institutionally disposed to resist any such change. But this explanation is not sufficient. Under the 1911 Act discussed here the Commons possesses an authority that it could probably use to impose further reform on the Lords if it were determined enough to do so. Yet successive governments have followed the pattern set by the Liberals in 1911 of appearing to back some kind of elected or at least partially elected second chamber, but not regarding it as a priority, and perhaps in reality seeing it as a potential threat. Members of the Commons have often proved reluctant to help create a more powerful rival to their chamber that might call into question the primacy they enjoy. Possibly now some of them also have in mind where they might like to spend their retirement.[55]

Section 1 of the Act deals with the 'Powers of House of Lords as to Money Bills': the issue that precipitated the constitutional crisis. The section stipulates that once the Commons has passed a Money Bill and sent it 'up' to the House of Lords, the Lords has a month to agree to it, at which point—unless the Commons decides

---

[54] See: Chris Ballinger, *The House of Lords 1911–2011: A Century of Non-Reform* (Oxford, Hart Publishing, 2012); and Dorey and Kelso, *House of Lords Reform Since 1911* (n 51).

[55] For an account of the content, workings and legality of the Parliament Acts see: House of Lords Select Committee on the Constitution, *Constitutional Aspects of the Challenge to the Hunting Act 2004*, (HL 2005–06, HL 141) (London, Stationery Office, 2006).

otherwise—it is presented for Royal Assent, without need for approval from the Lords (section 1(1)). Given that the Act gives such authority to the Commons with respect to a 'Money Bill', the definition of this kind of measure is important. The Act tells us that a Money Bill is 'a Public Bill which in the opinion of the Speaker of the House of Commons' deals with any of a series of specified matters relating to the raising of money by central government (section 1(2)). When it passes to the Lords, or to the monarch for Royal Assent, the Speaker attaches to every measure that he (or now she or he) so defines a signed certificate endorsing it as a Money Bill. The Act requires the Speaker 'if practicable' to 'consult' with two specified Members before doing so (section 1(3)).

The Act then moves beyond financial measures to deal with 'Restriction of the powers of the House of Lords' on other kinds of Bills. It sets out the circumstances in which a Bill can receive Royal Assent regardless of the wishes of the Lords. The original 1911 version of the Act stipulated that, first, the House of Commons must have passed 'any Public Bill ... in three successive sessions'—even if they straddle different parliaments (that is, if a general election intervenes). The Lords can reject or alter it on the first two occasions. But on the third, provided two years have passed since the initial 'second reading' of the Bill and its final departure from the Commons, unless the Commons relents, it can go forward to the monarch (section 2(1)). The Parliament Act 1949 amended the 1911 Act so that only two sessions and one year need to elapse before it is possible to circumvent the Lords in this way. Rejection includes outright veto, or the passing of amendments with which the Commons does not agree (section 2(3)). As with a Money Bill, the Speaker must sign a certificate stating that the Bill has met the requirements of section 2 when it is presented to the monarch for Royal Assent without Lords agreement (section 2(2)).

Section 2 provides two exceptions from the procedure it creates for bypassing the Lords: for a Money Bill (dealt with in section 1) and for a Bill 'containing any provision to extend the maximum duration of a Parliament beyond five years' (section 2(1)). It is the Act itself that sets the five-year time limit on a Parliament, which was previously under the Septennial Act 1715 seven years (section 7). The intention lying behind the exclusion of this measure from the section 2 procedure was to provide a safeguard against a majority group in the Commons abusing the Act to prolong the hold it possessed on power. Section 2 also leaves intact the power of the Lords absolutely to reject (but not amend) secondary legislation, that is, subordinate law issued under the authority of a parent Act. Furthermore, since sections 1(1) and 2(1) refer to a Bill 'passed by the House of Commons', it is not possible to use the override in relation to a Bill that began its progress through Parliament in the Lords. Also requiring Lords approval are Personal and Local Bills, and (as specified in section 5) technical measures known as Provisional Order Confirmation Bills.

Taken together the complex stipulations of section 2 of the Parliament Act 1911 (now, as noted, amended by the Parliament Act 1949) comprise the nearest equivalent to a UK constitutional entrenchment provision and amendment procedure.

One reason for this resemblance is the protection section 2 introduces for the five-year term limit on a Parliament. A subtlety in the way it seeks to achieve this objective needs recognition. It does not create a more demanding requirement for the extension of the length of a Parliament. Rather, it introduces a general relaxation in the rules governing the passage of a Bill into law, but exempts a particular provision from this broad easing, leaving it subject to the same amendment procedure as it was already. Before the Act, it was necessary to obtain the approval of the House of Lords for all Bills before presenting them for Royal Assent. After the Act, it was possible for public Bills (and of course Money Bills) to bypass the Lords, except in specified cases, most notably those that involved elongation of the parliamentary term.

Though the Act brought about this special status for a particular feature of the constitution in a negative way, exempting it from a change, it nonetheless represents a default form of entrenchment, the overcoming of which requires a particular procedure. But it possibly contains an ambiguity that a sufficiently resolute majority group in the Commons could manipulate. It is surely not possible to use section 2 directly to force the elongation of a Parliament upon a resistant Lords. Yet the Commons could, under section 2, drive through an alteration of section 2 itself that deleted the protection for the five-year limit, and then, using section 2 again, prolong Parliament and postpone a general election. It might then fall to the courts to decide whether this approach was legal, though the government and its supporters in the Commons would probably dispute the authority of the judiciary to adjudicate on this issue. At this point, the Parliament Act, introduced to resolve a constitutional crisis in an earlier era, would itself be at the centre of a similar breakdown.

Alongside the question of how effective the section 2 protections might be, the substance of the coverage they provide is noteworthy. The Act deems only the five-year maximum length of a Parliament to be in need of entrenchment under the regime it creates. No other measures: the remnants of Magna Carta still on the statute book; the Bill of Rights; the Act of Settlement; the Acts of Union; or the Acts providing for the franchise enjoy the same protection. Indeed, while it is possible to view the Parliament Act 1911 as performing some of the functions of a constitutional amendment clause, it does so in a double-edged sense. On the one hand, it leaves one rule more difficult to change than other legislative arrangements. On the other hand, a central purpose of the Act was to make constitutional change in other areas *easier* to bring about, rather than harder, as might normally be expected from an amendment clause. In particular, the Liberal Government had a political imperative to bring about Home Rule and judged—rightly—that the Unionist majority in the Lords would never pass such a measure.

Another sense in which the Act deals with issues that a written constitution might address, but does so in a way that contradicts the provisions of many such documents, is in its approach to the legal status of the certificate the Speaker of the House of Commons must issue to authorise the circumvention of the Lords. Section 3 states that 'Any certificate of the Speaker of the House of Commons given under this Act shall be conclusive for all purposes, and shall not be questioned in any court of law'. Many written constitutions invite—either implicitly or explicitly—judicial involvement to uphold adherence to their provisions. The Parliament Act 1911 seeks specifically to preclude this kind of engagement.

In the period since it passed into law the Commons has used the section 2 powers to bypass a resistant Lords on seven occasions, with all three main parties having utilised it. The Acts passed through this method are: the Welsh Church Act 1914; the Government of Ireland Act 1914; the Parliament Act 1949; the War Crimes Act 1991; the European Parliamentary Elections Act 1999; the Sexual Offences (Amendment) Act 2000; and the Hunting Act 2004. Nearly all of these Acts had a constitutional quality to them, and some of them engaged issues that might have been the subject of a written constitution, if one existed. They support an interpretation of the Act as a means of securing constitutional modification. What do they tell us about the impact of the Act upon the relationship between the Commons and the Lords? Though it has done so sparingly, the Commons has proved willing to use the authority it obtained in 1911. Harder to quantify but surely real are modifications in the behaviour of the Lords that the anticipation of an override have brought about. Nonetheless the Lords' power temporarily to stall legislation was still important, particularly as the end of a Parliament, and the prospect of a possible change in the group that held a majority in the Commons, drew closer.

One of the uses of the bypass facility contained in the 1911 Act was to secure the Parliament Act 1949, to alter the terms of the 1911 Act, enabling the Commons to impose its will more quickly. The 1949 Act subsequently became the focus of legal uncertainty surrounding the measures for forcing through Bills under the two Parliament Acts. A theory existed that it was not possible to use the 1911 Act to amend itself in the way it had been in 1949. If this view was correct, the 1949 Act, as well as legislation it brought into being, would be void. However, following a challenge to the Hunting Act 2004 the Law Lords did not find favour with this interpretation. They concluded that legislation enacted using the 1911 Act was legitimate primary law.

The Lords weakened in another way. The Labour Government that introduced the 1949 modification had already secured an agreement, in 1945, that the Conservatives would not obstruct Bills giving effect to proposals contained in the manifesto on which it had won the general election of that year. Eventually this accord developed into what is arguably a constitutional convention, known as the Salisbury–Addison agreement, named respectively after the Conservative and Labour leaders in the House of Lords who struck it. It has subsequently expanded, some hold, to cover the entirety of a government programme, whether or not referred to in a manifesto. This change suggested a further shift in the balance of power towards the Commons. A compounding tendency apparent since the first half of the nineteenth century was the rise of more tightly disciplined groupings in Parliament, linked to mass national parties. The Commons—or rather whichever government-marshalled group was predominant within it at a given time—which had, because of its changing nature, been better able to drive the expansion in its powers, was also better placed to deploy them effectively. An unbalancing of the constitution had, in the mid-seventeenth century, encouraged some Levellers to develop the idea of a written constitution as a safeguard against parliamentary tyranny. Perhaps another destabilisation, creating an increasingly dominant Commons, was taking place.

The UK was the product of two deliberate actions approximately a century apart. Driving both was the threat of a hegemonic France. The state they created in the shadow of Louis XIV and Napoleon was centralised, though discussion of more dispersed models had taken place and some concessions were made, especially to Scotland. Alongside security issues, a key motive for the constitutional model utilised was the desire to establish a single market, with uniform regulatory measures applying across the territory. Religious discrimination was prominent within the make-up of this state, and the Crown was attached to a German dynasty. Texts were central to the two Unions, but they were not full written constitutions like those that began to appear internationally from the late eighteenth century.

A different principle captured the imagination: parliamentary sovereignty. It achieved its most celebrated expression in a text that, though the work of a private individual, acquired quasi-constitutional status. Yet doubts always existed about the desirability of this doctrine. Over time its intellectual coherence, too, has become subject to challenge; yet it was for some a feature of UK or 'English' superiority. The Parliament Act 1911 made more firm the principle that the House of Commons was the primary wielder of parliamentary sovereignty. Events leading to this legislation revealed problems that could arise within the unwritten constitution. By the end of this period the UK was an outlier in a number of ways. Principles of limited government were important to its constitutional culture. Yet it had never provided for them in a written constitution, because a sufficient imperative to do so had never manifested itself. There was a connection between this lack of a fundamental text and the rise of the UK as the main global imperial power. Later in the twentieth century, UK power collapsed. What would happen to its constitution?

Part II

A System in Turmoil

6

The Dynamic Constitution

T HE UNITED KINGDOM (UK) is passing through a prolonged period of radical constitutional transformation. This incidence of change has in turn produced a fierce resistance. The ongoing contest is of historic importance, and remains in the balance. While the ultimate outcome remains uncertain, one of the range of possible resolutions is a written constitution for the UK. The chapters that follow in this part of the book consider first, in the present chapter, the nature of this period of reform. It includes some detailed case studies, and considers the processes by which change takes place. Successive chapters then focus on particular dimensions of the morphing constitution and their current condition, dealing in turn with the European perspective, the nations and regions that constitute the UK, and the role of the judiciary. The final chapter in this section considers where this process might be leading.

Constitutional change in some form is always present in any society: even if textual declarations are static, judicial interpretations and practical habits can modify. Since the Union first formed in 1706–07, it has seen important alterations in the organisational structures and principles underpinning it. These developments include the addition of Ireland to the state in 1800–01 and successive expansions of the franchise from 1832 onwards. Periods of intense, compound pressure upon and reform of existing models have occurred. From the later decades of the nineteenth century through to the early 1920s, multiple challenges appeared: demands for Home Rule in Ireland and elsewhere; campaigns for extension of the franchise, most notably to women; and a clash between the House of Commons and the House of Lords following the formation of a Liberal Government in 1905. The outcomes included: the Parliament Act 1911; Representation of the People Act 1918; and independence for much of Ireland, combined with devolved governance for the remaining six counties in the north.[1]

The way the UK is governed, then, has never fully been constant, and upheaval has occurred in earlier times. However, it is possible to identify, starting from the 1950s, a phase of constitutional dissent, debate and change without equal in its depth and breadth in UK history. This period has been one of sustained pressure upon the existing system, sometimes lasting for decades, producing dramatic

---

[1] For an assessment of constitutional reform in the 20th century, see: Peter Catterall, Wolfram Kaiser and Ulrike Walton-Jordan, *Reforming the Constitution: Debates in Twentieth-Century Britain* (London, Frank Cass, 2000).

outcomes.[2] Perhaps the most far-reaching development of all was membership from 1973 of the organisation now known as the European Union (EU), then the European Economic Community (EEC). Participation in the EU has posed a challenge to conventional accounts of a doctrine many hold as central to UK arrangements: parliamentary sovereignty. It has also had numerous indirect consequences for the understandings and practices involved in the way we are governed. A number of false starts towards constitutional change followed in the 1970s and 1980s. One involved devolution. Proposals for devolution to Wales and Scotland both fell at the referendum stage in 1979. The idea of a UK Bill of Rights also gained ground from the late 1960s, but lost impetus within government in the early 1980s. Yet even in the 1980s the position was never entirely fixed. Judicial review of the decisions and actions of public authorities became an increasingly potent practice, and the reformed House of Commons select committee system, introduced in 1979, established itself. Various pressure groups and think tanks kept up the momentum, lobbying for change and devising proposals. European integration progressed, making a surge forwards following the 1986 Single European Act, aimed at the attainment of a European Single Market.

In the 1990s new strands of change developed, especially following the formation of a Labour Government in 1997. From this point a batch of enactments followed in close succession, the scope of which was such that it still remains difficult fully to assess its significance. A selective overview gives an idea of the sheer range and importance of the measures. The Human Rights Act 1998 provides a degree of entrenched protection in UK law for the rights set out in the European Convention on Human Rights (ECHR), an international treaty to which the UK was an inaugural signatory in 1950 (ratified the following year and coming into force in 1953). Like membership of the EU, the Human Rights Act calls into question the doctrine of parliamentary sovereignty. The territorial distribution of political authority within the UK altered more dramatically than ever before with the introduction of devolution to Northern Ireland, Scotland and Wales. An Act of Parliament of 1999 removed most of the aristocracy from the House of Lords. The Freedom of Information Act 2000 gave the public a statutory right to apply for access to official information. The Constitutional Reform Act 2005 created a UK Supreme Court, separate from the House of Lords, which became operational in 2009, supplanting the old Law Lords. While Labour lost office following the 2010 General Election, momentum continued under the coalition that succeeded it. Indeed, constitutional change was intrinsic to the deal between the Conservatives and Liberal Democrats that included measures such as the introduction of five-year fixed-term parliaments, brought about through the Fixed-term Parliaments Act 2011, central to the cohesion of their political arrangement.

---

[2] For overviews, see: Vernon Bogdanor, *The New British Constitution* (Oxford, Hart Publishing, 2009); Martin Loughlin, *The British Constitution: A Very Short Introduction* (Oxford, Oxford University Press, 2013).

It may be tempting to demarcate a shorter time span for this phase of constitutional change, perhaps beginning with the formation of the Labour Government of 1997. Certainly this event marked the beginning of a particular set of initiatives of exceptional importance. However, to insist on this starting point is to separate the New Labour and Coalition measures both from the longer-term processes of which they were a fruition (for instance, in the case of devolution) and from changes of at least equal significance to those introduced under Tony Blair and his successors (such as EEC membership). Furthermore, using this longer period makes it possible to understand more clearly the resistance that some of the more recent reforms have encountered, since it has already manifested in similar form previously.

CONSTITUTION AND SOCIETY

An explanation of this phase of change should begin—though not end—with the collapse of the British Empire that took place to a significant extent in the two decades or so from the end of the Second World War.[3] Some historians have attempted to underplay the consequences of the existence of the Empire for domestic culture, and have claimed that, by extension, when this global entity passed away, the repercussions for the metropolis were not as great as an event on this scale might suggest. A prominent advocate of this 'minimal impact thesis' Bernard Porter, specifically singles out the area under consideration in this work. He writes: 'decolonization ... caused no French-style constitutional convulsions, certainly not in the political structures and processes of the time. They went on as always, scarcely affected by this apparent revolution'.[4] Yet this statement leaves open the possibility that there were 'constitutional convulsions', but taking hold over a longer period. The narrative of change in the UK outlined above certainly fits this description. Might it be that the end of empire helped bring about a phase of transformation so profound and protracted that it has been difficult for contemporary historians fully to appreciate, since they operate from within its midst?

While emphasising the importance of avoiding crude causality, this work identifies an era of post-imperial constitutional flux. In using this description it refers to an extended period from the 1950s (roughly speaking, late on in the decade) onwards, that continues today. The definition I apply here encompasses tendencies and changes that were a consequence of the passing of empire, or that had roots in the Empire itself and appeared or continued to exhibit as it ended. The category also extends to the secondary outcomes of these trends and occurrences. Most obviously, the phase began when the Empire was undergoing a final

---

[3] For a recent account of this occurrence see: John Darwin, *Unfinished Empire: The Global Expansion of Britain* (London, Allen Lane, 2012) ch 11.

[4] Bernard Porter, *The Absent-Minded Imperialists: Empire, Society, and Culture in Britain* (Oxford, Oxford University Press, 2004).

disintegration as a meaningful force. Admittedly, this observation alone does not establish that the Empire and its collapse helped bring about what followed. However, it is possible to establish a variety of links. Imperial decline contributed to a mood in which criticism of UK constitutional arrangements among opinion-formers rapidly became pronounced, with long-term implications. Moreover, there is evidence of an impact at a more popular level. One recent study, for instance, has suggested a connection between the end of empire and the rise of the nationalist movement in Scotland, a trend with immense consequences for the structure of the UK. As the author Bryan S Glass puts it: 'nationalism only appeared as a legitimate force in Scotland in the 1960s as the last vestiges of empire collapsed ... the implications for the sustainability of the British state are still unfolding today'.[5] From some perspectives, the historic development of the UK was itself the product of English colonialism.[6] In this sense it might be seen as apt that the unravelling of the 'English Empire' could follow the fall of the British.

Other constitutional tendencies have imperial connections. In the immediate post-war period, the UK was vulnerable to criticism that as an imperial power it was a violator of human rights, a term the decolonisation movement deployed heavily (though perhaps not with the same meaning the phrase implies today). A desire to counteract this negative perception was one of the motives for the UK promotion of what became the ECHR. The UK applied this agreement internally and to its overseas territories. Initially, the government anticipated that the Convention was for other countries, and that it would never be found in contravention. But violations came to be identified, both in overseas possessions (Cyprus) and domestically. The ECHR went on to have huge consequences for the UK constitution during the post-imperial era, unforeseen at the outset.[7] The imperial heritage manifested itself once more when theorists placed the UK within a so-called 'New Commonwealth Model' alongside New Zealand and Canada, for the way in which it incorporated the ECHR into domestic law in 1998 through the Human Rights Act. A further significant development was that the ending of empire, and large-scale inward migration from territories that had formed part of it, prompted the legal definition and redefinition of one of the most crucial concepts in any society: citizenship.[8]

The Empire and its loss were also part of an overall shift in the external orientation of the UK with substantial implications for its internal mode of governance. There were definite (if complex) connections between the passing of the UK as a world power and its eventual attainment of membership of the EEC, an event of

---

[5] Bryan S Glass, *The Scottish Nation at Empire's End* (Basingstoke, Palgrave Macmillan, 2014) 1.

[6] Jim Bulpitt, *Territory and Power in the United Kingdom* (Manchester, Manchester University Press, 1983) 70–103.

[7] See: AW Brian Simpson, *Human Rights and the End of Empire: Britain and the Genesis of the European Convention* (Oxford, Oxford University Press, 2001).

[8] See: British Nationality Acts of 1948 and 1981. The later Act narrowed the meaning of citizenship as part of an immigration control programme.

unsurpassed constitutional consequence.[9] The decline of the Empire took place within the same global-strategic framework—involving, for instance, instability in the European power balance—that inspired the continental unification project, in which the UK eventually joined. Furthermore, as Chris Gifford writes, the 1960s saw the 'British state' begin to pass through a 'post-imperial crisis over modernisation. The decision to join the European Community was part of the solution to this crisis'. Yet, Gifford goes on, 'despite the achievement of membership in January 1973, constraints and limitations on Britain's involvement in the integrationist project, reflecting the underlying structure and crisis of the state regime, became increasingly evident'.[10] The post-imperial phase, therefore, produced both impetus for and restraints upon constitutional change associated with European incorporation—and in other areas. As the next chapter shows, participation in European integration also went on to trigger a series of further systemic reorientations.

Decolonisation had implications for parliamentary sovereignty. The doctrine had historic origins that predated the Empire. But there were important associations between the two. The European and international balance of power that facilitated UK global predominance during the nineteenth century were also connected to the persistence of an unwritten constitution, of which parliamentary supremacy became increasingly recognised as a defining feature. Foreign invasion might have led in time to a written constitution that supplanted parliamentary sovereignty. But conquest did not take place. Furthermore, the existence of empire, as previously discussed, may have helped lessen potentially destabilising social pressures that otherwise could have led to a break in continuity necessitating a written constitution. Parliamentary sovereignty acquired added grandiosity during the era of British ascendancy, exponentially multiplying its geographical pretensions. It deflated along with the Empire. It is fitting that the 2002 'Metric Martyrs' legal judgement (discussed later in this book), that provided grounds for the questioning of the viability of parliamentary sovereignty, should have involved a clash between the desire of some individuals to retain the use of 'imperial' measurements and the stipulation to the contrary under European law.

Moreover, there was a theoretical conundrum: if Parliament had surrendered control over a territory within which it had previously been supreme, what did this event mean for its supposed sovereignty? With the Canada Act 1982, for instance, the Westminster Parliament provided for the 'patriation' of the Canadian Constitution. In section 2 of the Act, the UK Parliament appears to limit its own future legislative ability, stating that in future: 'No Act of the Parliament of the United Kingdom ... shall extend to Canada as part of its law'. This provision potentially offers support to the 'self embracing' school of parliamentary

---

[9] For consideration of these issues, see: Alan S Milward, *The UK and the European Community*, Vol 1: *The Rise and Fall of a National Strategy, 1945–1963* (London, Frank Cass, 2002).

[10] Chris Gifford, *The Making of Eurosceptic Britain: Identity and Economy in a Post-Imperial State* (Aldershot, Ashgate, 2008) 49.

sovereignty, according to which Parliament is able to dispense with its own power. If parliamentary sovereignty could disappear in this manner in one part of the world, could it do the same anywhere, even within the UK itself?

Empire and its end offer interpretative value in further senses. They provided some of the framework for constitutional discourse. An important point of discussion surrounding the merits of participation in European integration was the implications for remaining colonial possessions and for UK attachment to the Commonwealth, an imperial legacy organisation. The imperial perspective helps assist an appreciation of some of the particular changes introduced. During the phase assessed here, schemes came into force that were the culmination of ideas already under consideration in the UK in the high imperial era of the mid- to late nineteenth century. From this time a tradition of federal thought had developed in the UK.[11] Broadly speaking, this doctrine involves advocacy of the sharing of power between different tiers of government. As such it represented a challenge to parliamentary supremacy. As we have seen, in 1706 the Scottish commissioners requested a 'federal union', under which the Estates would continue to exist alongside the English legislature, but the model was not clearly conceived at this time. Subsequently the concept became more sophisticated. Federalism in the UK took a variety of forms. One involved interest in the idea of internal layers of governance for the UK, to accommodate Irish and to a lesser extent other forms of nationalism, and to reduce the workload of the Westminster Parliament. Another subject was the possibility of incorporating the British Empire on federal lines. A further proposition was for some kind of Atlantic model, merging the United Kingdom and United States. Finally, some thinkers in this school promoted the idea of European integration. An important motive for this stream of thought in earlier eras was a desire to enhance, maintain or restore the international strength of the UK. Ideas it proposed found belated concrete expression in the very circumstances that initial advocates hoped to prevent.

The empire perspective, then, while it does not explain the entirety of this phase, is essential to any understanding of a period of change that remains with us. But what exactly were the dynamics at work in this post-imperial environment? From the late 1950s vehement and sustained criticism of domestic social institutions and practices began at elite level in the UK. Deference became less pervasive. A decline school appeared, comprising commentators who found numerous faults with what they often labelled 'the establishment'. Hugh Thomas, in an influential 1959 volume he edited with this precise title, described this entity as 'the English constitution, and the group of institutions and outlying agencies built round it to assist in its protection'. In his analysis the 'establishment' was intent upon protecting the values of an era, between 1830 and 1870, in which Britain had been 'the greatest nation in the world'. He concluded that for the UK to achieve its potential in future 'the fusty Establishment, with its Victorian views and standards

---

[11] See: Michael Burgess, *The British Tradition of Federalism* (Madison WI, Fairleigh Dickinson University Press, 1995); John Kendle, *Federal Britain: A History* (Oxford, Routledge, 1997).

of judgement, must be destroyed'.[12] The emergence of such views inaugurated a period of multiple pressures upon the UK constitution. A literary genre depicting political-constitutional malaise persisted over subsequent decades.[13]

Within the constitutional system itself friction increased between different branches of government. The courts, for instance, became more willing (and able) to challenge other public authorities over the way they exercised their powers, while MPs of the governing party became more disposed to vote against the whip. There were political divisions over constitutional issues, not only between but within parties. Most prominent among these sources of controversy was European integration, but in the period since the late 1950s they have also included devolution, voting systems, provision for the protection of human rights (an issue with European connections), and the future of the House of Lords. In every case, parties might take opposing lines to each other, and might also disagree internally, with potentially damaging consequences for their cohesion as electoral forces.

Approaches could fluctuate. Labour and the Conservatives had tended to be unenthusiastic about constitutional reform, for a variety of reasons including self-interest: why change a system within which they were leading forces? Their outlook did not survive the period. The Conservatives brought about membership of the EEC in 1973, the most radical constitutional change of the era. Labour, which became increasingly disaffected with prevailing arrangements during an 18-year period of opposition from 1979, executed a massive programme of reform from 1997, while the 2010 Coalition (comprising Conservatives and Liberal Democrats) introduced measures including the Fixed-term Parliaments Act 2011. Other parties were more naturally inclined towards constitutional change. For example, it was in the essence of nationalists in Wales and Scotland to seek alterations to the structure of the UK, and a full package of systemic reform was central to the programme of the Liberal Democrats (as they are now known)—as it was for the Green Party. The stances of others, such as the British National Party and the United Kingdom Independence Party, engaged constitutional issues. Within the general climate of change which these different groups helped generate, reforms took place that provided them with new political openings, for instance the opportunity for election to the European Parliament or devolved legislatures.

Changing attitudes and patterns of behaviour extended beyond opinion-formers, policymakers and party leaderships to the wider population. Over time, popular participation in traditional political activities—such as party membership and voting—declined. In the early 1950s individual membership of the Conservative and Labour Parties was at an historic high: for the former, 2.8 million in 1953; and for the latter, more than a million at the same time. There are some problems with the reliability and comparability of figures, and

---

[12] Hugh Thomas,'The Establishment and Society' in Hugh Thomas (ed), *The Establishment* (London, Anthony Blond, 1959) 14–15, 20.

[13] See eg: David Marquand, *The Unprincipled Society* (London, Fontana, 1988); Will Hutton, *The State We're In* (London, Jonathan Cape, 1995).

the movement was not always in one direction. But dramatic overall decline is certain. By the beginning of the second decade of the twenty-first century, the Conservative total stood at somewhere between 130,000 and 170,000, while for Labour it was 193,000. In 1983, the proportion of the electorate in the UK who were members of one of the three main parties (Conservatives, Labour or Liberals, later merged with the Social Democratic Party, eventually becoming the Liberal Democrats) was 3.8 per cent. It had sunk by 2010 to 1 per cent. Offsetting the trend there has been a rise over the last 10 years for some of the smaller parties.[14] Yet it may be that parties are in general a less appealing proposition. Opinion research suggests that over the past three decades the tendency for individual electors to feel attached to any particular one has declined.[15]

This trend may have some connection with another pattern involving the exercise of the right to vote. In the General Election of 1950, turnout was 83.9 per cent. In 1997 it stood at 71.4 per cent, and the following General Election of 2001 saw a fall to 59.4 per cent. After this post-Second World War low there has been a recovery, but not to earlier levels (2005: 61.4 per cent; 2010: 65.1 per cent). The underlying pattern is generational: successive cohorts with decreasing likelihood to vote, even as they grow older.[16] These trends are part of wider European currents, though the UK is even within this context at the low end of the scale on measures such as party membership and electoral turnout. Some activities including petition signing and contacting MPs have increased.[17] But the fall-off affecting key modes of traditional political participation is a challenge to the viability of the representative form of democracy.

Coupled with a decline in propensity to vote, support has dispersed away from the two largest parties. Not since 1970 have the Conservatives and Labour both achieved more than 40 per cent at a general election. Parties including the Liberal Democrats, nationalists and Greens have gained. The fracturing of the two-party system casts doubt on the continued appropriateness of the 'First-Past-the-Post' (FPTP) voting system used for Westminster elections. Even as their overall support has dropped, the number of safe seats possessed by the Conservatives and Labour has increased. At the same time, other parties have made some parliamentary progress, and both the Conservatives and Labour seem less able to win a General Election outright than they once were: FPTP has, therefore, become less likely to deliver one of the core benefits its advocates have claimed for it: single party governments with secure majorities in the House of Commons. Consequently, coalition government returned after a 65-year gap in 2010, itself creating further constitutional tensions. The FPTP system is a source of instability through its tendency to exacerbate territorial polarisation. For instance, it makes

---

[14] Feargal McGuinness, *Membership of UK Political Parties* (London, House of Commons Library, 2012).

[15] *British Social Attitudes: The 30th Report* (London, National Centre for Social Research, 2013) 64–65.

[16] Aliyah Dar, *Elections: Turnout* (London, House of Commons Library, 2013).

[17] *British Social Attitudes: The 30th Report* (n 15) 68.

the Conservative Party appear even less popular than it is in Scotland, since the minimal seat haul the party obtains at general election time is disproportionately small. Similarly, Labour is under-represented in the South East of England outside London.

The Union—or at least the centralised form it took—suffered a loss of appeal. Support for devolution and for Celtic nationalist parties in Great Britain grew. As noted above, the collapse of empire may have removed a reason for the existence of the UK state. Allan I Macinnes, historian of the formation of Great Britain, writes that from the point of view of Scotland 'Political incorporation was not an end in itself. The fortunes of the Union have been umbilically linked to the Empire'. As this global construction disintegrated, 'Union … moved from a constitutional fixture to a constitutional option, particularly within the context of' ongoing European integration.[18] Economic difficulties in the UK during the period under examination fell particularly heavily in Celtic areas, and seem to have prompted further discontent with the existing system. Moreover, measures pursued under the Conservative Governments of 1979 to 1997 aimed at reversing perceived decline probably further exacerbated hostility towards the Union, or at least its existing configuration. Other types of social change had consequences for the Union. International unrest of the late 1960s found one outlet in Northern Ireland. It formed part of a chain of events that led on to an upsurge in violence and then institutional experiments aimed at achieving a lasting settlement in the Province.

The extent and nature of religious belief created a further moving picture. Adherence to the official faith, Anglicanism, declined.[19] So too did subscription to Christianity as a whole. For instance, between the final quarters of 2004 and 2010, the Labour Force Survey showed a fall in the number of Christians in Great Britain from 44.8 million to 41.4 million. At the same time, the total with no religion rose from 9 million to 13.4 million. Generational shifts seem to have been important again: new waves appearing who were less likely to subscribe to Christianity, and seemingly relatively settled in this position as they grew older. Non-Christian religions have seen an increase, mainly attributable to migration patterns, another imperial connection. The combined shift is towards a multi-faith and no-faith society, with the privileged position for Anglicanism appearing anomalous.[20] Religious orientation was fundamental to some of the most important constitutional struggles in English history and to the formation of the UK as a state. With these changes, what now was the appropriate relationship between the public sphere and the realm of faith? There was also a renewed link between religious adherence and security concerns, especially following the terrorist

---

[18] Allan I Macinnes, *Union and Empire: The Making of the United Kingdom in 1707* (Cambridge, Cambridge University Press, 2007) 326.
[19] David Butler and Gareth Butler, *Twentieth-Century British Political Facts: 1900–2000* (Basingstoke, Macmillan, 2000) 558.
[20] Oliver Hawkins, *Religion in Great Britain* (London, House of Commons Library, 2012).

attacks in the US of 11 September 2001, followed by the London bombings of 7 July 2005. The nature of the threat in the UK involved communities with historic roots in the former colonial empire. In response the authorities brought forward numerous legal and policy measures that, chiefly because of their human rights implications, raised important constitutional issues.

The various patterns discussed here help provide a background against which we can better comprehend the structural changes that occurred. Overall the evidence conveys a sense of people being less likely to take part in traditional collective activities, yet possibly more likely to assert their individual interests (for instance through raising issues directly with their MP), and suggests an atmosphere of intensified questioning of official institutions and practices. These kinds of trends assist an appreciation of the relevance of a body such as the Parliamentary Ombudsman, set up in 1967 to handle complaints from members of the public against government departments. A purpose of the Ombudsman was to bring about more personalised public services, better meeting the needs of individuals and providing redress following failure. The establishment of the Law Commission in 1965 indicated a prioritisation of utilitarian principles over the preservation of heritage. As we have seen, it soon brought about the removal from the statute book of some of the last remaining provisions of Magna Carta.

Change itself could be self-sustaining. Enacted constitutional arrangements cannot operate independently of their surroundings, but at the same time they can impact upon them. A consideration of the phase of dynamism from the late 1950s supports this point. New institutions, as well as representing innovations in themselves, can create a platform for the advocacy of further reform. Commissions and other bodies established to perform constitutional monitoring roles could then advocate changes in their areas of interest. The Committee on Standards in Public Life, which appeared in 1995, took an interest in promoting reforms including placing the Civil Service on a statutory basis. This end finally came about in 2010. Reforms may not satisfy the public, and may leave it demanding more. In 1983, 34 per cent of respondents believed that the House of Lords required 'some change'; by 1994 the figure was 58 per cent; by 2012, 63 per cent.[21] Yet between 1994 and 2012, arguably more than 'some' change had taken place. However, while modifications can be dynamic, if they are culturally inappropriate or in some way problematic they may encounter difficulties. Enhancements in the constitutional role of the judiciary, for instance, have challenged ingrained views that elected politicians should be in a position of supremacy. Attempted innovations such as devolved assemblies for the English regions failed for lack of public support.

A problematic feature of constitutional reform dynamics is that they sometimes involve misdiagnosis. The period has seen a sustained narrative of political malaise. But all claims regarding supposed constitutional dysfunction merit close attention. For instance, recurring assertions—that predate the 1950s by decades

---

[21] *British Social Attitudes: The 30th Report* (n 15) x–xiv.

or even centuries—involving the idea of an ever more powerful Prime Minister are theoretically flawed and difficult to reconcile with the historical record.[22] Claims that the House of Commons is increasingly subordinate to government and whips are refutable simply by reference to voting records. Another idea enjoying unmerited currency is that politicians are somehow increasingly detached from the wider public they are supposed to serve. The real trend—as the increased propensity of constituents to contact their MP helps establish—is in the opposite direction. Casework has over past decades become a predominant part of the work of MPs. The experience of the present author working in a Westminster office suggested that representatives, rather than being distanced from electors, are constantly and widely engaged in life in all its lurid complexity. If there is a problem it is that MPs are too heavily burdened by day to day existence at local level, at the cost of other roles such as policy oversight and legislative scrutiny on behalf of the UK as a whole.[23]

The identification of trends in public opinion also demands caution. In 1973, when asked about their 'opinion of the present system of governing Britain', 14 per cent stated that it 'Needs a great deal of improvement'; 35 per cent that it 'Could be improved quite a lot'; 43 per cent that it 'Could be improved in small ways but mainly works well'; 5 per cent that it 'Works extremely well and could not be improved' (4 per cent did not know). By 1995, the percentage believing that the system required 'a great deal of improvement' had risen from 14 per cent to 35 per cent, and those thinking there was scope for improving 'quite a lot' increased from 35 per cent to 41 per cent. The 'mainly works well' group had shrunk from 43 per cent to 19 per cent of the total, and those who were entirely happy had decreased from 5 per cent to 3 per cent (3 per cent were in the 'don't know' category). Yet the movement of opinion was not solely in the direction of dissatisfaction. By 2004, 18 per cent rather than 35 per cent (as in 1995) identified the need for 'a great deal of improvement'. The proportion was roughly the same for 'Could be improved quite a lot': 42 per cent in 2004 as opposed to 41 per cent in 1995. The 'mainly works well' group had expanded from 19 per cent to 34 per cent. Those who saw no room for improvement made up 2 per cent rather than 3 per cent, with those who did not know 4 per cent.[24] Sophisticated analysis and sometimes qualification is essential. Nonetheless, a variety of tendencies combined from the 1950s to produce immense challenges to the UK constitution. They led in turn to major changes. Any consideration of the system as it is now must place it within the period of upheaval identified here. Some detailed case studies give an idea of how these complex tendencies can play out.

---

[22] See: Andrew Blick and George Jones, *Premiership: The History, Nature and Power of the Office of the British Prime Minister* (Exeter, Imprint Academic, 2010).

[23] Scott Kelly, *The Slow Death of the 'Efficient Secret': The Rise of MP Rebellion, its Causes and its Implications* (London, The Constitution Society, 2014).

[24] Hansard Society, *Audit of Political Engagement 6: The 2009 Report* (London, Hansard Society, 2009) 30.

PARLIAMENT

Parliament has a special prominence at the heart of the unwritten constitution of the UK. Changes to it are, therefore, of exceptional importance. During the phase of dynamism such alterations have been plentiful and in some cases drastic. Yet some conflicts between the pressures of the post-imperial era and pre-existing systems remain unresolved, with consequent instability. Public representations of Parliament usually focus on one component within it: the House of Commons. In its dealings with the government, the Commons has provided evidence of the disappearing deference that has come to characterise some relations between different organs of government. Contrary to regular claims about supposedly increasingly obedient MPs, the data point in the opposite direction: MPs from the governing party (or parties) are far more likely to disobey the whip than they were in the 1950s. Some of the most prominent rebellions have focused on controversies of a constitutional nature, particularly involving European integration.[25] This change may be partly attributable to changing social patterns identified above: MPs have a more direct and individual relationship with people living in their constituencies, dealing with particular issues they raise. This kind of engagement, encouraged further by electronic communication methods, has loomed increasingly large in comparison to the collective party attachment of MPs. The concern to maintain a specific personal connection with voters possibly applies more in marginal seats that are liable to be won and lost in a general election. As noted, the number of constituencies not realistically likely to change hands has risen. Yet at the same time the growing cohort of MPs in safe seats have less to fear from the possibility that disunity will have a negative impact on the general popularity of their party.[26]

Some might welcome increased independence on the part of MPs, on the grounds that it is appropriate for them to exercise their judgement on behalf of their constituents, whose views they should also take into account and prioritise over adherence to party discipline. Yet it could weaken lines of democratic accountability. At the time of a general election, competing parliamentary candidates run for particular parties with distinct manifestos and approaches. If rebelliousness in the Commons weakens these attachments, it becomes harder for voters to make informed choices between different individuals presenting themselves on polling day. Furthermore, as party cohesion declines, the government may be tempted to rely increasingly on problematic methods aimed at combating this tendency. In the eighteenth century, before the clearer development of more disciplined groupings, what we would now see as financial corruption was common. In the present age, devices available include the expansion of the 'payroll vote'— ministers and Parliamentary Private Secretaries, comprising a bloc of support for the government within the Commons. In 1983 the payroll vote totalled 122;

---

[25] Philip Cowley, *The Rebels: How Blair Mislaid His Majority* (London, Politico's, 2005).
[26] Kelly, *The Slow Death of the 'Efficient Secret'* (n 23).

by 2010 it had reached 140.[27] The Commons Public Administration Select Committee has identified the 2000s as one of three decades since 1900 that saw a surge in the number of ministers, the other two being the 1930s and the 1960s.[28]

The increased assertiveness of the Commons—along with, in some cases, mistaken claims that it is a declining force—have helped bring about a series of changes in structures and practice. They have in turn enabled MPs to pursue their own agendas more forcefully still. After earlier experiments, in 1979 a permanent body of select committees formed with the task of monitoring the expenditure, policy and administration of individual departments. Over time their resources and coverage of government activity have grown and their work has become more formalised. They have themselves often taken an interest in constitutional matters, and made reform proposals.[29] Up to 2010 the whips played a lead role in determining who sat on these bodies, limiting their autonomy from government and partisan influences. However, party groups in the Commons now elect committee members, and the whole House votes for their chairs, strengthening the independence of this system of oversight. This reform came as part of a package that also included the creation of a Backbench Business Committee, a body giving the House control over a block of time not reserved for government business.[30]

The Commons has seen further important reforms that enhanced its ability to hold the executive to account, in particular in the period after Labour assumed office in 1997. Pre-legislative scrutiny, a practice enabling examination of draft Bills, developed; as did post-legislative scrutiny, meaning the consideration of the implementation of Acts of Parliament after they came into force (the House of Lords could also participate in these activities). The introduction of public bill committees has enabled the more informed scrutiny of Bills during their regular passage through the House, with a new practice of taking expert evidence on the measures involved.[31] Commons select committees obtained the right to hold pre-appointment hearings with individuals chosen to fill a range of senior public posts, and submit a (non-binding) view on the selection.[32] From 2002 the then Prime Minister, Tony Blair, began attending twice-yearly evidence sessions with the Liaison Committee, a body comprising the chairs of select committees. It enabled a more measured and in-depth examination of the premier than that carried out at the largely theatrical weekly Prime Minister's Questions. At the same

---

[27] Keith Parry and Richard Kelly, *Limitation on the Number of Ministers and the Size of the Payroll Vote* (London, House of Commons, 2012) 6.

[28] Public Administration Select Committee, *Too Many Ministers?* (HC 2009–10, 457) 3.

[29] For a recent assessment of the select committee system, see: Liaison Committee, *Select Committee Effectiveness, Resources and Powers* (HC 2012–13, 697).

[30] For the source of these changes, see: Reform Committee, *Rebuilding the House* (HC 2008–09, 1117). See also: Political and Constitutional Reform Committee, *Revisiting Rebuilding the House: The Impact of the Wright Reforms* (HC 2013–14, 82).

[31] See eg: Jessica Levy, *Strengthening Parliament's Powers of Scrutiny? An Assessment of the Introduction of Public Bill Committees* (London, The Constitution Unit, 2009).

[32] See eg: Peter Waller and Mark Chalmers, *An Evaluation of Pre-Appointment Scrutiny Hearings* (London, The Constitution Unit, 2010).

time, the Commons faced challenges (shared by the Lords). Over this period, a rise occurred in the use of secondary legislation, of which parliamentary scrutiny is generally meagre or non-existent, though committee reforms have taken place in an attempt to reduce this shortfall. Further difficulties arose with the distancing of ministers from the management of large sections of the Civil Service, creating new possibilities for the evasion of responsibility for controversial incidents when it suited ministers to do so.[33]

During the period considered here, a number of attempts took place to introduce a directly or indirectly elected House of Lords (for a time, the Labour Party favoured outright abolition). At the 2010 General Election, all three of the main parties supported either a mainly or wholly elected second chamber. Yet none of these plans has yet succeeded. Nonetheless, the composition of the Lords changed radically. The second chamber is less reminiscent of one of the Houses of an Estates General of late-medieval Europe than it was in the mid-1950s. The Life Peerages Act 1958 provided for the appointment of individuals who were created members of the Lords, but could not pass this position down to their descendants; it also provided for the admission of women into the Lords. Under the Peerage Act 1963 it became possible for an individual who wished to do so to disclaim a peerage, leaving the House of Lords. Most dramatically of all, 1999 saw the removal of all but 92 hereditary peers. Another important departure involved the transfer of the Law Lords to the UK Supreme Court in 2009. The 26 Anglican bishops remain. The shift towards membership by appointment rather than birth left the Lords collectively feeling more legitimate. It came increasingly to challenge legislative proposals passed by the Commons, leading to a rising partnership between the two chambers. This trend to some extent offset the rise of the Commons discussed in the previous chapter, but certainly did not fully negate it. The Lords developed new committees, including a body charged specifically with overseeing the constitution: the House of Lords Select Committee on the Constitution. In the course of its work, it began to develop an identifiable set of constitutional values.[34] Another significant innovation was a joint committee of Commons and Lords on human rights, responsible for scrutiny of legislative proposals, assessing their compliance with the ECHR, and holding other inquiries.[35]

A third component of Parliament, though it is not generally perceived in this sense, is the monarchy. This institution is often held to enjoy greater public popularity than other constitutional entities. Yet it has not been immune to the pattern of deteriorating deference. While opinion research shows a large majority agreeing with the continuation of the monarchy, a significant minority of republicans exists. Support for the preservation of the institution declined during the 1980s

---

[33] See: Select Committee on the Constitution, *The Accountability of Civil Servants* (2012–13, HL 61).

[34] Jack Simson Caird, Robert Hazell and Dawn Oliver, *The Constitutional Standards of the House of Lords Select Committee on the Constitution* (London, The Constitution Society/The Constitution Unit, 2014).

[35] For a recent work on the House of Lords, see: Meg Russell, *The Contemporary House of Lords: Westminster Bicameralism Revived* (Oxford, Oxford University Press, 2013).

and 1990s. Recent events, beginning with the marriage of the Duke and Duchess of Cambridge in 2011, seem to have prompted the upturn in popularity which the monarchy has enjoyed. Yet some analysis suggests that this spike is within the context of another generational shift, with the underlying pattern being for each new group to be less favourable towards the monarchy.[36] It is also important in itself that the asking of questions about whether to retain the monarchy is now deemed proper. Media scrutiny of the lives of members of the Royal Family has been intense and sometimes critical in recent decades. Attention has also focused on the way in which the Royal Household is financed, with modifications introduced.[37] The Succession to the Crown Act 2013 removed gender discrimination from determining who could become head of state, and religious discrimination regarding who their spouse could be. Yet monarchs remain heads of the Established Church, with which they have to be in communion, and they are not allowed to be Roman Catholics. Moreover, as almost throughout the history of the UK, they have to be descendants of Sophia, Electress of Hanover.

THE CIVIL SERVICE

In the era of constitutional flux, one of the first institutions of government to come under sustained attack was the instrument that enables UK ministers both to think and act: the Civil Service. Its development had strong imperial connections. The term 'civil service' originated as a means of describing administrative as opposed to military personnel attached to the East India Company. As part of a long historical process the administrative machine in the UK had acquired a collection of characteristics, some first developed in India in the mid-nineteenth century. It employed staff on a permanent basis. Changes in holders of ministerial office, or in the partisan complexion of government, did not mean removal of permanent officials from their posts. The corollary was a requirement to be impartial, serving different political chiefs equally well, without displaying personal or party political attachments. Officials were to avoid public identification with particular ministers or policies. A cult of the 'generalist' existed within the Civil Service, with a principle that administrators should possess the qualities of an all-rounder, not prior knowledge or skills specific to the task in which they were engaged. At the centre of the Whitehall machine was the Treasury, wielding pervasive influence over policy formation, and also responsible for management of the Civil Service itself.[38] Any government seeking to be effective needed the cooperation of the Civil Service. A particular area of influence was in constitutional matters. In earlier periods, counsellors who held office under successive political leaders—such as Wulfstan, Archbishop of York in the eleventh century—

---

[36] Ipsos MORI Social Research Institute, *Understanding Society* (London, Ipsos MORI, October 2013) 32.
[37] See: Sovereign Grant Act 2011.
[38] See: Peter Hennessy, *Whitehall* (London, Pimlico, 2001).

were able to present with authority accounts of what were the proper standards of governance. The UK Civil Service has similarly been able to advise on procedure and precedent, of which they can claim to be the keepers, and which takes on exceptional prominence under an unwritten constitution.

From the late 1950s the Civil Service, its values and organisation became the subject of criticism. Harold Wilson, who first became Labour Prime Minister in 1964, presented himself as a modernising scourge of the old order, though he could at times admire traditional institutions. One of the targets of the innovating side of Wilson was Whitehall. He and his advisers drew on intellectual traditions within the Labour movement stretching back as far as the 1920s, and a positive assessment of administrative methods utilised in Whitehall in the emergency circumstances of the two world wars. Currents of change that began in the 1960s continue to run today. A contingent of temporary aides, often with clear party political connections, appointed by and working directly to ministers appeared within the Civil Service in 1964. Known as special advisers, they subsequently grew in number, combined influence and notoriety. A greater openness to recruiting expertise developed. Responsibility for managing Whitehall split from the Treasury, moving first to a purpose-designed Civil Service Department (in 1968) then, by 1983, to the Cabinet Office. Successive reform programmes sought to instil new management techniques and greater efficiency.[39]

From the late 1980s the Next Steps initiative brought about dramatic structural transformation, transferring swathes of government business to executive agencies distanced from the continuous oversight of secretaries of state. This shift, while possibly desirable from a management perspective, presented difficulties regarding the maintenance of a core principle of the UK constitution: that ministers were accountable to Parliament for the work that went on as part of their portfolios. Under the Tony Blair governments, concepts such as 'joined-up government' and 'delivery' sought to ensure that officials worked in a more coordinated and more effective fashion. Because Blair drove them from the prime-ministerial centre, they raised further questions about accountability: in particular whether No 10 or a given secretary of state was primarily responsible for policy. An attempt at stabilisation came with the Constitutional Renewal and Governance Act 2010. It gave a grounding in statute to core traditional principles of the Civil Service: impartiality and recruitment on merit through open competition. In doing so, it belatedly put into effect a recommendation included in the so-called 'Northcote–Trevelyan Report' of 1854. Often this text is regarded as the foundation of the Civil Service. In implementing a Northcote–Trevelyan proposal the 2010 Act arguably resisted the tide of change. Yet the Act also provided for the existence of special advisers, who had since 1964 represented a challenge to orthodox Whitehall values.

---

[39] Andrew Blick, *People Who Live in the Dark: The History of the Special Adviser in British Politics* (London, Politico's/Methuen, 2004).

The most recent instalment in the process of bureaucratic change is the Civil Service Reform Plan that the Coalition launched in 2012.[40] It was not as original as the authors seemed to believe, recalling earlier initiatives dating back as far as the 1960s. Furthermore, the extent of its implementation in practice was not entirely clear. But it took to a new degree of intensity the challenge to which older Civil Service values have been subject since the Wilson era. One method advocated as part of the plan amounted to the outsourcing of policy development to non-public bodies beyond Whitehall. Another, the 'Extended Ministerial Office' involved enhanced discretion for ministers in constructing the inner team surrounding them, including the incorporation of outsiders.[41] This idea helped demonstrate the inescapably European nature of the UK constitution. When observing supposedly better performing countries elsewhere in the world from the late 1950s onwards, critics inferred that their administrative arrangements were a reason for success. A particular subject of praise was the French model. It involved the use of the ministerial *cabinet*, a customised support unit comprising career officials and temporary appointments. The UK system has edged towards the *cabinet* model ever since, and the 'Extended Ministerial Office' could take it closer than it has been before. Developments in the Civil Service demonstrate that the onslaught of constitutional change since the 1950s is more than a random succession of initiatives, though at times it may seem such. It has involved the manifestation of consistent pressures. While old arrangements do not yield immediately, the impetus of change and the rationale lying behind it persist. We can find similar patterns in areas such as devolution, finally introduced (or reintroduced in the case of Northern Ireland), following many decades of discussion and consideration, the recommendations of the Royal Commission on the Constitution in 1973, and the referendum failures of the late 1970s. Some ideas persist.

THE PROCESS OF CHANGE

Though it could generate discomfort, constitutional transformation became by the early twenty-first century a standard, continuous function of UK governments of different parties. Sir John Baker, a Cambridge professor of constitutional law, has noted that the establishment of a Department for Constitutional Affairs in 2004 created the impression of the political system itself as a public service subject to continuous government management and reorganisation.[42] Seemingly intent on proving his point, the Coalition formed in 2010 introduced a post of Minister for Political and Constitutional Reform. The holder was responsible for delivering a series of targets and reform objectives listed online. Moreover, on the

---

[40] HM Government, *The Civil Service Reform Plan* (London, Cabinet Office, 2012).

[41] Cabinet Office, *Extended Ministerial Offices: Guidance for Departments* (London, Cabinet Office, 2013).

[42] John Baker, 'Our Unwritten Constitution' (Maccabaean Lecture in Jurisprudence, British Academy, 24 November 2009).

government website, amid the detail about changes already accomplished and yet to come, there was no projected or even implied end to this process.

This protracted shifting of ground draws attention to the flexible nature of the UK constitution.[43] Processes involved in bringing about change are far less stringent in the UK than in states with written constitutions. Those who oppose recent alterations on the grounds that they undermine core established values of the UK polity must, therefore, confront a conundrum. It is one of the most prominent and vaunted features of the traditional UK model—its mutability—that has enabled these very alterations in its underlying nature to take place with relative ease. A corollary is that those less enamoured with the hallowed principles have seen features of the constitution they may dislike deployed in pursuit of reforms they support. Central to the capacity for casual, rapid transformation is the supremacy of the UK legislature. Broadly speaking, the Westminster Parliament is able—in theory at least—to accomplish any constitutional modification using regular legislative procedures, involving simple majorities (subject to qualifications considered elsewhere in this book). Indeed, Parliament has been able, through this straightforward approach, to introduce statutes that some hold have compromised the doctrine of its own sovereignty, possibly making some kinds of constitutional change a more demanding task in future.

Within Parliament the House of Commons has the ability, under the Parliament Acts of 1911 and 1949, to bypass the House of Lords (in most cases), and the Commons has a broader position of primacy over the Lords, resting on convention. The consequence of this arrangement is that the leaders of the grouping that predominates in the Commons, who form the government, and by extension the officials who advise them, are in a privileged position with regard to constitutional law-making. They have the ability to initiate change, and their cooperation is essential for others seeking to bring it about. In some cases ministers can affect constitutional modification—such as the formation and abolition of departments of state—through secondary legislation that receives a far lower level of parliamentary scrutiny than does a full Bill. Ministers can also wield powers that have no statutory basis and over which Parliament has little or more often no direct formal control, existing under the Royal Prerogative, a residue of monarchical authority. Under this constitutional source it is possible, for instance, to enter into international agreements (since 2010 subject in theory to limited parliamentary control) that have constitutional implications (though any consequential changes to domestic statute require parliamentary approval in the normal way). For instance, in December 1965 the UK Government allotted to adopt the system of individual petition under the ECHR. The constitutional implications—with hindsight at least—were immense, since the change meant that individuals would be able to assert a set of positive rights, if only through

---

[43] For the following, see: Andrew Blick, David Howarth and Nat le Roux, *Distinguishing Constitutional Legislation: A Modest Proposal* (London, The Constitution Society, 2014).

an international agreement. Yet, because its execution took place under the Royal Prerogative, the approval of the legislature for this seismic development was not required—a position which might have given cause to question what precisely the supposed sovereignty of Parliament was worth. Wider consultation with the public did not occur, and there was not even any debate in the Cabinet or in any sub-committee thereof.[44] A further source of influence for the Commons executive leadership arises because key components of the UK constitution rest in conventions. Their existence is amorphous and the process by which they change can be opaque. Amid the uncertainty, ministers are able to play an important role in defining, interpreting and enforcing conventions, activity which can bleed into changing them.

It is unsatisfactory for any one group to become predominant within these change processes, potentially making them subordinate to its material imperatives. One effect of the balance of constitutional authority in the UK has been to facilitate an increasing encroachment from the centre into policy areas previously within the remit of local government, in England in particular. Another specific case merits attention as illustrating dangers inherent in the UK skewed system of constitutional alteration: that of the Fixed-term Parliaments Act 2011. Interlocked party political imperatives that underpinned the Coalition formed in 2010 were the main driver of this change. The central provision of the legislation—for a standard period between elections of five years—was a means of making the arrangement between the Conservatives and Liberal Democrats more stable. From the perspective of officials in Whitehall, the prospect of a secure government was probably appealing in the particular circumstances, and in general a more predictable political timetable might have been attractive to them.

Outside the executive, reformers had long argued for fixed-term parliaments, often on the grounds that the previous arrangement gave an inappropriate advantage to sitting prime ministers, who were able to determine the timing of the poll to suit their own needs. No doubt some within government shared this principled view. But the immediate reason for the implementation of the idea was the necessity of fastening the coalition. The manner in which the government developed the measure and saw it passed into law, at a pace inappropriate to its significance and not allowing for sufficient consultation and parliamentary scrutiny, betrayed the political urgency underpinning it. The Lords could in theory have blocked the Bill under the Parliament Acts (since it created the potential for the extension of a Parliament slightly beyond the five-year limit). But it did not use this power. Not only were there problems with the process. In as far as the Act did deliver on reform ideas it did so imperfectly, and was distorted by party-political objectives. The length of parliamentary term it prescribed—five years—was longer than many supporters of such a change wanted, with four a preferred figure. Parliaments normally lasting half a decade would mean less frequent engagement

---

[44] Anthony Lester, 'Human Rights and the British Constitution' in Jeffrey Jowell and Dawn Oliver (eds), *The Changing Constitution*, 7th edn (Oxford, Oxford University Press, 2011) 75.

in the political process by many members of the public, a democratically undesirable consequence of the Act. From the Coalition point of view, it provided the maximum possible time in which to achieve an economic recovery before facing the judgement of voters. The Fixed-term Parliaments Act, then, arose from the narrow concerns of a party political negotiation that took place in 2010, with more expansive engagement in the decision and its implementation resisted. Yet it dealt with issues that were of fundamental importance, involving when elections take place and the processes for triggering them. In other countries, a written constitution would provide for these rules, and altering them would probably involve adherence to special amendment procedures.

Though excessive stewardship of the constitution from the parliamentary-executive leadership bloc is possible, recognising this difficulty should not lead to the conclusion that this group is omnipotent. It cannot fully manipulate circumstances around systemic change. Reforms are likely to have complex consequences. For instance, the Fixed-term Parliaments Act entailed a cession of authority by the Prime Minister, who lost some latitude in determining the timing of general elections. Furthermore, governments must always take into account the views of groups including backbench MPs; the party beyond Parliament; the media; the general public; the business community; and relations with foreign states and supranational organisations. Ministers may feel that commitments they made before they took office bind them to act. Constitutional change, including in its current phase, has complex underlying causes. Often the parliamentary-executive leadership is responding to and channelling external forces, not commanding them or initiating change entirely of its own accord. It is difficult for it to conjure momentum from nowhere. If this group is divided or the government is suffering from a lack of political capital, it may become more susceptible still to outside contingencies. A government may in some circumstances (though it may be mistaken in its judgement) see no option other than to countenance changes to which it is opposed, as with the acceptance in London of the Scottish Independence Referendum held in 2014. Agreeing to this vote was an illustration of the limitations on the parliamentary-executive bloc and the potential for powerful outside forces to intrude. The circumstances of the campaign underlined these points further. They drove the Prime Minister, along with other party leaders, to commit through the 'Vow' to a package of change he would never have chosen on his own account. However, in another sense, the Vow exemplified the capacity for making major constitutional commitments without consultation.

With such limitations in mind government leaders often deem it necessary to subject their theoretically immense power to additional legitimising processes. In the post-Second World War period, a convention appeared to the effect that legislation of 'first class' constitutional importance should be dealt with in detail by a full meeting of the Commons, with its 'committee stage' being taken by a committee of the whole House, not the small legislative committees that usually dealt with Bills. However, the rationale for the application of the 'first class' definition was not clear and this procedure was not necessarily a model for meaningful scrutiny.[45] Governments have sometimes submitted proposals of constitutional importance to other special procedures. For instance, before the UK joined the EEC it held three Commons votes on the principle of membership, the first two of which were entirely free (that is, un-whipped), the third partially so, with the Labour Party (in opposition) whipping against, though with a large rebellion taking place within it. Some have queried how meaningfully the parliamentary debates addressed the key constitutional issues, however. Finally, successive governments have utilised referendums as decision-taking devices, considered in more detail later. It should be noted here that such plebiscites can be deployed in a manipulative manner. In 1975, the Labour Prime Minister Harold Wilson used a vote on continued EEC membership as a political management tool. In 2011, the holding of a referendum on the possibility of adopting the Alternative Vote for elections to the House of Commons arose from the contingencies of coalition formation, and denied the public a meaningful choice by excluding the possibility of a more proportionate system.

Some means of adding authority to a constitutional change proposal are dubious. For instance, the justification for abolishing the Greater London Council came from a short passage included in the Conservative Party Manifesto for the 1983 General Election. The proportion of voters who were aware of this pledge, one among many in a document they may well not have read at all, may not have been great. Even if they did know about it, those who opted to support the Conservatives did not necessarily agree with the plan. Whether voters outside London should have had any part in such a decision was debatable. Anyway, although they won the election in question comfortably, the Conservatives received the support of well under half of those who voted. Yet the government felt it had a sufficient mandate to strip a group of people of arrangements for their self-governance, without their specific consent.

Experience suggests that the parliamentary-executive group can benefit from a more considered, consultative approach to constitutional change, and that to avoid such a course can be at the cost of the political acceptability and practical viability of the measure involved. The Blair period illustrates this point well. A number of earlier reforms under his governments rested on inclusive, careful deliberation. Scottish devolution, for instance, drew on the work of the Scottish Constitutional Convention, a cross-party and civil society body first formed in 1989. A number of other changes derived from pre-1997 talks between Labour and the Liberal Democrats, leading to the so-called 'Cook–Maclennan' agreement, named after its leading brokers, Robin Cook for Labour and Robert Maclennan for the Liberal Democrats.[46] Then in June 2003 the government unveiled a package of proposed changes that involved abolishing the office of Lord Chancellor

---

[45] Robert Hazell, *Time for a New Convention: Parliamentary Scrutiny of Constitutional Bills, 1997–2005* (London, The Constitution Unit, 2006).

[46] See: Robin Cook and Robert Maclennan, *Looking Back, Looking Forward: The Cook–Maclennan Agreement, 10 Years On* (London, New Politics Network, 2005).

and forming a UK Supreme Court. There were strong arguments in favour these changes, and support for them certainly existed. A problem was that they were tied up with a Cabinet reshuffle. They did not involve prior consultation; the announcements came in statements to the press rather than Parliament. This mishandling of the attempted reform provided those who disliked the substance of the change with a means of resisting it while appearing impartial. Such was the level of protest from within the legal community that the government had to cooperate with prolonged and intense parliamentary scrutiny of its plans, leading to their substantial revision.[47]

The process had taken place in reverse. To have begun with a wide formal canvassing of views on the subject, accompanied by a general steer about what the government had in mind, would have been more appropriate for a number of reasons. Not only would this sequence have been more acceptable from a principled perspective, it could well have meant that when firm proposals did appear they were more viable and credible. Under a written constitution, a change on this scale would probably require conformance to some kind of heightened amendment procedure. A government contemplating it would need to consult fully to ensure it had the consensus needed for it to pass; the procedure it used to do so would probably entail a degree of scrutiny of the proposal (indeed this approach could be mandatory), possibly involving an expert input, that would test its robustness and help enhance it. In the UK, the possibility of acting more informally creates a temptation for governments. If they act upon it they can bring their own proposals into disrepute, along with constitutional change and the constitution itself. Specific and firm amendment requirements, then, could protect both the system from the parliamentary-executive leadership, and the parliamentary-executive leadership from itself.

Another important feature of any constitutional change is the connection it may have with other reforms that could be under way, and the system as a whole. A criticism of modifications in the UK is that they are piecemeal and that more holistic assessments do not take place.[48] This idea merits close examination. Consideration—within and outside government—of reforms has sometimes taken into account their implications for each other: for instance, those contributing to the development of devolution schemes introduced from the late 1990s considered the possible consequences for EU policy. Organisations such as the pressure group Charter 88 (and its successor group, Unlock Democracy) and the academic think tank, the Constitution Unit, have given attention to the relationship between individual reform packages and the whole. However, compartmentalisation has certainly taken place. For instance, the Royal Commission on the Constitution established in 1969 did not range as widely as its title might suggest and confined itself largely to issues of territorial governance. The consideration and execution of House of Lords reform has often seemed not to give proper

---

[47] For an account of the handling of this proposal, see: Dawn Oliver, 'Constitutionalism and the Abolition of the Office of the Lord Chancellor' (2004) 57(4) *Parliamentary Affairs* 754.

[48] See eg: Matthew Flinders, *Democratic Drift, Majoritarian Modification and Democratic Anomie in the United Kingdom* (Oxford, Oxford University Press, 2010) 287–88.

attention to the implications for the relationship with the Commons. Central government has tended to treat each devolved system as a discrete entity, and each territorial model differs significantly from the other. This divergence, it should be noted, does not stem exclusively from attitudes within the UK executive, with influences such as the particular political and cultural characteristics of the areas involved playing an important part.

During the early period of the Coalition formed in 2010, simultaneous government plans existed to carry out a major alteration in the number and structure of parliamentary constituencies; establish a new form of voter registration; hold a referendum on electoral reform; introduce an elected House of Lords; and create fixed-term parliaments. No official attempt took place formally to link assessment of these packages, despite their obvious connections and their combined implication for Parliament as an institution. Nor did the UK Government appear fully to consider the implications for the UK as whole of the referendum on Scottish independence held in 2014. Once again, pronouncements from the main pro-union forces during the campaign tended to treat Scotland and arrangements for its governance in isolation, without proper reference to the whole. The culmination of this compartmentalisation came with the Vow, made to the people of Scotland, yet impacting upon the entire UK.

There also appears to have been a failure within policy-forming circles and beyond fully to appreciate the need to reassess traditional constitutional understandings. For instance, the doctrine of parliamentary sovereignty as once conceived, in legal and practical terms, needs significant modification, or else abandonment. A wide and overt acknowledgement of this necessity has not yet taken place, partly because there is room for doubt about what precisely has ever been the meaning of this concept. If fundamental principles and associated practical arrangements were contained in a written constitution, understanding their nature might be easier; altering them would require adherence to a specified procedure and an alteration of the words in the document. Under such circumstances, it would be harder to avoid recognising the advent of change. Furthermore, the transformation of recent decades has been of such a scale that it could be argued a new constitution has come into existence.[49] If this interpretation is correct, then this fresh entity has yet to undergo consideration, let alone receive approval, through a specific, single official procedure.

The lack of specific constitutional entrenchment in the UK could suggest that the many changes that have occurred are not secure and might be reversed as readily as they came about. The strict legal position would seem to be that a Parliament intent on doing so could abolish any of the innovations introduced. In 1983, the Labour Party General Election Manifesto committed the Party, if it formed a government, to negotiating an exit from the EEC, with no mention of a special domestic process being involved. The Conservative Party has committed to repealing the Human Rights Act 1998 and possibly withdrawing from the ECHR, creating a similar impression that they would be straightforward actions

---

[49] Bogdanor, *The New British Constitution* (n 2).

not demanding a higher level of consent than normal, beyond some kind of consultation with devolved institutions. But in practice, many of the transformations under consideration here have gained a protected position. In some cases the way in which they were executed has helped entrench them. The holding of referendums on continued EEC membership, and on the different manifestations of devolution, has contributed to an idea that they could be overturned only on the basis of further such plebiscites (notwithstanding the Labour pledge of 1983). Furthermore, the European Communities Act 1972, providing for UK participation in European integration, and the Human Rights Act 1998 are legally entrenched up to a point, as we will see. It is an irony that a torrent of constitutional alteration, possible partly because of the flexible dimension of UK arrangements, has contributed to the limited development of quasi—but not yet explicit—constitutional entrenchment.

This initial consideration of the frenetic but coherent period of constitutional change dating from the 1950s prompts a preliminary observation. It is often held that the introduction of a written constitution requires a crisis such as invasion or revolution. The lack of such an upheaval in the UK, it is held, explains the absence of a written constitution. This book has already recounted how English and UK history is littered with texts arising from circumstances of extreme disruption. The UK as a state came into being, set out in the Union documents, with a key object being to avert French peril. Moreover, a closer consideration of recent history points to a different conclusion regarding the idea of the lack of a crisis with fundamental constitutional implications. In fact the rapid loss after the Second World War of the largest ever formal and informal imperial network was a crash that helped trigger an elongated constitutional upheaval. Spectacular loss of status helped transform the country into an arena for debate about—and sometimes vicious conflict over—constitutional change, and a laboratory for experimenting with it. An ongoing constitutional convention, undeclared and disorganised, began.

In some accounts constitutional reform is a tedious subject or an abstract distraction from more important day to day issues. Yet whatever those who express such views may purport to believe, the nature of our system of government has been a central political concern for half a century. Some of the most important tendencies and events in recent UK history have influenced this trend, and it has in turn impacted upon them. Constitutional controversy has helped split and create parties, and both destroy and bring to power governments. It is connected to monumental shifts in social behaviour. Regardless of the assertions of those who dismiss constitutional discourse, it is part of the essence of the UK. The problem is not a lack of excitement or relevance, as they claim, but an excess. Discussing the way the UK is governed, and changing it when appropriate, are both healthy activities. But the period of transformation is associated with certain growing tensions. Perhaps the best way of moving beyond this episode of post-imperial constitutional trauma would be widely to recognise what has been occurring, and bring it to a conclusion through the introduction of a written constitution.

7

European Integration and its Consequences

THE UNITED KINGDOM (UK) is European. Since the earliest times there has been a circular flow of constitutional influence between, on the one hand, England (and subsequently the UK) and, on the other hand, the wider continent that includes England/the UK within it. In some respects and at certain times in their history England/the UK may appear to have displayed exceptional qualities and a domestic cult of peculiarity has developed. This outlook influences—or infects—present-day constitutional discourse. The analysis already conducted in this book has shown a need to expunge this fetish of difference. For instance, much is made of the undoubtedly real English tradition of empiricism. Associated with it is a tendency to ground constitutional declarations in history, rather than abstraction. It is held that such qualities mark out England—and by extension, the UK—as peculiar.[1] Setting aside that England, which ceased to exist as an independent state in 1707, does not equate entirely with the UK, other qualifications and reservations are necessary. Philosophers such as Edmund Burke do not monopolise English thought: the chief contemporary opponent of this Irishman, after all, was Thomas Paine, born in England. Moreover, the appeal to tradition in key texts from Anglo-Saxon times onwards was often misleading and could provide inspiration abroad for revolutionary constitution-builders of the future. The producers of these English documents were susceptible to wider European intellectual influence (and able in turn to impact upon such thought), and the texts came about in the context of intra-continental historical dynamics. Furthermore, in the mid-seventeenth century, England set itself apart in a way that contradicts the stereotype: in both thought and practice, it innovated through moving away from the need for a constitution to rest in custom and precedent.

In place of a thesis of separateness, therefore, should come an understanding of the present characteristics of the UK constitutional culture that locates it within the historic settings of the UK, the wider continent and the interaction between the two. Ongoing European developments, including the process of continental integration, emerge from a past in which the UK has shared, and in this

---

[1] See eg: Martin Loughlin, *The British Constitution: A Very Short Introduction* (Oxford, Oxford University Press, 2013).

sense they cannot be alien to it. Indeed, the European unification concept is to a significant extent an outgrowth of UK currents of thought. Moreover, the UK as a state shares important constitutional characteristics with the project of European union. Nonetheless, the aforementioned school of supposed UK distinction is relevant, though not as a tool of analysis, but as a phenomenon in its own right requiring investigation. This cultural trait, regardless (or perhaps because) of any weaknesses in its intellectual grounding, creates problems for the UK in its engagement with the post-Second World War pattern of European incorporation. It is an important part of why the UK is different. But the UK is still European, since all European countries are in their own ways distinct from each other. They all occupy particular spaces on an assortment of European spectrums of analysis.

It is certainly the case that in some important ways the UK is an outlier, particularly in its lack of a written constitution and the continued prevalence within it of the doctrine of parliamentary sovereignty. Membership of the European Union (EU) has caused constitutional trauma within the UK. To explore these complex phenomena, the following chapter begins with a consideration of the European integration project, and the relationship between it and the UK. Next there follows a consideration of the direct impact of UK membership of the EU in terms of constitutional arrangements and debates surrounding them. Finally, the chapter considers the varied and powerful secondary consequences of the EU for the UK constitution.

EUROPEAN INTEGRATION AND THE UK CONSTITUTION

Some of the direct impetus for the commencement of post-war European integration came from the horrific experience of 1939–45 and the desire to avert its recurrence. At the same time individual states saw the project as a vehicle for their particular objectives. The concept received positive encouragement from the United States, and the negative motivation of fear of the Soviet bloc. Those who promoted this scheme sought through shared supranational institutions to establish a secure environment in which democracy could flourish, banishing the dictatorships of previous decades, and prosperity grow. One early and distinct institutional outgrowth of this overall integration process was the Council of Europe. Winston Churchill had promoted the idea of the Council, and it formed in 1949 following an agreement made in London. It produced a key treaty, the European Convention on Human Rights, the following year. The development of the Council came to run in parallel with that of a separate organisation that is now known as the EU, the most important component of the European movement. It began as the European Economic Community in 1957 with six Member States (the European Coal and Steel Community of 1951 was an important precursor); it has now expanded to 28, with five actual and three potential candidates to join in future. Varied spheres of operation exist: justice and security; regional development; external policy, security and resilience; and culture. But it is the economic foundation that is the most important. The European single currency operates in 17 of the Member States.[2]

The EU has taken on some of the features commonly associated with a federation, a system under which powers are shared between different governmental levels.[3] There is a division of responsibilities between component states and the higher tier, the basic principle of which is expounded in Article 4(1) of the Treaty on European Union, one of the key documents setting out the structure and operation of the organisation. It emphasises that 'competences not conferred upon the Union in the Treaties remain with the Member States'. At European level there exists an executive (the Commission); a directly elected Parliament with growing powers; a body composed of the Member States (the Council of Ministers); and a court (the European Court of Justice (ECJ)). Unlike a typical federation, external policies are far more the business of EU Member States than the central organisation. Nonetheless, the use of the label 'federal'—a common part of the vocabulary of UK opponents of the EU—has substance to it. It is the implication that 'federal' simply means centralisation that is misleading, as the citation above from the Treaty on European Union suggests.

A major shortcoming in the EU—both for supporters and those less sympathetic—is the lack of democratic accountability for its central activities. The most obvious solution to this problem is to establish a clearer connection between outcomes of European parliamentary elections and the way in which the EU is governed. Doubters argue that since there is no European *demos*—that is to say, a self-aware European political community is absent—meaningful pan-European democracy is not possible. Consequently, they hold, the most appropriate level from which to derive democratic legitimacy is that of the Member State. The gap they identify is real. Perhaps the history of the UK offers an answer. Like the EU, the UK is a multinational entity, though not as diverse as the EU. In contrast to the gradual development of the EU, as Brendan Simms argues, the formal creation of Great Britain in 1706–07 was a sudden event, involving the Treaty and Acts of Union, establishing a state that was far more politically centralised than the EU has yet become.[4] At this early stage a sense of Britishness was not pervasive in the territories involved: it can be said there was no British *demos*. Cultural change followed institutional. An incorporation as sudden and far-reaching as that taking place with the inception of Great Britain in the early eighteenth century may not be possible. Indeed, given the difficulties experienced recently by the UK, it might not be desirable. But the establishment of a clear link between the casting of votes in European parliamentary elections and the occupancy of senior offices

---

[2] See eg: Desmond Dinan, *Europe Recast: A History of European Union* (Basingstoke, Palgrave Macmillan, 2004); Alan S Milward (with the assistance of George Brennan and Federico Romero), *The European Rescue of the Nation-State* (London, Routledge, 2000).

[3] See eg: NW Barber, *The Constitutional State* (Oxford, Oxford University Press, 2010) 172–81.

[4] Brendan Simms, 'Towards a mighty union: how to create a democratic European superpower' (2012) 88(1) *International Affairs* 49.

in Brussels and consequently the policies pursued there could add a new popular resonance to the European political sphere. Such was the rationale lying behind the nomination by European parties contesting the European parliamentary elections of 2014 of their favoured candidates for the presidency of the Commission. The UK stance in opposing the making of the appointment in this way was founded in the view that a European *demos* did not exist. Yet the UK approach, had it prevailed, would have represented a blockage to the possible development of the very quality it singled out as missing.

Further criticism of the EU centres on its role as a producer of economic and social regulations binding upon all participants. Those who raise these objections in the UK depict the EU as a body disposed towards intervention for its own sake, expanding beyond its appropriate remit and stifling economic vitality through the layering of unnecessary burdens upon business.[5] This scenario has clear constitutional connotations, and is part of the asserted case for the alteration of UK terms of membership of the EU, or for UK exit. It rests on fundamental misapprehensions. The key purpose and effect of these rule-making powers is to alleviate constraints applying to commercial concerns operating within the EU as a whole. The Single European Act 1986—a European initiative of which the UK Government under Margaret Thatcher was an important instigator—sought to create the conditions necessary for a single European market. Policymakers judged this development necessary as, while the European Economic Community (EEC) had removed internal customs barriers (and set single external tariffs), it remained possible for individual Member States to pursue protectionist policies through regulatory regimes that favoured domestic interests. The Single Market project consequently aimed to eliminate so-called 'non-tariff barriers'. It was to achieve this objective through the issuing of rules at European level, overriding those previously introduced by particular Member States, leading to the construction of a single regulatory system, facilitating a Single Market. While the production of new regulations may appear, when considered in exclusion, to be an addition to the overall volume of such rules, this impression is misleading, since they are the alternative to a multiplicity of measures, with each individual Member State able to follow its own path.[6] Nor is the idea of imposing homogeneity from above unknown to UK or English history: it is visible, for instance, in the Magna Carta stipulations about uniform weights and measures; and was intrinsic to the union of Scotland and England, and later Great Britain and Ireland.

Aside from the possible comparisons between the UK and EU, a subject of more direct importance to current UK discourse is that of the constitutional compatibility between the two. Though it is necessary to qualify theories of exceptionality, some features of the UK political system, and attachment to them, have created complications for UK participation in continental integration. Policymakers

---

[5] See eg: Mats Persson, *Out of Control? Measuring a Decade of EU Regulation* (London, Open Europe, 2009).

[6] Andrew Blick, *EU Regulation and the European Single Market: Incompatible or Inseparable?* (London, Federal Trust, 2013).

have in their deliberations been concerned about constitutional issues, such as the implications for national sovereignty. While such apprehensions are shared with other countries, one particular feature of its traditional arrangements—the doctrine of parliamentary sovereignty—has proved a problem for the UK that does not afflict other Member States in the same way.[7] Constitutional considerations have often figured prominently in 'Eurosceptic' narratives also, again with parliamentary sovereignty at their core. As Enoch Powell—an influential figure in this area—argued in 1976 when explaining his opposition to UK membership, participation was an exceptional problem for the UK among European states because 'in Britain self-government and independence are uniquely identified with the untrammelled authority of a representative assembly, Parliament'.[8] Powell identified a genuine psychological-cultural-constitutional barrier. Yet, on the other hand, another tradition of thought has existed in the UK, potentially more amenable to the existence of the sharing of authority between different institutional levels. This federal school included within it a European current. It merits close consideration as a corrective to possible caricatures of the UK in its relationship with the EU.

In 1871, the eminent historian John Seeley gave a speech to the Peace Society, later adapted as a journal article. His title was 'The United States of Europe'. Seeley insisted that: 'The nations of Europe must constitute themselves into some form of federation'. In his view the only way to 'abolish war in Europe' would be through the establishment of a 'completely new citizenship. We must cease to be mere Englishmen, Frenchmen, Germans and must begin to take as much pride in calling ourselves Europeans'.[9] A federal outlook was not unique in the UK in the nineteenth century, but those who subscribed to it were far more likely to focus on structures for empire[10] (which was the primary interest of Seeley himself) and the internal configuration of the UK. However, by the late 1930s, global–political circumstances had driven Europe to the front of the federal agenda.

In 1938 the campaign group, Federal Union, formed. Though there were different views within the organisation about what the geographical focus should be, prominent within it were supporters of the idea that the best response to the threat to democracy of the time was European integration, perhaps centring on a union of the UK and France. By mid-1940 Federal Union achieved a membership of more than 12,000, though it subsequently receded.[11] Clearly the organisation—and it still operates today—did not achieve its immediate goals. But it deserves

---

[7] Alan S Milward, *The UK and The European Community*, Vol 1: *The Rise and Fall of a National Strategy, 1945–1963* (London, Frank Cass, 2002) 442–50.

[8] Enoch Powell, *Reflections of a Statesman: The Writings and Speeches of Enoch Powell* (London, Bellew Publishing, 1991) 478.

[9] Michael Burgess, *The British Tradition of Federalism* (London, Leicester University Press, 1995) 133.

[10] See: Duncan Bell, *The Idea of Greater Britain: Empire and the Future of World Order, 1860–1900* (Princeton NJ, Princeton University Press, 2007); Duncan Bell (ed), *Victorian Visions of Global Order* (Cambridge, Cambridge University Press, 2007).

[11] Richard Mayne and John Pinder, *Federal Union: The Pioneers: A History of Federal Union* (Basingstoke, Macmillan, 1990).

to be taken seriously, particularly in this early phase, for a number of reasons.[12] Federal Union is representative of an important stream of constitutional thought. It was prescient regarding the future development of continental unification. The impact it made both at popular level and among the policy and opinion-forming community was swift and extensive, with extensive and approving press coverage. Federal Union attracted associates of impressive calibre. A cluster of leading intellectuals gathered around it, including William Beveridge, Lionel Robbins and Ivor Jennings. Friedrich von Hayek provided his own free market tilt on federalism, diverging from others attached to the movement who advocated economic planning. Two future Labour Prime Ministers, Clement Attlee and Harold Wilson, were supporters, though Federal Union had no specific party affiliation. The group helped generate the political climate in which the offer of union to France of June 1940, discussed in the introduction to this book, took place. Finally—and perhaps most important of all—Federal Union had an influence on the wider continent, both through contact with members of governments in exile in London during the war, and more specifically on one individual.

The largest structure in the European Parliament complex in Brussels today is called the 'Altiero Spinelli Building'. It takes its name from an Italian political campaigner, thinker and Member of the European Parliament, who lived from 1907 to 1986. He was over a period of four decades a crucial figure in the promotion of a federal Europe, and influenced the actual continental unification project, though he did not always regard it as sufficiently radical. Spinelli helped instigate the integration movement in the 1940s, and in the 1980s his campaign for a federal European constitution indirectly prompted the introduction of the Single European Act. It is important not to exaggerate the role of the European federalists in bringing about integration.[13] But neither should we dismiss their success in placing ideas on the agenda, thereby widening the conceptual framework of policymakers, and in shaping the programmes of European institutions once formed, the personnel of which could include those of a federalist inclination. Their work took place over the long term, and many of their ideas came into being, even if not always as an immediate consequence of their efforts. Beginning his political journey as a member of the Communist Party, the Fascist regime detained Spinelli for a period of 16 years from 1927 to 1943. During this period he drifted increasingly away from doctrinaire communism. While in the prison camp on the island of Ventotene, he was the main contributor to a text written in the middle of 1941 with a fellow prisoner, Ernesto Rossi, entitled *The Ventotene Manifesto*. Advocating a movement for the transformation of Europe into a 'steady federal state', it was a crucial initiating statement. Spinelli followed it up with further analysis and proposals and, after his release in 1943, political activism.[14]

---

[12]   See eg: Mark Mazower, *Dark Continent: Europe's Twentieth Century* (London, Penguin, 1999) 203.
[13]   Milward, *The European Rescue of the Nation-State* (n 2) ch 1.
[14]   John Pinder (ed), *Altiero Spinelli and the British Federalists: Writings by Beveridge, Robbins and Spinelli, 1937–1943* (London, Federal Trust, 1998).

While the manifesto might have been an incubus for all that UK 'Eurosceptics' dislike about the integration project and see as incompatible with their own domestic traditions, Spinelli wrote under the influence of UK thought. It reached him through a mentor, Luigi Einaudi, an economist of liberal inclination who went on to be the inaugural president of the post-war Italian Republic.[15] Einaudi had recommended European federation as early as 1918. He regarded the Union of England and Scotland as an admirable model,[16] and saw continental union as a means of furthering English constitutional values on a wider stage. Einaudi was one of a number in Piedmont at the time advocating such views. For this group, UK thinkers including Lord Acton (of mixed European background), James Bryce, Seeley and Henry Sidgwick were important influences. Because of his personal standing, the authorities allowed Einaudi to carry on correspondence with political detainees. The literature he dispatched to Ventontene included certain Federal Union publications he had acquired. These UK texts made a powerful impression upon Spinelli, who wrote in the 1970s that 'Their analysis of the political and economic perversion that nationalism leads to, and their reasoned presentation of the federal alternative, have remained to this day impressed on my memory like a revelation'. It seems that the fabled English practicality was at work in an unexpected way. Spinelli noted that he was 'looking for mental clarity and precision'. Consequently he did not find the 'foggy and contorted ideological federalism of a Proudhon or a Mazzini' appealing. Rather, he preferred 'the clean precise thinking of these English federalists', whose work provided both insight into 'the chaos into which Europe was plunging' and a means of 'devising alternatives'.[17]

After the Second World War, the UK eventually came to participate in a project it had helped inspire. By the early 1960s, UK policymakers began to see European integration as a success from which they could benefit, and could not afford to ignore. Admission to the EEC eventually came 10 years later. The UK has, in the decades that followed, often been less than enthusiastic about many features of the unfolding European project.[18] It renegotiated some of its terms of membership shortly after joining. The UK is not a member of the Single Currency. Successive UK governments have proudly achieved opt outs from EU spheres of activity in areas such as justice and home affairs. Nonetheless, the UK has been a member of the EU for more than 40 years, with unavoidably deep implications. An experiment to which the UK had made an intellectual and political contribution, but subsequently spurned, would from 1973 transform the UK constitution.

---

[15] Ibid, 2.

[16] Burgess, *The British Tradition of Federalism* (n 9) 173.

[17] Pinder, *Altiero Spinelli and the British Federalists* (n 14) 2–4.

[18] See: Hugo Young, *This Blessed Plot: Britain and Europe from Churchill to Blair* (London, Macmillan, 1998).

THE EUROPEAN COMMUNITIES ACT 1972

Taking part in European integration has posed fundamental challenges to key tenets of the UK system. It calls into question the doctrine of parliamentary sovereignty, creating a body to rival the law-making position of the Westminster legislature, qualifying the power of Parliament to amend and repeal an earlier Act, and making it possible for a court to disapply an Act of the UK Parliament. The organisation that the UK joined in 1973 had already developed the characteristics that would raise these issues.[19] Following the judgment of the ECJ in the *Van Gend en Loos* case of 1963, domestic courts of Member States were responsible for upholding rights that, under European law, were direct in their effect. With this principle in mind, as part of the judgment in the *Bulmer* case in 1974 at the English Court of Appeal, Lord Denning stated that 'the Treaty [giving effect to UK membership] is like an incoming tide. It flows into the estuaries and up the rivers. It cannot be held back'. He stated that Parliament had determined that 'the Treaty is henceforward to be part of our law'. When considering 'transactions which cross the frontiers' it would no longer be appropriate to 'speak or think of English law as something on its own'. Instead, the proper approach was to 'speak and think of Community law, of Community rights and obligations'. Moreover, 'we must give effect to them'.

The treaties establishing the EU do not explicitly deal with the matter of which takes precedence when European law conflicts with that of a Member State. However, it is essential to the effectiveness of the EU that its enactments supersede all others. In the *Van Gend en Loos* case in 1963 the ECJ found that 'the EEC Treaty has created its own legal system which ... became an integral part of the legal systems of the member states and which their courts are bound to apply'. The Court went on: 'the member states have limited their sovereign rights, albeit within limited fields, and have thus created a body of law which binds both their nationals and themselves'. With the *Costa* (1964) and *Simmenthal* (1978) cases the ECJ established that European law as applied in domestic courts overrode not only pre-existing legislation, but any new instrument passed at Member State level after the introduction of a European measure that it contradicts. Accompanying the Lisbon Treaty of 2007, 'Declaration 17' referred to the supremacy of EU law, stating that successive judgments had firmly fixed it (though as a declaration only it lacked full legal authority).

The incorporation of these principles into the UK system comes via the European Communities Act 1972. Section 2(1) makes the general provision that EU law—as contained in or provided for under treaty—is 'without further enactment to be given legal effect or used in the United Kingdom'. It will be, the Act

---

[19] For the following accounts of legislation and case law, see: Colin Turpin and Adam Tomkins, *British Government and the Constitution*, 7th edn (Cambridge, Cambridge University Press, 2011) 313–54; AW Bradley and KD Ewing, *Constitutional and Administrative Law* (Harlow, Longman, 2011) 125–44.

states, 'recognised and available in law, and … enforced, allowed and followed accordingly'. The European legal order finds its way into the law of Member States through a variety of means. Regulations, for instance, transfer directly, in full: in the UK, secondary legislation under section 2(2) of the 1972 Act performs this task. Directives allow Member States more leeway as to how precisely they will achieve a particular end goal. In the UK, ministers may decide that administrative action is sufficient, or opt to make statutory provision.

This complexity in the relationship between European and UK law helps make clear measurement of the former as a proportion of the latter impossible.[20] That the EU has made and continues to make an important contribution to the legal framework of the UK is certainly true. However, efforts—in particular on the part of those who are uneasy with European integration—to make precise claims regarding the percentage of UK legislation that is of European origin are doomed. It is not always clear whether a given UK measure is strictly and purely derived from European obligations. A government may use a directive as a cue to introduce a Bill containing provisions it wished to implement anyway, and its clauses may contain additional provisions that the European directive does not demand. Furthermore, there are problems in determining an appropriate counting method. For instance, should we go simply by numbers of instruments passed, or take into account their length, or seek to consider how many discrete tasks they perform (some of which may be 'European' in origin, others of which may not)? Moreover, resolving this particular difficulty would not help to assess the impact of individual provisions, both upon existing law and the environment they addressed. Finally, exercises of this nature focus on the production of legislation. Yet a full consideration of law must extend more widely, taking into account judicial decisions, which clearly have both European and domestic sources, but would probably be no easier quantitatively to measure.

A further controversy surrounding European law is qualitative in form. Section 2(4) of the 1972 Act states that 'any enactment passed or to be passed, shall be construed and have effect subject to the foregoing provisions of this section'. This stipulation provides a basis for European law to take precedence over other law, both predating and post-dating the 1972 Act, even Acts of Parliament. The *Factortame* cases of 1990 and 1991 were crucial to the realisation in practice of the pre-eminence of European law, and in particular the establishment of the principle that the courts will disapply an Act of Parliament in as far as it is irreconcilable with European law, even if the offending Act dates from after the European Communities Act 1972. In a passage from his judgment in the second *Factortame* case, Lord Bridge displayed a desire common in constitutional history: to seek to ground a decision that might seem radical in rules that were supposedly already prevailing. He held that a 'novel and dangerous invasion by a Community institution of the sovereignty of the United Kingdom Parliament' was not under way.

---

[20] Vaughne Miller, *How Much Legislation Comes from Europe?* (London, House of Commons Library, 2010).

His reasoning was that the supremacy of European law was either intrinsic to the treaties, or at least 'well established … long before the United Kingdom joined the Community'. Lord Bridge concluded: 'whatever limitation of its sovereignty Parliament accepted when it enacted the European Communities Act 1972 was entirely voluntary'. Debate surrounds the true implications of membership of the EU and cases such as *Factorame* for the position of the UK legislature.[21] Parliament almost certainly retains the ability to alter or abolish the European Communities Act if it passes an Act explicitly stating this purpose. In this sense parliamentary pre-eminence—or as some would have it, sovereignty—continues. However, the European Communities Act as judicially interpreted is clearly incompatible with the idea that a later Act always overrides an earlier one even when it does not specifically set out the intention to do so. Parliament in 1972 created a statute that has proved immune to implied repeal by Parliament in future. A key part of the Dicey version of parliamentary sovereignty was no longer sustainable. Other insistences by Dicey—that no body outside Parliament could rule an Act invalid or challenge its position of legislative supremacy—also appeared redundant.

Concerns about the constitutional implications of European integration, particularly its impact upon parliamentary sovereignty, have been a persistent theme in UK political discourse for longer than the UK has been a member of what is now the EU. In 2011, partly through a desire to reduce pressure over Europe from hostile Conservative backbenchers, the Coalition sought to use statute to protect the position of Parliament from subordination to a higher legal order. Informally known as the 'sovereignty clause', section 18 of the European Union Act 2011 is headed 'Status of EU law dependent on continuing statutory basis'. It states that 'Directly applicable or directly effective EU law … falls to be recognised and available in law in the United Kingdom only by virtue of' an Act of Parliament. It is not clear that this provision did anything more than state the existing position as most observers already understood it. Moreover, it is reasonable to question the logical basis for an Act of Parliament that declares the authority of Parliament. If this Act safeguards the authority of other Acts, from where is its power derived and why is it not present in those other Acts? Section 18, furthermore, failed to attain its political objective, with Conservative MPs becoming ever more troublesome. Consequently, early in 2013 the Prime Minister pledged that—if in a position to do so after the next general election—he would seek reform of the EU, and hold a referendum. It would offer a choice between continued EU membership under the terms he had obtained, or exit. This commitment draws attention to another change in the operation of the UK constitution with connections to European integration.

---

[21] For a recent discussion, see: Paul Craig, 'Britain in the European Union' in Jeffrey Jowell and Dawn Oliver (eds), *The Changing Constitution*, 7th edn (Oxford, Oxford University Press, 2011).

THE RISE OF THE REFERENDUM: 1975 TO THE PRESENT

Participation in the EEC—a development of the highest direct constitutional significance—began a chain reaction of further change. During the lead-up to membership in the early 1970s, controversy grew. It would be difficult to over-state how important the European issue, including the constitutional dimension to it, has been. The politics of Europe—which are inescapable inside or outside the EU—are dangerous. They have been a continuous source of deep and shift-ing division, not only between parties but within them.[22] As compared with their broad approaches at the time of entry, Labour is now more sympathetic to European integration than it was, the Conservative Party far less. At different times both parties have endured sustained periods of electoral failure at least par-tially attributable to Europe. A split in the Labour Party, beginning in the 1970s, led eventually to the formation in 1981 of the Social Democratic Party (SDP), a more centrist group that—in contrast with the Labour stance of the time—was supportive of the EEC. The Conservatives have suffered European convulsions, especially from the late 1980s. Though no full break of the SDP type occurred, the United Kingdom Independence Party has some of the characteristics of a Conservative splinter (though it has more complexity than this label captures), an objective of which has been to force the Conservative Party towards ever more radical stances regarding UK membership. The European issue is not solely a game involving the two main parties; it and the turbulence it induced were far more pervasive. Continental integration has been of great importance to others, such as the Scottish National Party, which has also held varied stances over time. Liberal Democrats have made a point of their pro-European outlook, though attitudes among party supporters are more divergent than formal policy stances might suggest. Parties such as the Greens have been able to make political progress at the European level through securing members of the Parliament, linking with similar groups from other Member States. The combined impact on the political scene has been and continues to be of an historic scale, matching the fundamental changes to the global role and domestic arrangements of the UK that membership of the EU engages.

Political turbulence intertwined with constitutional. The original basis for the legitimacy of UK membership was that there had been three votes of principle during the prolonged process leading to accession (the first two of which were entirely free from whipping). Ironically given the implications this approach was in keeping with the traditional doctrine of parliamentary sovereignty. By the early 1970s, opponents of joining were considering the idea of a referendum. It was an

[22] See: Nicholas Crowson and James McKay, 'Britain in Europe? Conservative and Labour Attitudes to European Integration since the Second World War' in William Mulligan and Brendan Simms (eds), *The Primacy of Foreign Policy in British History, 1660–2000: How Strategic Concerns Shaped Modern Britain* (Basingstoke, Palgrave Macmillan, 2010).

innovative proposition for the UK. Northern Ireland saw a border poll in 1973 and local authorities held plebiscites. But never before 1975 had a vote of this sort taken place on a UK-wide basis, though—another irony—they were common on parts of the continental mainland. The Labour Party contested the February 1974 General Election promising to renegotiate UK terms of membership of the EEC, then hold a plebiscite on whether the UK should stay in or leave. This was a ploy of the kind for which the Labour leader Harold Wilson was famous. He was able to exploit growing public hostility towards the EEC around the time of entry. At the same time he kept his options open as to what decision his government would recommend to voters. Crucially, it was possible for Wilson to finesse divisions in his own party about the issue, postponing the ultimate decision and to some extent transferring it from politicians to electorate. Eventually, after obtaining limited concessions in negotiations, the Labour Government allotted to advocate remaining within the EEC. Some ministers dissented and obtained by special arrangement the right publicly to express their views. On 5 June 1975 the campaign for a 'yes' to continued membership won, with 67.2 per cent of support on a turnout of 64.5 per cent. But it did not settle the issue for long, either within the Labour Party, which by the early 1980s came to advocate withdrawal; or in the country as a whole, where the idea of leaving has continued to attract significant support at various times.

The looming prospect of the referendum prompted the newly installed Leader of the Opposition, Margaret Thatcher, to give a perceptive and prescient speech to the House of Commons on 11 March 1975.[23] She began by identifying a need to give full consideration to the implications of introducing this device to UK politics. Applying referendums more widely to legislation, Thatcher held, would have meant 'no Race Relations Act, immigration would have been stopped, abortions would still be illegal and hanging still be in force'. In other words, in her analysis, direct democracy could produce different outcomes to the representative variety, reflecting the less liberal views of the wider public, as compared with those at higher level. Thatcher stressed that the proposed referendum would be the first to take place across the entire UK. Yet the government White Paper preceding the referendum, she complained, did not consider the constitutional dimension, and failed to clarify whether the outcome would have legal force. She observed 'how difficult it will be to frame a question which suits everyone and is regarded as fair by everyone'. For the Labour Government, Thatcher held, it was merely 'a tactical device to get over a split in their own party'. Forty years later, a Conservative leader, David Cameron, would be vulnerable to a similar charge. Given the perspective Labour had in 1975, Thatcher regretted, the impact upon the constitution was not a prominent concern. Here, then, was an exposition of how the unwritten UK constitution is vulnerable to party political abuse. Later in her speech, Thatcher pushed this thesis to its conclusion.

[23] HC Deb 11 March 1975, vol 888, cols 304–17.

While the government might seek to depict the referendum as a one-off response to an extraordinary circumstance, not for repetition, Thatcher cautioned that it was impossible to be so definite. 'Once the principle of the referendum has been introduced into British politics, it will not rest with any one party to put a convenient limit to its use'. She recalled the remark that the Labour Prime Minister Clement Attlee made in 1945, that referendums were 'a splendid weapon for demagogues and dictators'. Thatcher noted that both Dicey and Churchill could be 'prayed in aid on both sides' of the debate about referendums, and observed a tendency for opponents of a particular change to advocate referendums as a blocking device.

Thatcher acknowledged that the use of referendums occurred in other democracies. But she cautioned against superficial comparisons, and seeking to 'divorce one constitutional feature of a country from its whole content'. She proposed that the referendum be considered from four perspectives: parliamentary sovereignty, collective responsibility, 'representative Parliament', and 'the consequences for treaty obligations which have already been assumed'. She held that retrospective referendums on legislation would be a 'serious breach' of parliamentary sovereignty, that would create the impression of the introduction of a 'different rule to validate laws'. The holding of 'several' such votes would be sufficient to embed the practice and 'create a new rule'. In such circumstances the implication would be that certain measures necessitated approval in this way, but that 'others do not'. But in the absence of 'a written constitution one might ask: which proposals and what kind of measures?' She suspected that the answer to this question was 'in cases of constitutional change'. Yet there were difficulties inherent in precisely demarcating this category, since 'in the British tradition … so much depends on convention and precedent'. The use of referendums could be satisfactory if provided with 'a proper constitutional foundation' setting out the circumstances in which it was appropriate to use it. Yet fulfilling this condition would entail 'like many other democratic countries, going as far as a written constitution or at least part of the way'. She held that the implications of such a development for parliamentary sovereignty would be immense. Yet 'if our sense of constitutional rules and conventions is weakening, there may come a time when some such course should be considered'.

The 1975 vote arose from political contingencies of the time but had a lasting constitutional impact. While precedent for it was slight, the 1975 referendum itself served to provide a legitimising example for the future. Referendums have become an accepted feature of UK politics, used for constitutional decision-making. Since 1975, plebiscites have taken place in Northern Ireland, Scotland, Wales, Greater London and the North East region of England over the issue of devolved governance. Local authorities have held referendums about their structure and on policy issues. In 2011, the second UK-wide plebiscite took place, on the voting system used for elections to the House of Commons. Then in 2014, Scotland voted on whether to remain within the UK. Many of the concerns Thatcher had raised were valid. But for some kinds of decision—such as the setting up of new tiers of governance, or the secession of territory—they were the most appropriate device available. It is the political circumstances surrounding the plebiscite that determine how satisfactory and effective a mechanism it will be.[24]

As Thatcher observed, referendums represent a challenge to parliamentary sovereignty, in practice if not in a strict legal sense. Initially, Parliament, when providing for the holding of these votes, made them advisory rather than binding. But it would be politically difficult to reject a decision taken in this way. In every case Parliament has abided by referendums (though it has sometimes required more than a simple majority to be in favour of change). Then in 2011, referendums held on the extension of Welsh devolution and electoral reform were legally binding. Parliament retained a theoretical power after the votes to repeal or amend the Acts creating these obligations, thereby releasing itself from them. Yet this scenario is probably even less plausible than an evasion of a verdict under the earlier kind of referendum arrangement. The European Union Act 2011 marked a further development. Rather than providing for a one-off referendum on a single contemplated action, it created a referendum requirement for a range of possible future actions entailing the pooling of further responsibilities at EU level. The Act was another manifestation of the impact European integration has had upon the UK constitution. Some at the time noted the irony that the Act containing this measure also included in section 18 an attempt to assert parliamentary sovereignty.

A 2010 report from the House of Lords Select Committee on the Constitution, *Referendums in the United Kingdom*, was remarkable for the extent to which it accepted a surrender of influence by Parliament. The committee identified 'significant drawbacks to the use of referendums'. Yet, it went on, 'we acknowledge arguments that, if referendums are to be used, they are most appropriately used in relation to fundamental constitutional issues'. The implication was that the more important the decision, the more likely it was that Parliament was not equipped to take it. While it was not 'possible to provide a precise definition of what constitutes a "fundamental constitutional issue"' the committee had a list of measures it believed came within this category. They were: abolition of the monarchy; leaving the EU; the departure of any of the nations of the UK from the Union; the abolition of either of the Houses of Parliament; a change in the electoral system used for the House of Commons; a change in the currency used in the UK; and the introduction of a written constitution. The committee stressed that the list was not definitive. But it was certainly extensive and suggested a serious reduction in the practical extent of parliamentary sovereignty.[25] In 35 years, the referendum had made progress from a supposed one-off extraordinary measure to form part of the working constitution.

---

[24] See: Matt Qvortrup, *Referendums and Ethnic Conflict* (Philadelphia PA, University of Pennsylvania Press, 2014); Vernon Bogdanor, *The People and the Party System: The Referendum and Electoral Reform in British Politics* (Cambridge, Cambridge University Press, 1981).

[25] Select Committee on the Constitution, *Referendums in the United Kingdom* (HL 2009–10, 99) 27.

THE FRACTURING OF COLLECTIVE RESPONSIBILITY

The Harold Wilson schema for managing the political environment produced by UK entry into the EEC had a further constitutional strand. He managed to secure a Cabinet decision in advance of the 1975 referendum that the government would recommend to the public the option of continued membership. But the only way he felt he could secure this agreement while avoiding damaging ministerial resignations was through allowing public dissent by those who disagreed with participation in the EEC during the lead-up to the vote. By convention, free and frank discussion about important matters takes place inside Cabinet, which is the ultimate decision-making entity within the UK Government. But all ministers, Cabinet-level or below, are required to maintain an outward united front, and if they cannot, they must resign. They are not permitted, when their personal opinions differ from official policy, to reveal that this discrepancy exists. The precise way in which a conclusion came about is to remain private. This overall principle is known as 'collective responsibility'. Developing from the eighteenth century, it made possible the appearance of a cohesive body of ministers who could through their solidarity resist interference from the monarch, and answer as a group to Parliament, and in turn the electorate. While it may often have strained around the edges, it is crucial to the UK constitution, and any clear modification to it is a serious development.

In the mid-1970s, the party Wilson led, and the Cabinet he chaired, were divided on a range of core issues including the EEC. Holding a unified line was a continuous challenge. On 14 May 1974 Wilson felt it necessary to minute all ministers in charge of departments to remind them of 'the principle of collective responsibility of the Cabinet, as it applies to Ministers in their dealings with the Labour Party'.[26] Then on 21 January 1975, the Cabinet agreed that it would need to decide by the end of March whether—in advance of a referendum—it would advocate remaining within or leaving the EEC. It concluded that those of its members who did not share the view of the majority in Cabinet would be allowed publicly to express their views during the campaign, subject to rules to be laid down. Wilson announced this decision to the House of Commons on 23 January.[27]

The government had a clear precedent for this arrangement. In January 1932 the National Government had agreed a suspension of collective responsibility over the issue of tariff reform. On that day the office of the Prime Minister, Ramsay MacDonald, issued a statement that members who could not agree with 'conclusions arrived at by the majority of their colleagues on the subject of import duties and cognate matters [were] to be at liberty to express their views by

---

[26] The National Archive/Public Record Office (TNA/PRO) PREM 16/437, Prime Minister's Personal Minute, Harold Wilson to ministers in charge of departments (14 May 1974).
[27] Ibid, CAB 193/192, 'Membership of the European Community: Agreement to Differ', Memorandum by Cabinet Office (undated).

speech and vote'.[28] In justifying the decision to the Commons, Stanley Baldwin, the Conservative leader and Lord President of the Council, asked rhetorically: 'Who can say what is constitutional in the conduct of a national government? It is a precedent, an experiment, a new practice to meet a new emergency, and we have collective responsibility for the departure from collective action'.[29] Baldwin sought, therefore, to assert the maintenance of Cabinet cohesion on the grounds that the decision to disagree belonged to the whole group. At the same time he acknowledged that there was novelty in this arrangement. He was correct. The initial proposer of this suspension, Lord Hailsham, Secretary of State for War, had claimed when advancing it that it had a precursor. He told Cabinet he 'recalled a case during the [First World] War when [the Irish Unionist leader] Lord Carson had been allowed to vote against the Government's policy on a particular point'. But Cabinet Office staff investigating the matter in 1975 concluded that the supposed 'Carson Precedent' was a phantom.[30]

On 15 January 1975 the Cabinet Secretary, John Hunt, brought the 1932 arrangement to the attention of Wilson, and on 22 January sent him the relevant papers from the time. Both Wilson and the Foreign Secretary, James Callaghan, sought a 'fuller knowledge of any earlier occasions on which the Cabinet had departed from the application of the doctrine of collective responsibility'. The Foreign and Commonwealth Office historical adviser drafted a paper for them on this subject.[31] Wilson had the antecedent he wanted, claiming in a Commons debate of 23 January 1975 that 1932 offered a 'sound' precedent for his intended course of action.[32] But the flaws in this approach to legitimising constitutional rules and practice are clear. The problem with justification from history is that somewhere in the chain of regression there must be a beginning, an occurrence or a statement of a principle that was new. If it lacks a precursor, then how can it be proper, and in which case, how can it bear the weight of providing justification for that which comes after it? If, however, it is possible to legitimise an original practice or claim by some other means, such as reference to abstract principle, then references to the past become redundant. While the decision taken in 1975 had a clear precursor (from 1932), the 1932 episode itself did not, though Lord Hailsham groped for one. Moreover, while Wilson—unlike Ramsay MacDonald—had a precedent, he introduced some significant modifications to the 1932 approach. In 1932, ministers who disagreed with policy were able both to make speeches and vote in Parliament in accordance with their views; in 1975, they could only vote. In 1932, opponents of the official policy were not allowed to carry out a campaign against it; in 1975 they were. Indeed, their ability to do so was part of the essence of the agreement.

---

[28] Ibid, CAB 107/711, 'Modifications of collective responsibility of the Cabinet', Memorandum by Rohan Butler, Historical Adviser to the Foreign and Commonwealth Office (22 May 1975).

[29] Ibid, CAB 193/192, 'Membership of the European Community: Agreement to Differ' (n 27).

[30] See generally: ibid, CAB 107/711 'Modifications of collective responsibility of the Cabinet' (n 28).

[31] Ibid, CAB 193/192, 'Membership of the European Community: Agreement to Differ' (n 27).

[32] Ibid, CAB 107/711, 'Modifications of collective responsibility of the Cabinet' (n 28).

On 18 March 1975, when Cabinet agreed to recommend a vote to remain within the EEC, seven of its members dissented and gave notice of their intention to utilise the exemption as discussed in January. Wilson informed Parliament on 20 March, through a written answer, who they were; on 24 April he added to the list two ministers outside the Cabinet. The 'agreement to differ' became operative as soon as the Prime Minister announced the Cabinet recommendation about the referendum on 18 March. Wilson informed the Commons on 13 May that it would run until 5 June, the day of the vote, once polling had ceased.[33] He circulated final guidance on ministerial conduct inside government on 3 April,[34] and informed the Commons of the main features of it on 7 April. It permitted ministers to set out a position contrary to the government outside but not within Parliament, and not on foreign trips. On 8 April, Cabinet agreed additionally that while ministers could not speak against the government in Parliament, they could vote as they chose on the Cabinet recommendation. It was 'essential that all Ministers—whether supporting the Government recommendation or not—should avoid personalising, trivializing, or sensationalising the argument'. The rules prohibited ministers from directly confronting each other in public. On 15 May, Cabinet agreed that this prohibition could not apply to broadcasts that constructed confrontations through editing, and also lifted this ban as it applied to radio and television appearances from 1 June until 5 June, the day on which the vote took place. Further detailed provision dealt with issues such as parliamentary activities and the role of civil servants.[35]

It was not long before further suspensions of collective responsibility proved necessary. Once again, the EEC was the motive. During 1977–78, James Callaghan, the Labour Prime Minister who had succeeded Wilson in April 1976, authorised a degree of open dissent among Cabinet members. He did so first over the principle of direct elections to the European Parliament, a crucial step in the direction of a more federal Europe. Second, it was necessary to loosen collective responsibility over the choice of voting system for those elections. A larger gap followed before the next formal relaxation, though not quite as long as that between 1932 and 1974. When it came it went further than before. The Conservative/Liberal Democrat Coalition formed in 2010 introduced generalised provision for an opt out, rather than a more contained and specific exception. Though Europe was not a direct issue at first, the suspensions of the 1970s certainly helped make the arrangements followed from 2010 seem respectable. Under the Coalition, the suspension of collective responsibility became established as a standing possibility and regular occurrence. Three different documents—the *Ministerial Code*, the *Cabinet Manual* and the *Coalition agreement for stability and reform* all referred to collective responsibility applying 'save where it is explicitly set aside'. While there

---

[33] Ibid, CAB 193/192, 'Membership of the European Community: Agreement to Differ' (n 27).
[34] For the guidelines, see: ibid, CAB 103/711, 'Referendum on membership of the European Community', Note by the Prime Minister (3 April 1975).
[35] Ibid, CAB 193/192, 'Membership of the European Community: Agreement to Differ' (n 27).

was thorough documentation of the possibility of breaking with a collective line, there is no evidence of the provision to Coalition ministers of clear guidance of the sort Harold Wilson issued in 1975 regarding how they should conduct themselves when an exemption was in force.

The Coalition *Programme for government* published at the outset of the government stipulated five initial issues over which the partners in the government might openly disagree: which side to support in a referendum on the introduction of the Alternative Vote; higher education tuition fees; the possibility of renewing the trident programme; nuclear power; and the introduction of taxation incentives for marriage. The possibility of public disagreement did not end with these issues. Indeed it became difficult to discern all the areas in which the exemption applied, and if there was prior agreement to allow open discrepancies, or if they were embarked upon unilaterally. In the period from 2010 a clear difference appeared from previous arrangements for open dissent. Where previously—in 1975, for instance—the Cabinet had made a decision, with some registering their disagreement, there were now cases where there was simply no agreement—surely a weakening of Cabinet as the supreme body of government.

Attacks on collective responsibility came from multiple angles. The tendency was partly connected to the trends leading to more independent MPs and an increased occurrence of backbench rebellion. Early in 2013, a breach occurred that Cabinet seems not to have preordained. It came about after the Coalition dropped its House of Lords reform programme. Strong opposition to the proposal had come in the Commons, including from Conservative backbench MPs. Liberal Democrat front- and backbenchers—strong supporters of a change to the Lords—voted to delay a change in the number and boundaries of Commons constituencies that the Conservative Party favoured and to which it had previously gained Liberal Democrat agreement as part of the Coalition compact. In effect, Liberal Democrat Cabinet members were—without collective agreement—releasing themselves from the discipline of Cabinet unity to carry out an act of retaliation against the Conservative Party. The defence that Stanley Baldwin had offered in 1932, that the group as a whole had released itself from a constraint, was not available in this case.

Later in the same year it was the Conservative contingent of the Coalition that departed from the weakening framework of collective responsibility. In May 2013, the Prime Minister authorised a free vote on an amendment disapproving of the Queen's Speech for its failure to include reference to legislation providing for a referendum on the EU, a measure the Conservatives wanted but the Liberal Democrats opposed. In the end, no ministers took part in the division, but in theory they could have supported criticism of the programme of their own government without resigning from Cabinet, and they did fail positively to oppose a rebuke. This occurrence suggested that Cabinet practice had modified to the point that it was no longer always necessary for its members fully to support the legislative agenda that they had as a group produced, and given to the head of state to present to Parliament.[36] Once again controversy over Europe was placing pressure on UK constitutional arrangements. Other attacks on collective responsibility included the tendency of the Liberal Democrats to claim credit for particular policies with which they wished to be associated, thereby compromising the confidentiality of discussions.[37] The degree of mutual denunciation and reference to supposedly confidential decision-making procedures taking place by the time of the party conferences in October 2014 suggested that collective responsibility had ceased to exist. Some might hold that a coalition made this trend inevitable, particularly when a general election drew near. Yet multi-party arrangements were common in earlier eras, and a higher degree of Cabinet cohesion was maintained. Perhaps the changed social context made discreet coexistence more difficult. Whether discipline might fully restore under a single-party government or different coalition is at present a matter of speculation.

In the current phase of rapid constitutional development, the European dimension has been critical. Changing global circumstances drove a reassessment of the position of the UK within the continent, but the process proved painful and tumultuous. As in earlier eras, two-way constitutional influence between the UK and the wider continent continued. The UK provided a model for and influence upon European integration. Joining this project has in turn had a transformative impact upon the UK. Traditional constitutional understandings tumbled, though an instinct to claim continuity, however tenuous the case, sometimes manifested itself. Difficulties emerged for the doctrine of parliamentary sovereignty. A device of direct democracy—the referendum—came to coexist alongside the pre-existing representative apparatus. Collective responsibility had to stretch—or perhaps tear—to accommodate the European issue. European integration has been a challenge. It has involved cultural and political readjustment in the UK. Full reconciliation with the new position has not come about. As part of a wider controversy, critics have objected to various constitutional consequences of EU membership. Partly because of this particular strand of resistance, the UK may yet fully or partially leave the EU. However, just as those who seek to deny the occurrence of change are mistaken, so too are those who might imagine that the constitutional past is recoverable. Neither the UK, nor Europe, are what they were in the 1950s or 1970s.

[36] Select Committee on the Constitution, *The Constitutional Implications of Coalition Government* (HL 130, 2013–14).
[37] Scott Kelly, *The Slow Death of the 'Efficient Secret': The Rise of MP Rebellion, its Causes and its Implications* (London, The Constitution Society, 2014).

8

The Multination State

THE UNITED KINGDOM (UK) is not a nation state: multination state is probably a more appropriate term. At present it comprises three sub-nations: England, Scotland and Wales, and another entity—Northern Ireland—the definition of which is more complex.[1] They each have their own combinations of languages, cultures, political traditions and histories. When assessing the nature of nationality in the UK, the best starting point is the views of the people living within it. The existence of groups in Northern Ireland, Scotland and Wales who do not want to be part of the UK at all is well known. But it is also possible to measure degrees of connection to the UK state. The idea of belonging specifically to the 'UK' or 'United Kingdom'—meaning, in full, the United Kingdom of Great Britain and Northern Ireland—receives no attention from those conducting opinion research. They may be wise in this omission. The terms 'United Kingdom' or 'UK' have little resonance. As Linda Colley puts it: 'No one has ever proudly and seriously referred to himself or herself as a "UKanian"'. Indeed, Colley notes, the use of the initials 'UK' only came into frequent use as recently as the 1970s.[2] Polling questions focus instead on the relationship between 'British' and sub-UK identities. They produce intricate results. Particular self-definitions can vary in their connotations in different parts of the UK, and across communities within a given area. Yet certain general conclusions manifest themselves. The concept of being British has a degree of salience. Some groups—Protestants in Northern Ireland, the 'Black and Minority Ethnic' (BME) category in England[3]—stand out for their tendency to affiliate to Britain. But 'Britishness' fails to provide a full account of national attachment in the UK, and to many is either of lesser importance, or irrelevant.

As of 2012, according to the British Social Attitudes Survey, 23 per cent of respondents in Scotland regarded themselves as 'Scottish not British'; 30 per cent 'more Scottish than British'; 30 per cent 'equally Scottish and British'; 5 per cent 'more British than Scottish'; and 6 per cent 'British not Scottish'. In Northern Ireland, when required to choose between three possible identities in 2012, among

---

[1] Richard Rose, *Understanding the United Kingdom* (London, Longman, 1982) 10–34.
[2] Linda Colley, *Acts of Union and Disunion: What has Held the UK Together—and What is Dividing It?* (London, Profile, 2014).
[3] Richard Wyn Jones et al, *England and its Two Unions: The Anatomy of a Nation and its Discontents* (Institute for Public Policy Research, London, 2013) 24–25.

Protestants 69 per cent were 'British'; 3 per cent 'Irish'; and 24 per cent 'Northern Irish'. Within the Catholic community, 9 per cent identified as 'British'; 68 per cent 'Irish'; and 16 per cent 'Northern Irish'. In England, 17 per cent said they were 'English not British'; 12 per cent 'more English than British'; 44 per cent 'equally English and British'; 8 per cent 'more British than English'; and 10 per cent 'British not English'.[4] When the 2011 Census presented Welsh respondents with a range of options, it revealed that 57.5 per cent regarded themselves as only 'Welsh'; while 34.1 per cent categorised their identity as 'not Welsh at all'.[5] Evidence exists suggesting that attachment to Britain has generally been weakening over time, though the movement has not always been in one direction. When asked to select one or the other (a 'forced choice' question), respondents in Scotland in 1974 favoured Scottish over British identity by 65 per cent to 31 per cent. By 2005, the gap had widened, reaching 79 per cent to 14 per cent. In Wales in 1979, 57 per cent opted for 'Welsh' and 33 per cent 'British'; by 2003, the figures were 60 per cent and 27 per cent. In 1992, those identifying as 'English' made up 31 per cent and 'British' 63 per cent. By 2005, 40 per cent were 'English' and 48 per cent 'British'.[6] The 'forced choice' is problematic in that it can create an artificial dichotomy for some respondents. However, in this instance it does suggest that not only was 'Britishness' often a less powerful attachment for individuals than their sub-identity, but that it may be growing less pervasive. This perceptual trend accompanies major alterations in constitutional structures.

DEVOLUTION AND ITS IMPLICATIONS

The cultural variety of the UK, though it may be intensifying at present, has been an underlying quality of the state from the outset, and has always found expression in some degree of constitutional diversity.[7] Northern Ireland, Scotland and England have had distinct legal systems (and in post-devolution Wales discussion is ongoing about the possibility of a legal jurisdiction separate from that of England).[8] England and Scotland both have (different) established churches, while an 1869 Act of Parliament disestablished the Church in Ireland, and Acts of 1914 and 1919 did the same for the Church in Wales (though not quite fully). Each component of the UK has different official provisions for languages. Scotland has had its own systems of local government and education. Long before the term 'asymmetry' gained currency in the late 1990s, it would have been apt

---

[4] *British Social Attitudes: The 30th Report* (London, National Centre for Social Research, 2013) 139–49.

[5] *2011 Census: First Results for Ethnicity, National Identity, and Religion for Wales* (Cardiff, Statistics for Wales, 2012) 6–7.

[6] Ian Cruse, *Britishness* (London, House of Lords, 2008) 14.

[7] For the following, see: Andrew Blick, *Devolution in England: A New Approach* (London, Federal Trust/Unlock Democracy, 2014).

[8] National Assembly for Wales Constitutional and Legislative Affairs Committee, *Inquiry into a Separate Welsh Jurisdiction* (Cardiff, National Assembly for Wales, 2012).

to apply it to the configuration of the UK system of government. Observers often describe the UK as a 'unitary state'. The Royal Commission on the Constitution, for instance, used this term in 1973, then went on unintentionally to make the case against such a label by listing various anomalies and variations characterising the UK.[9] Taking into account the internal divergences, others assert that the label 'union state' is more appropriate than 'unitary'.[10]

This terminological dispute predates the Labour Government that took office in 1997. Yet the devolution programme pursued from this point became a further source of constitutional variety within the UK. It has created greater discrepancies between particular systems of governance across the UK. Devolution also entails diversity in a further sense: it has established poles of authority other than that of the UK Parliament, with expansive constitutional connotations. The origins of the devolved model can be traced at least as far back as the attempts to introduce Home Rule to Ireland from the late nineteenth century, which some came to believe should combine with similar provision for national or regional self-government across the UK. Though the first three attempts at Home Rule for Ireland failed, a devolved Parliament and executive operated in Northern Ireland from 1921 until its suspension in 1972. The idea of applying this principle in other parts of the UK did not completely disappear. For instance, a mass campaign promoted the 'Scottish Covenant' of 1949, calling for a Scottish Parliament. During the elongated phase of post-imperial constitutional upheaval, possibilities opened up for the renewed pursuit of this approach. Prompted by the rise of nationalist parties in Wales and Scotland, key areas of Labour support, Harold Wilson established in 1969 the Royal Commission on the Constitution. It recommended (though not unanimously) devolved government for Scotland and Wales.[11] However, when referendums eventually took place on the introduction of this system in the two nations at the end of the 1970s, they did not receive the necessary levels of support, and various attempts to reintroduce self-government to Northern Ireland failed.[12]

Then the late 1990s saw a breakthrough. Wales, Scotland and Northern Ireland now each have their own elected legislative assembly and executive responsible to it, with assorted other institutions. A variety of policy remits have transferred to them from the Westminster Parliament and Whitehall executive. This development has created further divergence. A gap opened up between the areas where devolution is now in force, and England (perhaps excluding Greater London, and soon Greater Manchester) where it is not. Furthermore, each set of devolution arrangements has its own distinctive qualities. Every one has had a different

---

[9] Royal Commission on the Constitution, *Report*, Vol 1 (Cmnd 5460, 1973) 19.

[10] Elizabeth Wicks, *The Evolution of a Constitution: Eight Key Moments in British Constitutional History* (Oxford, Hart Publishing, 2006) 167–68; Stein Rokkan and Derek W Urwin, *Economy, Territory, Identity: The politics of West European peripheries* (London, Sage, 1983) 187.

[11] Royal Commission on the Constitution, *Report* (n 9) 5.

[12] For the history of these issues see: Vernon Bogdanor, *Devolution in the United Kingdom* (Oxford, Oxford University Press, 2001).

genesis. In Northern Ireland, devolution—which is up to a point a restoration of the self-government that existed previously—was one element in a broader attempt to bring peace to the Province, involving an understanding between different parties in Northern Ireland and between the UK and Republic of Ireland.[13] Complex negotiations led to the Belfast or 'Good Friday' Agreement of 1998, an international treaty implemented in domestic UK legislation through the Northern Ireland Act 1998. The Agreement was an important moment in a long, violent history. Referendums in Northern Ireland and the Republic of Ireland both endorsed it. In the north, on a turnout of 81.1 per cent, 71.1 per cent voted 'yes'; in the Republic, the turnout was lower (56.26 per cent), but the proportion of support higher (94.39 per cent). The Agreement has facilitated a reduction in the level of conflict, though there have been subsequent difficulties including long suspensions of devolution.

The immediate pre-history of devolution in Scotland involved a broad-based movement for self-government that found expression in the Scottish Constitutional Convention, first established in 1989. Participants in the Convention included the Labour and Liberal Democrat Parties, individual members of other parties (though the Conservative and Scottish National Parties officially rejected participation), and trade unions, churches and other civil society representatives. It put forward firm plans for devolution, while other research work and behind-the-scenes political negotiations supplemented its efforts. In a referendum on 11 September 1997, on a turnout of 60.4 per cent of Scottish voters, 74.3 per cent endorsed the establishment of the Scottish Parliament and 63.5 per cent that it should have a limited ability to vary taxes. To a large extent the proposals of the Convention found their way into the Scotland Act 1998. In Wales, the process immediately leading to devolution was not as inclusive as in Scotland, and was largely an internal Labour Party matter. Nor was support for self-government as great. In a referendum held the week after the vote in Scotland, on a 50.1 per cent turnout, Wales produced a narrow 'yes' vote of 50.3 per cent.

Just as the genesis of each of the devolution systems diverged, so did the details of their specific configurations. In Northern Ireland, elections to the Assembly use the Single Transferrable Vote (STV), while the Scottish Parliament and Welsh Assembly utilise the Additional Member System (AMS). Even the precise details of the application of AMS vary between the latter two devolved nations. Each legislature has a different number of members. The organisation of the executive government differs in all three cases. Northern Ireland, for instance, has complex procedures to ensure cross-community power sharing at government level that are specific to the needs of the peace process and therefore not required in Scotland or Wales. The precise powers available to each assembly are different. So are the ways in which their legislative scope is defined. For Wales, the Assembly is able only to do that which the devolution legislation sets out positively as available to it. Arrangements for Scotland are less restrictive. Certain powers are 'reserved'

---

[13] Wicks, *The Evolution of a Constitution* (n 10) 182–83.

to UK level, with the Holyrood Parliament (a title signifying that it is more than an 'assembly') able to operate in any area not specifically prohibited to it. It is possible (through secondary legislation at UK-level) to delete items from the reserved list, and thereby devolve them (and by the same means to add policy areas, consequently removing them from the purview of Edinburgh). Finally, for Northern Ireland there is a list of 'excepted' matters that cannot be passed down, and of 'reserved' powers that can be devolved, but have not yet been; the remainder is by implication the business of Stormont.

Another key feature of the devolution schemes, related to their diversity, is that they are dynamic. All of them have changed in important and distinct senses since they first appeared. The St Andrew's Agreement of 2006 presaged changes to the internal arrangements of the Executive in Northern Ireland, and new provisions for the promotion and support of the Irish and Ulster Scots languages. In some ways the most dramatic shifts have taken place in Wales, including in the area of legislative authority. Initially, the National Assembly for Wales possessed only the powers previously attached to the UK Secretary of State for Wales. It could issue secondary but not primary legislation. Under the terms of the Government of Wales Act 2006 the Assembly took on new law-making roles. The first expansion under the 2006 Act involved being able to pass 'measures', with some similarity to Acts of Parliament, on particular 'matters' within devolved 'fields'. The transfer of matters to the Assembly required the approval of the UK Parliament on every occasion—a significant restriction. However, the Act allowed for a further extension in the scope of the Assembly, extending beyond creating measures dealing with individual matters. Subject to authorisation through a referendum in Wales, the Assembly would be able to pass 'Acts' falling anywhere within one of the available fields, without the requirement for further permission from Westminster. In a vote that took place on 3 March 2011, on a 35.2 per cent turnout, 63.49 per cent supported this expansion of authority. The Scottish Parliament from the outset had a tax varying power that the other devolved legislatures did not. However, it was small in scope and never used. Having chosen to remain part of the UK, Scotland will, in 2016, as set out in the Scotland Act 2012, take on more substantial fiscal discretion; and fulfilment of the 'Vow' of September 2014 will further add to its powers. While the expansion of legislative authority on the part of the National Assembly for Wales depended on agreement through a referendum, extensions of Scottish devolution have not yet involved this form of express approval (though the independence referendum of 2014 became in practice a choice between more devolution or departure from the Union).

Despite the differences between these systems in their historic backgrounds, the initial forms they took and their patterns of development, certain general observations are possible. Devolution is politically entrenched. A degree of party political consensus surrounds these systems. The Conservative Party, that was initially hostile to devolution in Scotland and Wales (though not in Northern Ireland, around which there has been partisan cooperation) came to accept it, and the idea of it intensifying. Most important of all, devolution in practice has achieved popular approval. In the Welsh referendum of 2011, for example, a far higher percentage of those who voted agreed with the extension of the legislative powers of the Assembly than had backed a more modest form of devolution at the outset in 1997 (though the turnout in 2011 was lower than in the earlier poll). In Scotland, some time before the referendum and the Vow, opinion research suggested clear majority support for devolution, and for its further extension in areas including taxes and social security.[14] Fulfilment of such desires is coming.

The evidence of the devolutionary experience is that self-government can create a momentum for more of the same. Though there have been obstacles—prolonged interruptions in Northern Ireland, and tortuous progress in Wales—the general direction of movement has been towards the increasing downward transfer of powers from UK level. Indeed, despite their differences, all three systems could be converging on a model of heightened autonomy. This pattern of development demonstrates that, while the success or failure of constitutional structures can rest to some extent on prevailing political cultures, it is also possible for the former to influence the development of the latter. Devolution has created institutions and fresh methods of operation, and encouraged popular perceptions that have both perpetuated its existence and created momentum for further change of a similar ilk. It is, therefore, both self-sustaining and self-aggrandising. Devolution in the UK can be seen as having definitely passed through a first tentative phase into a second, in which the systems have become firm fixtures, and the legislatures have achieved basic primary law-making powers. A third stage is now beginning, in which the devolved legislatures take on new fiscal powers, and other extensions to their authority. Scotland is doing so following its decision to remain within the UK; and Wales will follow along this path. The exact outcome of these changes is hard to predict, but they could well significantly alter the political dynamics not only of the nations in which they apply, but of the UK as a whole.

Judged on its own terms, in many ways devolution has proved a success. It has brought important parts of government activity closer to those it directly affects (though it may in some instances have led to an upward transfer of responsibility from local authority to devolved level). Systems and policies more closely tailored to the characteristics and desires of particular areas are possible. In Northern Ireland, institutions help accommodate the complex requirements of different, often exceptionally antagonistic, groups. In Wales, further provisions for a bilingual nation have been possible. Devolution has helped offset a frequently criticised quality of the UK constitution: its centralised nature. Major deviations have appeared between policies pursued by the UK Government for England—in such important spheres as health and education—and those favoured in the devolved territories. Regardless of whether particular decisions have been right or wrong, the important point is that these choices are available, and can impact upon wider UK political discourse. Strong focal points outside London are emerging. It is becoming increasingly possible for leaders to become figures on the UK stage

---

[14] *British Social Attitudes: The 30th Report* (n 3) 151.

without being based in Westminster. Modes of political operation other than the adversarial approaches that dominate in Westminster have gained space to flourish. There have been serious attempts to attain appropriate gender balance in representative institutions. Innovative public engagement mechanisms have appeared.

One area in which devolution has not delivered on the intentions lying behind it is in its failure to create a more cohesive UK. The evidence of some kind of decline in 'Britishness' was discussed above. Connected though not synonymous with the issue of sub-UK identity is that of secessionism. In Scotland in particular, some hoped that Home Rule would quell demands for independence. After initial signs that this expectation was well founded, the opposite proved to be the case. In 2006, a Scottish Liberal Democrat policy document identified 'changes in the political landscape' that the introduction of devolution had triggered. Among them was a 'vote decline' for the Scottish National Party (SNP) and their replacement by the Liberal Democrats as 'Scotland's second party'. Within the SNP, the paper held, some were now contemplating 'options other than independence for Scotland's future'.[15] This assessment proved premature. Only the following year, the SNP formed its first (minority) government at Holyrood. In 2011—surprisingly given the existence of an electoral system designed partly to stop this outcome—the party won a majority in the Scottish Parliament. The SNP, though it did not cooperate with the movement for the introduction of devolution, benefited from it. The newly established institutions gave it fresh political opportunities, and ultimately the chance to take office and hold an independence referendum in 2014. Though the SNP did not win on this occasion, it should not be assumed that the cause has suffered a final defeat, and in fact it seemed to gain impetus. Furthermore, that a significant group within one of its nations has expressed the desire to leave is in itself significant for the UK as a whole. Moreover, it is conceivable that devolution will accelerate to a point that the UK begins to fragment without a formal declaration of independence by any constituent part taking place.

The bedding down, expansion and success of devolution have served to present a challenge to longer-established constitutional practices and understandings. Across a wide range of policy areas elected legislatures in Northern Ireland, Scotland and Wales have now supplanted the UK Parliament (and associated executives have replaced the UK Government). A large volume of legislation produced in Westminster applies only to England, or in some cases England and Wales. In a strict legal sense Parliament retains the ability to legislate in areas that fall within the remit of the devolved legislatures. When passing the Acts establishing devolution, Parliament explicitly reserved this power. For instance, section 28(7) of the Scotland Act 1998 states that the creation of a Scottish Parliament with the ability to introduce Acts does 'not affect the power of the Parliament of

---

[15] Steel Commission, *Moving to Federalism—A New Settlement for Scotland* (Edinburgh, Scottish Liberal Democrats, 2006) 18.

the United Kingdom to make laws for Scotland'. The inclusion of such statements is not suggestive of self-confidence. Should a truly 'sovereign' Parliament need to remind us what it is? In protesting too much, Parliament displayed an awareness that it was creating systems that might challenge it. The ability of Parliament to intervene unilaterally in devolved business, or to alter or abolish the institutions without agreement from those involved, is in political terms seriously circumscribed. Referendums held in advance of the establishment of the systems give them a degree of entrenchment. In 1989, the Scottish Constitutional Convention Claim of Right asserted the entitlement of the people of Scotland to choose their own constitutional future. A rule—known as the 'Sewel Convention' in its application to Scotland—has appeared in the devolution era that Westminster will not normally legislate in a devolved area without the approval of the Assembly or Parliament involved through a 'Legislative Consent Motion'. The Vow appeared to embed the Scottish Parliament more explicitly, though in itself it did not have legal force. It is likely an Act of Parliament will seek to express the permanence of the Holyrood legislature and government, and enshrine the Sewel Convention. How this provision will fit with the general concept of UK parliamentary supremacy, and section 28(7) of the Scotland Act in particular, is an interesting question. Alongside the UK Parliament, the discretion of the Whitehall executive is subject to practical constraints. The Memorandum of Understanding, a non-statutory code first issued in 2000, sets out principles, practices and mechanisms intended to ensure that both the devolved and central administrations behave in a mutually respectful fashion.[16]

In practice, then, devolution has constrained the established doctrine of parliamentary sovereignty. Is it possible to identify a new system supplanting it? The three devolved territories are now subject to arrangements similar to a written constitution, as contained in the Acts of the UK Parliament providing for their systems. In each case, a process involving exceptional levels of inclusion and scrutiny has taken place. In Northern Ireland, the devolution package arose from cross-community and intergovernmental negotiations. Scotland had the Constitutional Convention. In Wales, the Labour Party dominated discussions that led to the initial programme. However, partly because of the system introduced, creating a likelihood of some kind of power sharing, a more open review of devolution then took place. The Richard Commission, running from 2002 to 2004, was in a sense a substitute for the process that might have taken place prior to devolution.[17] While the proposals it produced became a subject of dispute within Labour and were not fully implemented, the Government of Wales Act 2006, a substantial overhaul of Welsh devolution, was a response to the Commission. Other reviews of aspects of Welsh devolution, consulting widely, have followed. Similarly, investigations into

---

[16] For the latest edition, see: *Memorandum of Understanding and Supplementary Agreements* (London, Cabinet Office, 2012).

[17] Commission on the Powers and Electoral Arrangements of the National Assembly for Wales, *Report of the Richard Commission* (Cardiff, Richard Commission, 2004).

existing devolution arrangements in Scotland have taken place, most significantly with the Calman Commission on Scottish Devolution,[18] a body that sat from 2008–09, leading to the Scotland Act 2012. The Northern Ireland Human Rights Commission assessment of a possible Bill of Rights specifically applying to the Province rested on exceptionally inclusive and considered methods, though political blockages have prevented progress towards its ultimate goal.[19] Only the 'Vow' and the Smith Commission that followed it in 2014, bringing forward further devolution proposals for Scotland, arguably did not meet these same standards of inclusive decision-taking.

Consideration of the content of the devolution statutes strengthens the written constitution analogy further. They create institutions of government, including legislatures and executives, and prescribe how they should operate. At the same time, they impose constraints on the bodies they establish. As section 6(1) of the Northern Ireland Act 1998 iterates when setting out the legislative powers of the Northern Ireland Assembly: 'A provision of an Act is not law if it is outside the legislative competence of the Assembly'. The Assemblies in Northern Ireland and Wales and the Parliament in Scotland cannot legislate in subject areas that remain exclusively in the remit of the UK Parliament. One consequence of this restriction is that it is not possible for the devolved legislatures to alter the structure of the system within which they operate. A further limitation is that they cannot contravene—either by implication or explicitly—European law, or the European Convention on Human Rights (ECHR). In providing the means by which the latter stipulation is enforced, the Human Rights Act 1998 resembles a full Bill of Rights for these systems. Devolution, therefore, presents an example of how a written constitution might work in place of a UK Parliament with purportedly unlimited legislative power. A feature of the pro-independence campaign in Scotland was to propose the introduction of a full written constitution for the putative new state, the further extension of an already established pattern.[20]

Devolution is suggestive of a new constitutional model not only for the territories directly concerned, but the UK as a whole. It entails the increased assumption by the UK of federal characteristics. A federal system, broadly speaking, involves the apportioning of powers between different tiers of governance that are equal under the constitution in their respective spheres of operation.[21] There is a single federal set of institutions and below that a group of states. The core tasks likely to be reserved to the centre include external policy, defence, security and intelligence, and macroeconomics. Areas of public policy that may well reside mainly

---

[18] Commission on Scottish Devolution, *Serving Scotland Better: Scotland and the United Kingdom in the 21st Century* (Edinburgh, Commission on Scottish Devolution, 2009).

[19] Northern Ireland Human Rights Commission, *A Bill of Rights for Northern Ireland: Advice to the Secretary of State for Northern Ireland* (Belfast, Northern Ireland Human Rights Commission, 2008).

[20] Scottish Government, *The Scottish Independence Bill: A Consultation on an Interim Constitution for Scotland* (Edinburgh, Scottish Government, 2014); *Scotland's Future: from Referendum to Independence and a Written Constitution* (Scottish Government, Edinburgh, 2013).

[21] For a classic account see: KC Wheare, *Federal Government* (London, Greenwood, 1980).

at a lower level include culture, economic development, education, infrastructure, health, agriculture and fisheries, and some degree of fiscal power. A degree of overlap and cooperation can take place. Typically the respective areas of responsibility are set out in a written constitution, probably also including a Bill of Rights, and upheld by a Supreme Court, that has full power to negate all actions and legislation it deems to be without the scope of the institution involved, as defined in the text. Often mechanisms exist to provide the states with a firm role in federal decision-making, such as their inclusion in a chamber of the central legislature. Changes to the federal constitution are not within the power of any one institution, and involve some kind of exceptional approval procedure. Federal systems have particular value in providing expression to strong sub-identities within a given state, while maintaining a degree of overall coherence. For this reason states with a multi-national character, such as Canada, sometimes take this approach to the organisation of their systems of governance.[22]

Federal constitutions can come about because a group of smaller units decides to develop a closer association, while still preserving a degree of autonomy, as took place with the drafting of the US Constitution in 1787. They can also come into being because of an opposite dynamic: as a means of de-concentrating power within an existing system, while maintaining its existence, as has happened in Belgium, that formally became federal in 1993. In both the US and Belgian cases, the federal constitution formed avowedly and at a particular point. Other entities have come by stages increasingly to assume federal characteristics. Arguably the European Union (EU) represents the gradual, incomplete, appearance of a federation out of a collection of pre-existing existing sub-polities. Gradual federalism can also involve movement away from a more centralised system within a single state, to allow for regional or national diversity, as has occurred lately in Italy, Spain—and the UK, once again developing in accordance with wider European patterns.

As already discussed, UK political thought has a federal strand within it. Moreover, many federal constitutions worldwide have drawn upon UK influences. The framers of the US Constitution saw it as a means of realising ideas of freedom with a clear English derivation. Former UK colonies have adopted federal constitutions, with London providing encouragement and Whitehall supplying assistance. It may be that a UK product once directed only towards the export market is now gaining a domestic footing. Within the UK constitution as configured today the devolved territories can be seen as forming a tier equivalent to the 'state' level within a federal system. Since it became operational in 2009, the UK Supreme Court has assumed responsibility (previously possessed by the Judicial Committee of the Privy Council) for handling legal disputes involving devolution, just as the Supreme Court in a more fully federal system might rule on demarcation issues. As noted above, the devolved legislatures cannot exceed their proper

---

[22] Alain G Gaignon, *The Case for Multinational Federalism: Beyond the All-Encompassing Nation* (Oxford, Routledge, 2009).

spheres of operation, or violate the ECHR, or European law. However, while a federal legislature might be subject to the constitution in the same way as a state legislature, the same legal limits do not apply to the UK Parliament.

Another set of structures displaying certain federal characteristics exists. The Belfast Agreement created the British–Irish Council, a body through which the governments of the UK, Republic of Ireland, Northern Ireland, Scotland, Wales, Channel Islands and the Isle of Man meet to consider possible joint areas of activity. The British–Irish Parliamentary Assembly (up to 2008 known as the British–Irish Inter-Parliamentary Body) has since 2001 provided a forum for the legislatures of all these territories to carry out discussions and investigations (it first appeared in 1990, comprising only the UK Parliament and Irish Oireachtas). These bodies do not take binding decisions and are not exclusively of a UK composition. But they could represent the embryo of future mechanisms for combined decision-taking between 'states' at a federal level in the UK. Indeed, even if Scotland one day became independent, it is likely it would participate in coordinating institutions of this kind, as part of a web of archipelagic federacy.

A further sense in which devolution has a federal dimension is on the European stage. Across the EU a rise in regional (or in some cases, national) autonomy is in progress, in the UK as elsewhere. Regions (and in practice sub-Member State nations) have an entrenched legal position within the EU, with a Committee of the Regions to represent them—though it has not yet achieved a pronounced impact. A significant portion of the activities of devolved governance has a strong European dimension, hence the emphasis in the UK Memorandum of Understanding on the need for ministers to consult with their devolved counter-parts positions taken in EU negotiations. In a sense, the importance of the EU to their business restricts the devolved institutions, since they do not have the final determination of the stance the UK takes in EU negotiations. But nonetheless, the EU forms for the devolved territories a wider community, in which their significance is acknowledged and provided for. They are part of a whole, in which the UK tier and its Parliament can appear as just one level among others.[23]

Devolution is associated with a further blurring at the edges of the UK. As noted, arrangements in place for Northern Ireland are a component of the Belfast Agreement of 1998, a treaty between the Republic of Ireland and the UK. Elizabeth Wicks describes how the Agreement (incorporated into UK law through the Northern Ireland Act 1998) is exceptional—or perhaps even alone—internationally for the lengths to which it provides the population of Northern Ireland with self-determination.[24] Article 1(i) states that the respective governments 'recognise the legitimacy of whatever choice is freely exercised by a majority of the people of Northern Ireland'. They may decide to continue to be part of the UK, or join with the Republic of Ireland. Annex A 1(1) sets out that a referendum is the means

---

[23] See: Elke Cloots, Geert de Baere and Stefan Sottiaux, *Federalism in the European Union* (Oxford, Hart Publishing, 2012).
[24] Wicks, *The Evolution of a Constitution* (n 10) 183–84.

by which a choice may be made. The inhabitants of the Republic also figure in the decision, since Article 1(ii) describes how 'it is for the people of the island of Ireland alone' to opt, if they wish, for a 'united Ireland'. The existence of an 'exit clause' for Northern Ireland, that dates to the 1940s in statutory form, provides further evidence that not only is it difficult to describe the UK as a unitary state, but that the looseness of constitutional arrangements exceeds that normally associated with federal structures, as do other qualities of the UK, such as the multiple legal systems in operation. The right to secede seems to be expanding. Devolution made possible the forcing of the issue in Scotland, though it would entail independence rather than joining with another state. Might we be witnessing the emergence of a principle that any part of the UK can leave the Union? It is plausible that it will apply to Wales in time. Could it eventually extend to England as a whole, or even areas that are presently sub-components of England, such as Cornwall?

Devolution, then, suggests constitutional models and perceptions that serve to challenge prevailing arrangements and ideas. Yet in so doing, it is not wholly alien to the UK. As we have seen, various historic documents—some of which remain in force—share features with a written constitution, and federalism has a place in the UK intellectual tradition. Furthermore, the growing federalisation of the UK can be seen as a reasonable reflection of its national makeup. Countries facing similar challenges to the UK, such as Spain, have also opted for solutions of this sort. But the introduction of a full federal system would have to overcome resistance. Perceptions of the concept are contaminated. This problem began with the application of the 'federal' label to European integration as a term of abuse, eventually spreading to stigmatise federalism as a whole, not just in the European context. Indeed, some have portrayed different varieties of federalism as comprising a single threat. As the Conservative MP Eleanor Laing asked during a Westminster Hall debate on a possible federal UK in 2008: 'Why would we want a federal system? Would it be so that it would fit in with the idea of a European superstate or so that the United Kingdom could be divided into bite-sized chunks, ready to be gobbled up by a federal Europe?'[25] The independence referendum, however, made unionists more willing to consider federalism in as far as it might apply to the UK. In a paper published the day after the vote, for instance, the Society of Conservative Lawyers called for the formal establishment of a 'quasi-federal' system.[26] Yet there remains a practical barrier to attainment of a federal UK: England.

ENGLAND LEFT BEHIND

All of these dramatic developments that have such important consequences in the territories involved, and for the UK constitution as a whole, have largely excluded

---

[25] HC Deb 18 June 2008, vol 477, col 254WH.
[26] Society of Conservative Lawyers, *Our Quasi-Federal Kingdom* (London, Society of Conservative Lawyers, 2014).

the part of the UK in which the overwhelming majority of the population (approximately 54 million of a total of 64 million) lives: England. This gap is the most prominent feature of the debate about the so-called 'asymmetrical' quality of the UK constitution after devolution. The Labour Government elected in 1997 had hoped to extend this form of self-government by stages to nine administrative regions in England. In 1998, a referendum in Greater London approved the introduction of a Greater London Authority, including a directly elected mayor and assembly. The 'yes' vote was 72 per cent, with a 34.1 turnout. Had the Labour project for democratic governance in the regions been successful beyond Greater London, it would have involved further development in a federal direction, since it would have meant that every part of the UK had a form of government with some similarities to the 'state' tier within a federation. The powers initially envisaged for devolved regional English government were modest, even when compared with the system first introduced to Wales. However, as we have seen was the case for the devolved nations, the existence of directly elected assemblies and other institutions can help create a demand for more powers, and generally be self-entrenching. The Greater London Authority is firmly established, and has enhanced its range of responsibilities.

But the Labour plan for regional devolution in England failed the challenge of achieving sufficient initial public support. As for Northern Ireland, Scotland and Wales, the government deemed that the introduction of the system envisaged for England would require the agreement of the populations of each of the areas involved, expressed through an affirmative vote in a referendum. The North East region seemed to be the most receptive to the idea of a directly elected assembly, so it was there that the first such vote took place late in 2004. The electorate overwhelmingly rejected the plan (77.9 per cent voted 'no' on a 47.7 turnout), prompting the government to abandon the other referendums it had intended to stage. If it came so far short of winning in the North East, the chances of achieving a different outcome elsewhere seemed negligible. Some observed that the campaign was badly run, and lacking in proper support from the Labour Government, leaving the Deputy Prime Minister, John Prescott, an isolated advocate. A further problem identified was that not only were the powers vested in the intended assembly slight, but if they were introduced it would have had a centralising effect, drawing responsibilities upward from local government rather than downward from the centre. Opponents of the North East Assembly were effective in depicting it as a pointless additional layer of bureaucracy.

There was a wider difficulty with the regional agenda as a whole. The territories generally lacked historic or cultural resonance. They had appeared as the areas served by a set of Government Offices of the Regions in 1994, and the Labour government attached Regional Development Agencies to them under a 1998 Act. Their populations lacked the shared identity of the Welsh or Scots (the Northern Ireland case is more complicated), or even that of English counties such as Yorkshire or Cornwall, or of English cities such as Manchester or Birmingham (hence Greater London being more viable). It was difficult to turn them into a focus for enhanced autonomy. Another objection some raised was that they represented a dismemberment of the English nation.

The government did not fully abandon the regional agenda after the North East defeat. It continued with the use of representative but not directly elected assemblies, which had oversight functions in relation to Regional Development Agencies. As Prime Minister from 2007 to 2010, Gordon Brown appointed ministers for the English regions, accountable to a series of specifically created regional Commons select committees comprising Members from the area concerned. But such plans did not amount to the introduction of institutions with clear democratic accountability to the areas they served, achieved through directly elected bodies, as characterises devolution elsewhere in the UK. During the post-North East referendum period, interest rose in Whitehall in the possibility of using a different kind of division, the city region. These units focus on large conurbations, but extend beyond their immediate administrative boundaries to take into account their various social networks and connections. City regions can have more meaning from the point of view of their inhabitants than the English regions. However, problems could arise in determining what should be their precise geographical demarcations. Moreover, prospective city regions could overlap with each other. Furthermore, it might be difficult to achieve complete coverage of England, meaning that some parts would still lack this kind of devolved government. It is not clear, for instance, what would be an appropriate city region within which to place Cornwall. Some inhabitants might object to possibilities such as Plymouth or Bristol.

The Coalition Government that took office in 2010 dismantled most of the existing paraphernalia of regional administration. In place of Regional Development Agencies, it introduced 39 Local Enterprise Partnerships that once again suffered from a lack of clear democratic accountability to voters in the areas they served. The regional agenda continued to lurch on. In 2011, the government triggered referendums in the largest English cities on the introduction of directly elected mayors. Few powers not already possessed by city councils were on offer. Arguments advanced in favour of these proposed new office holders included that they would provide a public focus for governance in the areas involved, stimulating greater political engagement, allowing clearer accountability, and leading to the downward transfer of more authorities. But voters were generally unconvinced and the only city that decided it wanted a mayor was Bristol. A further development in directly elected regional government, of a sort, came with the introduction of Police and Crime Commissioners to each England and Wales police area outside London (41 in total), under the Police Reform and Social Responsibility Act 2011. Turnouts in the votes held for these offices on 15 November 2012 were spectacularly low, averaging 15.1 per cent. Nonetheless, it is conceivable they could offer an embryo for a wider form of devolved governance in the future. In November 2014 the city region idea received impetus with the unveiling of an agreement between the Chancellor of the Exchequer, George Osborne, and Greater Manchester local authority leaders for the transfer of powers from the centre to a Greater Manchester Combined Authority, and the introduction of a directly elected mayor.

LOCAL GOVERNMENT IN ENGLAND

None of these changes provided the people of England with the kind of self-government possessed in other parts of the UK. Even the Greater London Authority is considerably short of this level. Though it has significant access to money—including through the congestion charge—it lacks other powers possessed by devolved institutions. The London Assembly is not a legislative body (and indeed is seriously circumscribed in performing its supposed function of holding the Mayor to account). This lack of devolution in England is a much worse problem than it might otherwise be because of the lack of autonomy for local government. In its 2009 report *Devolution: A Decade On*, the House of Commons Justice Committee noted that: 'Prior to devolution, the United Kingdom was probably the most centralised state in Western Europe, and after devolution England continues to have a high degree of centralisation in its form of government'. The committee identified the 'constitutional doctrine of the sovereignty of Parliament and the absence of a written constitution' as reasons for the persistence of this quality in England, manifestations of which included the 'abolition of the Greater London Council in 1986 and in the ability of central government similarly to direct the policies pursued by local authorities'.[27]

Many commentators have long acknowledged the subordination of local government to Westminster and Whitehall. Successive UK governments as far back as the 1930s have pursued policy initiatives that have had the effect of siphoning power to the centre. Areas in which local authorities once played an important role, such as education—some of the very fields that are devolved elsewhere in the UK—have increasingly come within the purview of Whitehall and Westminster. Alongside the loss of control over policy, local authorities have had fiscal independence progressively stripped from them. Regular central reorganisation of the structure of local government over the decades has emphasised this position of dependency. The direction of travel has been towards a reduced number of local authorities, serving larger populations, from whom the institutions therefore become more remote, and to whom they are less meaningful. The centre has also imposed new organisational models. Under the Local Government Act 2000 local authorities were required to introduce a new executive system, in place of the old committee approach, using a Cabinet and possibly a directly elected mayor. This change distanced councillors now classed as backbenchers from decision-making. As at city council level, the hoped-for popular enthusiasm for mayors has not materialised.

---

[27] Justice Committee, *Devolution: A Decade On*, Vol 1 (HC 2008–09, 529-I) 5.

A recent statement of the position came in the 2013 House of Commons Political and Constitutional Reform Committee report, *Prospects for codifying the relationship between central and local government*. It found that local government was not free to pursue its own policy objectives. Every (presumably English) authority was subject to a minimum of 1293 statutory responsibilities, over 50 per cent of which had appeared during the previous decade-and-a-half. The period between 1979 and 1996 provided 39 per cent; 8 per cent came from before 1979. Alongside this tightening corset of legal obligations, local government lacks fiscal autonomy. The same Commons committee report cited figures from 2010 showing that UK local government (with England clearly making a major contribution to the overall pattern) raised only 12.7 per cent of its income from taxes, making it dependent on funding from the centre. No other democratic system for which the committee gave figures had such a small figure for local fiscal income. Denmark, for instance, stood at 34.3 per cent; Germany (including state and local levels) 57.8 per cent; Italy 40.1 per cent; and Spain 44.2 per cent (again comprising both the regional and local tiers).[28] The figure for the UK may have risen since, but it is because of huge cuts in subsidies from the UK central government, rather than an increase in autonomy at local level.

While the coalition and the Labour governments before it have pursued initiatives supposedly aimed at revitalising and empowering local government, cumulative movement has been in the opposite direction. Local government is the closest level of democratically controlled administration to the people of England (and of the rest of the UK). It remains responsible for the public functions most important to day to day life, such as waste collection and road maintenance. But it has seriously reduced discretion in how it should go about performing these tasks on behalf of its electors, and over how it might raise the money to do so. A centralising political culture stretching beyond the official institutions compounds the constitutional problems. The media has a tendency to call upon UK ministers to act to deal with issues that in other parts of the world would not fall into the generally accepted remit of central government. While Westminster and Whitehall are subject to strong practical restraints in exercising the theoretical power to interfere in devolved matters, no such considerations have served to protect English local government. The doctrine of parliamentary sovereignty is the ultimate weapon in the hands of those determined to trump the local democratic mandate. A form of social organisation allowing for people to direct their own affairs that in its origins predates Parliament and Magna Carta has been compromised. In the post-Scottish Independence Referendum environment, senior politicians of all parties began committing themselves to a bolstering of local government. Whether this mood will manifest itself in a genuine and substantial transfer of policy and fiscal power, with which the centre cannot interfere at a later date, is uncertain.

---

[28] Political and Constitutional Reform Committee, *Prospects for codifying the relationship between central and local government*, Vol I (HC 2012–13, 656-I) 8–9, 30.

THE ENGLISH QUESTION

The absence of devolution in England introduces further tensions. Almost as long as the idea of Home Rule for one or more parts of the UK has existed, observers have noted a potential problem with it. If not extended to cover the whole UK, it can produce an anomaly at Westminster. Members of the House of Commons elected from constituencies in areas that have this form of self-government will be able to continue to vote and take part in debates on devolved policy fields that do not directly affect their electors. Yet MPs returned from territories lacking devolution cannot have the same influence over devolved areas. It is even possible that a law may pass despite lacking majority support from MPs in the area to which it applies. The label often attached to this dilemma is the 'West Lothian question'. Another issue is that, while Scotland and Wales as nations have clear institutional and political means of expression, and mechanisms are in place intended to accommodate the divided national outlooks of Northern Ireland, England is not provided for in this way. If these problems only worried academics and commentators, they would not matter as much. But there is evidence of concerns beginning to spread. Work published by the Institute for Public Policy Research has recently identified evidence of heightening political consciousness in England. Increasingly, a body of resentment regarding the supposed unfairness of constitutional arrangements and their consequences has developed. A particular focus is upon Scotland as supposedly receiving treatment more favourable than it merits in areas such as finance. Support for existing arrangements for the governance of England has dropped, though opinion has perhaps yet to gather clearly around a single model for reform.[29]

For those who accept that the exclusion of England from devolutionary development is a problem, all of the possible solutions widely discussed to date raise certain difficulties. The regional agenda has already encountered difficulties. Another possible response, favoured by the Conservative Party, involves changes to procedures in Westminster. The idea has long antecedence and is presently known as 'English Votes for English Laws' (EVEL). It involves separating out Bills or clauses within Bills that have effect only on England (or sometimes England and Wales). They might then, at some point in the legislative process, be voted on only by MPs from English (or English and Welsh) constituencies. Assuming it is possible to surmount the technical challenges this idea raises, further queries are possible. Is it appropriate to create different classes of MP? Is there a danger of undermining the position of MPs as representing not only a particular territory, but forming part of a collective that deliberates on behalf of all? Would this kind of arrangement be likely to undermine such cohesion in UK identity as exists? If UK MPs as a whole continued to vote on the Budget, how could 'English' legislation be detached from the spending it was likely to incur? Perhaps

---

[29] Richard Wyn Jones et al, *The Dog that Finally Barked: England as an Emerging Political Community* (London, Institute for Public Policy Research, 2012).

the most problematic feature of EVEL is the possible scenario it raises in which one party or group has a majority of UK MPs, but not among English MPs. There might then be difficulties in forming a viable government, since it would not possess a parliamentary majority in important areas such as health and education. Therefore, while the EVEL idea may answer the West Lothian question it raises others in the process. Moreover, while it also deals to some extent with the lack of English representation, it does not bring about meaningful devolution of power within England.

Another way forward might be the introduction of an English Parliament. Representing a clear step towards a fully federal UK, it could sit alongside its Scottish and Welsh equivalents as the legislature of one of the three complete nations of the UK. It would provide the English with a concrete, institutional expression of their political identity that they have previously lacked. However, it would not deal in any significant way with the pronounced centralisation of political power in England, since a UK Parliament representing a population of 64 million would be devolved to an English Parliament serving around 54 million. Moreover, while it might seem that England could form an appropriate component in a federal UK, the preponderant size of the English population, along with English predominance in other areas such as the economy, might well have a destabilising effect. There is no example internationally of a successful federation containing such a disproportionately large unit. If federal institutions provided England with a share of power proportionate to its population or electorate, it could overrule all the other participants combined. This arrangement could prove unacceptable to Northern Ireland, Scotland and Wales. Yet English opinion could be hostile to a lower weighting. An English Parliament and executive would also be likely to pose a challenge to their equivalents at UK level, whether controlled by the same or a different party or coalition of parties.

For these reasons, some kind of English regional model could, in theory at least, be more workable. Within such a system, no one regional or national unit within the UK need be so large as to dwarf the others, threatening the stability of the constitution. Nor would any 'state' be relatively so small as to face the threat of irrelevance. This vision of a federal UK is similar to that once put forward by Winston Churchill before the First World War. However, it does not enjoy strong popular support at present. In 2012, when English respondents chose from four options, 21 per cent favoured retaining current arrangements; 36 per cent the system known as 'English votes for English laws'; 20 per cent a full English Parliament; and only 8 per cent elected regional assemblies in England.[30] A new approach advocated in some quarters is to utilise existing local government structures as a vehicle for devolution. It has apparent merit, and would be valuable regardless of what happens at other levels. However, if it involves pooling of responsibility between authorities, it might lead to problems of democratic

---

[30] Wyn Jones et al, *England and its Two Unions* (n 3) 14.

accountability. Moreover, it would leave some issues untouched. For instance, it would not address the lack of political and institutional expression for England as such (if such an outlet is regarded as necessary), and assuming local authorities did not attain primary legislative powers, could not fully answer the West Lothian question. No perfect solution to present problems exists, therefore, and any resolution will involve careful consideration and compromise. A process that can provide these qualities is required.

Territorial diversity has been an important quality of the UK constitution from the outset. The Union of 1706–07, though it was a dramatic fusion, took care to preserve some distinctive features of Scotland and not simply to swallow it into England. Fewer protections applied with the arrangements for Ireland in 1800, but subsequently the conflicts associated with its presence within the UK forced a variety of changes. While principles such as parliamentary supremacy are undeniably important, we should not allow them to create an overriding sense of UK constitutional uniformity. Moreover, theoretical challenges to more unitary conceptions have long lineage. In the present era of dynamic change, the forces of sub-UK divergence gained in strength and eventually manifested themselves in the devolution systems introduced in the late 1990s.

Devolution has proved from important perspectives to be a successful experiment: one that entrenches and extends itself. It challenges further still conventional constitutional notions, and is suggestive of different models, possibly involving a written constitution setting out a federal system. Yet the system has possibly undermined cohesion with respect to the participation of Scotland within the UK. Furthermore, England (other than Greater London) has played no part in this process. As a consequence it is subject to political over-centralisation. There is no significant layer of governance between the central and local, and the latter is clearly subordinate to the former. The positions of Scotland and of England mean that, for a number of reasons, the post-devolution UK suffers from unsatisfactory features.

Nonetheless, devolution gives us the clearest view of a possible future for the UK, with a federal system, provided for in a written constitution. Of the central changes discussed in this part of the book, it is the most secure, with EU membership and the Human Rights Act subject to serious challenge. How likely is a step towards a fully federal system? Two official inquiries, four decades apart, tasked with considering issues relating to the territorial governance of the UK, have expressly rejected this option. The Royal Commission on the Constitution opened the section of its 1973 report dealing with this possibility by stating, 'There is very little demand for federalism in Scotland and Wales, and practically none at all in England. Few of our witnesses advocated it, and people who know the system well tend to advise against it'. One of the problems the Commission identified was that 'A federation consisting of four units—England, Scotland, Wales and Northern Ireland—would be so unbalanced as to be unworkable'. The 'overwhelming political importance and wealth of England' would predominate; the Parliament in England would pose a challenge to that of the UK, and it would be difficult to give England representation in a federal legislature sufficiently small that the other territories represented could override it. Furthermore, any attempt to create a series of sub-units within England 'would be unacceptable to the people of England'. Other objections the Commission presented included that 'Federalism was designed and is appropriate for states coming together to form a single unit, and not for a state breaking up into smaller units'. The Commission also found that a federal approach would necessitate 'a written constitution, a special procedure for changing it and a constitutional court to interpret it'. It held that 'None of these features has been present in our constitutional arrangements before, and we doubt very much whether they would now find general acceptance'.[31]

In February 2012, the Coalition Government established a commission to consider 'how the House of Commons might deal with legislation which affects only part of the United Kingdom' in the era of devolution. It reported in March 2013. The mandate of the body did not directly address the idea of possible federal models, but they offered a potential solution to the problems with which it was concerned, so it felt a need to consider them. Nonetheless, the final report dismissed the possibility of a federal system in two paragraphs. It rejected a model using English regions by citing a general lack of demand and holding that it would not address concerns applying to England as a whole. The Commission then noted that the idea of a single English Parliament as part of a federal UK had 'vociferous advocates' and seemingly greater support than the regional approach. However, most opinions expressed to it on this subject opposed the English Parliament model. The first problem the Commission identified was that the relative size of England would make the system unworkable. Second, a federal arrangement would necessitate 'a delineation of competences ... arbitrated by a supreme court that would be able to overrule the UK parliament'. In other words—though the Commission did not use the exact terms—a written constitution supplanting parliamentary supremacy or sovereignty. It felt this approach to be a 'radical departure from UK constitutional practice'. The disruption involved 'would not appear a proportionate response to the current sense of disadvantage in England'. Finally, the Commission doubted whether the public would find acceptable an expansion in the number of politicians and the cost entailed. Ultimately it opted to propose dealing with asymmetric devolution at the level of the UK Parliament. It asserted the principle that

> decisions at the United Kingdom level with a separate and distinct effect for England (or for England-and-Wales) should normally be taken only with the consent of a majority of MPs for constituencies in England (or England-and-Wales).[32]

Both commissions ruled out a UK federation, and for similar reasons. But the underlying tensions they addressed remained. It may be that the UK is inherently

---

[31] Royal Commission on the Constitution, *Report*, Vol 1 (n 9) 159, 157, 158.
[32] *Report of the Commission on the Consequences of Devolution for the House of Commons* (London, Stationery Office, 2013) 5, 24–25, 38.

unstable, that expressing the diversity of the constituent parts is irreconcilable with the practical dominance of England. An easy federal solution is not on offer, or at least has not become apparent in well over a century of consideration, but neither have the other methods deployed brought about firm resolution. Indeed they have generated momentum for more change, either within the framework of the UK or through secession from it. Furthermore, even reforms conceived and presented as the alternative to a federal option have led the UK increasingly to take on federal qualities. Barriers to a federal UK are both cultural (the special position of the Westminster Parliament and the lack of a written constitution) and practical (the relative size of England). The two Commissions cited above lacked the will to overcome these obstacles. A body with a broader remit, not bound by the same degree of adherence to constitutional tradition and emerging from a recognition that more radical reform was necessary, might produce a different outcome. The continuation of the UK could at some point depend upon it.

9

The Rule of Law, Human Rights and Constitutional Conflict

A THRIVING CONSTITUTION subsists on more than legalism alone. Nonetheless, law will always play a central part in any such system. Legal rules and the institutional mechanisms established to uphold them are part of a wider culture. They depend upon this broader environment for their effectiveness, and must at times change to take it and its dynamics into account. Yet this culture needs and draws influence from the law. Given this interconnection, it is not a surprise that the present period of constitutional change has encompassed the legal system. The Constitutional Reform Act 2005 is a prominent example of alteration in this area, worth elaborating on here. The genesis of the Act was, as we have already seen, an example of the unsatisfactory approach that can be taken to constitutional change. Its substance exemplified the immense scope of the ongoing transformation. Prominent provisions within it were for the establishment of a Judicial Appointments Commission, alterations to the role of the Lord Chancellor, and most of all the creation of a UK Supreme Court. Comprising 12 judges, this court became operational in 2009, replacing the Appellate Committee of the House of Lords, and is the final civil court of appeal for the entire UK, and for criminal litigation in Wales, Northern Ireland and England.

Like many changes in the present period, this alteration was of immediate significance. It was part of an overall process of the constitution becoming more juridicial as opposed to political in nature, pointing to a different possible model for the UK. The removal of the judicial function from the House of Lords was important both for legislature and judiciary. Though the Supreme Court possessed few powers that its predecessor institution had not, over time, judges sitting on this court, partly by virtue simply of being there, but also with the encouragement of other provisions in the 2005 Act, might develop an increasingly independent outlook. In expressing this developing attitude, the judiciary might utilise certain instruments it has already fashioned for itself, of increasing sophistication and effectiveness. Any such action, of course, brings consequences with it. The legislature and executive might react to what they perceive as inappropriate assertions of judicial power, and public opinion may play a significant role. A confrontation of this kind would be a problem for the functioning of a democratic polity. As this discussion suggests, a consideration of the legal and judicial dimensions of the dynamic UK constitution is essential. It begins with an account of one of the most fundamental constitutional doctrines of all.

THE RULE OF LAW IN THE UNITED KINGDOM

A primary component of any democratic constitution is the rule of law, another phrase that Dicey popularised in English. It has origins in pre-democratic societies, and tensions are possible between it and facets of democratic systems of government. Yet the rule of law and democracy—though distinct concepts and both ends in their own right—are mutually dependent for their full realisation. Without democracy, the rule of law is limited by the exclusive nature of political processes; and without the rule of law, arbitrary action inimical to democracy remains possible. But what is the rule of law? Both a simple and complex concept, its precise nature is contested. It requires all actions to be subject to a system of rules. The fulfilment of this principle is necessary to a secure, stable and confident society, in which individuals and groups can have a degree of clarity about their position and what they can expect of others. A desire to meet some of these needs is detectable in the earliest of English constitutional documents, from Ethelbert's law code onwards.

The rule of law concept rests on certain requisites.[1] If it is to have any value it must involve more than simply a requirement for conduct to be in accordance with the law, whatever the law is at any given point and however it is enacted. Otherwise the path is open to tyranny through control of the production, content and interpretation of legislation. A meaningful version of the rule of law must seek to fulfil certain standards. All people should be equal before the law and must have access to it, otherwise the concept of an all-embracing order of justice is not attained. Arbitrary alteration of the law is to be prevented. A failure to guard against such practice means that those able to trigger changes as they see fit might be able to rule through the law, more than being subject to it, and do so at the expense of others, denying them protection. Democratic forms of government and an independent judiciary are important barriers to the subordination of the law to particular groups or individuals. Clarity is essential: the law must be knowable. Any authorities, duties and limits that the law establishes have to be defined with precision. Expansive and vague powers are undesirable. Public institutions play an important role in ensuring that the rule of law is upheld, but it is vital that they themselves are subject to this same principle otherwise there is a risk that they become predators, inflicting arbitrary rule. This dimension of the rule of law has a long heritage, discernable in documents such as those to which Cnut committed early in the eleventh century—and most famously of all, John in 1215.

It is possible to broaden—or 'thicken'—the concept of the rule of law further still to take into account human rights such as freedom of expression and association. A society in which individuals could be subject to unmerited restrictions in these areas could hardly be said to be fulfilling principles of legal equality.

---

[1] For a definitive account drawn on here, see: Tom Bingham, *The Rule of Law* (London, Penguin, 2011).

Furthermore, the exercise of such rights is an important strand of democracy that is in turn supportive of the rule of law. Advocates of the rule of law generally regard it as incompatible with the use of barbaric punishments, however defined. It is also possible to make a case for the inclusion of certain socio-economic rights. Access to the law and the political processes that generate it requires, for instance, that individuals are properly educated and are not destitute. We should be aware of the danger of conflating preferred particular policy objectives with essential components of the rule of law. Just as an excessively thin interpretation can deny meaning to this doctrine, so too can an account of it that is too thick. Nonetheless, there is an undoubted connection between social inequality and restrictions on the pervasiveness of the rule of law.

Given that it is an essential underlying component of a democracy, an obvious way to provide for the rule of law is through including key facets of it in a written constitution. This approach can insulate these principles against the abuse of the democratic mandate concept. Such threats involve populist measures that might in the process damage the very democratic system from which the pseudo-justification for this action will have derived. A written constitution can protect provisions supporting the rule of law against excessively easy alteration, and establish their superior position in the systemic hierarchy. This option is not yet available in the UK: so what does the rule of law mean here and how is it upheld?

Explicit statutory reference to this doctrine came with the Constitutional Reform Act 2005. As radical documents often have, this transformative Act of Parliament made reference to the continuation of long-established practice. Section 1 of the Act stated that the changes it brought about did not 'adversely affect' either 'the existing constitutional principle of the rule of law' or the 'Lord Chancellor's existing constitutional role in relation to that principle'. It did not inform us what this 'existing constitutional principle' actually was, or specifically the 'existing constitutional role' of the Lord Chancellor towards it. Nonetheless, the Act required the oath of the Lord Chancellor to include a promise to 'respect the rule of law' (section 17).

Referring to the rule of law but not at the same time specifying what it means is not unique to the UK. The Basic Law for the Federal Republic of Germany of 1949 (for example, in 16(2)) and the 1996 Constitution of the Republic of South Africa (1(1)(c)), for instance, both do the same. In this sense, section 1 of the Constitutional Reform Act is similar to the kind of provision found in such a text. Yet those documents often also seek to provide a wide and firm underpinning for the concept, even if they do not make this express connection when they do so. The 2005 Act certainly promotes some features of the rule of law, for instance through its provision for 'Continued judicial independence' (sections 3–4). The Lord Chancellor and other ministers are required 'not to seek to influence particular judicial decisions through any special access to the judiciary' (section 3(5)); and the Lord Chancellor must take into account 'the need for the judiciary to have the support necessary to enable them to exercise their functions' (section 6(b)). But further important dimensions of this doctrine are expressed outside the 2005 Act.

Consequently, provision for the rule of law is more diffuse than it might be under a written constitution.

Some provision for the principle is found in other statutes. Support for judicial independence, for instance, comes not only from the Constitutional Reform Act, but the Act of Settlement 1701. The Equality Act 2010 is a more recent legislative advance. It consolidates prohibitions on discrimination in a wide range of environments, defining a series of 'protected characteristics' such as gender, race, religion or lack thereof, and sexual orientation. In making more firm the position of these groups as equal members of society, one of the achievements of the 2010 Act is to enhance the rule of law. Beyond statute, there is a partial dependence upon convention: that ministers, legislators and judges will generally perform their public duties in such a way as to support the rule of law. But reliance on this constitutional source always carries with it the potential for doubt and confusion, and for abuse by those in positions of authority. For instance, confusion surrounds precisely whether the prohibition on ministerial interference extends beyond the specific statutory veto on using 'special access' to influence specific outcomes. Might it be inappropriate, for instance, publicly to condemn an individual decision once made, or to make a more generalised criticism of the outlook of the judiciary or of the legal profession? A written constitution, of course, would not necessarily answer all such questions.

Another indispensible dimension to the maintenance of the rule of law has been the common law. Judges have developed on a case-by-case basis their ability to carry out judicial review of the decisions and actions of public authorities. It is now established that the courts can appropriately consider such activity on a variety of grounds. First, they can assess whether it is legal, that is, within the scope of existing statutory authority. Clearly if this kind of control was not in place then the abuse of authority, with public bodies defining their powers in ways that suited them, would follow. Second, the courts may consider the reasonableness of an action. All institutions and individuals are capable of irrationality at times, and it should be guarded against. Third, procedural fairness is required. For instance, if rules exist governing how decisions should be arrived at, those exercising powers should adhere to them, and not arbitrarily circumvent them at certain points. If a court finds a violation on one or more of the grounds set out above, a number of responses, depending on the particulars of the case, are available. They include annulling a decision, quashing secondary—but not primary—legislation, and making a body do or not do something, as well as granting damages. An important principle of judicial review is that a court does not specifically usurp the role and responsibilities of other public authorities, second guessing them or substituting its judgment for their own. Rather, it assesses the legality of the decision or action they have taken. In practice, however, this distinction can become blurred, and a standard accusation against the courts is that they are improperly expanding their remit into the political field.

Dynamics connected to the present phase of constitutional change in the UK have manifested themselves in the practice of judicial review. The public has become more inclined to challenge decisions. In 2012, a Ministry of Justice consultation complained that the annual rate of applications made for judicial review had risen from 160 in 1974, to 4250 by 2000, to in excess of 11,000 by 2011. The main source of this increase was an expansion in the volume of asylum and immigration cases.[2] The judiciary too has become more assertive, developing new ways of challenging the executive. For instance, a case in 1985, considering the government ban on trade union membership at the Government Communications Headquarters (GCHQ), produced the new idea that the courts could enquire into the manner of the exercise of Royal Prerogative, rather than just whether it existed in a particular area. The clear signs of cultural change in the judiciary may magnify over coming years and decades, encouraged by such developments as the establishment of the UK Supreme Court.

Under the weight of these challenges governments have contemplated restrictive measures, becoming attracted to the idea of the 'ouster clause', a statutory measure intended to remove the application of judicial review in certain areas.[3] The possibility of constraint draws attention to a tension within the UK constitution. In many ways the doctrines of the rule of law and parliamentary sovereignty are complementary. In upholding the latter tenet through enforcing the law, the courts generally support the former principle. But it remains theoretically possible that Parliament could produce statute that tampered with or compromised principles of the rule of law. Under traditional orthodoxies the courts would have no option but to accept such an Act of Parliament regardless of its content.

THE HUMAN RIGHTS ACT

A further expansion in the scope of judicial review came with the Human Rights Act 1998. This enhancement came at the invitation—or on the instructions—of Parliament. The European Convention on Human Rights (ECHR) had been in force as an external commitment upon the UK since 1953. Initially the UK did not accept the provision contained within it for individuals to seek redress under the Convention, only agreeing to the possibility of actions initiated by other states against it. Then in 1966, the UK assented to individual petition, anticipating that there would be little consequence. But the cases, and findings against the UK, began to flow, covering areas from counterterrorism powers to corporal punishment of children to surveillance by the security and intelligence agencies. A clear anomaly was that people living in the UK could not access their Convention rights in domestic courts, and could only seek to uphold them through the European Court of Human Rights in Strasbourg. The Human Rights

---

[2] Ministry of Justice, *Judicial Review: proposals for reform*, Consultation Paper CP25/2012 (London, Stationery Office, 2012) 9.

[3] See: Anthony Lester, 'The Constitutional Implications of Ouster Clauses', speech to the Administrative Law Bar Association (Inner Temple Parliament Chamber, 26 February 2004).

Act set out to provide for Convention rights while preserving certain traditional constitutional norms.[4]

There was a long tradition of English common law freedoms that courts sought to protect unless clearly overridden by statute. Nonetheless, the 1998 Act represented a definite shift towards the positive protection of rights within the UK. Section 2 states that courts or tribunals when interpreting the Convention 'must take into account any' judgments, decisions and opinions emanating from organs of the Council of Europe. In other words, the Act imports not only Convention rights into UK law, but a body of case law associated with it. Yet while the word 'must' creates an obligation to consider the findings of the Council of Europe, the phrase 'take into account' is less than a definite instruction to follow them. Nonetheless, opponents of the Human Rights Act have often singled out section 2 for particular criticism, regarding it as subjecting UK law to an undesirable external influence.

Section 3 is another source of controversy. It requires that 'So far as it is possible to do so' both primary and secondary legislation 'must be read and given effect in a way which is compatible with the Convention rights'. This provision—that covers laws passed both before and after the 1998 Act—is important to discussions about the balance of power between the courts and Parliament, and the supposed 'sovereignty' of the latter. It creates the potential for considerable latitude on the part of the judiciary, since the courts are able to stretch the meaning of legislation to render it compatible with the Convention—even to the point of reading into it words that are not present in the text. In 2004, the House of Lords decided that the phrase 'as his or her wife or husband' in schedule 1, paragraph 2(2) of the Rent Act 1977 should become in their interpretation 'as if they were his wife or husband'. Taking place in the era when only opposite-gender marriage was permitted, the case involved whether a person in a same-sex relationship had the right, upon the death of a partner, to inherit protected tenancy under the 1977 Act as did someone who had been married. The Human Rights Act enabled the judiciary to decide that they did, using a novel interpretive method.[5]

If the interpretative efforts of the courts with respect to subordinate legislation fail to reconcile it with the ECHR, it is possible for them to rescind it. But this approach is unavailable for primary legislation that the judiciary cannot construe as in accordance with the Convention. In such circumstances, section 4 of the 1998 Act activates. It provides for a court to make a 'Declaration of incompatibility' between a 'provision of primary legislation' (a category within which Acts of Parliament are the main component) and a 'Convention right'. It 'does not affect the validity, continuing operation or enforcement' of the measure, nor is it 'binding on the parties to the proceedings'. A court cannot under the Act disapply or

---

[4] See: Anthony Lester, 'Human Rights and the British Constitution' in Jeffrey Jowell and Dawn Oliver (eds), *The Changing Constitution*, 7th edn (Oxford, Oxford University Press, 2011); Elizabeth Wicks, *The Evolution of a Constitution: Eight Key Moments in British Constitutional History* (Oxford, Hart Publishing, 2006) 111–36.

[5] Hilaire Barnett, *Constitutional and Administrative Law*, 9th edn (Oxford, Routledge, 2011) 405.

void an Act of Parliament, or any individual provision within it. It falls to the government and Parliament to respond to a declaration of incompatibility. Section 10 provides a means by which ministers, if they deem it necessary, can move swiftly to resolve conflicts between an Act of Parliament and the Convention, once all possibilities for appeal are exhausted. They can, by order, alter the primary legislation that is found in violation of the Convention. But while the ultimate ability to resolve conflicts does not rest with the courts, in practice ministers have accepted declarations of incompatibility when made.

From the point of view of high constitutional theory, the Human Rights Act1998 is protected from implied repeal: later Acts of Parliament do not amend or repeal the 1998 Act, unless they expressly state that they do so. However, as a corollary, the 1998 Act cannot by implication alter earlier Acts. Furthermore, Parliament retains the ability to amend or repeal the 1998 Act if it does so explicitly. Nonetheless, the Act has the effect of creating a legal rule that conflicts with the doctrine of parliamentary sovereignty, at least as Dicey envisaged it.[6] Though this change was daring for the UK, it amounts to weaker review and entrenchment than available under numerous written constitutions. To go further in the UK would be more controversial still. The impact upon parliamentary sovereignty had long been a concern for those considering some kind of charter of rights in the UK. In 1980, in accordance with a manifesto commitment the Conservative Party had made at the 1979 General Election, the Cabinet agreed on 24 April 1980 that the Home Secretary would establish an interdepartmental group of officials to 'consider the implications of a Bill of Rights for existing legislation'. One of the subjects the Interdepartmental Group of Officials discussed was the possibility of 'Full legal entrenchment' for a Bill of Rights 'for example allowing changes to be made only by a two-thirds majority in both Houses of Parliament'. It concluded that such a measure 'would be unlikely to be effective under our constitution with its recognition of unqualified Parliamentary legal sovereignty'. However, it might be that a convention could emerge that it was possible to abrogate the Bill of Rights only 'under certain conditions'.[7]

The Human Rights Act took into account such concerns, and they have persisted. While the interdepartmental committee of 1980 focused on amendment, a connected issue was enforcement. When considering the idea of a specific UK Bill of Rights in 2008, the Joint Committee on Human Rights stated in 2008 that it was opposed to a Bill of Rights affording the ability to the courts 'to strike down legislation'. The committee found this approach 'fundamentally at odds with this country's tradition of parliamentary democracy'.[8] In its 2009 assessment of the

---

[6] For diverse views on this issue see: Alison Young, *Parliamentary Sovereignty and the Human Rights Act* (Oxford, Hart Publishing, 2008); Aileen Kavanagh, *Constitutional Review under the UK Human Rights Act* (Cambridge, Cambridge University Press, 2009).

[7] The National Archive/Public Record Office HO 342/328, 'A Bill of Rights', Report by the Interdepartmental Group of Officials, draft, 18 August 1980.

[8] Commission on a Bill of Rights, *A UK Bill of Rights? The Choice Before Us*, Vol I (London, Commission on a Bill of Rights, 2012) 61.

options for a possible UK Bill of Rights, the Ministry of Justice was concerned to stress that it would not alter the position of Parliament. The Ministry stated that Parliament would remain 'free to legislate' and that 'the courts would have no power to strike down or rewrite future legislation'. The paper added that 'it is the Government's clear view that Parliamentary sovereignty must remain as the cornerstone of the UK constitution'.[9] Finally, in 2012 the Commission on a Bill of Rights, appointed by the Coalition, issued its final report. The Commission found favour with the approach contained in the Human Rights Act involving 'declarations of incompatibility'. In the view of the Commission, this mechanism maintained 'a sensible balance between, on the one hand, the ultimate sovereignty of the UK Parliament and, on the other, the duty of courts to declare and enforce the law'. Any UK Bill of Rights, it found, should follow this method.[10]

Beyond the way in which it approaches the review of Acts of Parliament, the 1998 Act encourages a culture of human rights in the UK. Section 6 makes it 'unlawful for a public authority to act in a way which is incompatible with a Convention right'. This stipulation makes it necessary for institutions across the UK to consider their actions from a human rights perspective. A gap in coverage has appeared involving the precise definition of a 'public authority'. Though the Act states that section 6 applies to 'any person certain of whose functions are functions of a public nature', case law has determined that private or voluntary sector organisations providing public services can be exempt from the section 6 requirement. The effect could be arbitrary variations in the extent to which human rights are protected, according to the particular organisation that was providing a service to any given recipient. With this omission in mind, the Commission on a Bill of Rights noted in 2012 'the growing prevalence of the outsourcing of once traditional publicly provided functions to private and third sector providers', and recommended considering altering the meaning of 'public authority' accordingly, if a UK Bill of Rights came about.[11]

Nonetheless, the legal regime set out in section 6 is important. It creates not only a negative obligation—preventing incompatible behaviour—but can extend to requiring an authority positively to guarantee rights: it specifically defines 'act' as including 'failure to act'. Furthermore, it can reach beyond what are termed 'vertical' relationships—interactions between individuals and institutions of governance—and into 'horizontality', that is the responsibilities and rights that people possess in their relationships with each other. It achieves this effect—albeit to a limited extent—through applying expressly to 'a court or tribunal'. These bodies, in adjudicating on disputes between individuals, must act in accordance with Convention rights, and therefore in the process they condition horizontal relationships towards greater conformance with the values of the ECHR.

---

[9] Ministry of Justice, *Rights and Responsibilities: developing our constitutional framework* (Cm 7577, 2009) 57.

[10] Commission on a Bill of Rights, *A UK Bill of Rights?*, Vol I (n 8) 22.

[11] Ibid.

Section 6 specifically omits Parliament from its coverage, presumably in defer- ence to the doctrine of parliamentary sovereignty. However, it does create a mech- anism that incorporates the consideration of compatibility or otherwise with the Convention into the legislative process at Westminster. Section 19 requires ministers responsible for a particular Bill, early in its passage through Parliament, either to issue a 'statement of compatibility'—that is, to assert the opinion that it conforms with the Convention, or to explain that while believing it violates the ECHR, nonetheless the government intends to proceed with it. This device forces government specifically to consider legislation from the point of view of human rights, and provides a basis for Parliament to do the same. To help the legislature to perform this function, since 2001 a committee of both Houses—the Joint Committee on Human Rights—has assessed Bills for their compliance with the Convention, alongside carrying out wider enquiries into human rights matters.

PROTECTED RIGHTS, THEIR LIMITATIONS AND THEIR IMPACT

The precise Convention rights that the Act incorporates into UK law are listed in schedule 1. Article 2 is the right to life. It means that no one shall be killed except in accordance with the law. Article 3 is the prohibition of torture, inhuman or degrading treatment or punishment. It reflects one of the provisions of the 1689 Bill of Rights. The Article means not only that the UK public authorities cannot use these methods, but that they cannot be complicit in their application else- where. For instance, the Article has the effect of prohibiting the use of evidence in legal proceedings obtained by these means, and the deportation of individuals to places where there is a risk of their exposure to such practices. These rules, arising from European Court of Human Rights case law, are a logical extension of the basic prohibition, since without them the UK could legally become an accessory to, or possibly outsourcer of, torture. They have also proved a source of public contro- versy in the present era of international terrorism, since they have created obstacles to the prosecution or deportation of individuals judged to be security threats.

Next, Article 4 prohibits slavery and servitude. Three Articles then follow that clearly and consciously echo Magna Carta. Article 5 protects liberty and security. It states: 'Everyone has the right to liberty and security of person. No one shall be deprived of his liberty save … in accordance with a procedure prescribed by law'. Any individual placed under arrest 'shall be informed promptly, in a language which he understands, of the reasons for his arrest and of any charge against him'. The Article stipulates that anyone subject to arrest or detention 'shall be brought promptly before a judge or other officer authorised by law to exercise judicial power and shall be entitled to trial within a reasonable time or to release pending trial'. Such an individual will also 'be entitled to take proceedings by which the lawfulness of his detention shall be decided speedily by a court and his release ordered if the detention is not lawful'.

Article 6 deals with the right to a fair trial. It states that all are 'entitled to a fair and public hearing within a reasonable time by an independent and impartial tribunal established by law'. Furthermore 'Judgment shall be pronounced publicly' and there will be a presumption of innocence. The accused have certain basic rights: to know the nature of the charge against them; to have the proper opportunity to defend themselves; to be able to represent themselves or choose their own advocate; and, if they do not have the material means to pay for the legal support they need, to have it provided for them. They should be able to question those giving evidence against them, and be able to summon people in the same way that the prosecution can. Article 7 iterates that there shall be no punishment without law. An individual cannot be found to have committed a crime that did not exist at the time they carried out a given act, and punishments cannot be made more severe than they could have been at the point at which a particular transgression occurred. The Article is careful to stipulate that it does not prevent prosecution for actions that contravene 'the general principles of law recognised by civilised nations'—that is, crimes against humanity.

Article 8 provides for respect for private and family life; Article 9 for freedom of thought, conscience and religion. Freedom of expression comes in Article 10, and freedom of assembly and association in Article 11. Article 12 covers the right to marry and have a family, while Article 14 forbids discrimination against individuals in securing the Convention rights on 'any ground such as sex, race, colour, language, religion, political or other opinion, national or social origin, association with a national minority, property, birth or other status'. Article 16 records the proviso that the authorities can limit the 'political activity of aliens', notwithstanding Articles 10, 11 and 14. Article 17 rules out the use of the Convention as providing grounds for undermining the rights it protects, while Article 18 stipulates that the use of limitations on rights allowed for under the Convention shall only serve the ends set out in the Convention itself. Three further Articles come in the First Protocol. Article 1 protects property, securing the 'peaceful enjoyment of ... possessions'. The right to education comes in Article 2, and to free elections in Article 3. In another passage reminiscent of the 1689 Bill of Rights, this latter Article calls for 'free elections at reasonable intervals by secret ballot, under conditions which will ensure the free expression of the opinion of the people in the choice of the legislature'. Once more, the connection between individual rights and democracy is apparent. Finally, Article 1 of the Thirteenth Protocol abolishes the death penalty.

An initial observation regarding these rights is that the particular way in which they have effect varies. They fall into three general categories. First come rights that are 'absolute'—that is, there are no circumstances in which withholding them is possible. Within this group are the right to life (Article 2), the right not to be subject to torture or inhuman or degrading treatment (Article 3), and the prohibitions of slavery (Article 1(1)) and of punishment without law (Article 7). Second are the 'limited' rights. They include Articles 4(2) and 4(3) dealing with forced labour, and Article 5, the right to liberty and security. In these cases, constraints can apply to the rights, but only in specific and circumscribed ways. Finally, 'qualified' rights involve balancing the position of the individual against the broader interests of society. Among this category are freedom of expression (set out in Article 10), freedom of assembly and association (contained in Article 11), and the right to property (provided for by Article 1 of Protocol 1). This is a sophisticated framework, then, allowing for flexibility where appropriate, and one that has become richer over time as case law has extrapolated its contents.

A further quality of these Convention stipulations is that they broadly fall into the category known as civil and political rights, and engage social and economic matters less. This emphasis and the omissions it might produce require consideration. The earliest English legal statements of the Anglo-Saxon era could deal with issues such as ensuring welfare provision. Yet over time, this feature of traditional legal norms gradually came to be overlooked. However, the concept of economic and social rights gained ground internationally from the mid-twentieth century. In 2008, promoting the received more than the historic view of Magna Carta, the parliamentary Joint Committee on Human Rights held that

> the rights which have been gradually conferred over the last 60 years or so by the welfare state, such as the right to health, housing and education, are now seen in the popular imagination as being just as fundamental as what are perceived to be the ancient rights in Magna Carta.[12]

The UK is signed up to treaties such as the United Nations International Covenant on Social, Economic and Cultural Rights. But this agreement is not incorporated into UK law—nor does it have the same supranational enforcement mechanisms as the Convention. But there is some provision in this area. In 2004, the parliamentary Joint Committee on Human Rights found that although specific protection of economic and social rights as such was lacking in the UK, various statutes in effect dealt with aspects of them, including 'housing, healthcare, employment relations and discrimination'. Furthermore, the committee noted that it was not possible to establish a 'clear line of demarcation between the substance of rights classified as civil and political, and those classified as economic social and cultural'. The Human Rights Act, though primarily aimed at the former category, supplied some protection for the latter. Article 3 of the ECHR prohibiting inhuman and degrading treatment, could 'guard against the worst forms of destitution'. Other ECHR rights—such as those involving physical integrity, personal autonomy and privacy—could engage access to health care. Provision for freedom of association under the ECHR applied to trade unions and their members (and those who did not wish to join them). The First Protocol of the ECHR, moreover, covered education and property rights.[13]

Just as the idea of making rights more enforceable or entrenched met with resistance, so did the prospect of introducing more explicit socio-economic provision. If any party might support such a proposition, it would—one might

---

[12] Joint Committee on Human Rights, *A Bill of Rights for the UK* (2007–08, HL 165-I, HC 150-I) 43.
[13] Joint Committee on Human Rights, *The International Covenant on Economic, Social and Cultural Rights* (2003–04, HL 183, HC 1188) 10–12.

imagine—be Labour. In 2009, the Labour Government issued a paper on a possible Bill of Rights for the UK. On the subject of whether economic, social and cultural rights should have equal force in such a document it argued that they involved matters that were more appropriately the business of 'democratically accountable elected representatives', not the judiciary. The choices involved normally entailed 'politically sensitive resource allocation'. To deal with them in the courts would undermine 'democratic accountability' and 'the separation of powers between the judiciary, the legislature and the executive which underpins our constitutional arrangements'. The government would not, consequently, advocate the full inclusion of economic, social and cultural rights in a Bill of Rights. It would, however, countenance some kind of declaratory iteration of core values.[14]

The 1998 Act, in international comparison, was neither firmly enforceable nor heavily entrenched; and in accordance with the Convention it provided for some kinds of rights more than others. But it has made a pronounced impact. Most dramatic of all have been the declarations of incompatibility. Between 2000 when the Act came into force and 2013 there were 27 issued, eight of which were reversed after appeal, 19 which became, in part or in their totality, final. The government description of the substantive matters involved in these cases is a fascinating piece of literature. It suggests that the Act has been creating a special legal space for the private and public realisation of the essence of humanity, and a respect for the ability of others to do the same. While all deriving from this theme, the issues engaged are expansive, including: the decision-making procedures of public authorities as they impact upon people; the detention of individuals in custody; sexual freedom; due process of law; safety in the workplace; transgender rights; and more.[15] The broadness and importance of these matters are manifest. But some of the most significant impact of the Human Rights Act has been away from the headline declarations of incompatibility, and indeed from legal action at all, and beyond the direct realm of civil and political rights. Research by the British Institute of Human Rights marking the tenth anniversary of the Act found that it had fostered different modes of behaviour among practitioners in public services providing support for the most vulnerable members of society, taking into account their basic dignity as human beings.[16] At work here was precisely the kind of cultural change that legal-institutional alterations can foster.

The 1998 Act arrived shortly before the commencement of a challenging period for some of the values it represented. Less than a year after it became operational, the terrorist attacks on the US of 11 September 2001 took place. This event marked the beginning of a period in which the Labour Government that had facilitated the Act pursued a series of security measures that strained

---

[14] Ministry of Justice, *Rights and Responsibilities* (n 9) 43.

[15] Ministry of Justice, *Responding to human rights judgements: Report to the Joint Committee on Human Rights on the government response to human rights judgements 2011–12* (Cm 8432, 2013).

[16] Lucy Matthews et al, *The Human Rights Act—Changing Lives*, 2nd edn (London, British Institute of Human Rights, 2008).

traditional understandings of legal due process and civil and political rights.[17] Challenges to aspects of its counterterrorist policies took place under the Human Rights Act. From one perspective, this dynamic demonstrated how important the Act was. However, the Act does not have a secure future. The Conservative Party in particular is now committed to repealing it, replacing it with a substitute, and seeking to reduce the application of the ECHR as an international treaty to the UK. Furthermore, resentment of the role of the Council of Europe for supposedly interfering in UK matters, particularly over the issue of prisoner voting rights, extends beyond the Conservative Party.

A flavour of some of the thought influencing the Conservative Party is found in a pamphlet by Michael Pinto-Dushinsky, published by the Policy Exchange think tank in 2011. It shows how the Human Rights Act and other developments discussed in this work could figure in narratives of an undesirable compromising of constitutional principles. In his publication, Pinto-Dushinsky warned about the possibility of members of the judiciary becoming 'politicians in robes', and of the concept of human rights expanding to the point that they became meaningless, singling out the use of the prohibition on torture against the 'spanking' of minors as an example of misapplication. The author argued that 'the doctrine of parliamentary sovereignty deserves deep reverence' and was a 'cornerstone of our democracy'. Yet it was endangered by 'elite circles of human rights experts, lawyers and employees of public interest lobbies'.[18]

In his recommendations, Pinto-Dushinsky stressed the need for governments to avoid violations of human rights and of the rule of law. At the same time, he held that Parliament should have a role in the appointment of Supreme Court judges, taking into account the attitudes of the individuals involved and the interpretations they might therefore apply to the Acts that Parliament passed. Pinto-Dushinsky's favoured option was for the Prime Minister to select these senior judges from shortlists of up to three, with parliamentary agreement required. He also believed that the UK should seek to ensure that the balance of the membership of the European Court of Human Rights became more closely proportionate to the numbers of people living in the Member States of the Council of Europe, and that the Court should be more restrained in changing over time the way in which it interpreted the ECHR. Other Pinto-Dushinsky proposals for the Court included that it should leave more discretion to domestic courts. If the UK could not obtain the changes it wanted, he suggested, it might choose to exempt itself from the scope of the Court.

Pinto-Dushinsky put forward a plan for amending the Human Rights Act to end the requirement for judges to do their utmost to interpret Acts of Parliament

---

[17] For a comprehensive account of legislation in this area, see: Clive Walker, *Terrorism and the Law* (Oxford, Oxford University Press, 2011).

[18] Michael Pinto-Dushinsky, *Bringing Rights Back Home: Making Human Rights Compatible with Parliamentary Democracy in the UK* (London, Policy Exchange, 2011) 5.

in a fashion that meant they were congruent with the ECHR. Pinto-Dushinsky objected to the discretion this provision afforded the judiciary. He preferred, if necessary, the use of declarations of incompatibility, since they left the last word with Parliament. To ensure fuller consideration of such judicial decisions in Westminster, Pinto-Dushinsky advocated the abolition of the expedited procedure for amendment of primary legislation found to be in violation of the ECHR. Regular procedures should apply. The author discouraged accession to further international human rights instruments without thorough consideration and a guarantee that they lacked legal force. He was particularly reticent about economic and social rights, and called for a debate about the difference between central and more peripheral rights.[19]

A further Policy Exchange pamphlet by Thomas Tugendhat and Laura Croft appeared in 2013. It extended beyond the concerns about internal constitutional integrity that Pinto-Dushinsky had raised and argued that the changing constitutional role of the courts, again with the ECHR and Human Rights Act at the centre, undermined the ability of the UK to guarantee its security against external threats. Developments in case law had extended the application of the Human Rights Act to cover territory overseas that was under effective control of the UK, and to armed forces personnel taking part in battle. Growing emphasises were on 'the rights of detainees, duty of care and the Right to Life'. The authors, though stressing that rules of some kind should apply to combat, concluded that this trend had an undesirable impact upon the way in which the military procured equipment, trained its staff and deployed them in the field. Major wars in future, they found, could be difficult to fight because of the use and threat of legal action. Recalling Stalin's question, 'How many divisions does the Pope have?', Tugendhat and Croft wrote: 'Today, the question is: how many divisions does the judiciary have?'.[20]

Views expressed in these pamphlets came to influence Conservative policy. They were reinforced by evidence that some members of the senior judiciary were coming to resent the influence of the European Court of Human Rights. In October 2014, the Conservative Party brought forward proposals for changes to the position of human rights in UK law. The Conservatives complained that 'Labour's Human Rights Act undermines the sovereignty of Parliament'—the value of this doctrine was apparently axiomatic. They also held that the Act was detrimental to 'democratic accountability to the public'. The party committed to abolishing the Human Rights Act but at the same time including the ECHR in an Act of Parliament. The Conservatives would then 'Clarify the Convention rights, to reflect a proper balance between rights and responsibilities'. The stated intention of this exercise was to ensure the attainment of the initial purpose of the Convention and to fit with 'mainstream understanding' of its provisions. It gave

---

[19] Ibid, 70–73.
[20] Thomas Tugendhat and Laura Croft, *The Fog of Law: An Introduction to the Legal Erosion of British Fighting Power* (London, Policy Exchange, 2013) 54.

three examples of the difference it might make in practice, all of which involved deportation of foreign nationals. Human rights legislation would only apply in 'the most serious cases'—defined as 'criminal law ... the liberty of an individual, the right to property and similar serious matters'. Courts in the UK would in future have less latitude in interpreting legislation, adhering to its 'normal meaning and the clear intention of Parliament'. To protect the armed forces from litigation involving operations abroad, the Conservatives would limit the scope of human rights law to the UK. An amendment to the Ministerial Code would make explicit the requirement upon ministers to adhere to the intentions of Parliament.

The paper emphasised the idea of freeing the UK legal system from Strasbourg. It promised to remove the obligation upon UK courts to consider the decisions of the European Court of Human Rights, and that the European Court would no longer be able to require changes in UK law, with its views 'treated as advisory'. If the Council of Europe did not provide prior agreement that the Conservative approach was valid, withdrawal from the ECHR, the paper insisted, was an option. It acknowledged that there would be consequential implications for the relationship with the European Union (EU). However, the presentation of these proposals neglected the possibility of a clash over the interpretation and application of rights at domestic level, between the UK judiciary and politicians in Whitehall or Westminster. They seemed to amount to a horizontal power-grab—from UK courts to Parliament—as much as a vertical—from Strasbourg to the UK. While the idea of repelling foreign interference was useful for rhetorical purposes, other types of tension are plausible. The prescriptive nature of these policies, seeking to limit the discretion of the judiciary in an area of fundamental importance, could in fact induce such a confrontation.[21]

A CLASH OF MODELS

The controversy surrounding human rights provision in the UK is part of a wider cleavage. Various tendencies discussed above suggest the rise of a new constitutional paradigm. Members of the public are increasingly willing to use the courts to challenge public authorities. The judiciary is more ready to support such efforts and develop tools to enable it to do so. Courts have a new role in reviewing Acts of Parliament, thanks both to membership of the EU and the Human Rights Act. This Act has also made the ECHR more embedded, in legal terms, as well as in institutional, political and cultural senses. Other changes discussed in previous chapters, such as the introduction of devolution, have given to the courts a greater constitutional role than they once had. They have come far closer to the position they might occupy under a written constitution, in which all public authorities, even when they produce primary legislation, can be subject to a set of rules contained in the document, as interpreted by the judiciary. The courts do not yet

---

[21] *Protecting Human Rights in the UK* (London, Conservative Party, 2014).

carry out explicit constitutional review. However, in practice they now engage in the application of defined fundamental principles that take them close to this practice, in particular human rights.

Some within the judiciary believe they could go further still. As part of his judgment in the so-called 'Metric Martyrs' case, *Thoburn v Sunderland City Council*,[22] on 18 February 2002 Laws LJ made some comments that came to attract much interest from constitutional observers (and were perhaps intended to do so). They were *obiter*—that is, they were asides not directly pertaining to the specific decision—and therefore did not have legal force as such. Nonetheless, Laws LJ conveyed ideas of fundamental importance to arrangements in the UK. They suggested a scenario in which the judiciary takes upon itself the power to invent a new class of constitutional statute; to decide which enactments precisely came within this category; and to impose a new requirement on Parliament as to the form in which it should legislate in certain circumstances. Laws LJ held that the common law had developed to a point that it acknowledged rights it was appropriate to describe as 'fundamental'. This observation led to another: the existence of 'a hierarchy of Acts of Parliament'. Laws LJ suggested a distinction between '"ordinary" statutes and "constitutional" statutes'. He believed that a law fitting in the latter category was discernable if it '[a] conditions the legal relationship between citizen and State in some general, overarching manner, or [b] enlarges or diminishes the scope of what we would now regard as fundamental constitutional rights'. He expected that a statute meeting definition (a) would also fit with (b). Laws LJ gave examples of legislation fitting within the 'constitutional statutes' group: Magna Carta; the Bill of Rights; the Act [sic] of Union; the Franchise Reform Acts; the Human Rights Act; the Scotland Act 1998; and the Government of Wales Act 1998. Finally, the European Communities Act (which the 'Metric Martyrs' case engaged) 'clearly belongs in this family'.

A simple distinction was possible regarding legal status: 'Ordinary statutes may be impliedly repealed. Constitutional statutes may not'. In seeking to decide whether an Act altered a constitutional statute, a court would ask whether 'the legislature's *actual*—not imputed, constructive or presumed—intention was to effect the repeal or abrogation'. Laws LJ believed the most satisfactory way of fulfilling this requirement would be through 'express words in the later statute, or by words so specific that the inference of an actual determination to effect the result contended for was irresistible'. He felt that the 'ordinary rule of implied repeal' was not sufficient, and had 'no application to constitutional statutes'. Laws LJ regarded the appearance of constitutional rights and statutes as 'highly beneficial'. It conferred 'the benefits of a written constitution, in which fundamental rights are accorded special respects' while retaining 'sovereignty of the legislature and the flexibility of our uncodified constitution'.

How much reassurance these latter comments would provide to supporters of parliamentary sovereignty is questionable. Many within this still substantial

---

[22] *Thoburn v Sunderland City Council* [2002] EWHC 195 (Admin) para 102.

grouping regard their doctrine as under attack from the judiciary (and supra-national European forces). This tension is a source of constitutional instability. The executive—parliamentary response—given impetus by the counterterrorism security agenda, as well as populist campaigns over immigration, asylum seeking and aspects of European integration—could go as far as to include attempts to tamper with, or even compromise judicial review, and dilute legal protection for human rights. It is likely that serious controversy would follow. The immediate criticism that the Conservative proposals for the ECHR met with in October 2014 give an indication of the kind of argument that can erupt. Both sides would probably claim that they were defending the rule of law: one asserting that it was synonymous with parliamentary sovereignty, the other arguing that there is a need for limitations upon the authority of the legislature to preserve certain fundamentals. But how might the judiciary respond in practical terms?

It is possible that the courts would ultimately decide that they were subordinate to Parliament, partly depending on the political climate and the extremity of the measures being implemented. However, some judges within the so-called 'common law constitutionalism' school, have suggested radical action would be possible. Another attention-grabbing *obiter* comment came on 14 November 2005 from Lord Steyn. He gave his judgment as one of nine members of the House of Lords Appellate Committee deciding an appeal against the validity of the Hunting Act 2004.[23] It had passed into law only following the use of the Parliament Acts to bypass the Lords. Lord Steyn discussed the implications that would arise from acceptance of the proposition that it was possible to use the Parliament Acts for any legislative purpose whatsoever. In such a scenario, 'oppressive and wholly undemocratic legislation' would become attainable. Lord Steyn described how the two Acts could facilitate abolition of 'judicial review of flagrant abuse of power by a government or even the role of the ordinary courts standing between the executive and its citizens'.

But, Lord Steyn held, the UK did not have an 'uncontrolled constitution'. He listed what he saw as some constraints on the supremacy of Parliament: European law; the Scotland Act (that, Lord Steyn asserted, suggested 'a divided sovereignty'); and the ECHR as integrated into the domestic system by the Human Rights Act, creating a 'new legal order'. He concluded that the 'classic account given by Dicey of the doctrine of the supremacy of Parliament, pure and absolute as it was, can now be seen to be out of place in the modern United Kingdom'. Parliamentary supremacy remained the '*general* principle of our constitution'. Yet, it was, Lord Steyn asserted, 'a construct of common law. The judges created this principle. If that is so, it is not unthinkable that circumstances could arise where the courts may have to qualify a principle established on a different hypothesis of constitutionalism'. If, for instance, an attempt to 'abolish judicial review or the ordinary role of the courts' took place, the Appellate Committee or its successor the

---

[23] *Jackson and others (appellants) v Her Majesty's Attorney General (Respondent)* [2005] UKHL 56.

Supreme Court might need 'to consider whether this is a constitutional fundamental which even a sovereign Parliament acting at the behest of a complaisant House of Commons cannot abolish'.

Though he did not say so in specific terms, Lord Steyn was by implication depicting a serious constitutional crisis. Some of his reasoning was faulty. The Scotland Act 1998 has not yet developed into a formal constraint on the law-making authority of Parliament. But his general prediction could conceivably come about. If faced with an Act of Parliament that plausibly amounted to a major abrogation of the rule of law, it is understandable that the judiciary might be reluctant to apply it, or at least wish to interpret it in a way that contradicted the clear wishes of Parliament. This approach would replace one problem with another. To prevent an abuse of parliamentary sovereignty, a court might take on itself the right unilaterally to bring about an alteration in the basic constitutional order, an action for which it lacks legitimacy. Furthermore, it is likely that such an effort would meet resistance. A direct confrontation between the judiciary and legislature would take place. Depending on the issue, it might well be that the latter would have populist media support and public opinion to aid it. While victory for either side would be problematic, success for Parliament, possibly the more likely outcome, could have grave implications for the rule of law. It might be that such a battle would eventually drive the introduction of a written constitution for the UK. Pre-emptive action—which ensures that the rules are owned collectively and the sole property neither of Parliament nor the courts—is preferable.

10

Direction of Travel

THE UNDERPINNINGS OF the United Kingdom (UK) constitution are shifting. Changes such as EU membership, devolution, and an altered role for the judiciary—each important in its own right—are connected to deeper movements in the principles and powers on which the system of governance rests. Already, more traditional accounts of our arrangements, that always had deficiencies, are in key areas redundant. But where might this transition lead? One outcome worth considering is a written constitution. Some of the qualities of such an entity are already discernable in the UK today. Yet the same forces that may drive towards a text for the UK have prompted the assertion of other, conflicting values. Nonetheless, interest in and support for this reform among observers has grown. Policymakers have begun to take the idea of a written constitution more seriously. Furthermore, any attempt to put it into practice will be able to draw upon a number of draft texts that have emanated from different parts of the political spectrum.

CODIFYING CONVENTION AND LIMITING THE ROYAL PREROGATIVE

An important feature of constitutional transformation dating from the late 1950s has been not only the particular substantive changes that have taken place, but their cumulative impact in compromising a set of often interlinked core understandings and authorities. Parliamentary sovereignty, for instance, faces challenges both legal and practical. Assertions that the UK is a unitary state, always in need at the very least of qualification, are harder to maintain. Courts are more able and willing to challenge public authorities, and the limits on such judicial practice are unclear. Upholding collective Cabinet responsibility—particularly in the recent period of coalition government—has become increasingly problematic. Changes in the Civil Service and in the relationship between Parliament and government make the line of accountability from executive to electorate, via the legislature, less defined. Trends including a decline in traditional forms of participation create problems for the democratic legitimacy of the system. We can further illustrate this movement of reference points through consideration of two particular sources from which the constitution derives: convention and the Royal Prerogative.

In most democracies other than the UK the constitution rests on a single text that is in turn—in theory at least—an expression of popular sovereignty. In the UK, the sources of authority for public institutions and systemic rules are more diffuse. First, there are Acts of Parliament, such as the Parliament Acts 1911 and 1949, the devolution legislation, and the Fixed-term Parliaments Act 2011 (and sometimes statutory instruments issued under their authority, which can, for instance, transfer powers between the UK and Scottish Parliament). According to conventional accounts, Acts of Parliament trump other possible constitutional sources. But nonetheless some important powers have other foundations and do not rest in statute, though Parliament could provide them with such a basis if it chose. The internally enforceable rules of Parliament itself—known as its 'law and custom'—comprise one such non-statutory category. They are found in such places as the Standing Orders of the House of Commons. Judicial decisions, though those who make them present themselves as only applying the law, can in practice perform a constitutionally creative role. The judiciary, for instance, developed a variety of common law individual freedoms. More recent constitutional precepts such as the 'Carltona principle', determining that officials and junior ministers are able to exercise powers possessed by secretaries of state, originated in the courtroom (in this instance in 1943).[1]

Non-domestic influences can comprise a source of constitutional authority. The UK tends towards a dualist model—that is to say, international agreements do not become a full part of internal law other than through an Act of the Westminster Parliament. Nonetheless, courts in their deliberations take into account agreements to which the UK is party, even if not incorporated domestically; other international norms; and relevant judgments reached in proceedings abroad. The internal regulations of political parties can play a part in the functioning of the UK constitution at times such as coalition formation, or when a Prime Minister resigns midway through a parliamentary term. Doctrines such as parliamentary sovereignty, the rule of law and ministerial responsibility, provide a grounding for the constitution. So too does the work of authorities such as Dicey. Even public statements, such as the 'Vow' of September 2014, can take on an apparently constitutional character. Ongoing pressures of recent decades have made adjustments in understandings of all these sources necessary.

Another basis for the UK system of government is that of convention: rules that are not directly legally enacted or enforceable.[2] Conventions exist under all kinds of constitutions whether written or otherwise, but in the UK they provide for a number of arrangements that a constitutional text, if such an entity existed, would probably include. For instance, conventions to a large extent shape the role

---

[1] See: Cabinet Office, *The Cabinet Manual: A guide to the laws, conventions and rules on the operation of government*, 1st edn (London, Cabinet Office, 2011) 25–26.

[2] For the following, see: Andrew Blick and Peter Hennessy, *The Hidden Wiring Emerges: The Cabinet Manual and the Working of the British Constitution* (London, Institute for Public Policy Research, 2011); Andrew Blick, 'The Cabinet Manual and the Codification of Conventions' (2014) 67(1) *Parliamentary Affairs* 191.

of the head of state; determine the functions of the office of Prime Minister and the workings of the Cabinet; ordain the principles underpinning the formation of governments following general elections and their maintenance thereafter; and guide the dealings between devolved institutions and the centre. Conventions are amorphous in a number of ways. Disagreement surrounds how best to define them as a concept, and also the nature of particular conventions. Against this general background of both importance and uncertainty, further change has taken place.

Courts may now recognise the existence of a convention and take it into account in their deliberations. In this way these rules have moved a small distance towards resembling the judicially enforceable stipulations of a written constitution. Another development in conventions has involved the tendency for publicly available, official texts to include descriptions of them. Formerly, commentators depicted their not being explicitly set out in writing as central to their character. For instance John Stuart Mill made reference in 1861 to 'The unwritten maxims of the Constitution … These un-written rules, which limit the use of lawful powers'. It is now necessary to qualify such accounts. Increasingly accounts of conventions are written down in official documents, available in the public domain. In 2004, the former Cabinet Secretary and Head of the Home Civil Service, Lord Wilson of Dinton—in an assessment of the nature of constitutional conventions—noted the 'proliferation of Codes' that was under way. The texts to which he referred did not always deal solely with conventions—which are difficult precisely to identify anyway—but they certainly made up at least a portion of their content. Examples of these texts include the so-called 'Osmotherly Rules' containing guidance for civil servants on the provision of evidence to select committees, that first came became public in 1980, and the 'Armstrong Memorandum' of 1985, setting out the constitutional relationship between officials and ministers. In 1992, the Government published a previously internal document, Questions of Procedure for Ministers (since 1997 known as the Ministerial Code).[3] The Civil Service Code appeared in 1996 and the Code of Conduct for Special Advisers in 2001. Both of these documents now have a statutory source, under the Constitutional Renewal and Governance Act 2010. Potentially, this development could suggest a wider momentum from unwritten convention to code to Act of Parliament. While the Ministerial Code is not yet provided for through Act of Parliament, the equivalent document has such a basis at devolved level in Northern Ireland.[4]

The texts cited so far dealt with the inner workings and external relationships of the UK executive, which produced and owned them. Other constitutional branches have become involved in the practice of seeking to encapsulate—or perhaps create—conventions. Since 2000 the devolved and UK governments have operated a Memorandum of Understanding agreed between them, setting up non-statutory rules for their relations, involving mutual respect of spheres of

---

[3] Amy Baker, *Prime Ministers and the Rule Book* (London, Politico's, 2000).
[4] See: Northern Ireland Act 1998, s 28A.

operation, and the basis for cooperation in areas of potential overlap. A House of Commons document, *Core Tasks for Select Committees*, first appeared in 2002. In 2004, the Judges' Council issued the first edition of the *Guide to Judicial Conduct*. That there existed a requirement regularly to update and republish these documents was itself becoming by convention. Then in 2011 the *Cabinet Manual* appeared in its first full edition.[5] Another executive product, it found inspiration in a document of the same name from one of the few states other than the UK to lack a written constitution—New Zealand. The manual provided an expansive account of conventions ranging across the entirety of the constitution, from the executive perspective, and contained various references to other codes in its text.

Drivers of this codification phenomenon have included public pressure for greater transparency in official institutions, and the need to codify relationships between such bodies that might previously have functioned on a less formal basis. Declining deference on the part of the public towards official authorities, and between and within different institutions, may be connected to a breakdown in the effectiveness of tacit rules, creating a need for clearer encapsulation. Similar dynamics were at work in England in 1215. In as far as official versions of these understandings now exist in writing, again the UK constitution is increasingly taking on a textual form in the public arena. Those who issue them, including the executive, may create heightened political pressure to be seen to abide by the rules they set out. It is plausible that reference to a convention in an official document increases the chances of its playing a meaningful role in judicial review. Yet the processes leading to the production of these documents do not adhere to the standards of inclusive engagement appropriate to a written constitution. In many cases, the executive drafts them and—even if it does carry out public consultation—has ultimate control over the content.

This arbitrary quality would be a problem even if these texts merely described the internal position within Whitehall as it already existed. They do not. Often they involve the manner in which the executive deals with other institutions and groups, such as Parliament and the public, making the exclusive nature of their production more problematic. Furthermore, describing conventions in official documents inevitably leads to change of some kind, executed either unconsciously or deliberately on the part of the authors. The *Cabinet Manual*—and here is another point of comparison with Magna Carta—presented itself as stating already prevailing principles. The preface by the then Cabinet Secretary and Head of the Home Civil Service, Gus O'Donnell, claimed that its role was 'recording the current position rather than driving change'. But in reality it did more. In one area—the principle that the Cabinet Secretary could arrange Civil Service support for parties in negotiations following a general election with no overall winner— the manual, published in an early draft before the 2010 General Election, actually fabricated a rule and in the process allowed O'Donnell to supply this service in May 2010. Codification of conventions, then, presents some opportunity for

---

[5] See: Cabinet Office, *The Cabinet Manual* (n 1) 25–26.

alteration of the constitutional landscape by one party—often the UK executive—acting unilaterally. One recent and problematic exploitation of this potential occurred when the Coalition issued a document entitled *Consultation Principles* in 2013. Setting out the basis on which departments should engage the public in the development of government proposals, it superseded earlier guidance contained in the Code of Practice on Consultation that had first appeared in 2000. In the process, it diluted the more comprehensive requirements on government included in the earlier text and enhanced the discretion of the executive that produced it.

When they issue texts such as the *Cabinet Manual*, governments draw on a constitutional power source known as the Royal Prerogative.[6] It is of ancient origin, beginning as a set of authorities that monarchs wielded personally. As old as these powers is a tension associated with them, providing a central theme of the great historic constitutional conflicts. The idea that rulers can act alone has always met with some kind of resistance. Anglo-Saxon law codes made a point of stating that they were issued with the involvement of others. Abuse of the prerogative by John Lackland led to the attempt to restrain him and the appearance of Magna Carta. Many subsequent texts—including from the critical seventeenth-century period—sought to limit this authority. During the Cromwell era, written constitutions set out and regulated a group of executive powers equivalent to the Royal Prerogative. Parliament developed as the institution through which the monarch could legislate together with the Commons and the Lords, rather than alone. Eventually, in the post-Bill of Rights era, Parliament and its Acts attained definite supremacy over the prerogative.

Defeat for Stuart absolutism led on to a decisive alteration in the nature of the Royal Prerogative, but not an eradication of it. The strict position now is that entirely new manifestations of the prerogative cannot appear, and that the legislature can by Act of Parliament reduce its scope. In practice it is now largely ministers who utilise Royal Prerogative powers, though some remain personal to the head of state. Parliament has by definition never authorised them, and does not have a legal right of involvement in their exercise, unless it specifically provides itself with such a role through statute. However, ministers are in theory accountable to Parliament for the full span of their activities, and they must act subject to political realities. To ignore the views of Parliament is badly advised, and a government may regard it as appropriate to consult the legislature over a matter of Royal Prerogative even though not strictly required to do so. Furthermore, parliamentary approval is needed to raise the money required to fund any policy, regardless of the particular constitutional authority under which it is exercised.

Under the Royal Prerogative today, government can conduct diplomacy; declare war (though it has not done so since 1942); enter into armed combat without declaring war (which it certainly continues to do); direct the armed forces at home and abroad; ratify treaties (since 2010 subject—in theory—to

---

[6] For the following, see: Andrew Blick, 'Emergency powers and the withering of the Royal Prerogative' (2014) 18(2) *The International Journal of Human Rights* 195.

a parliamentary process); provide the basis for public corporations such as the BBC; and wield residual emergency powers. The Prime Minister and all government ministers are appointed under the Royal Prerogative. Honours and peerages (the latter entailing membership of the House of Lords) are conferred using this authority. Other powers—such as the right to force people into navy service— may or may not now be defunct. The list goes on, but there is no definitive official account of the extent of the Royal Prerogative. For this reason the courts can play an important part in identifying whether or not a particular power exists. In the process, they can act creatively—though they do not present their role in these terms—by adapting the prerogative to changed circumstances. Further discretion arises because a statute can only abolish a prerogative power expressly or by necessary implication. The judiciary may consequently need to decide whether it is possible for an Act and the prerogative to operate in the same general area, or whether the latter must defer to the former. Here is another example of the complex relationship between Parliament—and the sovereignty some believe it wields—and the courts. Where the will of the legislature ends and the latitude of the judiciary begins is not always clear. Traditionally, however, the courts have been more restrained in another sense. While it was accepted that they could consider whether or not a particular prerogative authority exists, they did not scrutinise the manner of its exercise. James VI/I seems to have had this limitation in mind when during a speech to the Star Chamber in 1616 he held that the 'absolute Prerogative of the Crown' was 'no Subject for the tongue of a Lawyer'.

Contemporary pressures for constitutional change have found one of their many outlets in reform of the Royal Prerogative. A good illustration of this pattern comes from consideration of the basis on which intelligence and security policy is conducted. During the 1980s and 1990s successive Acts of Parliament dramatically shifted its constitutional foundation. Investigative techniques including the tapping of telephones—that previously seemingly took place on a basis of the prerogative—became subject to the Interception of Communications Act 1985, a parliamentary enactment that simultaneously provided for these activities and created protections against their misuse. The Security Service Act 1989 provided the internal agency, commonly known as MI5 that had rested on the prerogative since 1909, with a statutory foundation. The Secret Intelligence Service (SIS, often known to the public as MI6)—that first came into being at the same time as the Security Service—acquired a new footing in an Act of Parliament through the Intelligence Services Act 1994, as did the Government Communications Headquarters (GCHQ). Both the 1989 and 1994 Acts established arrangements for the oversight of the bodies they mandated, such as tribunals and commissioners. The 1994 Act set up the Intelligence and Security Committee, comprising parliamentarians charged with considering the policy, administration and expenditure of the intelligence and security agencies. In 2013, through the Justice and Security Act, the committee transformed fully into a parliamentary body.

Thus the trend was for a sphere of government action to transfer from the Royal Prerogative and acquire statutory authorisation that in the process introduced greater public accountability to official operations within this sphere. Another transformation took place outside the realm of parliamentary legislative intervention. In 1984, the Law Lords, in a case involving the prohibition of trade union membership for GCHQ employees, disagreed with the view once propounded by James I/VI. They determined that judicial consideration of the prerogative could consider not only whether a prerogative power existed, but also the mode of its deployment. These changes had a variety of motives. Politicians and the media became more likely to challenge the actions and status of the covert agencies. Added impetus came from judgments under the European Convention on Human Rights (ECHR).[7] At the turn of the 1980s—1990s, the collapse of the Soviet bloc prompted further reconsideration of arrangements.

Unfolding external events continued to be important. The developing post-Cold War global security landscape helped create more challenges still for the maintenance of the Royal Prerogative. The UK became a more regular participant in military conflict abroad—the entry into and conduct of which takes place under this ancient executive privilege. At the same time it placed itself at the forefront of an international movement promoting an emergent legal doctrine eventually known as 'responsibility to protect' (R2P) that could both justify and encourage interventions. The operation to prevent atrocities in Kosovo in 1999 was an important practical contribution to this theory. Though few recognised it as such, R2P was a successor to earlier notions of a duty to intervene to prevent tyrannical rule in foreign lands.[8] The sense that England had an obligation to act to prevent Catholic repression of Protestants in the seventeenth century had—in sometimes complex ways—contributed at the time to immense constitutional tension and eventually curtailment of the prerogative. Initially in the twenty-first century, however, it was the Iraq War, the legal case for which was not primarily humanitarian, that drove constitutional reform.

The controversial nature of UK involvement in the action in Iraq in 2003 drew attention to the authority under which it took place. For political reasons, during 2002—03, the Government held three votes on its policy in advance of the full commencement of the operation. But it was under no legal obligation to do so. Increased pressure came from within Westminster and elsewhere to give Parliament a firmer role in military action. Some advocated an Act of Parliament, modelled on the US War Powers Resolution (or Act) 1973, itself in part a response to the way in which the White House had stretched its constitutional authority during the Vietnam War. Supporters of change in the UK hoped to create a requirement—whenever practically possible and appropriate—for UK ministers to obtain approval before deploying troops overseas in circumstances that were hostile, or potentially so. Reformers have not yet achieved this goal, but

---

[7] For the playing out of these tendencies in relation to the Security Service, see: Christopher Andrew, *The Defence of the Realm: The Authorised History of MI5* (London, Penguin, 2010).

[8] See: Brendan Simms and DJB Trim (eds), *Humanitarian Intervention: A History* (Cambridge, Cambridge University Press, 2011).

acceptance began to develop—including within the executive—of a convention to this effect, with the votes over Iraq providing an important precedent. The so-called 'Arab Spring' of 2011 and its consequences returned the humanitarian intervention issue to the forefront of the international political agenda. In turn it provided opportunities to test and shape the emerging rule about the role of the UK Parliament in military conflict.

The results were mixed. On 21 March 2011, a vote took place in the Commons over an action in Libya, but three days after it commenced. As is characteristic of understandings lacking in legal force, the position of Parliament was not firm; it depended on the cooperation of the executive. Yet in August 2013, the Government decided it wanted advance approval for a possible operation, and tentatively proposed the principle of intervention in Syria. The Commons rejected it. This episode demonstrated that the elected chamber was acquiring a new right. It also showed that it was a real power, since approval was more than simply a formality, and might not be forthcoming. Moreover, the vote had an impact on policy, and the outside world. In 2013, the Commons made it politically untenable for the UK Government to proceed with an action in Syria, and as a consequence discouraged the United States from such an intervention. None occurred. Here was proof that constitutional change is more than a theoretical, self-reflective exercise, and can have dramatic external outcomes, whether good or bad. A year later the government proved reluctant to recall Parliament when contemplating action against the Islamic State. In September 2014 it eventually sought and obtained approval from the Commons for air attacks in Iraq, on the condition that it would seek a fresh mandate if extending action to Syria.

The Iraq experience of 2002—03 also helped trigger more wide-ranging reform of the Royal Prerogative. As Prime Minister from mid-2007 Gordon Brown instigated an attempted overhaul of the UK constitution that included a review of the prerogative within it. For the first time a government was going further than simply reducing the scope of this set of powers. It was targeting the authority as a whole as inappropriate, on the grounds that it did not provide a proper role for democratic representatives in Parliament. In 2009 the Government published the fullest ever official account of the range of prerogative powers, though the list insisted it was not exhaustive. The Constitutional Renewal and Governance Act 2010 for the first time gave the Civil Service a statutory source, and provided Parliament with a role (though limited) in the approval of treaties (while ratification itself continued to take place under the prerogative as before). Retrenchment of the Royal Prerogative continued under the Coalition that formed in 2010. A product of the political necessities of the agreement between the Conservatives and Liberal Democrats, the Fixed-term Parliaments Act 2011 removed a power that had been personal to the monarch: to grant dissolutions of Parliament upon requests from the Prime Minister. The Royal Prerogative was—as I have argued elsewhere—withering. But important parts of it survived, such as the power to appoint ministers, to determine their precise portfolios, and to remove them. Armed combat, though subject increasingly to convention, remained a matter of

Royal Prerogative. So too did the conduct of diplomacy. Despite the introduction of the Civil Contingencies Act 2004, supposedly a comprehensive piece of legislation, the executive probably retained certain reserve powers for use in emergency circumstances. The Royal Prerogative has played a part in the creation and attempted entrenchment of a new press regulatory regime. Personal monarchical authorities remained also, including responsibility for choosing and dismissing prime ministers and for granting Royal Assent to parliamentary Bills. These functions were important (though only in extreme circumstances might contemporary monarchs seek to deploy or refuse to deploy them on their own initiative). Reform, then, was rapid and substantial—but incomplete.

A NEW MODEL?

Discussion in previous pages has suggested that, as the traditional constitutional models change and assumptions connected to them become subject to doubt, there are signs of a new structure surfacing in place of the old. Developments through the present period of change have led arrangements for the UK increasingly to resemble a written constitution. The Human Rights Act has similarities with a Bill of Rights. Devolution legislation has some of the quality of provision for the state tier under a federal system, and takes on a role akin to that of a written constitution in the parts of the UK where it applies. The Human Rights Act and European Communities Act have led the courts increasingly to perform tasks with some resemblance to constitutional review, asserting provisions and principles of fundamental importance. Developments in the common law have also involved the courts increasingly upholding principles of a constitutional character. The Constitutional Reform Act 2005 establishes the UK Supreme Court, with some of the features of a constitutional court. Membership of the European Union (EU) entails the acceptance of a legal hierarchy, via the European Communities Act, that in turn creates a system sharing some of the features of a written constitution. Though the draft European constitution signed in 2004 never came into force because of the inability of some Member States to ratify it, the two core documents of the EU today—the Treaty on European Union and the Treaty on the Functioning of the European Union—have some of the content of such a text, to which the UK has subjected itself.[9]

More widely, constitutional arrangements are to an increasing extent defined in writing in official documents of some kind. For instance, the Fixed-term Parliaments Act established precise rules about the calling of elections at a point other than the natural end of a Parliament. Increasingly the conventions of government, which once existed more in implicit form, have come to be defined in published codes. Between them the growing framework of statutes and codes are

---

[9] For a consideration of the EU as a constitutional order, see: Allan Rosas and Lorna Armati, *EU Constitutional Law: An Introduction* (Oxford, Hart Publishing, 2012).

developing into what could conceivably be an embryonic written constitution. The rise of the referendum as a device for taking decisions about systemic change suggests the introduction to the UK of a characteristic associated with written constitutions. It means in practice that some changes to the fundamental rules involve a procedure more demanding than the standard parliamentary legislative process. Another quasi-amendment procedure has appeared with the qualification of the doctrine of implied repeal with respect to the Human Rights and European Communities Acts. Parliament must follow a special procedure to alter or abolish these statutes, by using express terms. The two Acts therefore enjoy entrenchment, though of a relatively soft variety.

To assume the existence of inevitable momentum towards a written constitution, however, would be an error. Many of the changes discussed here met with resistance before and after they came about. Wider objections have appeared to the direction of development as a whole. An example of this school of thought came with a book that appeared in 2000, in the midst of the New Labour reform programme. Entitled *The Rape of the Constitution?*,[10] a picture of Tony Blair appeared on the cover, implying that he was the perpetrator of the alleged offence. The volume dealt with issues including the House of Lords, devolution, and the EU. Despite the sensationalist title, it contained serious contributions that between them expressed support for as well as opposition to change. But its premise suggested the idea of an interlinked set of changes violating a long-established system. The reverse jacket of the book contained advance comments. Vernon Bogdanor complained that 'Reform cannot be equated with rape without a considerable degree of terminological inexactitude'; while Margaret Thatcher regretted: 'I only wonder if you need that question mark in the title'. The outlook Thatcher expressed has survived her passing, and efforts to reverse constitutional change have intensified, with encouragement from significant sections of the print media. The future of the Human Rights Act, along with UK participation in the ECHR and the position of the UK within the EU, are all uncertain. Other reforms—in particular devolution—are more secure.

While some dislike and may seek to reverse constitutional change, others have denied it is taking place in as substantial a fashion as is sometimes held. Jeffrey Goldsworthy has mounted an impressive assertion of the continued viability of the doctrine of parliamentary sovereignty. For him, in contrast to Dicey, implied repeal is not essential. A sovereign Parliament must be able to change previous acts as it chooses. But if in a particular instance it requires itself to do so in explicit terms, it does not negate its underlying authority. Rather, it acts upon an ability 'to protect itself from its own inadvertence'. A requirement that it use express words in order to achieve a particular objective does not remove sovereignty, Goldsworthy holds, provided that it does not prevent it from legislating with respect to particular substantive issues, or seriously restrict its ability to make law.

---

[10] Keith Sutherland (ed), *The Rape of the Constitution* (Thorveton, Imprint Academic, 2000).

Goldsworthy also counters claims that sovereignty is derived from the common law. The theory with which Goldsworthy disagrees—known as 'common law constitutionalism'—points to the conclusion that the courts could, if they chose, dispense with that which they created.[11] Adapting the legal philosopher HLA Hart, Goldsworthy concludes that the legal authority of the legislature in fact rests in a consensus: acceptance by officials based in the judicial, legislative and executive organs of governance. Some judges may have lately expressed the view that they might in certain circumstances impose a different constitutional principle, perhaps by declining to recognise as law an Act of Parliament they believed seriously violated the rule of law. But, Goldsworthy holds, replacement of parliamentary sovereignty would require the establishment of a new consensus. The judiciary or any other party acting alone can break with a consensus unilaterally but cannot by this means establish a new one.

The intellectual achievement of Goldsworthy is great. But from the perspective of the development of the doctrine of parliamentary sovereignty as a whole, it can appear to involve post-rationalisation, a redefinition of boundaries to fit changing circumstances and perceptions. It seems that the way to preserve the authority of the *term* 'parliamentary sovereignty' is to dispense with key features of its content as previously accepted (in as far as all its adherents ever followed it in all its nuances). Dicey is sacrificed, yet to many he was inseparable from the doctrine. Furthermore, various changes—EU membership, the Human Rights Act, devolution, the use of referendums—have served to render parliamentary sovereignty simply less useful as a means of describing and understanding the UK constitution, regardless of its legal persistence or otherwise.

The consensus concept also requires further scrutiny. We know that a group within the judiciary has claimed that there are limits to the legal authority of Parliament, which the courts themselves might determine. Consideration of another constitutional branch, the UK executive, raises some interesting points. Externally, the executive insists that Parliament retains its sovereignty. However, it has—as we have seen—confused the matter by referring specifically to Dicey, whose particular version of the theory is no longer viable, if it ever was. Furthermore, as Goldsworthy notes,[12] in 2004 Lord Goldsmith, the Attorney-General, informed Parliament that it drew its 'legislative powers' from the 'common law'. These statements are only the public face of the executive: what might be the internal view? Cabinet Office files from the mid-1970s show that, with work under way to develop devolution legislation, there was concern within government about the extent to which Parliament was able to change the terms of the Union between England and Scotland, if devolution as designed should imply this effect. As we have seen, the language of some of the Treaty and Acts suggested unalterability. Some officials were concerned that a constitutional conundrum could

---

[11] See eg: Jeffrey Goldsworthy, *Parliamentary Sovereignty: Contemporary Debates* (Cambridge, Cambridge University Press, 2010) 182, 14–56.

[12] Ibid, 14–15.

arise if a Devolution Bill appeared to conflict with these earlier provisions.[13] This discussion shows that a settled and pervasive shared conception of parliamentary sovereignty as a viable legal doctrine was lacking within Whitehall. It is doubtful that it has developed in the intervening period, though access to files beyond the mid 1980s is restricted. When considering the idea of consensus across different branches of the government, it is necessary to note that not only have some members of one party to this agreement—the judiciary—openly suggested they do not fully subscribe to it, but another—the central executive—suffers from public confusion about its meaning and private doubts about its force.

A WRITTEN CONSTITUTION: PROPOSALS AND DRAFTS

Since the 1970s, in parallel with material developments, a literary genre has appeared. Authors working within it typically call for the introduction of a written constitution for the UK, proposing a general outline for it or even going so far as to produce a draft text.[14] They have been both group and individual efforts, with a broad span of political perspectives and motivations. An early entry came from O Hood Phillips in 1970. Then the distinguished Conservative politician Lord Hailsham (whose father we have encountered as the proposer of the exemption from collective Cabinet responsibility of 1932) gave in 1976 his celebrated lecture 'Elective Dictatorship', later published as a pamphlet. He argued that government by Parliament had proved a valuable system for 'our country' over a period of 'seven hundred years' (another conflation of the history of England and of the UK). However, it was now necessary to acknowledge 'how far this nation ... has moved towards a totalitarianism which can only be altered by a systematic and radical overhaul of our constitution'. He concluded that a written constitution was required to restrain the authority of Parliament, and gave an outline of the form he felt it should take.[15]

At this time the idea of a written constitution could appeal to the political Right as a means of limiting central government that from this perspective appeared to have become excessively interventionist. The converse of this logic was that for the Left the idea of a written constitution might be less attractive. Moreover, on this end of the political spectrum the judiciary could be a subject of suspicion and resentment for its social and political orientation, if not in a partisan sense then as a small 'c' conservative institution.[16] Among those who held such a

---

[13] See: The National Archive/Public Record Office CAB 198/427 'Devolution: Act of Union 1707 and Parliamentary Sovereignty', 15 January 1975–16 March 1977.

[14] For an earlier analysis of this school, see: Dawn Oliver, 'Written constitutions: principles and problems' (1992) 45 *Parliamentary Affairs* 135.

[15] Lord Hailsham, *Elective Dictatorship*, The Richard Dimbleby Lecture (London, BBC, 1976) 3, 14–17.

[16] See: JAG Griffith, *The Politics of the Judiciary*, 5th edn (London, Fontana, 1997), first published 1977.

disposition, proposals that might give a new role to the courts, perhaps involving ruling on the validity of Acts of Parliament, would be unwelcome. The experience of a long period of Conservative government from 1979 helped change attitudes. A different kind of 'elective dictatorship'—of the neo-liberal rather than socialist variety—manifested itself. A written constitution might entrench not only civil and political, but also economic and social rights. For Tony Benn, on the radical Left, writing in 1993, it was a means by which 'the people can wrench control of their own lives from the powerful'.[17] The provisions he called for included an extensive range of social and economic protections in a Charter of Rights. Unlike other proposals considered here, with his model Benn was concerned to ensure that Parliament was not ultimately subordinate to judicial interpretations of the constitution.

Benn produced a text of 54 clauses and four schedules, initially published in 1991, that he introduced to Parliament as a Bill (with no chance of actually passing into law). His effort was part of a trend of constitution-drafting taking hold at the time. John Macdonald had produced 79 articles for the Liberal Democrat Party in 1990.[18] This document seems to have been the earliest attempt at producing an actual text (at least in this era). It was also important because of its direct association with a party, rather than one figure within it. The Institute for Public Policy Research (IPPR) first issued its constitution of 129 clauses and six schedules in 1991.[19] It represented the entry of the moderate Left into the field, alongside the more radical vision of Benn. Then after a gap of nearly two decades (during which time a number of works appeared calling for such a text but not detailing its contents in the same way), Richard Gordon put forward a draft 248 clauses in length in 2010.[20]

As the work of Gordon, Hood Phillips and Macdonald demonstrates, an important source of contributions to the written constitution literary school was the legal community. Lord Scarman, a retired Law Lord, made the case in 1992. A central defect he identified in the existing UK system was the rise of the Commons relative to the monarchy and Lords, unbalancing the post-1688 settlement. He held that 'The rights of the people lack the protection of the law against oppression, tyranny and injustice if threatened by a prejudiced or frightened political party in control of the Commons'.[21] The rationale Lord Scarman offered was indicative of a tendency for advocates of written constitutions to justify their proposals as a means of preventing a potential disaster, or ending a crisis already

---

[17] Tony Benn and Andrew Hood, *Common Sense: A New Constitution for Britain* (London, Hutchinson, 1993) 123.

[18] 'A Draft Written Constitution for the United Kingdom' in *"We, The People ..."—Towards a Written Constitution*, Federal Green Paper No 13 (London, Liberal Democrats, 1990) App 2.

[19] The edition used here is: Institute for Public Policy Research (IPPR), *A Written Constitution for the United Kingdom* (London, Mansell, 1993).

[20] Richard Gordon, *Repairing British Politics: A Blueprint for Constitutional Change* (Oxford, Hart Publishing, 2010).

[21] Lord Scarman, 'Why Britain needs a Written Constitution', The Fourth Sovereignty Lecture (London, The Charter 88 Trust, 1992) 7.

under way. For instance, the Liberal Democrats in 2007 saw both a text and the process used to create it as a way of addressing twin problems: that 'People have become alienated from the political process' and that 'the Government is systematically undermining fundamental rights and freedoms'.[22] In advocating a written constitution in 2010, Gordon stated 'We cannot avoid the fact that we are living through a period of acute national misgiving'.[23] By contrast, nearly two decades previously, the IPPR had been deliberately more cautious. While acknowledging the existence of domestic tensions, it stated: 'we do well to be sceptical about claims of a constitutional crisis in the United Kingdom'.[24]

Aside from how grave a picture they presented of prevailing circumstances, most of the entries in this genre were clear that a written constitution was an opportunity to bring about substantive innovation. Some of the most dramatic changes were those that Benn envisaged in his plan for 'a democratic, secular, federal Commonwealth comprising the nations of England, Scotland and Wales dedicated to the maintenance of the welfare of all its citizens'.[25] The monarchy and Northern Ireland were absent from this constitution, and Benn published alongside it a 'Commonwealth of Europe Bill' intended to achieve the dissolution of the existing European Community and replace it with a broader-based intergovernmental organisation; or if failing in this implausible accomplishment, deny the European Communities Act 1972 its supremacy in the hierarchy of UK law. Even the more moderate proposals for constitutional texts tended to set out a shift towards a federal or quasi-federal configuration, a relatively dramatic development (particularly before the advent of devolution from the late 1990s). Yet it was also possible to present a written constitution as having a consolidating impact. In a pamphlet published in 1990 by the free market think tank, the Institute of Economic Affairs, Frank Vibert argued that such a text would 'help buttress institutions and practices not only from erosion from within the United Kingdom but from pressures from outside—notably from the European Community'. Vibert saw the creation of this document as an appropriate task to carry out after a series of alterations—for instance reforming the Lords and incorporating the ECHR—rather than as a means of attaining them.[26] However, a written constitution was in itself a radical proposal. As Lord Hailsham, after giving an account of the 'absolute sovereignty of Parliament' put it: 'Only a revolution, bloody or peacefully contrived, can put an end to the situation which I have just described'.[27]

---

[22] Liberal Democrat Party, *For the People, By the People* (Liberal Democrat Conference, autumn 2007) 1.

[23] Gordon, *Repairing British Politics* (n 20) 3.

[24] IPPR, *A Written Constitution for the United Kingdom* (n 19) 5.

[25] Benn and Hood, *Common Sense* (n 17) 92.

[26] Frank Vibert, *Constitutional Reform in the United Kingdom—An Incremental Agenda* (London, Institute of Economic Affairs, 1990) 21.

[27] Lord Hailsham, *Elective Dictatorship* (n 15) 4–5.

PRACTICAL STEPS: GORDON BROWN AND BEYOND

The contributions to this literary movement did not in their own right change the constitution of the UK. Yet they were part of an intellectual and political current. Such a phenomenon can help shape perceptions and create conditions for change. Adherents to the cause, who had varied motives and perspectives, were both prominent and diverse. Their combined force demands serious consideration. In mid-2007, the written constitution movement gained a sponsor at 10 Downing Street. Upon taking up his new office after 10 years as effectively the Prime Minister-in-waiting, Gordon Brown made constitutional reform his main objective. When unveiling his 'Governance of Britain' programme in his first speech as Prime Minister to the House of Commons in July 2007, towards the end of his statement he noted that the UK had a 'largely unwritten constitution', and that changing it would be 'a fundamental and historic shift'. He therefore called for the engagement of the population in a 'sustained debate' about the possibility of a 'full British Bill of Rights and duties, or for moving towards a written constitution'. Any such change would require 'a settled consensus'. The Secretary of State for Justice, Jack Straw, would lead a process involving cross-party talks, parliamentary discussion and public consultation across the UK.[28]

An important theme of the official 'Governance of Britain' paper published at this time was the lack of a UK written constitution. It related this absence directly to the persistence of the Royal Prerogative, in the context of this source containing powers that might otherwise be found in such a text. The paper noted that 'The vast majority of countries have codified, written and embedded constitutions. The UK has not'. Having established the peculiarity of UK arrangements in this respect, it then advanced a case for changing them. It was important to ensure that the UK continued to be 'a cohesive, confident society'. Other proposals in the paper were intended to facilitate a strong 'British' identity. There was a further requirement: to better define 'not just what it means to be British, but what it means to be the United Kingdom'. The outcome could be 'a concordat between the executive and Parliament or a written constitution'. The 'Governance of Britain' went on to stress that any such change would require a protracted, thorough and wide engagement with the public and that wide agreement over its content would be needed. Because of the overriding importance of the issues engaged it was essential to 'proceed with caution'.[29]

Any accusation of excessive haste would have been ill-founded. It took two years for Brown to make his personal preference explicit, though he did have the excuse of having to respond to an intervening global credit and economic crisis. On 10 June 2009, the day after the first meeting of the new Democratic Renewal Council, in effect a Cabinet committee with contributions from outside experts,

---

[28]   HC Deb 3 July 2007, vol 462, col 819.
[29]   Secretary of State for Justice and Lord Chancellor, *The Governance of Britain* (Cm 7170, 2007) 16, 62, 63.

Brown gave the Commons an update on the reform agenda. In the course of his account he remarked that observers often found it 'extraordinary that Britain still has a largely unwritten constitution. I personally favour a written constitution'. This statement suggested that the position of the government as a whole was not as definite. Once again Brown noted the magnitude of such a change, and promised thorough public engagement, stressing that 'the drafting of such a constitution should ultimately be a matter for the widest possible consultation with the British people themselves'.[30]

Brown gave a more detailed account of his ideas when he appeared before the House of Commons Liaison Committee—comprising the chairs of Commons select committees—on 16 July 2009. Alan Beith MP, chair of the Justice Committee, questioned him specifically on his plans. Brown expressed the view that 'we have got a written constitution for parts of the United Kingdom and for parts of the constitution, so the idea that our constitution is unwritten has never been true'. He illustrated his point by referring to the laws creating devolution, provision for EU membership and the Human Rights Act. As Brown saw it the issue turned on whether the appetite existed to deal with questions such as the appropriate content of a text, and the relationship between the courts and 'parliamentary sovereignty'.[31] When asked whether a written constitution should be subject to a heightened amendment procedure he said he believed it would, but acknowledged that this consequence meant entering into a debate about 'whether one Parliament can bind another Parliament'. He then recognised the existence of 'very difficult questions' around the position of the judiciary and expressed the view that it would not be 'the intention of a written constitution, in Britain at least … to give judges greater power over our democratic affairs'.[32] His comments on process suggested a lack of clarity about how he might reach his goal, making vague references to the Scottish Constitutional Convention and concluding 'I will listen to whatever ideas you have'.[33]

Between October 2009 and February 2010 the Ministry of Justice arranged a series of events across the country designed to probe in depth the views of the public using so-called 'deliberative' techniques. The main focus was on the idea of a 'Statement of Values' and a 'Bill of Rights and Responsibilities'. Organisers introduced the express subject of a written constitution part way through the process. They received mixed responses regarding the desirability of the idea.[34] Brown then came forward in public with a firmer agenda, this time at an event organised by the IPPR on 2 February 2010. In his speech on this occasion he outlined a number of prospective constitutional changes to Parliament, to the parliamentary electoral system, to promote political gender equality, and to enhance

---

[30] HC Deb 10 June 2009, vol 493, col 798.

[31] Q239.

[32] Q241.

[33] Q242.

[34] Ministry of Justice, *People and power: shaping democracy, rights and responsibilities* (London, Ministry of Justice, 2010) esp 52–54.

local government, before talking about 'a wider issue—the question of a written constitution'. Expressing the desire that the different political parties might collaborate on this matter 'in a spirit of partnership and patriotism' Brown informed his audience that he had that day entrusted the Cabinet Secretary, Gus O' Donnell, with a new task. The official would be responsible for a project 'to consolidate the existing unwritten, piecemeal conventions that govern much of the way central government operates under our existing constitution into a single written document'. Brown noted that the Ministry of Justice consultation had made apparent a lack of agreement about 'what a codified constitution would be for, on what it would encompass and on what its status would be'. Brown wanted to form a body that would consider this matter, which he hoped would have cross-party participation. In concluding he voiced the hope that 'if we are to decide to have a written constitution the time for its completion should be the 800th anniversary of the signing of the *Magna Carta* in Runnymede in 1215'.[35]

A private seminar on this subject took place at No 10 involving an array of constitutional experts from the worlds of academia and think tanks. Then, perhaps in March, the aforementioned Democratic Renewal Council took and seemingly agreed a paper from Jack Straw on the specific subject of making progress towards the goal Brown had identified. It considered some arguments for and against a written constitution, and then set out a process that might lead to its introduction. It would involve a main committee and sub-bodies, with all-party and expert participation. The tasks it undertook would include writing down and consolidating major conventions and prerogative powers. It would also discern the core principles necessary for inclusion in a constitutional text, reporting back to the government and Parliament with its findings. But the plan went no further. It seems to have lacked the kind of sustained impetus from within government that would have been necessary were it to have any hope of succeeding. The cross-party collaboration that Brown deemed essential proved unobtainable. Through most of his premiership Brown was in a position of political weakness. The global financial crisis must have made a focus on constitutional issues more difficult to achieve. His personal political style also may have been a hindrance.

Though it had already stalled, the idea featured in the Labour Manifesto for the General Election of May 2010. It pledged to 'set up an All Party Commission to chart a course to a Written Constitution'.[36] At the same time, the Liberal Democrats made a commitment—in accordance with their long-standing policy objective—to 'Introduce a written constitution. We would give people the power to determine this constitution in a citizens' convention, subject to final approval in a referendum'.[37] Two of the three largest parties were therefore committed in principle to a written constitution—an historic moment. (The Green Party also supported this goal at the same time.) Had Labour won the General Election,

---

[35] Gordon Brown MP, 'Towards a new politics', speech, 2 February 2010.
[36] *A Future Fair For All* (London, Labour Party, 2010) 9:3.
[37] *Liberal Democrat Manifesto 2010* (London, Liberal Democrats, 2010) 88.

or had—slightly more plausibly—a coalition between Labour and the Liberal Democrats come about in May 2010, perhaps this agenda would have revived. However, it did not figure in the agreement between the Conservatives and Liberal Democrats. The most significant legacy arose from the task Brown had entrusted to O'Donnell of compiling details of the existing constitution. A draft of part of this document appeared in February 2010, containing details of procedures around the formation of governments in circumstances of no overall majority in the House of Commons. Production of what became known as the *Cabinet Manual* survived the transition to the Coalition. A full draft followed late in 2010 and a first edition in 2011. It was a shadow of what Brown had intended ultimately to come about. While his public standing may not be high at present—a common misfortune for recently removed Prime Ministers—Brown is likely to be rehabilitated at some point. His endorsement of a written constitution could form a part of future reassessments.

The next development provided a demonstration of the tendency for a constitutional change to generate impetus for further such transformation. In 2010, following the General Election, the Commons began electing the chairs and other members of select committees. This new practice entailed wresting the determination of these appointments away from the whips. Without this change, it is hard to imagine that the Labour MP Graham Allen would have become chair of the Political and Constitutional Reform Committee (PCRC), set up to shadow the constitutional brief given to the Liberal Democrat Deputy Prime Minister, Nick Clegg, as part of the Coalition accommodation of May 2010. Allen, on whose staff I served from 2002—04 and to whom to whom I continued to act thereafter as an informal adviser, had a long record of pursuing radical constitutional goals. This track record would probably have been enough to rule him out under the old system of filling places on committees. He had also been a leading figure in the two largest backbench rebellions in parliamentary history, against the invasion of Iraq, in February and March 2003. As chair he knew he probably had a full five-year span to work in, owing to the Coalition plan for a fixed-term Parliament. He persuaded his committee to embark on a consideration of whether or not to introduce a written constitution for the UK, running over this whole period.

Allen had long advocated such a text. However, the enthusiasm he has for a written constitution makes him an exceptional figure in Westminster. Parliamentarians who are attracted to constitutional change tend to cluster around one or more individual issues, rather than advocating the introduction of a full systematic document. Since a written constitution implies new legal limitations on the legislature, reticence about the idea is to be expected among parliamentarians, many of whom take seriously the doctrine of the sovereignty of their institution. Nonetheless, before the PCRC project, certain parliamentary committees had made contributions with some relevance to this subject. The committee of both Houses set up to scrutinise the draft Civil Contingencies Bill produced in 2003 a recommendation that—though the government did not act upon it—would have provided a special status to certain enactments as being constitutional in nature. The draft Bill proposed to create a power for ministers—in emergency circumstances—to issue regulations that could accomplish the same outcomes as Acts of Parliament, but without being subject to the same degree of parliamentary control. The committee feared that 'In the wrong hands, it could be used to remove all past legislation which makes up the statutory patchwork of the British constitution'. It produced a list of laws of a constitutional nature it believed should be exempt from abolition or modification under the proposed Civil Contingencies Act, spanning from Magna Carta to the House of Lords Act 1999.

In 2008, a report from the Joint Committee on Human Rights, *A Bill of Rights for the UK?* engaged with many issues relevant to a written constitution. They included what should be the content of a UK Bill of Rights: its legal status and the role of the courts in enforcing it; the implications for Parliament; the connection with devolution; and the process that might lead to its introduction. Though the committee was sympathetic to the idea of a Bill of Rights, it was firm that it should not involve the judiciary ruling acts of Parliament invalid.[38] In 2009, the Commons Justice Committee noted the suggestions emanating from the Brown Government about the possibility of introducing a written constitution. It remarked that a substantial portion of the UK constitution already existed in writing, including in the devolution statutes, Magna Carta, the 1688 Bill of Rights, the European Communities Act 1972 and the Maastricht Treaty. Nonetheless, the committee was clear that a full text would represent a major development. Important issues it identified as arising from any attempt to introduce a written constitution were what its underlying values would be; how both to draft and amend it; the scope of its provisions; and its legal status and enforceability. Though it came to no definite conclusions the committee held that it 'would welcome a thorough debate' on the subject.[39]

These committee views were significant but did not amount to a major movement for a written constitution within Westminster. Given general attitudes prevailing in Parliament, there was never any chance that the PCRC would actually recommend the adoption of a text for the UK. Instead, Allen sought and succeeded in obtaining from his committee agreement to consider the cases for and against such a text; to discuss the process that might lead to its introduction, in the event of a decision to do so; and what might be its contents, if it came about. But despite the need to couch matters in the hypothetical, this inquiry mattered. It was the first official, public investigation held into this subject in Parliament—or anywhere else—in the UK. It could help place the subject more firmly on the agenda, and create a body of work on which parties or governments at some future point interested in pursuing a written constitution might draw. The inquiry innovated in methods as well as subject matter, obtaining external advisory support on a sustained basis from King's London staff, including Professor Robert Blackburn, Professor Vernon Bogdanor and myself. In July 2014, the PCRC published for

---

[38] Joint Committee on Human Rights, *A Bill of Rights for the UK?* (2007–08, HL 165-I, HC 150-I).
[39] Justice Committee, *Constitutional Reform and Renewal* (HC 2008–09, 923) 20–22.

consultation three different draft constitutional texts, each of which was the work of Blackburn. The title of the report was *A new Magna Carta?*[40]

Around this time, the written constitution idea was gaining salience from a further source: the Scottish referendum campaign. The Scottish Government made a written constitution a key part of its programme for the proposed independent state, issuing successive papers on the theme. Supporters of Scottish presence within the UK also deployed this concept. In June 2014, Gordon Brown published a book setting out proposals for a future UK with Scotland still within it. He proposed power-sharing arrangements for the UK, though stopping short of federalism. He expected a written constitution would eventually come about to enshrine the system he advocated.[41] As instigator of the Vow in September of the same year, Brown achieved more progress towards his constitutional goals as a backbench MP than he had ever managed as Prime Minister. Also in June 2014, a Conservative Member of the Scottish Parliament, Murdo Fraser, went further, proposing a federal UK as a means of establishing consensus between supporters and opponents of secession. His model would use English regions, and a states' chamber would replace the House of Lords. Fraser wanted to see the new arrangement set out in a written constitution. After the Scottish referendum, such views would gain far wider currency.

Post-imperial cultural and political pressures have disrupted older models. In some areas they have heightened already existing tensions, such as between the centralised qualities of the UK and its pronounced diversity as a multination state. Other previously more widely accepted features have become compromised, most notably parliamentary sovereignty. The heavy reliance on tacit understandings has experienced a decline with the move towards codified conventions. The Royal Prerogative, an extra-parliamentary power source, has depleted. On the new landscape we can discern some of the contours of a written constitution. Calls for a more overt adoption of such a system have become frequent and appeared from a diverse range of sources. They are more than simply fringe activity. A Prime Minister has taken up the cause, and two of what were then the three main UK political parties endorsed it at the 2010 General Election. A Commons select committee has conducted an innovative five-year inquiry into the subject.

Yet none of these propositions should convey the image of an inevitable and tidy progression towards a written constitution for the UK. Some deny the old order has cracked. Others regret that it has, and want to block further change, and possibly reverse earlier transformations. Moreover, the diverse nature of support for a text is potentially both a strength and a weakness. Those of this general disposition may disagree severely about appropriate content, given their varied political outlooks. Is, for instance, an underlying purpose of a constitution to

---

[40] Political and Constitutional Reform Committee, *A New Magna Carta?* (HC 2013–14, 463).
[41] Gordon Brown, *My Scotland, Our Britain: A Future Worth Sharing* (London, Simon & Schuster, 2014).

curtail the role of government in society, or to provide for certain minimum standards of welfare? While many envisaged a special role for the judiciary, for Benn a written constitution was a means of asserting parliamentary supremacy over the courts (and he also envisaged an end to existing arrangements for the upholding of European law). Consequently, those who seek the outcome of a fundamental text for the UK must consider how they might build a sufficiently powerful coalition to achieve this goal. They need to win the argument about the desirability of this change, in the face of a combination of hostility, indifference and incomprehension among the elite and the public. Advocates of a written constitution must also consider how they might go about creating it, and its possible content. In doing so, they will have the benefit of a structural and intellectual foundation that has emerged in the contemporary UK.

Part III

A Constitution for the United Kingdom

11

Advocating and Creating a Written Constitution

THE UNITED KINGDOM (UK) should create a written constitution. To help it to do so, it can absorb lessons from its own history and developments over time elsewhere. Ample examples are available of how both to devise and create such a text, and the possible form and content of the final product. Confounding popular views, the concept of a written constitution has an important basis in our historic thought and practice. It would not be a foreign imposition. The past, therefore, will be valuable to would-be UK constitution-builders. But reference to antiquity in itself will not provide them with the fundamental justification for the task they undertake. In fact, those purporting to reassert established principles have often done so to cloak innovation, that must in truth seek validation from somewhere other than precedent. This chapter begins by explaining why a written constitution is desirable, and then considers how it might come about and the mechanisms necessary for the task. The next chapter discusses the content of the text.

To argue that a political system must rest in first principles rather than supposed inheritance is not to call for a separation of the constitution from its history. While they do not in themselves provide the necessary justification, knowledge of earlier constitutional texts and their impact supports a consideration of what the appropriate underlying values might be. Furthermore, an understanding of that which has gone before is essential to an appreciation of where we are now, that is in turn a prerequisite for the successful construction of a constitutional text. The present is partly an accumulation of past events.[1] While the past should not hold the present captive, it is important to be aware of the extent to which any set of proposals represents continuity with or disruption of existing arrangements, and their relationship with any apparent dynamics of development. History can be the guide to where we are, how we came to be here, and why. Any written constitution, though it should aspire to be founded in universal principles, can only achieve expression within the specific environment into which its founders introduce it, and in which it operates at any given time thereafter, though it will itself impact upon this wider setting. The past should therefore inform attempts to construct

---

[1] See eg: JWF Allison, *The English Historical Constitution* (Cambridge, Cambridge University Press, 2007) 103–04.

a viable text. But this approach need not accompany a reluctance to bring about radical change. Rather, consideration of some features of constitutional development may point in the opposite direction. As Thomas Paine put it:

> Government by precedent, without any regard to the principle of the precedent, is one of the vilest systems that can be set up. In numerous instances, the precedent ought to operate as a warning, and not as an example, and requires to be shunned instead of imitated; but instead of this, precedents are taken in the lump, and put at once for constitution and for law.[2]

The caution Paine offers is apt. Yet as the historic survey in this work shows, there is much of value to extract from past efforts at setting out fundamental rules, and even when we do discard it, it should be after careful consideration.

THE POSITIVE CASE FOR A WRITTEN CONSTITUTION

Not least because written constitutions often purport to be expressions of popular sovereignty, the views of the public are important to a debate about this subject. Some evidence suggests that the UK population is supportive of the idea of a written constitution. The Joseph Rowntree Reform Trust (JRRT) has carried out a series of 'State of the Nation' polls including a question on this subject. When asked to respond to the assertion that 'Britain needs a written constitution, providing clear legal rules within which government ministers and civil servants are forced to operate' the percentage saying that they tend to agree or agree strongly with this view has generally been in the high sixties and low seventies. In 2000, the total was 71 per cent; in 2004, 80 per cent (a change in the available options seems to have contributed to this jump); in 2006, 68 per cent; and in 2010, 73 per cent. However, the framing of the question in this way is vulnerable to the charge that it is loaded in favour of 'yes'. Who indeed are those who make up this 30 per cent who do not want 'legal rules' that are both 'clear' and oblige those in positions of power to behave themselves? In circumstances in which a text for the UK began to appear as a possible outcome, less favourable views of the idea would receive coverage as well. Some would seek to place a question such as 'should unelected judges, applying European rules, be able to prevent elected politicians from deporting foreign terrorist suspects?' in the minds of the public.

A further qualification of the notion of powerful popular support for a written constitution is that the public seems not to perceive it as a priority, and many do not have clear opinions at all in this area. In 2008, the Hansard Society *Audit of Political Engagement* asked members of the public to name up to three of a selection of constitutional features as 'most urgently in need of change'.[3] Issues on the list included the practical operation of the Human Rights Act (that was

---

[2] Thomas Paine, *Common Sense and the Rights of Man* (London, Phoenix, 2000) 207.
[3] Hansard Society, *Audit of Political Engagement 5: The 2008 Report* (London, Hansard Society, 2008) 31.

most widely identified as requiring swift attention, at 26 per cent); UK participation in the European Union (EU) (23 per cent); the lack of a modern UK Bill of Rights (14 per cent); and 'powers that government can currently exercise without Parliament's approval', an allusion to the Royal Prerogative (23 per cent). The issue of 'Britain's unwritten constitution' came eleventh out of 11. Only 9 per cent singled it out, making it a less chosen option even than 'don't know' at 16 per cent. The Hansard Society also asked respondents to indicate how far they were either satisfied or dissatisfied with the same list of aspects of the UK constitution. Those who were either very or fairly satisfied with the 'unwritten constitution' totalled 19 per cent; while the figure for very or fairly dissatisfied was 18 per cent. The bulk—at 65 per cent in all—were either neutral or did not know.

At the turn of 2009–2010, as part of the Gordon Brown reform agenda, a series of Ministry of Justice public engagement events across Great Britain uncovered qualitative evidence. Among the various constitutional issues they addressed was the possibility of introducing a full constitutional text. Those taking part saw potential value in establishing more precision and intelligibility around arrangements. They regarded a written constitution as a potential rallying point for UK identity, reviving its democratic principles and attachment to them. It might provide a means by which new entrants into the country could understand the system and its values. Finally, a written constitution could protect rights from abuse by the authorities if they sought to alter the rules in an inappropriate fashion. Yet the deliberative process also found objections. Producing a document could prove to be wasted effort, simply duplicating law already in existence. A written constitution might be excessively rigid and unresponsive to wider developments. It could produce expensive legal action. Broadly a little more than 40 per cent of those who took part were favourable to a written constitution, while slightly less than 40 per cent disliked the idea (though the sample, as is in the nature of qualitative research, was not representative).

The overall picture then, is that a majority of the public agree with a written constitution in principle if the idea is put to them in a particular way. But they are unlikely to regard it as an immediate concern, and may not have strong feelings about it at all. When giving it closer attention they can identify arguments both in favour of and against such a document. Those seeking to promote a written constitution for the UK could have an estimable task of exposition and persuasion ahead of them. But the attainment of substantial and worthwhile goals is by definition a challenge. So what is the case for a written constitution? I will begin with the positive side of the argument, showing the possible benefits of such a change, before moving to the negative, outlining the potential problems it could help address or avoid. In the process I will identify and address possible counterviews.

The most obvious advantage is that a text could create greater clarity about which fundamental rules and principles made up the constitution.[4] At present the

---

[4] O Hood Phillips, *Reform of the Constitution* (London, Chatto & Windus, Charles Knight, 1970) 149–50; Lord Scarman, 'Why Britain needs a Written Constitution', The Fourth Sovereignty Lecture (London, Charter 88 Trust, 1992); Rodney Brazier, 'How Near is a Written Constitution' (2001) 52(1) *Northern Ireland Legal Quarterly* 7.

constitution derives from various sources such as doctrines and conventions, the Royal Prerogative, statutory and non-statutory codes, Acts of Parliament, judicial decisions, international agreements, the 'law and custom' of Parliament, the work of past constitutional experts feeding back into the very entity they sought to define, and even the internal rules of political parties. Consequently, it is difficult even for the full-time specialist to grasp in totality all the key components. Inevitably, others struggle to comprehend the overall quality of the constitution. The 2008 Hansard Society research cited above included a question on how far respondents felt they understood different features of the constitution. Of all the subjects highlighted, 'The constitutional arrangements governing Britain' came eleventh out of 11 for respondents saying they knew it 'very well or fairly well', with 20 per cent. The most understood was the relationship between the casting of votes and the balance of party representation in the Commons, with 49 per cent. Other items coming above 'constitutional arrangements' included 'How the Human Rights Act works in practice' (34 per cent), the EU (28 per cent), the debate about the possibility of introducing a UK Bill of Rights (28 per cent) and 'powers that government can currently exercise without Parliament's approval' (22 per cent).

In a democracy this low level of knowledge about the rules and values making up the core of the system should be a source of concern. There is surely a connection between this problem and the lack of a written constitution, framing expressly the key arrangements in a single, public document of the highest official status. The desire to achieve clarity in this way has motivated the production of documents in UK and English history, as far back as the time of King Ethelbert of Kent nearly fifteen hundred years ago. Of course, in practice the extent to which written constitutions are depictions of reality varies. In some cases, as with the constitutions of the Soviet Union and their commitments to individual freedoms, they can be deliberate travesties of reality. Even when they have a substantial connection to the practical working of the polity and command general legitimacy within it, they can only aspire to capture in full all the essential features of the system. Some portion of the rules will always remain tacit; practice, custom and convention must play a part. Other deeper, invisible, underlying legal principles may (or may not) exist. The concept of an 'unwritten constitution' exists in discourse around the US system, with a different connotation from that applying to discussion involving UK arrangements. In the United States (US) it conveys the idea of a fundamental set of rules beyond or perhaps beneath the text, possibly residing in common law.[5] Yet in the US, as in most other democracies, at least a text exists. It may not always function in practice, or may be interpreted in competing ways, or may be regarded as unsatisfactory, or working in parallel with or subject to other rules. But one advantage over the UK approach is that there is a single document around which an argument can take place. Identifiable problems

---

[5] See eg: Thomas C Grey, 'Do We Have an Unwritten Constitution' (1975) 27(3) *Stanford Law Review* 703.

of a disconnect between texts and reality do not so much undermine the case for a UK written constitution as emphasise the importance of designing it well, in good faith, proceeding in accordance with and in pursuit of democratic principles.

A related point is that producing a document would make it possible more clearly to distinguish between constitutional matters according to their degree of importance. The drafting process could determine what issues were and were not of pre-eminent status, and whether they should consequently be dealt with in the text. For instance, the basic powers of devolved institutions would be likely to find expression, but some of the precise details of their relations with Whitehall might not. An internal hierarchy might prevail within the document itself. Some portions of the text might be harder to amend than others. For instance, fundamental rights might have exceptional protection from casual alteration. The role provided to the judiciary in upholding the document (if it had this function) might vary across its content. There could be declaratory statements intended to have no direct status in court proceedings, and some rights might be more legally enforceable than others.

While none of them are perfect and their duration varies, written constitutions can act as a focus for the identity of a state, as in a way did Alfred's law code. For instance, the US Constitution—drafted in 1787—came early in its history as an independent state, and has continued to be an important tool for the attainment of national coherence ever since. Their instigation can carry a country through a challenging period. The Basic Law of the Federal Republic of (West) Germany of 1949 assisted post-war democratic recuperation and international rehabilitation. Later, in 1990, it proved able to sustain the absorption of the former (East) German Democratic Republic. The Constitution of the French Fifth Republic of 1958 helped deal with a colonial crisis that had spilled over into France itself. Texts can express core values underpinning the community as a whole as, for instance, does the South African Constitution of 1996, which also achieved success in bringing about a rebirth of the state in its post-apartheid era.

In countries with strong sub-identities—of which the UK is one—a written constitution can entrench the position of these parts, while at the same time locating them within the whole, through federal or quasi-federal structures. The Spanish Constitution of 1978 fits into this mould, with its provision for 'Autonomous Communities'. A written constitution might therefore accommodate the rich variety of the UK, pronouncing a multi-polar entity. Such a text could provide for multiple political identities—from local to national to UK level—and encompass them within a whole bound together by a shared set of values, providing the basis for a more clearly defined concept of citizenship. Those who oppose this approach might fear that to allow for differentiation is to court fragmentation and undermine cohesion. Yet the data on national identity previously discussed demonstrate that this position already exists, and suggest a need for structures that accommodate and channel the diverse streams of perception of the UK.

The constitution could also help ensure that self-government was available to all territories of the UK, not simply to those currently within the scope of the devolution process. Its impact in England in particular could be decentralising, through creating and entrenching devolution or its equivalent, and providing local authorities with a new, firmer, footing. Critics would argue that this latter change might have a negative impact upon service provision, that there are certain tasks that central government is better able to perform, and that the public do not want a fragmentation of responsibility. The exact division of tasks between different tiers would need close consideration. However, the UK and within it England, as already noted, is exceptional for the extent to which power is concentrated in Westminster and Whitehall, and the benefits of this arrangement for policy formation and delivery are not manifest. If we consider the example of Switzerland, the populations of some cantons number only in the tens of thousands, comparable to that of Rutland County Council, the smallest unitary authority in England. Yet in Switzerland substantial policy responsibilities are exercised at the cantonal level. The UK and Switzerland cannot be identical, but lessons can be learned. Furthermore, genuine democratic accountability is more plausible at the local layer, where a connection between those responsible for making and implementing decisions and voters is more clear and direct, within the context of a geographical area that is meaningful to the inhabitants. It may be that the existing devolved institutions pose a threat to the local tier below them, that could benefit from the protection of a written constitution. At the same time, a written constitution could place limits on as well as provide for decentralisation. Excessive devolution is a potential problem too, and a text could safeguard against it in particular by defining more clearly those functions it is essential to retain at UK level to ensure cohesion.

A further set of benefits on offer from a written constitution involve the introduction of constraints on governmental institutions, both in terms of their spheres of operation in relation to each other, and in their dealings with individuals. For instance, it could establish a clearer division of powers between the UK, devolved, and local tiers. Furthermore, the document could include within it provision for fundamental individual rights, shielding them from violation by the executive and Parliament. The JRRT opinion research that has suggested strong public support for the idea of a written constitution used a question that conveyed the idea of a limiting device upon ministers and officials. This concept of a text as a restraint on public agencies is powerful. The received version of Magna Carta emphasises this dimension to the agreement reached in 1215. Placing limits on official authority, ensuring it conforms to legal norms, is of fundamental importance. Yet, as closer consideration of Magna Carta has demonstrated, another more positive constitutional perspective, with attractions of its own, exists. The 1215 text sought to ground institutional mechanisms, such as a process of consultation for tax raising and a committee for the enforcement of its own provisions, and to enshrine privileges for certain social groups such as widows and 'free men'. Similarly, a UK constitutional text would create as well as restrict. It would provide a new basis for the spheres in which different democratic institutions support those they represent. In the process, it could form entirely new powers. It might, for instance, establish more significant tax raising authorities at devolved and local authority levels. Moreover, a written constitution would seek to entrench and protect rights. It might create obligations for official bodies not only to refrain from violating these freedoms, but to act positively to ensure their fulfilment. Government engagement is required to ensure civil and political rights, such as the right to life and the right to freedom of assembly, for instance through ensuring police protection is available. If a written constitution provided for social and economic rights, then it might entail some kind of active official role in these areas also.

Another prospective benefit of a UK text is the process that its introduction would require. More than simply a means to an end, the steps involved in the creation of this document could have intrinsic value. Ideally, they would involve the widest possible engagement of individuals associated with different groups, of diverse social backgrounds, and of varied geographical origins. The people of the UK have never had an opportunity to take part in the creation and approval of the main features of their constitution as whole. They cannot hope properly to own the constitution until a document is devised in this way. The need for legitimacy through participation is detectable in earlier texts, including the Anglo-Saxon law codes with their insistence that they are founded in consultation with the magnates of the kingdom. In a democracy this basic principle requires expansion. A constitution-building process with an appropriate level of public involvement should facilitate a healthy public discussion about constitutional issues, many of which are the subject of controversy. It would need to consider such contentious issues as the nature of devolution and its consequences; the relationship between ministers and Parliament on the one hand, and the courts on the other; provision for individual rights; and—possibly—the position of the UK within supranational organisations, in particular the EU. Some might argue that it is better not to raise these disputes since they will not be resolvable. But these divisions are already with us. A major constitutional debate—or set of parallel and connected discussions—has been taking place since the late 1950s. The UK is divided over fundamental issues, as the referendum on Scottish independence and the prospect of a further plebiscite on EU membership demonstrate. A full constitution-building process might enable discussions to be held in a more considered, interlinked way, and reach a more satisfactory resolution, partly through educating the public more fully about the issues involved.

Another concern raised about a constitution-building process is that it would become diverted into unnecessary discussion by those with such agendas as the abolition of the monarchy and disestablishment of the Church.[6] But such matters—which engage the way in which the occupant of the role of head of state is determined, and the principle of freedom of belief—should be at the heart of

---

[6] For a discussion of this possibility, see: Dawn Oliver, 'Towards a written constitution' in Chris Bryant (ed), *Towards a New Constitutional Settlement* (London, Smith Institute, 2007) 146–47.

a serious debate about our constitution. Those who fought Stuart absolutism in the seventeenth century, helping establish in England the principle of limited government in the process, recognised the importance of these issues, whatever we may think of the precise conclusions these activists reached. Some among their number sought to establish a new system set out in a written constitution. It is understandable that supporters of the Established Church and the monarchy might be uncomfortable with a thorough and rational scrutiny of these institutions. But it would be incorrect to suppose that the issues engaged lack salience. In the contemporary UK, both religion and the monarchy are more pressing contemporary constitutional issues than some might acknowledge. Changing patterns of belief, disbelief and unbelief, combined with domestic and global security issues, make a thorough consideration of the relationship between public authority and faith entirely apt. It could consider, for instance, the proper place of religion in educational institutions, and other issues such as the presence of Anglican bishops in the House Lords.

Another religious issue has connections to the monarchy: the discrimination in the succession rules, devised in the late seventeenth and early eighteenth centuries to keep a Catholic Stuart away from the throne. Are there any other matters involving the head of state in need of consideration, or is it a sufficiently stable and popular institution not to require scrutiny? Whatever the present condition of the monarchy, a major flaw in it (aside from its undemocratic character) is that it is exceptionally dependent upon chance as to the character of the individual who comes to fill the post. Greater definition of and constraints upon the role of monarch, such as a written constitution could provide, might be a greater necessity under a future head of state. Dealing with such a contingency in advance would be the preferable course of action. It might seem disrespectful to carry out a public debate centring on possible developments in an era after the death of the current monarch. However, she would not be in her present role were it not for the decision made to establish the otherwise tenuous Hanoverian claim on the Crown through the Act of Settlement 1701 (restating it in the Union texts of 1706–07), and at the same time to constrain members of this dynasty when ruling their new kingdom—a measure devised while Anne lived (and before she even took the throne), but specifically anticipating her passing. The presence of these kinds of issues on the written constitutional agenda would be welcome, but the precise decisions made about them would require a degree of consensus. In a properly conceived process, capture by small groups and their agendas would not be possible; they would have to persuade through open argument, that those who felt they had better ideas would have the opportunity to contest. It is in fact present constitutional discourse that is vulnerable to appropriation in pursuit of particular agendas, especially by those hostile to the EU and the nature of human rights enforcement in the UK.

As well as securing wider ownership and promoting healthy debate, a constitution-building process could enable an holistic approach, leading to a more rational outcome than that which characterises the present constitution.

Structural and institutional tensions abound. The doctrine of parliamentary sovereignty is in potential or full conflict with other features of the constitution such as adherence to the rule of law, devolution and participation in the EU. Democratic institutions coexist with a monarchy possessing immense theoretical legal strength, bound only by conventions, and with an unelected House of Lords. In addition to offering the possibility of resolving these internal tensions, the process of devising a written constitution could consider the disjuncture between present arrangements and the wider contemporary society within which they exist. For instance, transformations in the way people involve themselves in political processes—with traditional routes such as parties and voting in elections less pervasive than they once were—point to a need for changes in the mode of interaction between government and public. Technological developments—including the rise of electronic communications and the increased use of surveillance equipment in public places—raise a variety of constitutional issues in need of consideration. Concerns involving international terrorism and connected conflict and instability in various regions have a strong constitutional dimension. They engage issues including the place of religious faith in society, the powers under which governments engage in military action abroad, the accountability of the Intelligence and Security Agencies, and the impact of domestic security measures upon human rights. Some might claim that a written constitution would represent a hazardous limitation on the pursuit of proper responses to pressing dangers. The perils are real. But a systemic text could provide a means of approaching them in an even-handed way and retaining the values that the struggle against terrorism seeks to preserve.

The creation of a text for the UK could have a beneficial effect on the way constitutional change takes place.[7] First-order alterations would become more visible than they are at present. Alterations equivalent to the recent establishment of a Supreme Court, or the introduction of fixed-term parliaments, or the possible future abolition of the Human Rights Act, would involve altering the written constitution itself, and as such rightly be perceived as more momentous than if involving regular legislative enactment (or, as is sometimes the case, even more casual processes, such as the emergence of the convention during the twentieth century that prime ministers must sit only in the House of Commons, and never the House of Lords). Such amendments would, moreover, probably be subject to special procedures, requiring a higher level of agreement than ordinary law, and possibly some kind of expert review, to assess the viability of proposals. The likelihood of modifications taking place that were not widely and fully appreciated, were poorly devised, or that particular groups forced through to serve sectional ends, would diminish.

---

[7] Frank Vibert, *Constitutional Reform in the United Kingdom—An Incremental Agenda* (London, Institute of Economic Affairs, 1990) 21; Rodney Brazier, 'Enacting a Constitution' (1992) 13(2) *Statute Law Review* 122.

It is true, as some will point out, that the constitution could alter without the words of the document needing to change. Judicial decisions can bring about new interpretations, and the development of conventions can change the way that the provisions work in practice. However, these shifts take place within an overall setting that the core text creates. Another claim emanating from sceptics is that a written constitution would lack the flexibility that is held to be beneficial to the UK, on the grounds that it makes modification, when required, a relatively easy task. However, the purpose of a text would not be to prevent change altogether. The attempts of Magna Carta and the Treaty and Acts of Union to assert their perpetuity would be too crude if applied today. It would be better to follow the model developed from the mid-seventeenth century and allow for amendment if certain requirements are met. The purpose of the procedure adopted would be to regulate change and make it take place in a more appropriate fashion, not prohibit it. Indeed, amendment mechanisms could take a form that made them more open to groups outside the UK executive that is presently predominant in the immediate instigation of change. Furthermore, the fluidity of the UK constitution as presently composed should not be overstated. Certain groups—particularly the executive and Parliament—possess the ability to veto as well as initiate alterations. For instance, on a number of occasions over the past century, the wholly unelected status of the House of Lords has seemed likely to end. Yet it still persists, in large part because of reluctance on the part of the Commons to permit a change that could create a second chamber rivalling its own position more seriously.

Introducing a text offers the possibility not only of protecting constitutional arrangements from inappropriate alteration, but also ensuring that they are legally enforceable, something those who imposed Magna Carta on John Lackland in 1215 sought to do through its 'security clause'. At present, key constitutional principles and institutions, including the rule of law, individual rights, free and fair elections on a universal franchise, devolved and local government, and the courts, can, in theory at least, be subject to modification or outright assault through one institution—Parliament—acting unilaterally. (Indeed, Parliament can even alter its own composition and rules determining the way it operates.) An enforceable written constitution could create a barrier to abuse, through rendering normal legislative measures that conflicted with it unlawful. It could also ensure that, unlike at present, the actions of all public authorities were subject to review specifically on a basis of whether they complied with the constitution and, if they failed to do so, would face annulment.

The need to uphold the text would probably involve a special role for the judiciary. Inevitably some would depict this prospect as undesirable on the grounds that it would draw officials lacking an electoral mandate into matters of political controversy that are more appropriately the business of those in possession of their own democratic legitimacy, acquired from a more direct relationship with voters.[8]

---

[8] See eg: Robert A Dahl, *How Democratic is the American Constitution?* (New Haven CT, Yale University Press, 2001); Adam Tomkins, *Our Republican Constitution* (Oxford, Hart Publishing, 2005) 25.

This criticism deserves serious consideration. Numerous responses, calling into question the idea of a straightforward clash between the democratic and the non-democratic, are possible. A first point to be stressed is that within Parliament, only the Commons—and not the other two components, the Lords and the monarch—is elected. Furthermore, when it wields the special power that the lack of a written constitution affords it, Parliament is sometimes interfering in the business of other levels of governance, particularly local government in England that is itself elected. The Commons mandate may be up to five years old, while a democratic institution that is constitutionally subordinate to it may have been returned more recently, and the particular matter involved may clearly be one that is appropriately dealt with at a more local level. In such circumstances, the judiciary—if it were making a constitutional ruling—should be seen as adjudicating between two different democratic institutions, rather than illegitimately asserting its will over elected authority. Moreover, the highly disproportionate electoral system used for the Commons further undermines parliamentary claims to a democratic trump card: a group that received less than 40 per cent of votes cast can win an absolute majority of seats, and some parties receive far less representation than their share of support. Furthermore, the proportion of votes received by the 'winning' party has broadly declined over time. The claims of the Commons—and by extension, the case against a written constitution—are weakening further still with turnouts in general elections lower than they were in earlier decades. Finally, the legitimacy of parties, that individually or in coalition with each other dominate the Commons and Parliament, is damaged by their declining membership.

There are further grounds for doubting any democratic dichotomy raised by judicial constitutional enforcement. In many instances it is likely the courts would be reviewing the constitutionality of the behaviour of appointed public officials, not parliamentarians or elected office holders at another level of governance. The judiciary would in such instances be seeking to ensure that such agents are operating in accordance with their democratically determined constitutional roles, not obstructing the will of those that the electorate has selected. Even when a decision is formally that of a minister, in practice civil servants may well have at least heavily influenced it. Perhaps most fundamentally, we need to acknowledge what may seem a perverse quality of democracy: that it must both provide outlets for and restraints upon majoritarianism. The latter are required to safeguard against the overriding of individual rights that are in turn essential to wide and meaningful democratic participation, and to create a barrier to the unpicking of the democratic system itself. Such checks may at times appear to amount to a frustration of the elected by the unelected, but they are indispensible.

The power provided to the judiciary by the constitutional review role is less than sometimes imagined. An argument subsequently attributed to Alexander Hamilton retains force (though it was framed with the 'separation of powers' model in mind). It came in a series advocating the proposed US Constitution, undertaken in 1787–08 alongside James Madison and John Jay, jointly using the pseudonym 'Publius', and known collectively as *The Federalist Papers*. In entry number 78, Hamilton/Publius explained that of 'the different departments of power ... the judiciary, from the nature of its functions, will always be the least dangerous to the political rights of the Constitution; because it will be least in a capacity to annoy or injure them'. While the executive 'dispenses the honours' and 'holds the sword of the community' the legislature 'commands the purse' and 'prescribes the rules by which the duties and rights of every citizen are to be regulated'. The judiciary, conversely, was able to 'take no active resolution whatever'. It lacked both force and will and had 'merely judgement', being reliant upon the support of the executive 'even for the efficacy of its judgements'.[9]

There are further reasons, beyond the imbalance that Hamilton noted, to doubt a thesis of excessive judicial authority under a written constitution. Though judicial interpretation can provide extensive discretion, judges would have to found their decisions in the constitutional text and give public accounts of their reasoning. Furthermore, the constitutional importance of the judiciary is in some ways problematically great under the *present* system, and a written constitution could actually restrict it in certain ways. The lack of such a text creates a vacuum that not only Parliament may fill, but also at times the courts. For instance, the task of the judiciary in discerning the extent of the Royal Prerogative can provide it with notable room for manoeuvre. The Human Rights Act—designed to reconcile protection of individual freedoms with prevailing doctrines of parliamentary sovereignty—has led to a position, with which some are uneasy, in which the courts can add their own words into Acts of Parliament to make them compatible with the European Convention on Human Rights (ECHR). Moreover, some within the judiciary believe that it may be appropriate for them at some point to overturn constitutional orthodoxies and replace them with their own versions of what the fundamental norms should be. It is no more desirable that the courts should be able unilaterally to define the constitution than Parliament using its regular procedures, and probably less so. A written constitution, though it would probably provide to the judiciary an important role in upholding the text, would force the courts to operate within a more clearly defined framework than presently exists, and remove some problematic areas of latitude.

Another likely objection to the possibility of a written constitution enforced by the courts is that it would lead to the politicisation of judicial appointments: that is, since judges would be placed in a position of making decisions with important implications for public policy and the balance of power between different levels of governance, parties would seek to ensure that those promoted to senior judicial posts shared their particular outlook; international evidence, for instance from Germany and the US, supports this view. This outcome is undesirable in as far as it can lead to a constitution at times becoming subordinate to party political

---

[9] Alexander Hamilton, James Madison and John Jay ('Publius'), *The Federalist Papers* (New York, Mentor, 1961) 465.

dynamics, thereby diminishing it, since it is supposed to stand above and regulate such interactions.

To avoid this problem, a written constitution could contain a stipulation that judicial appointments should not be partisan. Ultimately adherence to it would depend on self-restraint. Yet under the existing system we are also similarly reliant on convention, and should not imagine that the judicial and party political spheres have ever, or can ever, be hermetically sealed, any more than an absolute separation of powers is possible. English and UK constitutional history illustrates the point well. The appointment of politicians to judicial posts has ample historic precedence in the UK: the old office of Lord Chancellor represented a fusion of legislative, executive and judicial roles at the highest level. Moreover, critics from the Left and the Right have long complained that the decisions of judges reflect definite political orientations, if not necessarily involving attachment to a specific party. According to such analysis excessive judicial power is a concern not because it might lead to politicisation, but because politicisation already prevails. There is also presently some interest on the Right in providing Parliament with direct involvement both in judicial appointments and decisions. This development would not require a written constitution and is attractive to those who would be hostile towards this kind of text; it is also entirely possible within the parameters of the doctrine of parliamentary sovereignty. Those, therefore, who criticise the idea of a written constitution on the grounds that it threatens judicial politicisation should consider that under widely accepted interpretations of prevailing principles, the courts and all they do are ultimately subject to a legislature within which parties are the dominant force. Indeed, in terminology no longer used, Parliament was once known as the 'high court of Parliament'.

Advocates of a UK written constitution should be careful neither to oversell nor misrepresent their cause. Not all of the positive values discussed above could be realised immediately or perfectly at the first attempt, but a journey towards them would begin. It is possible to find numerous cases of texts from around the world that have failed or at least experienced operational problems. Yet given that nearly all countries—democracies and otherwise—have a written constitution, that some of them have difficulties is not a surprise and contributes little to the present debate. We do not necessarily know in every case that the text is the underlying cause of a malfunction, or that not having a document at all would have helped avoid it. Furthermore, since the collection of states without such a text is so small—common wisdom has it that the UK, New Zealand and Israel are the significant members of this group—a meaningful comparison between the two categories, those with and without written constitutions, as an aid to discerning the preferable approach, is difficult. This disparity should, however, at least give cause for consideration in the UK as to whether the overwhelming majority of states have followed the correct path. Moreover, whatever difficulties some of these countries may have, while they may alter their fundamental text—possibly frequently—they do not seem to contemplate abandoning it altogether. Individual defects, then, do not discredit the concept of the written constitution, and their identification should be welcome to those who desire a document for the UK, since it will help avoid the repetition of mistakes.

Another error for supporters of a written constitution to avoid is the assumption that it will reverse long-term social trends, such as those leading to lower engagement in more traditional political activities. Any notion that such patterns are a consequence of flaws in our arrangements, and that restructuring and reform can, for example, achieve a return to an era of mass party membership and higher turnout in general elections, requires careful scrutiny. The changed nature of engagement is connected to wider social developments in the UK and internationally, and involves generational shifts that are probably less pervious to redirection than such an outlook admits. Indeed, the very idea that trends of this sort are a problem in need of correction is only apparent from the perspective of an older order, the reference points of which are becoming less relevant precisely because of the change that its adherents might find regrettable. It is arguable that the debate over whether or not to introduce a written constitution is itself an outgrowth of this same declining system and modes of thought connected to it. However, the historic survey conducted in this book demonstrates just how enduring principles associated with this kind of text are. They have survived many social and political transformations. Further changes are always taking place. We cannot know precisely how the landscape will shift, or indeed what generations yet to come will add. But it is reasonable to assume that the concepts that can find expression in a written constitution will retain appeal and potential value.

Some trends of development enhance the case for a fundamental document. As discussed, declining turnout at general elections undermines the legitimacy of Parliament as a legally supreme body able to alter the constitution as it sees fit, subject to no overriding set of rules. Another pattern some research has identified is for an increased professionalisation of politics, by which is meant the rise of a career path beginning with an 'instrumental' apparatchik role preceding entry into Parliament and possibly ministerial office.[10] Adding to the impression of a formal career is the more structured nature of the daily role of the MP following the intensification of constituency casework. If politics is becoming more of a profession, perhaps it is time to regulate it as such, through a written constitution. While a text probably cannot reverse trends of development (even if to do so were desirable), it can make a difference by variously dealing with their consequences, embracing them, and even shaping their ongoing development.

THE NEGATIVE CASE FOR A WRITTEN CONSTITUTION

There is also a set of negative reasons for introducing a text: circumstances it could prevent from coming about, or bring to an end. They help deal with one

---

[10] See eg: Max Goplerud, 'The First Time is (Mostly) the Charm: Special Advisers as Parliamentary Candidates and Members of Parliament' (2013) *Parliamentary Affairs*.

of the main arguments deployed against a fundamental document: that, whatever the merits of it may or may not be, there is simply not a pressing need for one in the UK, which functions well as a democracy as it is.[11] Without powerful urgency, so the theory runs, the necessary urge will not exist to engage in such a complex and demanding task. Written constitutions are in part defensive barriers, entrenching key principles against abuse. They have not always worked, and it is even possible for governors of malign intent to turn a text on itself, as was the case with the notorious clause 48 of the German 'Weimar' Constitution, that helped facilitate the Nazi dismantling of democracy. Sometimes, constitutions are never intended to provide the values they claim to secure, such as the 1936 Soviet Union text. Yet extreme examples do not discredit the idea that a written constitution could, if properly conceived, act as a valuable protective measure for UK democracy. The present domestic system contains within it certain gaps in protective coverage that a properly conceived text could help fill. Their not being exploited often relies upon adherence to tacit understandings and other rules that lack the formal, enforceable status of a written constitution.

It might be argued that our political culture has proved effective as a means of upholding the integrity of the system, and that clearer rules included in a text are not required. But, as we have seen, what we would now regard as democratic dispositions within the UK owe much to earlier efforts at setting out principles and practices in documents. A renewed encapsulation is overdue. It may not seem urgent, but complacency is inadvisable. The previous part of this book identified growing tensions in the relationships between different institutions of governance, and in their dealings with the public. Levels of deference have declined. In these circumstances, the old tacit understandings or conventions have lost credibility. The relationship between the UK Parliament and English local government is instructive. Self-restraint was needed on the part of the former to prevent it from using its legal supremacy to invade the spheres of operation of the latter, but this protection no longer seems effective. Across the constitution more specific agreements have become necessary. This dynamic has motivated the shift towards the production of public, official codes dealing with various features of the UK constitution. They cover issues ranging from the principle of collective Cabinet government, to the rules surrounding government formation, to the responsibility of ministers to Parliament, to features of judicial independence and to the relationship between central and devolved governments. But they have not achieved complete coverage, and they do not always achieve desirable outcomes. Moreover, some rules are too important to leave simply to statements often lacking in wide ownership, and of unclear constitutional or legal status.

The drafters of a written constitution could express themselves in such a way as to clearly prohibit certain outcomes that, though they may seem unlikely, would be disastrous if they occurred even on a single occasion, calling into

---

[11] See eg: NW Barber, 'Against a written constitution' [2008] *Public Law* 11.

question the survival of the present constitutional order. Currently, for instance, the Civil Contingencies Act 2004 that provides delegated powers for responses to emergency circumstances, contains within it some potential for a government to compromise democracy. It allows ministers to issue regulations making 'provision of any kind that could be made by Act of Parliament' (section 22(3)), subject to a far lower level of parliamentary control than that involved in producing primary legislation (see section 27). Uneasy with the implications, the joint parliamentary committee considering this legislation when it existed as a draft Bill called for it to include protections for key constitutional statutes, stipulating they were not subject to interference or abolition under the Act. The government rejected the joint committee recommendation, though the final Act states that it cannot alter the Human Rights Act, or the relevant provisions of the 2004 Act itself, and it specifies that any provision introduced must relate to the emergency that has arisen and be a proportionate response to it (section 23).

A court could quash a regulation issued under the 2004 Act, but it would be on less firm ground in seeking to prevent constitutional abuse than it would if the 2004 Act contained an express list of laws the alteration of which was beyond its scope. How bold judges might prove in emergency circumstances is difficult to determine. It is a shame that an Act intended to deal with such a wide range of possible threats to the stability of the social system omits definite provision forestalling one particular danger: the undermining of democracy through the very powers the legislation creates to protect it. The scenario might seem only a remote possibility, but unlikely events are the business of laws of this kind. It is preferable that the limitations on emergency powers should be explicit. If a constitutional text existed, discerning the precise nature of the fundamental components of our arrangements would by definition be a more straightforward task. The document could both create authorities for use in circumstances of extreme threat, and set out the limits of their application, particularly as they related to the other provisions of the written constitution. It would replace the Civil Contingencies Act 2004 and the residual emergency authorities that lurk within the Royal Prerogative. The introduction of greater clarity about the proper and inappropriate use of such powers by an authoritative text would in itself act as a deterrent to abuse. Moreover, the courts would thereby have firmer guidance for their deliberations in this area, and hopefully greater legitimacy if it ever proved necessary to make difficult decisions.

The Civil Contingencies Act 2004 creates potentially immense executive powers that, according to the terms of the Act, require an emergency to become live. It is also possible for Parliament to pass Acts providing ministers with the ability by order to amend and repeal primary legislation not solely in defined extraordinary circumstances, but as a more regular practice, and again with circumscribed parliamentary involvement. It is important that the limitations on such powers should be tightly defined. The Legislative and Regulatory Reform Bill of 2006 initially set out to create a wide authority of this sort, acquiring for itself the nickname 'the abolition of Parliament Bill'. Ostensibly the purpose of this law was to enable the government swiftly and flexibly to reduce the regulatory burden applying to business through secondary legislation issued under a parent Act. One objection to the original Bill was that it would allow a minister to determine how stringent a parliamentary procedure would apply to any given measure issued under its authority. Another problem was that it contained relatively weak protections against abuse. In February 2006, a letter from a group of Cambridge legal academics appeared in *The Times*, positing a range of possible inappropriate uses of the proposed law. Among them were the creation of a new criminal offence carrying a prison sentence, the removal or restriction of trial by jury, the introduction of house arrest in the gift of the Home Secretary, the granting to the Prime Minister the ability to oust judges from their posts, the altering of nationality and immigration legislation, and tampering with the remaining provisions of Magna Carta.[12] Parliament modified the Bill before it passed into law, reflecting the extreme controversy that the original proposal generated. Then, under the Coalition, the Public Bodies Bill of 2010 as initially drafted created similar concerns. Again political pressure forced ministers to alter their plans. Yet it is possible that a future government might make a more determined pursuit of such a measure, creating an enhanced opportunity for casual systemic modification, and other inappropriate measures, through statutory instrument. A constitutional text could place clear limits on such activity.

Another attack on the constitution from within could come through legislation that sought to exclude judicial review from specified areas. The intended effect would be to prevent courts from considering whether the official use of powers was rational, fair and within the terms of the Act from which they purported to derive, and compliant with human rights standards. The Asylum and Immigration (Treatment of Claimants, etc) Bill of 2003–04 included what is known as an 'ouster clause', intended seriously to circumscribe judicial review of the operation of the system of asylum and immigration appeals. Fierce resistance followed, in the House of Lords and from the Joint Committee on Human Rights, as well as from pressure groups. The government eventually relented and dampened its original proposals.[13] Nonetheless, the episode provided an illustration of how the doctrine of a legally unlimited legislature can potentially conflict with the rule of law. A written constitution could provide for the basic principles of judicial review, creating a right of access to it, and prohibiting its ousting.

Another problematic proposition is that a government could, using simple legislative procedure, bring about the repeal of the Human Rights Act 1998 and—as an executive action under the Royal Prerogative—withdraw from the ECHR. As we have seen, the Conservative Party is now committed to the first course of action, and possibly the second, or as a minimum a reduction of the

---

[12] New Politics Network, *The Legislative and Regulatory Reform Bill 2006* (London, New Politics Network, 2006).

[13] See: Joint Committee on Human Rights, *Scrutiny of Bills: Sixth Progress Report* (2003–04, HL 102, HC 640) 7–35.

force of the Convention in the UK, though it plans to introduce a new 'British Bill of Rights' at the same time. Advocates of such policies tend to present them as a rejection of unwanted foreign and judicial interference in domestic, democratic decision-taking. Yet the ECHR, drawn up with a major UK input, explicitly derived its content from principles that had developed under the influence of UK (or English) ideas, and associated documents such as Magna Carta and the Bill of Rights. The likely outcome of this course of action would be a reduction in the width and depth of protection for the rights of everyone in the UK and in areas under the control of the UK. Simply defending the Human Rights Act seems to be a failing tactic. A more aggressive approach is needed from those who support the principles it encapsulates. A written constitution could make the curtailment of rights as envisaged by those who dislike the 1998 Act and the operation of the ECHR more difficult, or entirely prohibit it.

Further removal of rights would take place in the event that the UK left the EU. The effect would be to deny to people in the UK the protections and entitlements they presently possess as European citizens. Even if this outcome came about following support in a referendum, there are problems with the idea of majorities imposing such a decision on minorities against their will. We have seen how it is possible to cite John Milton as anticipating the fully formed doctrine of parliamentary sovereignty, and in this sense as an opponent of entrenched principles. Yet on another occasion he expressed a view that could encourage a different outlook, asserting: 'More just it is ... that a less number compel a greater to retain (which can be no wrong to them) their liberty, than that a greater number, for the pleasure of their baseness, compel a less most injuriously to be their fellow slaves'.[14] The sentiment these words conveys is an antidote to excessive majoritarianism, whether it finds expression in divisions in Parliament (as may be the case with repeal of the Human Rights Act) or referendums (for the EU).

A further threat might come from misuse of the Parliament Acts. A government could use its majority in the Commons to force through legislation amending the 1911 Act itself, with the effect of removing the ability of the House of Lords to veto extensions to the life of a Parliament beyond five years. It might then be possible for the government to elongate its own existence as it saw fit, bypassing the Lords. The Law Lords considered this possibility in the course of their assessment of the challenge to the Hunting Act 2004. Once again the threat may seem remote, but it is significant that during these proceedings the Attorney-General asserted on behalf of the government that it would be possible to use the Parliament Acts in this way. A written constitution could explicitly prohibit abuse through including and entrenching provision for the electoral cycle.

In many of the scenarios outlined above, the last defence against a government seeking through a Commons majority to commit constitutional abuse might be the courts. The judiciary might, for instance, strike down secondary legislation

---

[14] Cited in Mark Kishlansky, *A Monarchy Transformed: Britain 1603–1714* (London, Penguin, 1997) 190.

issued under the Civil Contingencies Act that modified constitutional Acts of Parliament in a way not in keeping with the original purposes of the parent legislation. Courts might also not accept that an attempt to prohibit judicial review in a given area was valid, or deny the ability of the Commons to use the Parliament Acts to remove the protection for the length of a Parliament. But because a written constitution is lacking, there is no text providing clear guidance as to when fundamental principles are being transgressed, necessitating firm resistance. On the one hand, this absence could provide the courts with too little strength. They are likely to be uncertain of their position, and faced with politicians possessing a more immediate democratic mandate, possibly marshalling a populist campaign. A reluctance to obstruct would be understandable, but possibly disastrous. On the other hand, an assertive court may feel in a position to discern for itself what the underlying rules are. This level of discretion is clearly inappropriate to attach to any one constitutional player. It is entirely plausible that the executive and legislature would not accept subordinancy to the judiciary or the principles it asserted. The implications of such a stand-off for the rule of law and the operation of the democratic system, as noted in an earlier chapter, would be grave.

The threats discussed so far primarily involve an ill-intentioned or at best misguided government. Problems could also emanate from another source. Under the Royal Prerogative the monarch remains able—in strict legal terms—to choose and dismiss prime ministers and to withhold Royal Assent from legislation. Any conventions limiting or prohibiting the use of these powers are not explicitly stated in the executive account of such rules: the *Cabinet Manual*. Moreover, the manual expressly iterates certain positive customary rights said to be possessed by the monarch. For instance, it asserts that 'he or she is entitled to be informed and consulted, and to advise, encourage and warn ministers'. The manual, typically of efforts to state the conventions in this area, emphasises the importance of appearances: 'By convention, the Sovereign does not become publicly involved in the party politics of government'.[15] However, the manual does not—presumably for reasons of etiquette—refer expressly to the need to safeguard democratic processes from royal interference, and clearly allows for behind-the-scenes influence on the part of the head of state, something that remains a regular feature of UK politics. Yet restraint of the monarchy lies at the core of the UK constitution. Blood was spilled winning this principle, and it involved the production of a series of constitutional texts. Action is needed to ensure that this value is realised in the contemporary context.

Elizabeth II has proved effective at avoiding engagement in controversial issues, at least visibly. However, it can never be certain that her successors will display the same self-restraint or public relations skills. For a monarch who wishes to pursue particular objectives, regular opportunities are available, such as the weekly

---

[15] Cabinet Office, *The Cabinet Manual: A guide to the laws, conventions and rules on the operation of government*, 1st edn (London, Cabinet Office, 2011) 3.

audience with the Prime Minister. A more dramatic opening might come after a general election producing no overall victor. George V was active in the formation of the National Government of 1931.[16] Perhaps one of his descendants may seek to emulate him. The wording of the *Cabinet Manual* leaves this possibility open with its statement that following an inconclusive poll, 'The Sovereign would not expect to become involved in any negotiations, although there are responsibilities on those involved in the process to keep the Palace informed'.[17] Some might even argue royal engagement in such circumstances would be desirable. In reality, it would be a disaster, both because of how it appeared, and because of what it meant.[18] Society is not what it was in the era of Ramsay MacDonald. Possibly monarchists should be the most worried about the consequences for the institution if the person who filled it became visibly uncontrollable. A written constitution should address this potential democratic breakdown either by making the monarchy subject to it, or other more radical means. It could reduce the potential for royal involvement in public controversy that the present system deems undesirable, and also perhaps eliminate the scope for private intervention that is, under existing rules, seemingly considered more acceptable. The desire to set out in writing what are the limitations on the personal prerogatives of the monarch, and in the process reduce them, was an important motive driving Magna Carta. It remains a worthwhile endeavour.

Another prospect that some—though not all—would regard as undesirable is a break-up of the UK. While Scotland may for the time being have decided to remain within the fold, the occurrence of a referendum on continued membership of the UK by one of its components is significant. It would be rash to predict that no further such votes will be held in Scotland or elsewhere. The UK is moving towards a relatively clear arrangement that parts of it have the right to secede if they choose, without requiring a more general authorisation from the state as a whole. If one of the Celtic participants in the UK were to leave, the constitutional consequences for those that remained might be difficult to shrug off, and could encourage further departures. Furthermore, specifically English identity, with a foundation in resentment over perceived systemic inequity, could increasingly find concrete political expression. If England were to create the impression that it was abusing its economic weight and population size at the cost of others, the Union could become untenable. Problems of this nature could develop if changes in parliamentary rules at Westminster meant that a government with the confidence of the House of Commons majority was rendered unsustainable because it

---

[16] See: David Marquand, '1942–1932' in David Butler (ed), *Coalitions in British Politics* (London, Macmillan, 1978) esp 61, 64.

[17] Cabinet Office, *The Cabinet Manual* (n 15) 3.

[18] For discussion of the rules applying in such circumstances, see: Robert Blackburn, 'Monarchy and the Personal Prerogatives' [2004] *Public Law* 546; Rodney Brazier, 'Monarchy and the personal prerogatives: A personal response to Professor Blackburn' [2005] *Public Law* 46.

did not possess a majority among MPs elected in constituencies in England. How a text might address these scenarios is discussed in the next chapter.

Similarly, major possible constitutional changes already noted above, for instance involving UK withdrawal from the ECHR, might be less popular in parts of the UK other than England, and create the perception that England was stripping people of their rights against their will. A referendum on continued EU membership that produced an overall majority in favour of leaving, but not in one or more of the Celtic territories, would be of questionable legitimacy. Both the ECHR and European law are explicit parts of the devolution systems, creating higher rules to which they are subject. To remove the UK from these systems or alter their application without express permission from the areas concerned would be to court controversy and alienation. During the Scottish Independence Referendum, a key component of the 'no' campaign was the claim that an independent Scotland would face uncertainty about its position within the EU, an outcome depicted as undesirable in such narratives. Yet remaining within the UK could now lead to similar insecurity, with the future effectively in the hands of the English electorate and a government with little support outside England. Membership of a union operating in this way would appear increasingly unattractive. A written constitution could provide different—more inclusive—approaches.

Some would hold that it is better not to speculate about such scenarios. They might argue that they are too unlikely to merit consideration. However, these gaps in the constitution exist regardless of whether or not we want to think about them. Furthermore, there is another nightmare setting: the one we inhabit at present. The UK constitution is in a condition of unresolved post-imperial turmoil, a chain reaction of systemic change that has not yet ended. Established assumptions and practices are subject to intense pressure. In some areas, there has been successful transition to different internal and external modes of organisation. But resistance persists, combined with efforts to reverse change. An insistence on clinging to certain constitutional peculiarities is often presented in terms of the specialness of the UK, and a supposed dichotomy between our values and those prevailing elsewhere in Europe.

Consequently, difficulties remain in achieving the full acceptance and realisation of various principles, even though they originate in part in the UK. An outline of some of them follows. First, there is a need to impose limitations on all institutions of governance, and for none of them to be a seat of absolute legal and constitutional power. Authority must spread widely across multiple poles, from central to local level. Second, major decision-making, particularly of a constitutional nature, should require meaningful input from the different sub-components of the UK, and no one unit should be able to dominate. Third, any provision for local, regional or national self-government should, as far as possible, be available throughout the UK, and not denied to some. Fourth, the ultimate source of authority is the population, though this principle should not be confused with a crude majoritarianism. Fifth, fundamental rights should be enforceable, and such an arrangement is a crucial component of democracy, not a challenge to it. Sixth, key constitutional principles should have a higher legal status than regular law. Seventh and finally, any constitution is porous, with an inescapable relationship of interdependence with the outside world. The act of establishing a constitution could provide opportunity for moving beyond the present reluctance to accept such understandings, through a full public consideration of what the UK is and should be. The ideas underpinning this new settlement could take into account previous UK constitutional documents, and the wider continuum of European democratic development. The text this exercise produced could serve as a focus for a reformed UK.

CREATING A CONSTITUTION

Arguing in favour of a written constitution is an easier task than introducing one. How might it come about? The present work is not one of prophecy. I will not attempt to set out precise circumstances in which a text would come into being, nor do I claim that it is an inevitable outcome. But it is plausible, not least because it is desirable. If a wide enough recognition of the potential value of a written constitution forms, then it will become possible. Political will is crucial. If it exists in sufficient depth and breadth, then the claim some may make that the objective of creating such a text is too demanding or problematic will become less relevant. The challenge cannot be more daunting than that facing the drafters of Magna Carta in 1215. Doubters should also consider whether anyone in, say, 1960 given a description of the UK constitution of today would have found it credible. We should not exclude this possible pattern of development, particularly when there is some precedent for it in the past of England and the UK, and such texts exist across the world.

A worthwhile area for consideration is whether an abrupt—even violent—dislocation is the only circumstance in which a written constitution might come about. When considering the related issue of a possible Bill of Rights for the UK, the Joint Committee on Human Rights found in 2008 that many such instruments had emerged from turmoil. It noted that the Declaration of the Rights of Man and the Citizen in France, the Bill of Rights in the US and the South African Bill of Rights were all 'forged in the heat generated by momentous conflicts and upheavals'. Similar observations, the committee remarked, were applicable to the United Nations Universal Declaration of Human Rights and the ECHR, both of which came about shortly after the Second World War, the experience of which left an imprint upon them. The attempted Northern Ireland Bill of Rights was part of a conflict resolution process. In the period after the committee reported, the world economic crisis has prompted attempts at major constitutional revision in two countries where it impacted most seriously: Iceland and Ireland. Yet the committee concluded that it was possible for a text to appear in more regular circumstances, citing the Canadian Charter of Rights and Freedoms of 1982, that came about because of the desire of the then premier, Pierre Trudeau, to 'bind the Canadian federation together' as opposed to 'any particularly momentous upheaval in Canadian society at that time'.[19]

Nonetheless, when speculating on possible circumstances leading to a written constitution, the idea that it might involve one or more problems is reasonable. Aside from the international evidence, UK and English history can support such a theory. Often there was an interaction between longer-term tensions and a more immediate crisis. In 1215, the overall nature of Plantagenet rule collided with military disaster under the objectionable John Lackland. Stuart absolutism was a problem for much of the seventeenth century that various specific disputes inflamed, prompting a number of texts. The Unions of 1706–07 and 1800–01 both came about when protracted concern about the nature of the governance of the archipelago became more pressing because of a threat of French hegemony on the continental mainland. A sustained tension involving the relative powers of the Commons and Lords turned into a constitutional battle when a radical Liberal Government took office, leading to the Parliament Act 1911. At present the UK is passing through an elongated phase of systemic flux. The interaction of a more immediate problem with the tendencies that have been at work over decades, thereby creating circumstances conducive to the introduction of a constitutional text, is plausible. It could involve, for instance, a clash between the courts and politicians, or between one and more of the territorial components of the Union and the centre, or a supranational connection such as the EU or ECHR. If changes in party voting patterns left the existing parliamentary electoral system seeming increasingly inappropriate, a serious legitimacy problem could appear. However, rather than waiting for an immediate crisis, it is better to act pre-emptively.

But how should those undertaking this task proceed? Much guidance is available from the past and from international experience, both of which the following discussion incorporates. Not all the case studies engaged with involve the creation of an entire constitutional text. None introduced such a document to a mature democracy that previously only had an unwritten constitution, the task that the UK would face (perhaps the closest equivalent is the 1982 'patriation' of the Canadian constitution). Some of the examples deployed here focus on a narrower range of subject matter, or even an individual issue. Yet nonetheless, instructive evidence is widely dispersed, and should be used where it has value. Drawing on this data, I consider below the ideal processes that might take place. In fact, a convoluted progression towards a written constitution may already be in hand, using some of the methods I recommend but omitting others. Reality is messy.

Preparatory Steps and Composition of a Convention

A crucial prerequisite to a written constitution would be a firm commitment by one or both of the two main UK political parties. Because of the way the political

---

[19] Joint Committee on Human Rights, *A Bill of Rights for the UK* (2007–08, HL 165-I, HC 150-I) 23–24.

system works, this necessity is inescapable. The proposal included in the Labour Manifesto of 2010 shows that potential exists, though it would have to form a more prominent and clearly established part of the programme than it did in this case—and the party concerned would have to go on to form at least part of a government. There would probably be a need for collaboration on this issue with at least one other party, given the need to proceed by some kind of consensus in these areas. Cooperation across partisan lines can be a valuable commodity, as it was, for instance, to the establishment of the Spanish Constitution of 1978, when a range of groups from diverse origins across the spectrum worked together after a prolonged period of dictatorship. With this principle in mind, the support of multiple parties would be ideal. Yet it would not be essential, and should not be achieved by compromising core principles. Nor should one intransigent group be able to deny a constitution to the whole. Furthermore, whatever position they each take on this issue, parties alone will not be enough. They simply cannot claim to represent the political community in the way they might once have; a reversal of this trend is not foreseeable. Some kind of civil society involvement while plans were still at a formative stage—as took place with the Scottish Constitutional Convention—would be valuable.

Discussion could then lead to a general statement of principles and an outlined programme of action in advance of a general election, with the endorsement of multiple parties and groups. If voters obliged by returning a House of Commons that was supportive of this policy, then formal action could begin. The important requirement would be that there had already developed momentum involving a broad coalition of extra-parliamentary, non-party political groupings and the more traditional institutions of political organisation and representation. Attaining a breadth of social support is crucial. In 1215, it was the combination of forces such as barony, Londoners and clerics that obliged John to accede (albeit in bad faith) to demands from below. Furthermore, their project survived, despite the actions of John and Innocent III, partly because it catered for a variety of interests and therefore could command wide backing.

Central government and its personnel will inevitably have a part to play in the production of a written constitution, but should be subject to careful restriction. A meaningful text would represent a threat to the degree of discretion possessed by the UK executive. Ministers might over time find the radical agenda on which they came to office less appealing, given the perspective of government. William of Orange, after taking power, seemingly became less enamoured with the principles of limited government with which he had associated himself before launching his military action in 1688. But the pressure he had unleashed and encouraged forced him in this direction anyway. In distancing themselves from a written constitution, politicians would probably receive encouragement from the permanent Civil Service, within which a concern would probably exist to protect the privileges of the central executive in general, and of Whitehall officials themselves in particular. It is not necessary to be a full-blown conspiracy theorist to recognise the strong likelihood that, given the opportunity, civil servants, being humans, might seek to blunt proposals for a written constitution. Moreover, they would be likely to promote particular stipulations for inclusion in any constitutional text that entrenched or enhanced their privileged position, as did senior church figures with Magna Carta and earlier texts dating to Anglo-Saxon times.

Towards the close of a 2005 article considering the pattern of constitutional change in the UK, the former Cabinet Secretary and Head of the Home Civil Service, Richard Wilson (Lord Wilson of Dinton), discussed whether it might be time to 'codify the British constitution'. He argued that it 'would be a formidable task' and if 'political will' was lacking it would take place over an excessively long period of time. Wilson concluded that the 'Piece-meal reform' already in hand was preferable, and that a 'Civil Service Bill would be a useful step', as well as a 'code of governance for central government'.[20] In other words, in place of a full written constitution, Wilson advocated a statute protecting the position of the institution with which he was associated, combined with seemingly another variant on the code of the sort Whitehall was already regularly producing.

Wilson had retired in 2002. But perhaps the view he expressed was representative of the kind of response Gordon Brown met with when, two years after Wilson wrote, Brown became Prime Minister and sought to pursue the introduction of a written constitution. If so, it would help explain why Brown achieved so little in this admittedly ambitious objective, and why two of the most significant measures he did achieve in the constitutional field involved legislation for the Civil Service and the instigation of the *Cabinet Manual*, perhaps akin to the 'code of governance for central government' Wilson had in mind. The permanent bureaucracy with its impartial perspective can play a crucial role in ensuring effective policy-making and implementation. A written constitution might well protect some of the core characteristics that make it a valuable institution. But the Civil Service is not the appropriate instrument for the creation of this document, and Whitehall is not the proper place for executing the task.

Just as it would need distance from the executive which it would serve to limit, the task of creating a written constitution would, for similar reasons, also have to be separate from Parliament. It is notable that some of the very earliest impetus for the concept of a written constitution in mid-seventeenth century England came from the army rather than Parliament, and an important motive lying behind it was a desire to restrict the legislature. A fundamental text should come from somewhere other than Westminster. The contribution Parliament could make would be through passing an enabling Act providing for the establishment of a constitutional convention. However, alongside the Act—and perhaps also included as a schedule to it—could appear a statement to the effect that the convention operated under the authority of and on behalf of the people as a whole. This stipulation would signify that the text, though the legislature would play a part in its initiation, was intended to transcend this legal origin and in the process supplant Parliament in its traditional role as the ultimate basis of constitutional authority in the UK.

[20] Richard Wilson, 'Constitutional Change: A Note by the Bedside' (2004) *Political Quarterly* 286.

The document could only achieve this status if it was perceived as having legitimately attained it, both in general public opinion and within the bodies responsible for the operation of the constitution, including executives, elected assemblies and the courts at their various tiers across the UK. Without public and institutional support, there is a danger the constitution would fail to command the authority it would need, and crucially that it would not be successful in binding the UK Parliament. The 'continuing' theory of parliamentary sovereignty could even lead to the conclusion that it is impossible to subject Parliament to a higher authority by any means, and that Parliament will always retain the ability to nullify any such effort by regular legislative procedure. This absurd proposition does not deserve countenance. Nonetheless, an effort properly to establish a written constitution would need to overcome the significant degree of adherence to the parliamentary sovereignty concept that—however vaguely conceived it is—persists.

Lawyers have offered ingenious solutions.[21] They include Parliament abolishing itself and creating a new legislature in its place that would be subject to a constitution. Fittingly, an exponent of the viability of parliamentary sovereignty has proposed the most convincing means of escaping the grip of this doctrine. Jeffrey Goldsworthy argues that it 'is a product of long-standing consensual practices that emerged from centuries-old political struggles, and it can only be modified if the consensus among senior legal officials changes'. He adds that 'it ought not to be modified without the support of a broader consensus within the electorate'. On this basis Goldsworthy praised the *Governance of Britain* Green Paper of July 2007, which set out the Brown programme, for its emphasis on 'an inclusive process of national debate' and 'extensive and wide consultation' that might produce 'a broad consensus'.[22] In accordance with this thesis a process for the creation of a written constitution must be widely based enough to achieve the required level of agreement.

Essential to the text achieving acceptance and consequently being a success is that the body devising it is of appropriate form and composition.[23] It cannot be an executive or parliamentary exercise, nor will one of the traditional techniques such as setting up a Royal Commission or Speaker's Conference suffice. Though it has precedents, a full, modern written constitution will be a new concept for this country, and demands in turn the use of an entity that the UK has not seen before: a specific constitutional convention. An innovative task calls for innovative

---

[21]   Oliver, 'Towards a written constitution?' (n 6) 149; Hood Phillips, *Reform of the Constitution* (n 4) 156.

[22]   Jeffrey Goldsworthy, *Parliamentary Sovereignty: Contemporary Debates* (Cambridge, Cambridge University Press, 2010) 7.

[23]   For a comparative analysis of constitutional conventions, see eg: Robert Blackburn (ed), *Case Studies on Constitution Building* (London, Centre for Political and Constitutional Studies, 2014), paper prepared at request of the House of Commons Political and Constitutional Reform Committee; Dawn Oliver and Carlo Fusaro (eds), *How Constitutions Change* (Oxford, Hart Publishing, 2011); and Alan Renwick, *After the Referendum: Options for a Constitutional Convention* (London, The Constitution Society, 2014).

methods. It should build on historic and international good practice, and add to it, returning the UK to the forefront of democratic development. Who should sit on the convention? I will deal with the wider public later, but an important point, that Alan Renwick makes well, must be grasped first. Though it should not be subordinate to them, the participation of representatives of political parties in the convention is a necessity. Their support will be vital to the constitution ever being implemented. A text is more likely to be acceptable to them if they have been involved in its production; and having taken part it may be harder for them to disassociate themselves from it, if they want to. The failure of the Icelandic Constitutional Council is instructive. It sat in 2011, comprising elected members drawn from without regular party political circles. The Council produced recommendations that never came into being, despite receiving endorsement through a referendum in 2012, because the Icelandic legislature did not put them into force. The make-up of the Council contributed to this outcome, as although it may have been legitimate from a purist perspective, it excluded the elite groups whose support or at least acquiescence was vital. Another reason for incorporating politicians into constitutional design is that if the document is enacted it is they who will be most directly involved in its ongoing operation. Consequently, their having investment in the text will be vital to its surviving and functioning effectively. Once again, the fate of Magna Carta is instructive. John Lackland never intended it to be successful, and ensured its swift demise, in its initial form.

Elite buy-in, then, is essential. The convention must take place away from Parliament and government, but incorporating figures from within these institutions. One way of co-opting high-level groups could be by appointing representatives of parties to the UK convention according to a formula possibly related to electoral support. Another approach could be direct elections. Of the 152 who sat on the Australian Constitutional Convention of 1998, for example, there was a bloc of 40 appointed members from state legislatures and the Commonwealth Parliament. One-third of the Irish Constitutional Convention formed in 2012 comprised appointed politicians. In the Swiss Canton of Geneva in 2008 elections took place for a constitutional assembly, charged with creating a new cantonal constitution. Within it 11 groups were represented, of which eight were connected to conventional parties.

The sub-components of the UK would have to participate each in their own right, since a viable written constitution would need to express the fundamentally multinational quality of the UK. The convention could incorporate members from the devolved assemblies of Northern Ireland, Scotland and Wales. But what of England? The English nation at present lacks political representation in its own right. This issue is not only a problem that a constitutional convention should seek to address, but also an obstacle to the successful pursuit of such an exercise. It may be that England needs to hold a constitutional convention of its own to determine how it might participate in a similar project for the UK as a whole. In different ways, Northern Ireland, Scotland and Wales have all had their constitutional moments; the UK as a whole cannot have its equivalent unless England does too. Resolving the English issue would enable full participation by the territorial sub-units. Earlier examples of such an approach include the sending by the states of delegates to the US convention in 1787 and the election by state parliaments of the members of the Parliamentary Council that devised the German 'Basic Law' of 1949. The circumstances are not identical, but it is important to try and secure participation from all parts of the UK. Canada has faced problems of constitutional legitimacy since, although it 'patriated' its constitution in 1982, it has never managed to establish arrangements that are satisfactory to the Province of Quebec without alienating others.

Given the previously discussed decline in traditional modes of political participation, party and governmental involvement in a convention would not be sufficient. Direct public engagement is required. One method currently attracting attention is known as online crowd-sourcing, something attributed to the recent Icelandic constitutional exercise. It involves soliciting views from the public electronically. However, it is not clear how far the methods genuinely influenced the direction of the Icelandic project, and to integrate them more thoroughly would require the commitment of substantial resources, though this concern should not preclude the practice. Participants in crowd-sourcing, moreover, would be self-selecting and not a representative sample of the population. Another approach to wider incorporation of the public is a method known as sortition. It is not new, and was employed in Ancient Athens. In the contemporary context there are examples of the use of sortition for constitutional design processes, such as the Citizens' Assembly that sat in British Columbia in 2005 to consider the electoral system in use in the Province. Sortition makes it possible to obtain a more representative social sample in such terms as gender balance and ethnicity than is often visible in legislative bodies, though an unavoidable filter is that of those asked, only people who feel disposed to take part and are able to do so make up the participants. Some may hold it undemocratic to place a randomly chosen group of people in such a position of influence. However, if it is appropriate to choose juries to deliver verdicts in criminal cases by this means, then the principle could appropriately be transferrable to a constitutional convention.

Remit, Working Methods and Ratification of the Text

What might it be appropriate to expect a UK constitutional convention to achieve, and what therefore should its exact terms of reference be? In truth, it is probably only once it has gathered that the dynamics and potentials will begin to become fully apparent to those taking part. The original specification for the convention that produced the US text in 1787 was purely to deliberate on enhancements to the existing confederal system. Ultimately it went far further. As Catherine Drinker Bowen remarks, it was initially called only a 'convention' and the 'notion of a new "constitution" would have scared away two-thirds of the members'.[24]

---

[24] Catherine Drinker Bowen, *Miracle at Philadelphia: The Story of the Constitutional Convention, May to September 1787* (New York, Little, Brown & Co, 1986) 4.

In Ireland, the Constitutional Convention of 2012–13 had eight specific items on its agenda but was able to stretch its remit more widely because of a final clause authorising it to consider other matters. The terms of reference of a number of the other more recent processes considered in this chapter are not as relevant. They were focused on an individual issue, or relatively narrow set of closely connected topics. In British Columbia, the electoral system alone was under consideration. In Australia, it was primarily the possibility of abolishing the monarchy. The task for a UK body, creating a fundamental text where none at present exists, would be of a different quality. It is important that the UK convention is not required to deliver more than it transpires is possible, and at the same time, if fruitful consensus is achieved, it should not find itself constrained by its formal brief. The main instruction should be to agree a constitution on behalf of the people of the nations and regions of the UK.

Nonetheless, certain basic requirements should apply. There should be a floor: provisions presently in force that the constitutional convention cannot remove and must incorporate into any document it produced in some form. These protected features would include individual rights as provided for through the Human Rights Act (if it still exists by this point), the possibility of judicial review and the independence of the judiciary, and the status of the devolved territories. While the document eventually produced might set out means by which such arrangements could change, the convention would not itself deal with these modifications. However, it could build upon some of these features of the UK constitution: for instance, by extending devolution, or making rights more enforceable. This kind of steering has applied before in the production of major constitutional texts. In 1948, the occupying powers in western Germany communicated through the 'Frankfurt Documents' certain obligatory require-ments that would bind the Parliamentary Council: the upholding of funda-mental rights, and a democratic, federal system. Ten years later, the Parliament of the French Fourth Republic passed legislation intended to provide general parameters of operation to the drafters of what would become the Fifth Republic Constitution. The law stipulated that the new text would include provision for individual rights, for the principle of universal suffrage, for judicial indepen-dence, the separation of the executive from the legislature, and the responsibility of ministers.

What precisely the mandate means in practice will be for the convention to determine. If it is satisfactorily composed, it will have the democratic authority to place an expansive interpretation on its remit. A likely starting point will be the Union, the position of the different parts of it, and their relations with the centre. This discussion will naturally connect to the status of the UK Parliament, and issues such as the composition and powers of the second chamber. The idea of a Bill of Rights and the legal system will be important. From here many other con-siderations could flow: local government, electoral systems, public engagement mechanisms, and so on. To make its project meaningful, the convention would need to consider how its constitution could be entrenched and enforced.

The way in which the convention goes about its business will be crucial to the content and viability of its end product. It should choose its own methods. A crucial decision will be whether to work from concrete proposals, or start with more abstract first principles (taking into account that there will be certain protected areas). Delegates at Philadelphia in 1787 followed the former path. A draft scheme known as the 'Virginia Resolves' or 'Virginia Plan' proved important to framing the debate and driving the convention forward. The Geneva Constitutional Assembly took the latter approach, using a method known as the 'blank slate'. Yet however they work, participants in the convention will not be able fully to exclude the existing system from their minds, either as an example to follow or to avoid, and may be under the influence of models developed prior to their meeting. The manner in which the different members interact will also be important. There is a danger that the professional politicians taking part could dominate, at the expense of other members, such as those chosen using sortition (if this composition technique is applied). It may be necessary to some extent to keep different groups separate, but mixing them when necessary. Another subject requiring attention involves how far the business of the convention should be public. Open proceedings may on the surface seem desirable, but it should be accepted making progress may at times require closed sessions, a method deployed throughout the 1787 convention in Philadelphia. The convention will not ultimately be able to hide its conclusions, but reaching them may require confidentiality at certain points. Records could possibly be retained for subsequent release via the National Archive after 20 or 30 years. Public sessions might include the taking of evidence. These events could form a focus for crowd-sourcing and other engagement components of the convention.

A further matter for resolution relates to the scale of the task entailed by creating a UK constitutional text. It seems practically unlikely that all the members together could work out the entirety of a possible text. After an initial programme of work was agreed, a series of subcommittees could form, which might then present their proposals to the plenary for approval or modification. One important concern for the convention, that should probably be included in its initial mandate, is that it meets a relatively tight deadline. There is a risk in losing momentum and coming to be regarded as irrelevant. A firm date for completion will help focus the attention of those involved. Though its task would be considerable, the convention should certainly not sit for longer than the duration of a Parliament, and probably under three years. The principle of swift action, however, has limits beyond which it becomes counterproductive: the Australian Constitutional Convention of 1998 had only 10 days in which to deliberate. But the period of operation suggested here for a UK body is feasible when it is considered that the Irish Constitutional Convention of 2012–13 had only 12 months in which to conclude.

Having made efforts to ensure a widely based convention, it is important to guard against excessive dependence on any one unmediated sectional interest dominating during its proceedings. One important concern in this regard is information. Who would present it, how and in what form? Expert involvement is a complex area. Pressure groups will want to have a role, and it is right that they should. However, by definition they have predetermined agendas. In practice, another group of bodies that will engage with a convention—think tanks and research institutions—are also likely to be partial, though they may present themselves as otherwise. The academic community presents its own problems. It will tend not to offer straightforward answers. Divisions exist between and within disciplines, as do disputes involving personalities. But the many providers of evidence will between them amount to a rich resource. The constitutional convention must be sure to consult as widely as possible, and come to its own conclusions. This requirement suggests another concern. In processing the information supplied to it, and in its other functions, the convention will need administrative support. Those who fulfil this duty will be in a position to exercise influence, through the way in which they filter submissions, their contribution to the setting of agendas, the organisation of business, the advice they supply and in many other ways. Who will perform this task? Wherever personnel come from, they will bring particular institutional dispositions. For this reason it is probably wise to mix staff from a variety of origins, including different tiers of governance in the UK, and from outside the official world altogether. Legal advice, to ensure the text is viable and drafted in a way that a court would find recognisable, would be essential.

All the technicalities of committees, procedures and institutional support mechanisms are important. But amid them is another necessity. Somewhere on the constitutional convention, either among the full members or on the staff, should be one person or more with the ability to produce flowing prose, and at least one other person able to edit it effectively and sensitively. (It will also be important to be able to produce the words in at least two languages, Welsh and English, possibly more. All versions will be official, and none will be a 'translation', but the drafting of any given passage will have to begin in one of the languages.) Unavoidably some parts of the text will be drier than others, comprising more technical, legally worded passages, but it must include at least some inspiring content. Without the presence of the skills needed to add this quality, the entire enterprise could fail. It may be that a single individual will play the central role in drafting, as Thomas Jefferson did with the American Declaration of Independence of 1776, or that it will be more of a collective product, as was the French Declaration of the Rights of Man and Citizen of 1789.[25] No set model exists, but the convention must possess the requisite ability in some form. Where precisely it will come from is difficult to predict. What matters is that those who aspire to produce a written constitution need to be able to write. In doing so they should not let history weigh them down. They are not producing a piece of parchment, but a text that most will access online and navigate electronically. The language, structure and presentation should reflect this reality. The most appropriate way to honour the example

[25] For this comparison, see: Lynn Hunt, 'Introduction' in Lynn Hunt, *Inventing Human Rights: A History* (New York, WW Norton & Co, 2007).

of Ethelbert of Kent will be to emulate his success in simultaneously advancing the frontiers of constitutionalism, technology and communication, not in producing a document born with a grey beard.

Finally, one of the most difficult issues regarding process is how to obtain formal approval for the document once drafted. An Act of Parliament would be insufficient and inappropriate. The purpose of the convention would be to establish a constitutional source that supplanted Parliament in its traditional role. Moreover, if this document was to be entrenched against amendment by regular legislative procedures—as it should be—a special procedure for establishing it in the first place would probably be necessary. Inevitably, some will argue that the most appropriate—or only—way to ratify an instrument purporting to express popular sovereignty, and supplant the supremacy of Parliament, is through the electorate voting for it in a UK-wide referendum. Indeed, it is possible to argue that for such an important change, it would be necessary to secure the consent of more than a simple majority of those voting, and that a super-majority requirement of some kind would be necessary. If the constitutional text itself included provision for the holding of referendums in certain circumstances, particularly for its own amendment, it might follow that for a plebiscite to be required to alter something, it needs to be approved in this way in the first place. Moreover, perhaps it would be improper to deny the people as a whole a direct role in the process, ceding it to the small group who were members of the convention. A referendum can help establish a firm basis for a constitution, as it did at the outset of the French Fifth Republic, when 82.6 per cent voted in support of the text on a turnout of 98.9 per cent.

However, as already discussed, referendums have their drawbacks. These votes are often a crude instrument of public engagement; they can undo earlier good work. The recommendations of the British Columbia Citizens' Convention fell because, though obtaining 58 per cent assent in 2005, they failed to meet a supermajority stipulation (a second referendum in 2009 lost outright). As much as opening proceedings up to the people, a constitutional referendum might place it at the mercy of those who, in pursuit of their own agendas, could mount a nihilistic public campaign against the constitution. The core arrangements being overturned have never been subject as a whole to a referendum. If the convention was constructed and conducted itself in an appropriate way, it could represent the public and engage them in a more balanced procedure than that facilitated by a referendum campaign. It might possess popular—rather than populist— legitimacy of its own. Possibly the convention could approve the text on its own in a plenary vote that might involve a supermajority. Another way forward, particularly if the document set out arrangements of a federal nature, might be for each of the components of the UK to provide assent, perhaps via their elected assemblies, if they have them. The approval of three of the four territories might be sufficient, or perhaps unanimity might be necessary. It could be for each area to determine internally how it decided on whether to agree to the constitution, and indeed whether a referendum was necessary within its own territory. The German

Basic Law of 1949 required approval from two-thirds of state parliaments (and obtained the consent of all but Bavaria). After it was adopted, those members of the public who objected to the UK constitution in some way could seek to alter it, particularly if the amendment procedure was not overly demanding—and did not involve the holding of referendums. Yet it seems likely that the demands for a UK-wide plebiscite would be difficult to resist. Furthermore, while the referendum—like any another democratic mechanism—has drawbacks, at times it is the best means available for popular decision-taking, particularly if preceded by extensive and meaningful public debate and negotiation between different groups.

There are powerful positive and negative arguments in favour of a UK written constitution. Yet objections, both legitimate and less serious, also need to be overcome. The public may appear supportive if asked about a text in a particular way, but hostility is no doubt possible. A general lack of comprehension and of sense of urgency is also widespread. Convincing people in sufficient numbers that a written constitution is needed will be a challenge. The introduction of a text will either involve particular circumstances interacting with existing trends, or a concerted effort from a number of political groupings collaborating with each other and building connections with wider civil society. If progress is made by some means, the process employed to devise and propose the text cannot be of the more traditional variety such as a Cabinet committee, Speaker's Conference or Royal Commission. It must recognise that the nations and regions that make up the UK are part of its constitutional essence, and that the structures of representative government and party politics do not represent the public as well as in previous times. The introduction of a UK constitution will be an extraordinary event. But this realisation should not encourage dismay among supporters of this outcome. They only need to succeed once.

12

The Constitution

TO WRITE THE United Kingdom (UK) constitution will be to change it. The mere existence of a text with the explicit title 'constitution' will influence perceptions and consequently behaviour. Regardless of the specific arrangements for enforceability, statements and arrangements included in the document will acquire a special status. Therefore, even a document that sought to describe the system rather than alter it, or perhaps had limited or no legal force, would inevitably make a difference: and if it did not, what would be the purpose of it? If a text sought to set out conventions, as publications such as the *Cabinet Manual* has done, it is likely to end up modifying some of them along the way. A document that is in some way entrenched or legally superior will also, by definition, have brought about transformation, regardless of the substantive content of its provisions. Furthermore, the pressure exerted on a constitution-building process to bring about change, from multiple directions and interests would be immense. A constitutional convention might overtly seek to do so anyway. The perception of constitutional texts, especially from the English and UK perspective, can be that they are primordial, restating or reviving the ancient. Their authors from Anglo-Saxon times onwards have deliberately promoted this idea. But the impression is deceptive: in their time they were innovative, and a true emulation of them should be the same.

The following chapter, then, takes as its starting assumption that a written constitution will entail substantial systemic alteration. Change, prospective or actual, has been the defining feature of UK arrangements for five decades. It will continue to be so with or without a written constitution. But this kind of text offers a chance to channel this tendency, and regulate its future course, in a more satisfactory fashion. The coming pages discuss the choices that the drafters will have to make over a variety of issues when constructing a constitution, and the implications of their selections. In certain areas I indicate preferences and elaborate on reasons for the desirability of a written constitution, particularly if those who write it make particular decisions. Ultimately, however, it will be the work of whatever group is constructed to produce it. Given the transformative perspective taken here, the focus is on the prospect of a full constitution, not weak substitutes such as non-legal codes. Its radicalism, however, has limits: for instance I assume the persistence of parliamentary government, though a proposed presidential model for the UK exists.[1] I also suspect a likelihood that the monarchy would

---

[1] Graham Allen, *The Last Prime Minister: Being Honest about the UK Presidency*, 2nd edn (Exeter, Imprint Academic, 2003).

be retained, in altered form, for the time being at least. Connected to but not synonymous with this judgement, I avoid proposing a complete delineation of a UK 'state' in place of the existing 'Crown', its nearest equivalent under present arrangements.[2] Others, however, are welcome to outbid me. I hope they do.

PRESENTATION, WRITING STYLE AND PREAMBLE

Many or most people reading a UK constitution, if introduced, will do so first on a computer monitor screen, having found it using an internet search engine—the name of which does not need free advertisement here. It could also be available as a mobile phone app. The presentation, layout and internal design of the text should reflect this reality, with an alternative printable version. If historians are correct to tell us there was no master copy of Magna Carta—only multiple duplicates of which four survive—then we can continue this tradition in a different way: there will be no physical original of the UK constitution since it will come into being as electronic data. Because of this quality the text will be widely accessible, but it is also important that hard copies are made available in schools, libraries and other public buildings, to maximise distribution.

The style of the text is crucial in two senses. If the UK is to engage in the demanding exercise of producing a fundamental document, it should at least ensure it is well written. As discussed in the previous chapter, it is important that the constitutional convention includes within it the talent able to carry out this task. Existing officially in at least two languages, Welsh and English, the end product must excite and capture the mind of those it seeks to represent, protect and bind together: the inhabitants of the UK. At the same time, if it is to have effect as a legal document, parts of it will need to be technical, and at times detailed. Declaratory passages may be helpful to the wider impact of the text, but will probably not be justiciable. Moreover, the drafters will need to consider how much discretion they wish to leave to the courts in those passages clearly intended to have full legal force. The more precise they are in their intentions, the less scope for creative judicial interpretation there will be. However, in seeking certainty, the document will become longer and more difficult for the public to comprehend. The appropriate balance is a matter of judgement, informed by the type of constitution that is desired.

An opportunity for an immediate attention-securing flourish comes with the preamble. Not all documents of this kind have an introductory statement: for instance, the Netherlands text commences without one. But if properly devised it can play a vital role in seizing the imagination and setting the tone for what follows. Preambles can expound what is the source of the authority of the constitution, its purpose, and its values, connecting the particular circumstances of

---

[2] See: Maurice Sunkin and Sebastian Payne (eds), *The Nature of the Crown: A Legal and Political Analysis* (Oxford, Oxford University Press, 1999).

its origin with universal principles. The United States (US) has provided some of the most inspirational efforts. Though not strictly a constitution, the Declaration of Independence of 1776 contains powerful opening phrases, including the statement:

> We hold these truths to be self-evident, that all men are created equal, that they are endowed by their Creator with certain unalienable Rights, that among these are Life, Liberty and the pursuit of Happiness—that to secure these rights, Governments are instituted among Men, deriving their just powers from the consent of the governed.

Drafted 11 years later, the US Constitution had a shorter preamble than the Declaration of Independence. Its greatest impact came from the first three words that denoted popular sovereignty. It read in full:

> We the people of the United States, in Order to form a more perfect Union, establish Justice, insure domestic Tranquility, provide for the common defence, promote the general Welfare, and secure the Blessings of Liberty to ourselves and our Posterity, do ordain and establish this Constitution for the United States of America.

The American revolutionaries set a high standard to which future drafters could aspire. Some have chosen simply to copy the opening triplet of the US Constitution: for instance, the opening of the South African Constitution of 1996 uses the 'We the people' formulation—though it adds a comma after the 'We'. The Institute for Public Policy Research (IPPR) draft UK constitution also opened with the phrase 'We the people of the United Kingdom', and borrowed further from across the Atlantic with a reference later on to 'life, liberty and the pursuit of happiness'. A flaw in the IPPR overture, however, is that it is excessively long and tries to cover too much ground.[3] The Richard Gordon constitution preamble, that also deploys the phrase 'We the People of the United Kingdom', is more succinct.[4]

But ideally the UK would find a striking line for itself. It was in this spirit that in 1999 the Australian Prime Minister, John Howard, proposed a preamble (that never came to fruition) to the Australian Constitution including the term 'mateship'. Like Ethelbert of Kent in an earlier millennium, Howard sought to use the vernacular to express a fundamental principle. The quest for a preamble could provide a UK constitutional convention with a valuable focus for public engagement. Many proposals could be obtained, though some would certainly be perverse, and the exercise could encounter cultural resistance. In 2007, *The Times* held an online contest for a possible statement setting out the essence of 'Britishness'. The winner was 'No motto please, we're British'.[5] Some may regard such comments as funny or clever. But they lead to a tyranny of informality,

---

[3] Institute for Public Policy Research (IPPR), *A Written Constitution for the United Kingdom* (London, Mansell, 1993) 31–32.

[4] Richard Gordon, *Repairing British Politics: A Blueprint for Constitutional Change* (Oxford, Hart Publishing, 2010) 42.

[5] For a discussion of preambles see: Joint Committee on Human Rights, *A Bill of Rights for the UK* (2007–08, HL 165-I, HC 150-I) 34–35.

stifling attempts at rational discussion of the political system. One of the tasks of the drafters of a UK constitution would be to overcome these attitudes and establish that a written expression of fundamental principles should be as important to this country as any other.

A FEDERAL UNION

A core issue the text would need to address would be the position of the components of the UK: Wales, Scotland, Northern Ireland and England (or English regions of some kind). It is difficult to escape the conclusion that the UK would take on a decisively federal form, whether or not it adopted this explicit label. Drafters of proposed UK constitutions—from Lord Hailsham to Tony Benn to the IPPR—have united in this view (the Gordon constitution stands out for not making this provision). To reflect the principle of a state composed of equal autonomous parts, the appropriate name for it would be 'the United Kingdom of Wales, Scotland, Northern Ireland and England'. The 'United Kingdom' abbreviation would continue—unless changes to office of head of state rendered the second of the two words inappropriate.

The UK constitution would entrench what are presently the devolved systems of Northern Ireland, Scotland and Wales, probably reducing their divergence from each other in certain ways, and strengthening them. The position of England would derive from the conclusions of the English constitutional convention discussed in the previous chapter, subject to the agreement of the full UK deliberation process. Either England would participate in the UK as a single unit, or as a group of regions—a decision considered below. The text would allot responsibilities between what we can term the 'federal' (ie, UK) and the 'state' or 'national' levels of government. To guarantee the position of the states, the best approach might be expressly to define only the powers exercised at the centre. This method would thereby create the presumption that a function lay below the federal tier, overridden only if the constitution explicitly stated otherwise. The sorts of areas likely to be reserved to the UK Parliament and government are: foreign affairs; defence, security and intelligence; immigration; and macroeconomic policy. The lower level would be left with areas including: health; education; housing; culture; economic development; agriculture; and the environment. Both tiers would have the ability to raise taxes. However, it might also be possible to share some responsibilities between them. This latter kind of arrangement might be part of an attempt to create a culture of cooperation rather than separation. Yet harmonious overlap can bring difficulties, namely in identifying who should be answerable for the way in which particular shared powers are exercised. For this reason the UK constitution should establish an 'accountability principle': that for every public policy decision and programme, there should be a clear line of responsibility leading from an individual or group back to voters or the courts (that in turn applied the constitution and upheld the rule of law).

States would have sub-UK constitutions of their own. The UK document might stipulate their basic arrangements, but allow the territories concerned to change them in accordance with defined procedures. States might, for instance, choose their own electoral systems, or introduce rights supplementary to those provided for under the full UK constitution. Northern Ireland and Scotland would presumably continue to have their distinct legal systems, while Wales might develop one if it chose. At present, the devolved legislatures have responsibility for local government. However, it is advisable for the UK as well as 'state' level constitutions to make provision in this area, as for instance both the Benn and IPPR drafts do. Some policy areas not reserved to the federal tier, such as the running of schools and hospitals, could by this means be exercised at local rather than 'state' level. Local authorities would have guarantees for their fiscal autonomy and their geographical and hierarchical position. Making detailed stipulations about the rights of local government might go beyond the more generalised statements of other constitutions internationally, but at the same time it seems the only remaining way of bringing the UK into line with actual practice in other countries. One of the greatest potential democratic benefits of a UK text would be a downward dispersal of power through this means.

The changes entailed by the full establishment of a federal UK would appear more dramatic in some parts of the country than others. For the devolved territories, they would involve expanding upon and making more formal already existing tendencies, and enhancing local government. The advantages in these cases would include the clearer protection of self-government, an end to constant and possibly wearing constitutional churn, and greater autonomy at local level. This latter quality would be a valuable protection against the tendency of the devolved institutions to centralise power within their own territories. For England there would be a more dramatic break with the past. For the first time (with the arguable exception of Greater London) it would have a set of democratic institutions between the local and UK level. But in what form would England participate in the new UK constitution? Would it be as a single, national unit, or several geographical blocks? Both models have attractions and difficulties. If the English constitutional convention could agree on a set of regions, then this approach would be best. It would deal with the need for decentralisation and avoid the potential instability attendant upon a single English component in a federal UK.

There is no perfect set of internal English boundaries awaiting discovery. But a central theme of this book is that the viability or otherwise of constitutional arrangements does not depend entirely upon their fitting with their pre-existing environment. Causality can flow in both directions. Texts such as Magna Carta and the Treaty and Acts of Union of 1706–07 attained immense influence, shaping perceptions and creating expectations that can in turn encourage further changes. More recent examples of constitutional innovation transforming the wider culture include devolution from the late 1990s. Democratic institutions introduced to the English regions would not rest on the same base of prior cultural identity as existed in, for example, Wales in the late 1990s (though the position in Wales was itself complex). But a federal constitution could initiate a trajectory of development towards self-aware communities, centring on the new bodies, their procedures, their policies and the political dynamics surrounding them. Furthermore, as the example of Germany demonstrates, it is possible to establish a successful federal constitution within which some states have a stronger pre-existing identity than others.

If England preferred inclusion in a federal UK as a single participant, certain issues would arise, as discussed earlier in this book. Consequences of the decisions that England took as a political entity would spread decisively beyond the English border, regardless of the formal position. England would dwarf the other UK states and perhaps present a challenge to federal authority. A consideration of mechanisms for the involvement of the different states in UK-level decision-taking follows later in this chapter. But whatever systems were in place, creating a federal UK with a single English component would be an experiment. Whether the imbalances involved would create insuperable problems is difficult to predict. Yet some might hold that providing England with national political expression in this way, alongside that of other parts of the UK, is the most or only satisfactory option for the future.

Aside from issues specifically involving England, a possible more general criticism of a federal constitution is that it would accelerate the fragmentation of UK identity and encourage a disintegration of the country itself. Devolution was intended—in Scotland and Wales at least—partly as a means of making continued presence within the UK seem more attractive. Yet in Scotland in particular the independence movement subsequently made substantial political progress. An extension of the process begun with devolution might augment these trends further. It is true—and argued repeatedly in this work—that constitutional changes can precipitate wider changes in the surrounding environment. They have done so in the case of devolution. Yet in this instance they channelled already powerful social forces that predated the existence of the UK in their origins, and intensified in the post-imperial era. Attempts to contain these urges within the more traditional constitutional model were democratically unsatisfactory, and inflammatory. Any problems devolution caused arose from those it addressed. Furthermore, a written constitution will not create more difficulties than would otherwise exist. Devolution continues to intensify under the '*un*written' constitution. However, it does so in an unstructured fashion that creates problems for the overall system, and within which England is not yet provided for satisfactorily.

A more stable and formalised division of powers could increase the potential for a twin identity: one with an outlet at 'state' level, the other at federal level (with a third 'local' identity also a possibility). It might become more viable to claim, for instance, that Scottish autonomy was not in conflict with participation in the UK, but that they were both provided for within the same constitutional document, and were complementary. When people are forced by questionnaires to choose between being British or having a sub-UK identity, they often opt for the latter. It is better to provide a constitutional structure that avoids imposing this binary decision upon them, and encourages both attachments simultaneously. The text would need to include further provisions to attain greater unity, such as a statement of a principle of financial redistribution between the richer and poorer 'states'. It would probably not set out the precise equation employed, but could iterate a basic doctrine and establish mechanisms to oversee its application. An arrangement that pleases everyone is impossible, but the introduction of a new, more transparent system based on clear values, replacing the current 'Barnett Formula', could help develop a shared consciousness around a UK constitution based on mutual benefit and obligation. The constitution could also require the production of codes agreed between the various tiers to ensure they deployed their powers in ways that supported the stability of the whole.

A federal UK constitution, then, would offer the chance for a UK that was cohesive both through variety and commonality. It would ensure that federal and state levels had sufficient but not excessive power. One mark of the strength of this system would be that, in accordance with the principle of a voluntary union of autonomous parts, the text would allow for secession and set out the steps involved in attaining it. A procedure already exists for Northern Ireland to leave, set out in the Belfast Agreement and implemented in domestic UK law through the Northern Ireland Act 1998. Scotland has obtained, once, the ability to decide whether to become independent, and could presumably do so again. The constitution would need formally to adapt the Northern Ireland provisions to the whole of the UK, presumably including England or its regions. In creating such a permissive system with respect to possible departure, the UK constitution would be exceptional, perhaps one of a kind, internationally. Yet to do so would be to recognise a reality that is already developing, with Northern Ireland leading the way, and Scotland now following. Viewed from one perspective, such an arrangement invites instability and creates weakness. But as well as being unavoidable, it could become beneficial. It will encourage federal and 'state' governments to take into account the interests of all. If they do so successfully, the UK system could become a symbol of strength, of a country that remains together because its people choose to do so, with its written constitution the binding agent. On this foundation could rest a new positively defined citizenship, set out in the text.

THE UK EXECUTIVE

The document would create the UK-level executive, acting as the ultimate source of its authorities and regulating their use. One impact of the constitution would be to restrict central government. A federal system would remove some of the ability it possesses to determine policy below a certain level, in England in particular. In the areas that remained to it, requirements for specific parliamentary approval would increase. The scope for judicial review of its actions would probably expand expressly to take in the question of their constitutionality. A strengthened freedom of information regime would make the executive subject to greater public scrutiny, for instance through removing the right of ministers ultimately to override disclosure. The constitutional text could entrench the system of redress from maladministration by public authorities, and create certain obligations regarding consultation and other means of public engagement.

All of these apparent constraints are justifiable from a democratic viewpoint. Furthermore, though they might frustrate certain ambitions and cause some discomfort among ministers and officials in Whitehall, they will bring some benefits even from the perspective of these individuals. Some policy disasters of recent decades might not have happened under a written constitution of the type envisaged here, because they would not have been constitutionally possible.[6] Clearly falling within this category is the Community Charge or 'Poll Tax' that encouraged the defenestration of Margaret Thatcher in 1990. A properly devised constitution would not have allowed the UK Parliament to impose a form of local taxation in this way. The drive from successive governments unilaterally to prise responsibility for publicly funded schools away from local authorities—again something a written constitution worth the name would prohibit—may well come to appear a serious error. The potential for ill-judged reactive interventions in the business of local government, perhaps under media pressure, would lessen. Frivolous initiatives such as the 'Big Society' might no longer be possible. Furthermore, Whitehall would be better able to perform the reduced—but still immensely significant—range of tasks that fell to it.

In carrying out its responsibilities, the UK executive would be more accountable to Parliament, in public debate, and in legal terms through the courts. The text might strengthen principles of collective decision-taking at the highest level within government. Some might fear the loss of essential flexibility and confidentiality. But it must be possible—at least from the point of view of those who subscribe to democratic principles—for accountability to coexist with discretion. Furthermore, evidence exists that the use of exceptionally exclusive and confidential policy formation methods that do not accord with established procedures can often lead to mistakes.[7] In such cases, the wisdom, knowledge and support of others that might have led to success were not obtained. The conditions a text would impose upon it could make the executive more effective.

One of the most important consequences of a written constitution for the executive would be the eradication of the Royal Prerogative. Certain powers presently derived from this ancient legal source would reappear in some form in the text, while others would not, and might vanish altogether. The former category of necessary functions for inclusion in a text would take in the appointment and removal of ministers and the allocation of their portfolios, the conduct of diplomacy and ratification of treaties, the granting, refusal and revocation of passports,

---

[6] For policy disasters, see: Anthony King and Ivor Crewe, *The Blunders of Our Governments* (London, Oneworld, 2014).

[7] See eg: Butler Review Team, *Review of Intelligence on Weapons of Mass Destruction*, Report of a Committee of Privy Counsellors (HC 2004, 898) ch 7.

and the ability to deploy the armed forces in potential or actual hostilities overseas (declarations of war, another Royal Prerogative, have become an archaic practice for most countries, though the document might need to refer to and regulate them). Among the latter group of authorities that would have no place in a written constitution—or perhaps anywhere else—are such items as exclusive rights for the production of the Book of Common Prayer and the Authorised Version of the Bible. A series of other prerogative powers may or may not still exist, but if they do, they need to vanish from the executive armoury, either because of their eccentricity or sinister quality. They include the royal right to wild swans, sturgeon and even whales as a source of income, and the power to force people into service in the Royal Navy.

The supplanting of the Royal Prerogative would entail greater clarity about what was the precise scope of executive action. It would create a more definite idea of the powers it possessed. They could become subject to greater direct and formal controls by the legislature. The constitution would not only specify that these authorities existed, it would facilitate judicial review of the manner in which the executive deployed them. The courts are already developing this practice in relation to the Royal Prerogative, but a written constitution would provide a firmer basis for it. Those concerned about judicial activism should be aware that in some ways the discretion of the courts could reduce if the existence or otherwise of certain powers became more clear following the introduction of a fundamental text.

The idea of expunging the Royal Prerogative leads on to consideration of the office holder to whom it is formally attached, though who is in practice largely distanced from the powers wielded in her or his name: the monarch. It seems likely that a UK convention set up to produce a written constitution—perhaps depending on the precise circumstances in which it came into being—would continue the existence of the hereditary head of state. With the exception of Benn the recent proposers of texts for the UK have envisaged this outcome, at least in the first instance. But while retaining the monarchy a written constitution might alter it in a number of important ways. For instance, rather than the queen or king being a source of constitutional authority, the text could be the basis for the existence of the monarchy. Heads of state would be subject to the document. It would stipulate that they were required to uphold the constitution. They would make an undertaking to this effect in their oath of office, the wording of which the text would set out. These requirements would eliminate the latent problems entailed by existing arrangements, under which the monarch is subject in key areas only to vague conventions, creating a potential for democratic abuse, or at least for the perception that it has taken place. While the monarchy was retained, the term 'the Crown'—the closest equivalent in UK terminology to 'state'—could persist, though the text would redefine the different institutions and powers associated with it.

The constitution would set out the rules determining who came to hold the post of head of state and the procedures required for their removal. Assuming the monarchy was maintained initially, it could nonetheless be possible at some point in the future, if so desired, to alter these regulations so as to remove the hereditary principle. The post might, for instance, become directly or indirectly elected, or an official might perform the role. Those who produced the IPPR Constitution deliberately allowed for the possibility of such transitions.[8] If it stops short of ending the hereditary principle, the constitutional convention should remove religious discrimination from the rules of succession—with implications for the Established Church. It should provide for a same-sex couple one of whom is monarch to have a status equal to that of a different-sex couple in the same position, including provision for their children, biological or adopted, to succeed them.

A task allotted to the head of state under the constitution could be the confirmation—perhaps a better word than appointment—of the head of the UK government, presumably known as the Prime Minister. The most appropriate procedure would be for the lower House in the legislature (assuming the persistence of bicameralism) to choose who should hold this post from among their own number, after a general election or the departure of an incumbent in mid-term, with endorsement from the head of state then a formality. Similar arrangements apply to the appointment of first ministers in Wales and Scotland.[9] At present in the UK a premier is appointed, with a public vote in the Commons to approve the government following afterwards. In circumstances where it is not entirely clear who could form a government, whoever is chosen thereby gains an important initiative, handed to them by an undemocratic institution. If the head of state were elected in some way, a more active role in proposing a candidate to Parliament—as takes place under Article 62 of the German Basic Law—could be appropriate.

The adoption of prior parliamentary approval would shift the focus to the Commons, with symbolic as well as practical implications. It would emphasise that governments—both single party and coalition—derived their position from elected representatives. Parliamentarians would in turn be responsible to voters for their decision to support or oppose the formation of a given ministry. Governments would be more keenly aware of their need to take into account Parliament, while MPs might find it harder to disavow governments the heads of which they had approved. Making the appointment of the Prime Minister subject to a parliamentary vote would also reduce the chances of a head of state exercising an improper role in the formation of a government in circumstances when there is no single party majority in the Commons. While the UK retains the monarchy it is exceptionally important that procedures are in place to ensure that the office is kept separate from such party political processes. Critics might complain that advance approval of the Prime Minister by Parliament would make no difference to the choice made. If they are correct, this change will at least have caused no harm, and the symbolism is itself important. Another likely objection is that it would introduce a problematic delay to the establishment of governments. But

---

[8] IPPR, *A Written Constitution for the United Kingdom* (n 3) 188–91.
[9] See: Scotland Act 1998, s 46; Government of Wales Act 2006, s 47.

the periods of time involved need be no longer than those of other countries that have elections in their legislatures before the appointment of heads of government, with no apparent negative repercussions. Finally, some believe it would create a more powerful Prime Minister, imbued with specific personal legitimacy from the Commons, overpowering Cabinet colleagues at the expense of collective responsibility. Yet whether this modification would produce figures more commanding than, for instance, William Gladstone, David Lloyd George, Winston Churchill, Margaret Thatcher or Tony Blair, is doubtful.

The head of state would probably be responsible for granting assent to primary legislation, after it had passed through other stages (at federal level at least, though perhaps not 'state' laws). It seems unacceptable that a monarch should continue to possess even a theoretical power to exercise an absolute veto on Bills passing into law. Perhaps under current constitutional arrangements the ability to withhold Royal Assent could be a final defence against the introduction of oppressive Acts of Parliament. But a monarch would in such circumstances be vulnerable to the charge of abuse. Moreover, a written constitution akin to that envisaged here that overrode the Royal Prerogative could provide at the same time a more effective and democratically satisfactory set of protections for core principles and rules than a monarchical privilege that has remained latent for more than three centuries, the exercise of which might induce as much as avert a crisis. Perhaps a non-monarchical head of state, were such a post established, would possess a conditional veto that a parliamentary super-majority could overturn.

The idea of involvement—whether only formal or more active—of the holder of an executive office in the passage of Acts illustrates an important feature of constitutions. Though they perform distinct tasks, the concept of 'separation of powers' between the legislature, judiciary and executive, is misleading.[10] Even in systems where different branches have their own direct electoral mandates, points of contact are inevitable, and proper. For instance, the executive ought—in accordance with the principle of the rule of law—to be subject to some extent to acts of the legislature that the judiciary in turn upholds. Those designing a written constitution should accept that 'separation of powers' principles are in practice unrealisable and indeed undesirable. They should consequently direct their efforts towards ensuring that the inevitable institutional intersection is appropriately arranged and regulated. The judiciary, for example, cannot be entirely 'separate', but it can be 'independent' in the judgments it makes.

Another group of functions the constitution might attach to the head of state are those of appointments and patronage. Ministerial appointments could take place on the nomination of the Prime Minister, with formal approval made automatic: the theoretical right of a monarch that exists at present to refuse to agree to a particular selection would disappear. Practical constraints on premiers

---

[10] For a discussion of this concept, see: Mogens Hansen, 'The mixed constitution versus the separation of powers: monarchical and aristocratic aspects of modern democracy' (2010) 31(3) *History of Political Thought* 509.

in choosing who should and should not have places in government, and what their portfolios should be, would persist. The constitution might stipulate that ministers should be drawn from Parliament, or one chamber within it (for instance, a Chancellor of the Exchequer or finance minister would probably need to sit in the Commons). Confirmation votes in the legislature are a possible option. Further public appointments could similarly be made on the advice of ministers, or other bodies, possibly subject to parliamentary processes. The head of state would grant honours—if this system of awards continued—but would no longer appoint members of the second chamber of Parliament. Conferral of titles on individuals sitting in Parliament—and perhaps ex-members of the legislature as well—should be prohibited.

The constitution would provide for authorities in the field of external policy that are presently matters of Royal Prerogative. An important change that the text could introduce would be to make these functions clearly subject to parliamentary control. Ministers and officials would possess the ability to conduct diplomacy with foreign states, under the general supervision of Parliament. Treaties would become subject to scrutiny and express approval by the legislature before ratification, a task the head of state would perform as a matter of course (if a monarch and therefore not democratically accountable) following parliamentary approval. The constitutional convention might wish to consider whether this arrangement for the approval of international agreements implies the need for a further shift. Since all new treaties would be subject to full parliamentary authorisation it might be appropriate for the UK to move towards a monist system, under which international agreements entered into would automatically incorporate into the domestic legal hierarchy. This approach would differ from the present arrangement whereby treaties cannot in themselves change UK law (though courts can take them into account), with specific legislative action by Parliament required to achieve this effect.[11]

The head of state could be, as now, head of the armed forces, exercising this responsibility in the case of more regular activities in accordance with the advice of the relevant Secretary of State (presumably for Defence), but with overall policy subject to the oversight and approval of Parliament. Deployments outside the UK in actually or potentially hostile circumstances would require explicit authorisation—in advance whenever possible and appropriate—from Parliament, according to a specific time-limited framework. The constitution would need to define these operations so as to include those that could have a destructive effect even if not involving the movement of personnel, to cover such activities as cyber attacks and the use of Unmanned Aerial Vehicles (UAVs, or 'drones'). Declarations of war would also invoke the need for parliamentary approval, though they now appear to be defunct.

---

[11] David Feldman, 'The Internationalization of Public Law and its Impact on the UK' in Jeffrey Jowell and Dawn Oliver (eds), *The Changing Constitution*, 7th edn (Oxford, Oxford University Press, 2011). See eg: French Constitution, Art 55; Constitution of the Kingdom of the Netherlands 2002, Art 94.

A further area in which the UK executive would have important authority (potentially at least), yet be subject to clear parliamentary control, would be in the ability to issue emergency decrees in carefully defined circumstances. At present this power is largely provided for through the Civil Contingencies Act 2004, with some residual scope for action apparently existing under the Royal Prerogative. A change from arrangements under the 2004 Act might be an express limitation on the use of emergency powers to prevent their use to alter or bypass the constitution itself, except possibly in specifically defined ways. The text could also provide for the existence of the Intelligence and Security Agencies and the mechanisms for their oversight, including the parliamentary Intelligence and Security Committee.

The written constitution should contain a statement of the principle of ministerial responsibility—assuming it remains a component of UK arrangements—and make provision for measures to ensure it is realised in practice. It would cease to be a doctrine supported by a convention, and become a central part of the constitutional text. Collective responsibility of ministers would be the first part of this doctrine set out in the document. The text would explain that senior members of the government determine major policy decisions as a group in Cabinet or Cabinet committees, and the outcome binds every government minister within and without Cabinet. It would describe the role of the Prime Minister as the chair of Cabinet. The second principle would be individual responsibility. The text would stipulate that ministers are directly answerable to Parliament for particular decisions within their remit and the departments beneath them. It would require them not to mislead the legislature, and state that they should resign office if exposed as doing so. When framing this general tenet, the drafters might also consider the extent to which the full range of governmental activity can truly be answerable to a single office holder, who in turn accounts to Parliament. Large-scale decentralisation to local and state level within a fully federal system could help lessen the scale on which UK central government operates, thereby making individual ministerial responsibility more plausible, though a recognition that practical difficulties with this idea will continue to some extent is essential.

The document might set out certain core principles of good governance intended to ensure general probity and effective, accountable policymaking practice within the executive. Those drafting a constitution would probably also provide for the position of the institution that supports ministers: the Civil Service. A text could set out its underlying principles, which could include impartiality, and recruitment and promotion on merit, as well as setting out the exceptions to these rules. While the full constitutional text could deal with general principles, it might also require the production of a single executive code containing more detailed provisions covering the ethical requirements and operational rules applying both to officials and ministers. It could supplant multiple texts, including the Ministerial Code and Civil Service Code that exist at present. Potentially this document could be subject to parliamentary scrutiny in draft form, and subsequent approval. This practice underlines the importance of Parliament—the institution responsible for both supporting government and holding it to account—to which this chapter now turns.

PARLIAMENT AFTER SOVEREIGNTY

In 2009 the then Secretary of State for Justice, Jack Straw, told the Commons Justice Committee that there were 'two models of a written Constitution'. One option, followed in many other territories, involved 'an entrenched and overarching Constitution which is more powerful than Parliament'. But Straw favoured a different approach. It was 'a text which seeks to bring together the fundamental principles, sometimes called conventions, of our constitutional arrangements, the most important of which is that Parliament is sovereign', alongside statutes such as the Parliament Acts.[12] Following the approach Straw advocated would be an interesting intellectual exercise. It would have perceptual consequences, and probably further unforeseen outcomes. But it would produce a text that was neither specially enforceable nor entrenched. Many of the merits of a written constitution discussed in the previous chapter would not be available, making its value questionable. The present work therefore focuses on the first model to which Straw referred, but which he did not favour. A written constitution should be superior to and binding upon all institutions, including the Westminster legislature. Superficially, it is possible to construe such a text as posing a threat to Parliament—a consideration that motivated Straw. Certainly, a written constitution that is worth creating is likely decisively to end the doctrine of parliamentary sovereignty as many conceive it, in as far as it has ever applied and continues to do so at present. Yet a written constitution, even as it stripped Parliament of its supposed sovereignty, could strengthen it. The text could do so through augmenting the democratic credentials of the legislature and enhancing its ability to hold the executive to account. A discussion of these changes follows.

The Composition of Parliament

At present Parliament comprises three institutions—the House of Commons, the House of Lords and the monarchy. Only the composition of the first is democratically determined, and even then it uses an electoral system that produces results so disproportionate as to undermine their representativeness. A written constitution could correct these deficiencies, conferring greater legitimacy upon the institution. First the head of state could become subject to clearly defined principles set out in the text. Second the House of Lords—if it persisted in largely appointed form by the time a UK constitutional convention sat—would need to change also, assuming the framers deemed a bicameral system necessary. Ideas floated from within the Lords itself, such as the possibility of retirement for peers, do not address the fundamental problem that individuals in effect appointed by the UK executive, whom it is almost impossible to remove, are directly involved in the legislative process. Alongside the general lack of democratic accountability, the

---

[12] Justice Committee, Oral Evidence, 14 July 2009, Q61.

lingering hereditary members and the representatives of one particular Christian denomination (that lacks the adherence it once possessed), serve further to deny legitimacy to the Lords and consequently Parliament. The option favoured among reformers at present is a directly elected upper chamber. The constituencies used might well be designed to provide representation to the 'states' of the UK, assuming a federal system were adopted—the approach taken in the US. But the alternative, following the German model, would be for the 'state' governments to comprise the upper chamber.

Whatever the precise arrangement devised for the second chamber, there would be wider implications. First, a House that was elected either directly or indirectly via the states would surely be more assertive in its dealings with the Commons than the current Lords, which has itself acquired an increased activism since the shift away from inherited membership. While there exist some hard regulations in the Parliament Acts (which themselves probably require clarification) interactions between the two chambers, and the primacy of the Commons within them, rest to a significant extent on convention. The constitutional text would need either to make the seniority of the Commons more firm, or the authors would have to accept greater equality in the balance between the two chambers. Second, if the reconstituted Lords provided for state input at federal level, the relative positions of the different components of the UK would need close attention. The chief challenge that those advocating a federal UK face arises from the relative size of England within the Union. If England were included as a single part of a federal UK, and the constitution accorded England a voting strength in the second chamber that reflected the size of the English population, it would exceed that attached to all the other states combined. Would such an arrangement be acceptable to Wales, Scotland or Northern Ireland? Or would England settle for anything less? One response to this problem may be to note that, in a directly elected second chamber, there is no reason to believe that members would generally vote on 'national' grounds, and would often divide along party lines that crossed internal borders. Another is that an institutional middle way could be found. Votes in the chamber might require the support of at least two state participants to pass. England, therefore, would have to obtain the agreement of one of the other components of the UK to achieve the outcomes it wanted in this House. If this body were involved in constitutional amendment procedures, the requirement might be more demanding still, as is discussed below.

Electing Parliament

As well as dealing with the composition of the second chamber, the constitutional text would fix a standard term for the parliamentary electoral cycle, and allow for early dissolutions as provided for at present under the Fixed-term Parliaments Act 2011. However, it would be appropriate to reduce the regular length of a Parliament as envisaged under the Act from five to four years. The length set in

2011 is, in international perspective, excessive. From the point of view of voters, a four year cycle would create a chance to participate in a key democratic activity more frequently. From the perspective of the elected components of Parliament and of government, if a democratic mandate loses force the older it becomes, a shorter term seems beneficial. Furthermore, four years is surely a sufficient period of time for the implementation of a programme.

The constitution would protect the right to vote in parliamentary and other elections, and should fix the minimum age at 16. This provision would extend to at least some prisoners. To underpin the integrity of the electoral process, the constitution would supply the basis for the existence of the Electoral Commission and Boundary Commission. It might not stipulate specific numbers for the membership of the Commons, nor the specific size of constituencies; however it might set out principles from which judgements about these issues by the relevant bodies could derive.[13] (If the second chamber was a federal 'states' assembly, the numbers or proportions might be fixed.) But what voting system or systems will apply? Often written constitutions do not deal specifically with this issue, a task consequently left to subordinate legislation. However, it seems likely that a UK constitutional convention would wish to consider this matter and cover it in the text it produced. The First-Past-the-Post system (FPTP) used for the House of Commons is a recurring subject of complaint. None of the devolved legislatures established in the UK use it. The Coalition proposals for a reformed House of Lords did not include FPTP. It seems unlikely that a constitutional process would arrive at this method of determining the composition of either chamber of Parliament. If a directly elected second chamber came about, it would be likely to use a system more proportional than FPTP, though if there was a federal weighting system it might complicate matters. The Commons might shift in a similar direction: indeed if it did not, its legitimacy could diminish relative to the second chamber.

Parliament and Accountability

Parliamentary sovereignty often appears to be a tool in the possession of the executive rather than the legislature. In ending this doctrine a written constitution could entrench a series of institutions, including Parliament, which would in the process become more able to hold the executive to account. The document could protect Parliament—that acts at times (though by no means always) almost as an executive automaton—from itself. In particular a text could place clear limits on the delegated powers that primary legislation can confer on ministers. At present, Parliament can undermine its own relevance through creating secondary authorities enabling the executive to implement certain important measures without

---

[13] See: Lewis Baston, *Electoral Collision Course: The Boundaries and the Register after May 2015* (London, The Constitution Society, 2014).

being subject to fuller parliamentary procedures. The written constitution could afford Parliament more control over its own actions. It could express clearly the principle that Parliament as an institution is responsible for its own timetable. The text could also deal with circumstances when Parliament is out of session. At present, if an emergency develops and Parliament is not meeting, it is dependent upon ministers to authorise a recall, something they can prove reluctant to do. The text could give the legislature the power to reconvene itself, perhaps following a request from a set proportion of its members. Some defined circumstances, such as contemplated military action, should automatically necessitate an immediate recall if practically possible.

Under a federal constitution the task of the UK executive, though it would continue to be demanding, could become more manageable. So in turn would the responsibility of the UK Parliament for overseeing government. The pressure on the parliamentary calendar could ease to some extent. So too might the demands on individual parliamentarians (partly depending on how many there were in the reconfigured institution). Policy areas that presently devour much time at Westminster (in particular in as far as they impact upon England) would become the concern of 'state' level governments and legislatures, and below them local government. Such issues as road repairs and disputes between neighbours— important parts of the daily work of MPs today—would firmly be without the scope of Parliament. Parliamentarians might object that they would be stripped of an important part of their role as representatives of a locality. But the time of MPs should be too valuable to waste on refuse collection, and equally, refuse collection is too important to leave to MPs.

The constitution should set out certain basic requirements of law-making procedures, and require their supplementation in more detail in a code. They should include a requirement that the executive, whenever reasonable to do so, facilitate a period of pre-legislative scrutiny, enabling consideration by parliamentarians of proposals at an early stage. This work need not involve a draft Bill, and it might be preferable if it used instructions to counsel, setting out the underlying principles, as the focus for scrutiny. Included in this process would be a consideration of likely compatibility with the constitution. It would take place on a basis of an explanation from the government of the purpose of the measure and its anticipated outcomes. The text would require ministers, before introducing a Bill, to obtain advice from the law officers over its constitutional compatibility, and to include a statement that they had done so and were satisfied that it was within the scope of the text. The legislative process would then begin with a further assessment of the proposed measure by a specific constitutional committee. A further innovation that the document could introduce would be to stipulate scrutiny by specialist bill committees with regular members, able to develop expertise in the areas with which they dealt.[14] They might also be able to achieve more effective

---

[14] See: Meg Russell, Bob Morris and Phil Larkin, *Fitting the Bill: Bringing Commons Legislation Committees into Line with Best Practice* (London, The Constitution Unit, 2013).

scrutiny of secondary legislation than exists at present. Hopefully the total volume produced of law of this type would lessen as a consequence of a fully federal UK, with many matters handled by state or local institutions. A final practice stipulated in the text could be that post-legislative scrutiny should take place at an appropriate subsequent point, assessing the impact of the Act and how far it had achieved the objectives hoped for it.

The constitution could stipulate the existence of select committees, including the system in the Commons responsible for overseeing the policy, administration and expenditure of particular government departments, with elected members and chairs. It would clarify their rights regarding the summoning of witnesses. The text need not specify in full which committees should exist. However, it might entrench certain bodies. First would be the Public Accounts Committee—along with the Public Accounts Commission, the Comptroller and Auditor General and the National Audit Office as a whole. The financial accountability role with which these institutions are associated is among the most fundamental of Parliament, and essential to the integrity of the system of government. To further safeguard these principles, the constitution would stipulate certain budgeting principles, including the need for regular statements, votes and the maximum transparency in the figures made available to Parliament and public. Second, the constitutional text could create certain specific committees, including ensuring parliamentary oversight both of treaty making and of engagement in military conflict. It might also establish a committee akin to the present Joint Committee on Human Rights, also building on the practices of the House of Lords Select Committee on the Constitution. The text would charge this body specifically with assessing the compatibility of Bills with the UK constitution, and conducting wider inquiries on constitutional matters. A further committee could form to provide oversight of executive activity during times of emergency when it proved practically impossible for Parliament to continue meeting or to recall, ensuring some degree of continuing accountability. The text might attach to committees operating in external policy fields the ability to set mandates for ministers before attending international negotiations.[15] Potentially this practice could apply to EU meetings also (assuming the UK has retained EU membership). However, there are limits to the extent to which each EU Member State can afford such power to its domestic legislature while retaining the flexibility required at supranational level. Furthermore, it would be regrettable if, having freed itself from detailed engagement at sub-UK level, the UK Parliament allowed itself excessively to become embroiled in EU matters. A directly elected European Parliament exists to deal with this business.

The constitution would make specific provision for meaningful public engagement with Parliament. It would deal with petitions received directly from the public, and not those passed on from government departments. The text

---

[15] For discussion of oversight of external policy, see: Simon Burall, Brendan Donnelly and Stuart Weir, *Not in Our Name: Democracy and Foreign Policy in the UK* (London, Politico's, 2006).

would establish a committee for dealing with such representations in a manner appropriate to their specific nature. Parliamentary responses to petitions could take a range of forms, from inquiries to Bill amendments to what is currently the default action (for petitions transferred from government): debates in Westminster Hall. The value of this flexible response would be that it properly integrated views from outside into the work of the legislature. It could also help educate the public on the complexities of the democratic policy process, and the limitations and opportunities it presents. Here the UK Parliament can derive lessons from, among other institutions, the Scottish Parliament. The overall impact could be to strengthen representative democracy through more direct engagement, rather than rival it.

Parliament would under the constitution have access to its own source of legal advice, to help it dispose of the new functions given to it, including for authorising treaty ratification and armed conflict. Beyond general provision in the constitution, the text would require the production of more detailed codes governing the organisation, operation, principles, and rules of conduct of the whole of Parliament and its members, included in a single publication, renewed as a whole with every new Parliament and updated as necessary. As well as expanding upon some of the arrangements discussed above, it would include regulations covering the ethics and probity of members, including contact with lobbyists. The full written constitution would also clarify the privileges of Parliament, such as the freedom of speech of members, currently derived to a large extent from the Bill of Rights of 1689.

FUNDAMENTAL RIGHTS

Human rights are an indispensible component of, and are only fully meaningful within, a democratic system. It is possible to find examples of written constitutions that do not contain specific and full provision in this area, for instance in Australia (at federal level). But a UK document should not make such an omission. What rights should it contain?[16] We have already seen that there is not a clear distinction between civil and political rights, on the one hand, and economic and social rights, on the other; and that even in as far as separation is possible, rights in both categories have an important part to play in the realisation of democratic values. For these reasons more traditional interpretations should not constrain the drafting of the 'Bill of Rights' contained within the constitution (assuming it is to have this title). It should include those rights contained in the European Convention on Human Rights (ECHR) that in practice have socio-economic connotations anyway. The text might add to these provisions certain entitlements some regard as important parts of English or UK values. They could include

---

[16] A key source drawn on here is: Joint Committee on Human Rights, *A Bill of Rights for the UK* (2007–08, HL 165-I, HC 150-I).

and right to trial by jury and to legal aid. The Bill of Rights could stipulate the requirement for individuals to receive equality of treatment regardless of their particular characteristics. It could also enshrine the obligation on public authorities to behave legally, in accordance with proper procedure, and rationally—in other words, the principles of administrative justice, as supported at present by traditional judicial review. A UK constitution could then set out a variety of more explicitly socio-economic rights, already included in international agreements to which the UK is a signatory, such as the United Nations International Covenant on Economic, Social and Cultural Rights (ICESCR). They could include rights to housing, education, work, fair employment conditions, social security, and health.

It is not inevitable that a constitutional convention would agree with the assessment presented here that this latter broad grouping of rights should acquire constitutional status. But it is important to stress that constitutional provision for economic and social rights would not mean an enforceable requirement for immediate access on demand to a full range of public entitlements. Aside from being unrealisable, this approach strays too far into attaching a written constitution project to a particular ideological outlook. It is reasonable for those of different persuasions to see varied potential benefits in the introduction of a text, and consequently to strive for different versions of what it should set out. But to subordinate a constitution-building exercise to a relatively narrow agenda is to exclude others, and devalue the project. Furthermore, it would enable those who dislike economic and social rights for their own ideological reasons to dismiss them through caricature. In fact they are attainable and exist in varied forms across numerous states, including in many parts of Europe and beyond—for instance in South Africa.

The true meaning of provision for these rights involves the existence of some kind of expectation that public authorities recognise their existence and act accordingly. This principle could involve a requirement for basic protections for certain vulnerable groups, a prohibition on the arbitrary removal of provisions, and a duty on public authorities to seek a fuller attainment of economic and social rights over time ('progressive realisation': a concept provided for under the South African Constitution and contained in Article II of the ICESCR). Varied models of justiciability exist. Hard enforcement, with courts even able to void primary legislation it finds non-compliant, may raise concerns about the judges becoming inappropriately involved in political decisions and in practice having an influence on the distribution of public money. Accordingly, the IPPR Constitution included social and economic rights, but proposed that—unlike their civil and political counterparts—they should not be accessible through the courts.[17] Another way of managing the controversy of this issue would be to allow for different states within the federal system to introduce additional Bills of Rights of their own, building upon but not lessening existing protections. Particular territories within the UK could then establish protections in accordance with their

---

[17] IPPR, *A Written Constitution for the United Kingdom* (n 3) 182.

particular political and cultural traditions and circumstances. They might even choose to extend beyond economic and social rights and into other areas such as cultural and environmental rights. However, a wide range of protections at UK level would seem a desirable balancing measure to guarantee certain standards, accompanying the pronounced decentralisation of political power that a written constitution should bring about. Individuals could be subject to the same basic social protections wherever they lived in the UK, though the means of providing and expanding upon them might vary immensely.

Many of the components of a Bill of Rights in a UK written constitution would apply to all people, not only citizens, within UK territory—including those in areas under effective UK control, such as countries or zones within them under military occupation. The constitution would make it explicit that human rights requirements applied in the same way to all providers of public services, even if the particular organisation involved was part of the private or voluntary sector. In addition to the protections contained in the UK Bill of Rights, people in the UK could retain rights under European law and the ECHR, ultimately accessible through supranational legal systems (if the UK continues its participation in these arrangements). The constitution would also entrench the existence of a Human Rights Commission, charged with monitoring developments and supporting legal challenges against suspected infringements. This discussion now leads to the issue of the means of enforcement of a Bill of Rights, alongside other components of the UK constitution.

THE COURTS, THE LEGAL SYSTEM AND CONSTITUTIONAL REVIEW

The courts should have a critical place within the UK written constitution. It would both establish their position, and should give them responsibility for upholding its stipulations. The text would presumably recognise the distinct legal systems in place in England, Northern Ireland and Scotland. The constitutional convention would need to address the possibility of a jurisdiction for Wales. Ultimately it would probably be for Wales to decide if it wants to follow this path. The text would set out the court system—with the UK Supreme Court at its summit—and the judicial appointments process. It could model the latter on the arrangements included in the Constitutional Reform Act 2005, with a Judicial Appointments Commission playing the central role.

The constitution would entrust the courts with a central role in upholding the rule of law. Certainly the text should refer to this principle—perhaps in the preamble—and might define it, though it should make clear the account it provided was not intended to be exhaustive. The document would iterate the need for judicial independence, and specifically prohibit executive or parliamentary interference in legal cases. Various provisions of the Bill of Rights included in the constitution, discussed above, could help underpin the rule of law. A right of access to justice could help ensure that the ability to obtain the protection of the law and the constitution was not denied to those lacking in material wealth. The words of Magna Carta could provide inspiration here. Other principles, if properly protected, would strengthen the rule of law. The constitution should provide for the ability of the courts to review administrative acts (up to and including secondary legislation) according to whether they are rational, procedurally fair and within the scope of existing legal power (within which adherence to the constitution would now be the ultimate requirement). Constitutional enshrinement of these principles would create a barrier to any attempt to restrict the ability of the judiciary to conduct judicial review. When considering the legality of actions the courts would apply the constitutional text, and take into account the contents of codes issued in accordance with it, as well as other legislation and norms. If a public authority was found to have violated any of the standards of administrative justice, the courts should have the ability, under the constitution, to quash the particular decision or action involved, and to require the necessary remedial measures. One of the benefits of this practice could be the introduction of clear judicially enforced limits on the ability of Parliament through primary legislation to vest ministers with inappropriately expansive delegated powers.

As it does at present, the role of the courts would also extend to the review of Acts of Parliament for their compatibility with European law, and disapplying them in as far as they were not (once again, assuming continued EU membership). The possibility of clashes between European law and the UK constitution are a complex matter.[18] Though they are unlikely we should not pretend they are impossible in the hope that they will not happen. A UK court, in the *Thoburn* case, has already considered this matter with respect to the UK constitution in its current form, though it was not a direct part of the judgment. The German judiciary, working with a written constitution, has also grappled with the issue. One approach may be for the creation of mechanisms—possibly in the UK Parliament—to monitor European measures for constitutional compliance while under development, and identify whether or not they might require a change to the UK text, in accordance with its amendment procedures. This kind of activity would be an area in which the UK legislature could usefully concern itself with EU business, adding value rather than unhelpfully duplicating the work of European institutions.

We have seen that the courts could enhance existing judicial review through the use of the constitutional text and its subordinate codes in ruling on the actions of public authorities. But what would be their approach to Acts of the UK Parliament? A constitution-building process that produced a document that was in no way binding upon the UK Parliament would be an exercise in time wasting. It should not be possible for regular legislative procedures at Westminster to circumvent the written constitution. The text should have some kind of special status in law. If the constitution is to achieve the transcendent status required of it, then it needs—in a legal sense as in others—to be something more than a regular Act of Parliament.

---

[18] See: NW Barber, 'Against a written constitution' [2008] *Public Law* 11.

If the constitutional framers decide to give the text protection of this sort, a series of questions arise. Need all of the document be justiciable? Should those parts of the text protected in this way be enforceable to the same extent? Which courts would the text empower to carry out this review? Would it be widely possible or reserved to the UK Supreme Court or another body formed to perform this task? Would it be possible for courts to carry out an assessment of the constitutionality of an Act in the abstract before it became operational? If so, how might such a process fit with the possible parliamentary constitutional scrutiny procedures discussed above? If a proposed Act is judged compatible at an early stage, would it be possible for individuals affected by it in particular ways once it was in force to mount a legal constitutional challenge to it?

While these matters are important, there lurk behind them more fundamental issues involving the position of Acts of Parliament within the constitution, and what precisely a court should be able to do when it cannot reconcile the former with the latter. One approach would be to adapt procedures from within the present UK constitution—in particular those associated with the Human Rights Act 1998 or the European Communities Act 1972. The document could be immune to implied repeal by future Acts of Parliament, as are both of these Acts. (Unlike the Human Rights Act, however, the constitution would probably need to repeal earlier legislation.) If there was a clash between the constitution and subsequent primary legislation, a court could issue a declaration of incompatibility akin to those available under the Human Rights Act. Ministers could then respond using a fast-track legislative process, or in some other way. Alternatively, reflecting the principles that have developed around the European Communities Act, the courts could deal with any incompatibility more directly, disapplying Acts in as far as they unavoidably violated the text.

But these kinds of protections would not be effective against a government and Parliament determined to abrogate a fundamental principle and willing to do so through using express terms in an Act. Under this system, an Act of Parliament could presumably either state that it took effect regardless of a particular constitutional provision that might conflict with it, or perhaps alter the constitutional document itself to remove the blockage altogether from the text. The entrenchment that is appropriate for a constitutional text as a set of fundamental rules would not be possible. Moreover, it is difficult, within the rationale of a federal system, to justify the UK Parliament not being subject to the rules to the same extent as the 'state' legislatures, if the constitutional position is supposed to be one of equality between the different layers of governance. For these reasons, it is preferable to provide the courts with full powers either to disapply for the particular instance concerned, or else completely void Acts of the UK Parliament they cannot read as compatible with the constitution, and to prohibit Parliament from overriding or unilaterally altering the constitutional text.

At this point the contours of the UK constitutional landscape would have shifted to the extent that even the most ingenious of scholars would have difficulty in making a plausible claim for the persistence of the doctrine of parliamentary sovereignty. Furthermore, even those who hold that this concept was always flawed, or has ceased to apply already, would acknowledge that a major transition had taken place. It would be clearly established that, on the range of issues the constitution covered, the UK legislature would no longer have the last word. In formal terms, this ultimate authority would have shifted to the text, as an expression of the will of the people of the UK: popular sovereignty. Some would characterise the true outcome in terms of a transfer of power from elected politicians to unelected judges. Hopefully a culture will emerge in which different players seek satisfactory non-legal resolutions of disputes. The document may even express this principle. Yet sometimes recourse to the courts on constitutional issues will be necessary, and even desirable, as a more definitive solution. We should accept that a written constitution would create new areas in which the courts might become a focus for decisions of political importance. In these circumstances they might wield important discretion through the particular way in which they interpret the text. Sometimes they will make decisions that are poor or are in clear contradiction of the wider social consensus. Yet at the same time, their power will be limited in important ways, in particular that they must account for the relationship between their judgments and the document. Moreover, if there is sufficient opposition to the way in which the judiciary has interpreted the constitution, it will be possible to reverse the decision through an amendment to the text that makes a different inference explicit. It is this process of constitutional modification that we consider next.

CHANGING THE CONSTITUTION

The most important component of any constitution is the provision it makes for its own alteration. This part of the text determines who is in control. It also helps—alongside constitutional judicial review—provide for the entrenchment of the document, properly guaranteeing it a heightened position in the systemic hierarchy. Opponents of a written constitution for the UK are likely to argue that if introduced it would remove valuable flexibility from the political system, making it difficult for it to adapt with sufficient speed to changed circumstances. An important challenge for those drafting a UK text is to establish procedures for constitutional amendment that reflect its fundamental importance, but do not bring about excessive rigidity. The effect should be not to block change, but to ensure that when it occurs it does so in a more inclusive and considered fashion than is often the case at present. A written constitution and constitutional flexibility are not necessarily conflicting concepts, and should be mutually enhancing. The process establishing the text in the first place might be a means of bringing about reforms, some of which have been surprisingly difficult under the present, supposedly more malleable unwritten system. Amendment procedures stipulated in the text could provide for groups that have tended to be marginalised from the process of change to have a clearer, more direct engagement, affording more responsiveness than exists at present.

What procedures might be involved? As with constitutional review by the courts, one option would be to build on already existing arrangements. At present, the Parliament Acts provide some entrenchment for the maximum length of a Parliament. They make it possible for the Commons to bypass the Lords in the production of primary legislation. At the same time, the Acts preserve the absolute House of Lords veto in areas including Bills seeking to extend the life of a Parliament beyond five years. A written constitution could apply this rule to a wider range of provisions, and also rule out the potential abuse of the Parliament Acts to remove the protections they provide. Constitutional change in specified areas would thereby always require the approval of both chambers of a bicameral Parliament. Depending on the composition of the second chamber, this method could potentially ensure that the different components of a federal UK were directly involved in amendments.

There is also now some precedent for legislative super-majorities, as included in the Fixed-term Parliaments Act 2011, which requires two-thirds of all MPs, including vacant seats, to support one form of early dissolution of Parliament.[19] A written constitution could adapt this practice as part of an amendment procedure. The European Union Act 2011 provides precedent for a blanket requirement that a range of possible changes should be subject to referendums. Here is another model that could create some kind of special protection for constitutional provisions. However, the text would need to deal with the issue that, within conventional understandings, probably neither the Fixed-term Parliaments Act nor the European Union Act are self-entrenching. That is to say, in theory, simple legislative processes could alter them, removing the heightened safeguards they provided.

Some combination of the ideas discussed above could help avoid potential problems such as England forcing the UK to exit the EU notwithstanding the possible objections of Wales, Scotland or Northern Ireland. In a referendum on change, a majority could be required not only in the UK as a whole, but in each of its components. In a federal second chamber comprising or representing the 'states', weighting and super-majority arrangements might ensure that the preponderant English population did not equate with an ability to dominate the approval of constitutional amendments. Some issues might require agreement from all the 'states', and as a minimum it should not be possible to impose an amendment directly affecting a particular component of the UK without its approval.

Once again we would be coming close to a point where it would be difficult to sustain claims for the persistence of parliamentary sovereignty. An argument is possible that conditions operating within Parliament, such as the stipulation that super-majorities are needed, are reconcilable with this doctrine. Nonetheless, in practice they could mean that Parliament has enormous difficulty in bringing

---

[19] See: Fixed-term Parliaments Act 2011, s 2.

about certain kinds of legislative change. Referendums (aside from their suitability or otherwise as decision-taking devices) are more problematic still from the perspective of the doctrine of parliamentary sovereignty, particularly if the requirement to use them before constitutional amendment becomes self-entrenching. If a written constitution applied external restrictions to Parliament in this way—backed up by the possibility of judicial review—then it would have destroyed the credibility of claims that parliamentary sovereignty retained viability.

While the entrenchment of certain core values is desirable, and a central reason for introducing a written constitution, it should not mean we are trapped forever with provisions that were badly conceived from the outset, or have become inappropriate in the light of changed circumstances. Alteration must be possible. It can be achieved partly through the development of conventions (in the sense of understandings lacking in direct legal force). We have seen how important these arrangements are to the operation of the UK system at present. While a constitutional text would deal with some issues previously covered by conventions, it is inevitable that new understandings of this kind would develop around it, though not involving matters as fundamental to democracy as at present. Since conventions can come into being, change and disappear without any formal process taking place, they are a means by which the operation of a constitution can alter in accordance with the requirements of the time, without a need to adhere to textual amendment procedures. Ideally, such practices should help realise the spirit of the constitution. They should not provide a means of negating the rules contained in the text. A further, and firmer, way in which the working rather than the wording of the constitution can change is through judicial interpretation and reinterpretation. Certain individual rights, for instance, can adapt, to match developing social values. Using existing texts for new purposes is—as the various applications of Magna Carta over the past 800 years attest—a venerable and potentially fruitful activity.

But sometimes, rather than twisting a document past recognition while claiming continuity, it is better to change the words. As a general principle, major alterations should follow full procedures and take place openly. Consequently, the constitution needs to be responsive to proposals for formal change. One means of ensuring flexibility would be to have at least some parts of the text subject to more than one kind of amendment procedure, to ensure that a single method—such as a referendum—did not serve in effect as a means of blocking alteration. Another is to make some parts of the text subject to less demanding alteration procedures than others, according to how fundamental they are. At the other end of the scale, some portions of the constitution may be deemed unamendable. For instance, in Germany the fundamental rights and the federal system are beyond alteration, while the French Constitution rules out change to the republican nature of the system.

To ensure that the text changes when needed, it needs to be under continual scrutiny, and this consideration must be both well informed and carried out in an inclusive fashion. With these ends in mind, the text should create a constitutional commission, permanently in session. In composition it would reflect the same principles as the constitutional convention, balancing the direct incorporation of members of the public through sortition with experts and individuals involved in operating the system, and having members from the different territories of the UK. The first concern of the commission might be dealing with issues specifically left aside by the convention that had drafted the constitution. It would keep the text and its practical functioning under permanent review, taking evidence as widely as possible and producing reports. It could also consider thematic issues from a constitutional perspective. They might include social trends and attitudes within the UK, global and domestic security, and the development of electronic communications and their implications in such areas as privacy and freedom of expression. Key institutions including the UK executive, or either chamber of the UK Parliament, or sub-UK legislatures and administrations, might refer matters to the commission for investigation. So too could the public through petitions. A special mechanism would enable the commission to propose constitutional amendments. It could be possible to initiate alterations through other routes, but a convention (in the sense of a custom) might develop that working through the commission was the appropriate means of bringing about change. The practices the commission used could ensure that the plans that emerged were sufficiently well conceived and consulted upon as to have acquired a degree of momentum even before formal procedures began. This work would mean that the constitution was not a constraint imposed by one generation on those yet to come, but a core set of values based in consensus of the time, and changeable in considered ways, using processes similar to those that created it in the first place.

The constitution outlined here draws upon, entrenches and augments many concepts and values deeply embedded in the English and UK past, and extrapolates certain developments presently underway. But nonetheless it would represent an abrupt discontinuity: and this quality would be a value central to the introduction of the text. A desire to remain within existing frameworks should not prevent the adoption of satisfactory approaches to issues such as judicial enforcement and amendment procedures. The concerns raised about them do not withstand close analysis, and do not justify toleration of the flaws in the existing system that are becoming more pronounced. Contrary to the claims of their advocates, it is concepts such as parliamentary sovereignty that represent an inappropriate imposition from the past on the present and the future, not a democratically-devised and implemented written constitution including sensible provisions for its own upholding and alteration. John Milton was correct to be concerned for the right of every generation to determine its own future, but not all decisions can be taken by the same procedures, and some processes should be more rigorous than others. With these principles in mind, the UK can through a written constitution mark an end to its long phase of post-imperial trauma and reconcile itself to a future as a federal European democracy.

13

Conclusion

T HE CONSTITUTION OF the United Kingdom has problems. They may prove terminal. The Scottish Independence Referendum of September 2014 unleashed pressures that threaten the systemic integrity of the whole. It is not yet clear how and if it will prove possible to form a settlement that offers satisfactory territorial-political autonomy while somehow accommodating the relative size of England. Other issues awaiting resolution involve the position of the United Kingdom (UK) within the European Union (EU); provision for human rights; and possible tensions between two doctrines: parliamentary sovereignty and the rule of law. The Scottish vote and its consequences marked an important moment in constitutional development. Yet they augmented tendencies that had already been playing out over a period of five decades. Moreover, possible solutions had even longer antecedence. The past is important, and it may not always be convenient. Preceding pages, taking Magna Carta as their cue and considering a series of texts both prior to and following it, have demonstrated this point.

They have shown that the idea of continuity as a defining characteristic of the English and then UK constitution is dubious. Internal upheaval has been important, including in 1215 and during the seventeenth century. Foreign invasion, threatened or actual, from Scandinavia, France or Holland, has forced progress at critical moments: under kings Alfred and Cnut, around the time of Magna Carta, in 1688, and at the time of the formation of the UK, for which fear of Louis XIV and later Napoleon provided impetus. The establishment of this state was itself a firm break in historic continuity in 1706–07 and then in 1800–01. England was subsumed within a larger entity on the former occasion, Great Britain on the latter. This observation introduces a further dimension to constitutional discourse in the UK. Though sometimes treated as such, the English and UK traditions are not synonymous. The latter is a complex multinational entity (though the former also fully incorporated Wales from the Tudor period) and an appreciation of this quality is essential to any understanding of it. Finding a satisfactory model for the governance of this complex state has proved a challenging task. In 1706, the Scottish proposed a vaguely-conceived federal or confederal compact. The English demanded a more centralised approach, though it may be that a version of the original Scottish proposal is now coming into being. Along the way, the union with Ireland created a UK polity rent by sustained conflict, prompting in turn a variety of constitutional innovations of lasting influence. The Irish dimension to UK history provides further cause to question the idea of smooth, peaceful development, and furthermore of the supposed superiority of the UK political system. Indeed, it could be the case that the UK is an inherently unstable state.

Further perceptions are recast. The conception of England or the UK as separate from Europe detracts from a full understanding of the constitutional development of all three. From the time of Ethelbert of Kent onwards, the European context—its ideas and events—was always important to constitutional texts. The Anglo-Saxons brought with them from the mainland methods and principles of social organisation that by the seventh century they had begun to write down, aspiring to what Bede termed the standards of the 'Romans'. Magna Carta—written in Latin, the European language—was initially the victim of an external institution, the Church in Rome, that later became an enforcer of the charter. More widely, Christianity was an important source of shared continental constitutional culture. The break from Rome under Henry VIII entailed not a withdrawal from Europe, but provided a particular perspective from which to approach and participate in continental struggles. Many monarchs who agreed key documents had connections with other parts of Europe, such as Cnut, the Normans, the Angevins, and William III. The Act of Settlement 1701 provided for Hanoverians to come to the throne, and set out the terms on which they could do so.

Events of 1688–89—in part entailing the incorporation of Dutch principles into English governance, via the Bill of Rights 1689 and other measures—provided inspiration for movements abroad, which in turn had constitutional consequences for the UK. Military conflict following the French Revolution, for instance, drove the union of Great Britain and Ireland. The invasion of 1688 demonstrates further the importance of outside intervention. During the seventeenth century England resembled a 'failed state', incapable of resolving its problems internally and in need of foreign assistance. It came from William of Orange, who deployed concepts similar to those used by present-day liberal interventionists, and that were also in keeping with Protestant thought of the time (as well as being advanced by Catholics). The so-called 'Glorious Revolution' helped create a context in which the UK formed. To this considerable extent the present day UK owes its existence and its principles of limited government and individual freedom to an intercession from the continental mainland, carried out on a basis of 'supranational' European constitutional values.

The preceding historic survey can help cast doubt on another commonly held theory of today. It is often argued that treating socio-economic matters in a fundamental text is inappropriate. Yet protecting the vulnerable was fundamental to some of the very earliest English documents (though reference to past practice does not in itself settle an argument). The Anglo-Saxons were clearly unaware of the so-called 'Anglo-Saxon model'. Magna Carta, furthermore, was closely concerned with material obligations and privileges, and the means of subsistence of the large bulk of the population. This dimension of the 1215 text is largely forgotten. Its recovery is essential to a fuller understanding of the nature of constitutions. A further negative depiction of constitutional provision for economic regulation presents it as a constraint upon market systems. This idea figures in criticisms of the role of the EU as issuer of measures binding upon and within the UK as a Member State. Yet like any other form of economy, the market system requires rules for it to function. It is a game necessitating the impartial enforcement of rules delineating ownership and defining proper modes of transaction. It is for this reason that the rule of law is regarded as so important to economic development. Furthermore, the present work has demonstrated that regulation is historically as well as logically prior to the appearance of contemporary market economies. The Anglo-Saxon texts variously sought to protect property and impose a single standard of currency. Magna Carta called for common weights and measures and equality of trading conditions, even for foreign merchants. The authors did not envisage a market system of the type prevailing today, but the measures they sought to impose were of a type vital to the emergence of any such model. The Union of 1706–07 and its successor of 1800–01 were of direct importance. Their combined terms expressed the aspiration for a single market across the Atlantic archipelago, which in time became a firmer reality, and provided inspiration for the European integration project.

A further observation, applicable to both the UK and EU systems, is apt. As noted, regulation is essential to a market economy. However, it is also the case that some measures can serve to undermine the viability of the system to which they apply, perhaps through imposing excessive compliance requirements, a frequent complaint from opponents of the EU. Yet a purpose of the treaty and Acts of Union (as well as earlier English texts such as Magna Carta) and of the European Single Market is to lessen the overall burden of regulation. Such interventions might create at a high level new measures or rule-making authorities. Yet the intended impact is to introduce a set of uniform regulations, each of which replaces a multiplicity of varied rules across the territory in which they apply. This approach enables the eradication of 'non-tariff barriers' constraining the free market. More is less. And less—for instance, the removal of European regulation—would prove to be more—that is, the proliferation of differential protectionist regulations across Europe. Entry into the vacuum would be swift.

A final problematic presumption remains. It is that the 'unwritten' quality of the UK constitution is a defining feature of it. A narrow, pedantic criticism of this outlook is that many parts of the system exist in written form somewhere or other. However, a more serious reservation is that the label 'unwritten'—though useful—should not lead to the abjuration of fifteen hundred years of history. English as a written language came into being as a means of expressing fundamental social rules. The text produced under Ethelbert of Kent around the turn of the sixth and seventh centuries shares features with a contemporary written constitution. So did many documents that came after it. The resemblances included a tendency to deal with a span of institutions, rules and fundamental values. They might arise from some kind of crisis, and be the work of a relatively inclusive production process. The texts could begin with a declamatory preamble. They might have some kind of legal force, and sometimes sought to entrench themselves, making future alterations either subject to a special procedure, or ruling them out altogether. Some of these instruments clearly anticipated the concept of the written constitution. Indeed the Instrument of Government of 1653—following on from earlier draft proposals of the late 1640s—was arguably the first text of this type. Others, such as Magna Carta and the Bill of Rights—though often subject to distorted interpretations—had immense impact on the later emergence of written constitutions and associated charters of rights.

Therefore, when we judge the UK to possess an 'unwritten' constitution, we do so by measuring it against a concept to which the UK and especially England has made a foremost contribution. Yet since the full appearance of the concept of a written constitution following events of the late eighteenth century in the United States and France, the UK has not yet made a decisive movement in this direction. Nearly all other democracies in the world have built upon theoretical and practical achievements made in England and the UK (and elsewhere) to this end. But international and social forces conspired to fail to produce circumstances sufficiently conducive to such a development in the UK. It is unwise to attribute the lack of a major overhaul of the UK to a supposed innate superiority, when fortune played such an important part. The United Provinces—an important source for some of the constitutional principles of the UK—had to start again following Napoleonic conquest; so too would have the UK in similar circumstances. But the UK has not yet found itself in this position. Increasingly from the late eighteenth century onwards it became possible to define the UK in contrast with other states that possessed fundamental texts, and the doctrine of parliamentary sovereignty attained wide acceptance. In some ways the existence of a supreme body comprising monarch, Lords and Commons was a successor to the concept of the Anglo-Saxon king issuing texts on the advice of senior magnates. Yet these documents predate the full emergence of Parliament as an institution, as does Magna Carta, and indeed local government. The path to such a pervasive concept of parliamentary supremacy was not pre-ordained, and it need not prevail forever. It is certainly not possible to claim that the idea of a written constitution is culturally incompatible with UK and English traditions.

As well as drawing our attention to a string of constitutional texts, consideration of Magna Carta encourages an historical conception of the present, that is, an appreciation of the contemporary as a phase rather than an instant. The UK is passing through a period of constitutional change of unsurpassed importance in its history. Traceable to the late-1950s, it is of post-imperial character. The post-imperial concept involves a process that found a trigger in the collapse of the British global enterprise, and that has connections to the Empire and its legacy. It has many dimensions, including European integration, the nations and regions of the UK, and the rule of law. The initial impetus from the passing of empire had various subsidiary consequences that brought into being a self-sustaining momentum. This phase has tested core established understandings of the UK constitution, such as the idea that the system is of exemplary quality, that it is unitary in nature, that it is an entity apart in Europe, that it tends to provide for rights in a negative, implicit sense, and that within it, Parliament is sovereign.

Challenges to orthodoxy have created controversy, with a desire in some quarters to preserve or restore traditional principles. The position is unstable. Government and Parliament may clash with the judiciary; the dispersal of power across the Union is shifting with unpredictable consequences. Membership of European supranational organisations is in doubt. A possible but not inevitable conclusion to this tumultuous episode in UK history is the adoption of a written constitution. It would break the final taboo, but its potential outline is already discernible. Increasingly the UK has taken on the characteristics of a federal system, particularly as a consequence of devolution. This constitutional model embodies many of the most controversial features of recent transformations in the UK. Yet it has deep roots in UK political thought. Ideas about multilevel governance dating back at least as far as the nineteenth century have found their way back onto the UK agenda via devolution and the EU.

A written constitution would be a means of attaining greater clarity, wider and deeper dispersal of power, and a firmer more enforceable set of principles and rules. It could help end or avert certain difficulties, and create a settlement that was an expression of the will of the people. Achieving these qualities in a meaningful way entails a curtailment of the legal authority of the Westminster legislature, though the effectiveness of this institution could at the same time increase. If parliamentary sovereignty existed, it would be necessary to abolish it. Whether it truly does exist is another matter, and almost beside the point. It is a doctrine that has to be qualified as soon as described, or else appear a potential instrument of oppression. An omnipotent legislature is not a problem, its advocates claim, because self-restraint and practical external forces ensure it does not deploy its authority inappropriately. Yet examples of misuse in the past, ranging from detention without trial on security grounds to the abolition of the Greater London Council, are apparent. The supposed checks and balances did not work on these occasions. Though it may in some ways serve as a means of realising democratic principles, parliamentary sovereignty can threaten values important to the sustenance of a democratic system. The democracy justification is, anyway, an historical post-rationalisation, since the idea of an unlimited legislature long predates such developments as a universal franchise and the current extent of predominance possessed by the elected chamber, the House of Commons. Parliamentary sovereignty is certainly not—as implied—essential to democracy. Other democracies internationally function well while limiting their central legislatures.

Difficulties may be intensifying. The old system of tacit understandings, claimed to be so important to limiting parliamentary authority, is clearly in decline. In the current climate, populist pressure on the UK legislature is likely not to restrain it, but to drive it towards greater assertions of its authority. Parliamentary sovereignty may appear to degenerate at times into a dictatorship of the *Daily Mail*. To challenge this constitutional principle is to invite hostility. It is curious that sections of the UK press often concerned to depict parliamentarians as corrupt, dishonest and incompetent are also determined that these same inadequate individuals should wield absolute power.[1] Parliamentary sovereignty has the quality of a sacred doctrine. As such it is perhaps not amenable to close intellectual scrutiny or, if it is, labyrinthine intellectual discussion is required, and it can promote fanaticism among its adherents, justifying and encouraging unpleasant actions in its name. Viewed from the perspective of the advances it made in the seventeenth century, it is a cousin of Jacobinism and Bolshevism: a revolutionary concept that filled a space previously occupied by absolute monarchy, taking on some of its qualities.[2]

An exercise in establishing a written constitution must eradicate any trace of parliamentary sovereignty. Hiding innovation behind continuity, an approach characteristic of earlier times, will not serve this objective. The past can provide guidance, but should not constrain for its own sake. Drafting of a constitutional text should have regard to the historically constructed environment into which it will enter, but should also take into account its ability to bring about cultural change. Like earlier documents in the UK and England, it will also benefit from external influences. The best tool for creating this text will be a constitutional convention, independent of government and Parliament, but incorporating party politicians alongside members representative of the wider public. Framers of instruments since Anglo-Saxon times have recognised the importance of a broad social base for their efforts. A strength of Magna Carta during its first decades was that a diverse range of social groups had an interest in it. A written constitution should be not simply a document, but an act: a statement by the people of the rules, values and institutions that should govern them. The convention must be composed in such a way as to speak for the whole, while producing a text that will prove viable.

But we have not yet reached the point of seeing a properly conceived constitutional convention established. How should those—of all parties and none—who support a fundamental document for the UK proceed? First, they should ensure that their objective is a basis for immediate action rather than paralysis. There will never be a convenient time to commence such a task. Other issues will always supposedly be more pressing: international security, the economy, improving public services, and so on. Yet the circumstances of the First World War did not preclude the introduction of the Representation of the People Act 1918, trebling the number of voters through including women (over 30) within the franchise, and removing most of the property qualifications applying to men. Furthermore, the ability of the UK to address multiple challenges is not enhanced by the persistence of present constitutional difficulties. Once it is recognised by all who support a text that the present is the appropriate time to begin a campaign, a suitable tactical approach is needed. Continual demands for a convention are not in

---

[1] This point was made in a conversation with Vernon Bogdanor (9 October 2014).

[2] For a work placing different European constitutional traditions in comparative perspective, see: RC van Caenegem, *An Introduction to Western Constitutional Law* (Cambridge, Cambridge University Press, 1995).

themselves sufficient. It is possible to make transitional demands, arising directly from the political circumstances of the time and forcing progress towards the goal. Devolution and its dynamic nature offer the best point of entry at present. Campaigners should exploit the new emergent multilayered environment and target their efforts at the devolved as well as UK level of governance. It might be useful to demand legally enforced entrenchment of all the devolved institutions, placing them decisively beyond the reach of Parliament. Another reasonable yet radical campaign would be to make withdrawal from the EU and abolition of the Human Rights Act 1998 subject to approval from all the territories of the UK, either from their legislatures or electorates in a referendum. Both changes would amount to the introduction of the most important feature of any written constitution: a special amendment procedure, possibly accompanied by full judicial-constitutional review. Introducing them would necessitate a constitutional convention.

Finally, throughout their campaign, advocates of a fundamental text must be able to exercise self-restraint and possess willingness to compromise. A coherent movement is needed. In the debates that took place in late October and early November 1647 at Putney, participants considered the idea of what we would now call a written constitution. The day before the Levellers produced their 'Agreement of the People', Oliver Cromwell sought to cast doubt on an earlier Leveller manifesto, 'The Case of the Army Truly Stated'. Simply assessing the merits of any given proposal, he observed, was difficult in itself. It required the attention of 'wise men and godly men'. But there was a further challenge still: 'How do we know if, whilst considering these things, another company of men shall [not] gather together and put out a paper as plausible as this? ... And not only another, and another, but many of this kind'.[3] Cromwell's eventual solution was an elite exercise in constitution-building. Its product, the Instrument of Government, was innovative—perhaps the world's first written constitution. But it failed to create stability and did not survive even four years. Those who support such a text for the UK must seek to disprove Cromwell's prediction. A full debate of the options, to which this book is an intended contribution, is essential. Certain principles, such as human rights and the position of the nations of the UK, should not be negotiable. But the various participants in this movement should avoid excessively detailed demands, and leave final decisions to the proposed constitutional convention. It will then be possible finally to move beyond Magna Carta.

[3] ASP Woodhouse (ed), *Puritanism and Liberty* (London, JM Dent & Sons, 1938) 7–8.

Index